PLENTIFUL COUNTRY

Books by Tyler Anbinder

Nativism and Slavery:
The Northern Know Nothings and the Politics of the 1850s

Five Points:
The Nineteenth-Century New York City Neighborhood That Invented Tap
Dance, Stole Elections, and Became the World's Most Notorious Slum

City of Dreams:
The 400-Year Epic History of Immigrant New York

Plentiful Country:
The Great Potato Famine and the Making of Irish New York

PLENTIFUL COUNTRY

The Great Potato Famine
and the Making of Irish New York

TYLER ANBINDER

LITTLE, BROWN AND COMPANY

New York   Boston   London

Little, Brown and Company
Hachette Book Group
1290 Avenue of the Americas, New York, NY 10104
littlebrown.com

First Edition: March 2024

Little, Brown and Company is a division of Hachette Book Group, Inc. The Little, Brown name and logo are trademarks of Hachette Book Group, Inc.

The publisher is not responsible for websites (or their content) that are not owned by the publisher.

The Hachette Speakers Bureau provides a wide range of authors for speaking events. To find out more, go to hachettespeakersbureau.com or email HachetteSpeakers@hbgusa.com.

ISBN 9780316564809
LCCN 2023949229

Printing 2, 2024

LSC-C

Printed in the United States of America

The first generation thinks about survival;
the ones that follow tell the stories.

—Hua Hsu, *Stay True*

Contents

CONTENTS

New York City in the Era of the Great Irish Famine

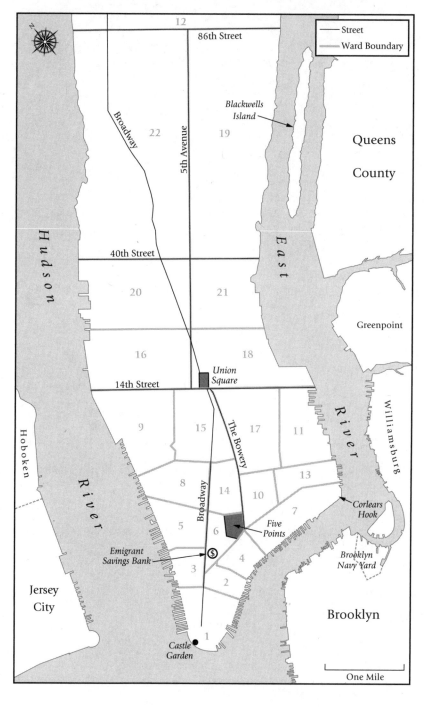

PLENTIFUL COUNTRY

Introduction

How had he fallen so far, so fast? Thomas D. Norris must surely have asked himself that question as he stood in Battery Park at the southern tip of Manhattan, probably in his dark blue woolen Civil War uniform, beseeching passersby to purchase an apple so he could support himself and his four children. Only a few years earlier, Norris had been an officer in the United States Army, commanding a company of nearly one hundred Irish American soldiers, whose uniforms and weapons he had paid for out of his own pocket. Norris had been able to do so because he was the proprietor of two successful lower Manhattan clothing shops. That he had managed to open those establishments less than a decade after fleeing Ireland's Great Potato Famine was even more remarkable. Yet now, Norris was hawking apples in rain and snow, heat and cold, just two blocks from the very spot where he had presided over his flagship retail location on South Street until the beginning of the war.

In his first decade in New York, Norris had been the very personification of the American Dream. Born in 1827 in Killarney, a town of seven thousand residents in mountainous southwest Ireland, Norris learned the tailor's trade in his teens and managed to survive four years of Famine before immigrating to the United States at age twenty-four in 1851. By that point, New York was already the garment manufacturing capital of the Americas, and Norris quickly found work for one of the city's hundreds of

3

clothing wholesalers or retailers. Not long after his arrival, Norris married Ann Hannon, who had also emigrated from Ireland in 1851. They had three children, two girls and then a boy, over the course of the next few years, and a fourth in 1863.

Norris could have continued working indefinitely for wages as a "journeyman" tailor in New York. Even though that job did not pay well by American standards, he and Ann would have been far better off than they had been in Ireland, where employment was never reliable and Catholics like the Norrises had few political rights. But Thomas was too ambitious to settle for the backbreaking, poorly paid life of a journeyman tailor. Instead, he and Ann scrimped and saved, and by 1855 they had accumulated enough capital to open their own clothing shop in Ward Nine on West Street at West Tenth Street, facing the northernmost, least-used Hudson River piers. Perhaps seeking more foot traffic, Norris soon moved the shop to 7 South Street, facing the southernmost East River docks and two busy ferry landings. This shop did so well that Thomas, now calling himself a "clothier" rather than a tailor, opened a second shop a few blocks away in 1858. Both were still operating when the Civil War broke out in the spring of 1861.

After the Confederate attack on Fort Sumter, Norris felt obliged to defend his adopted homeland and enlisted in one of the regiments that constituted New York's Irish Brigade, a unit made up of several thousand Irish immigrants. Norris fought at Bull Run a few months later and while he escaped that famous encounter unscathed, several of his friends were wounded, and the unit's commanding officer, Colonel Michael Corcoran, was captured. Having expected a quick war and easy victory, Norris and most of his comrades had been allowed to enlist for only three months, so immediately after Bull Run, Norris returned home to Ann, the children, and his clothing business.

Yet Thomas soon came to feel ashamed for having abandoned the Union cause and his Irish American compatriots who remained in the army. So in 1862, he sold his shops and used the proceeds to outfit a company of one hundred soldiers for Corcoran's Legion, a new Irish American infantry unit to be led by Corcoran, who had been released by the Confederates after several months captivity in Richmond. Norris, now a captain, played a prominent leadership role in the new unit and promoted the Irish contribution to the war effort by sending "letters from the front" for publication in New York's most widely read immigrant newspaper, the *Irish-American*.

Norris's first two years as an officer were relatively uneventful, but that all changed in 1864, when General Ulysses S. Grant took control of all the Union forces in the east and began aggressively pursuing General Robert E. Lee's Army of Northern Virginia. Norris's unit fought bravely at Spotsylvania Court House, North Anna, and in the assault on Lee's forces surrounding Petersburg, where Norris was wounded in the right shoulder and left thigh on June 16, 1864. Norris's regiment was present at Appomattox Courthouse when Lee surrendered there ten months later.

Captain Thomas D. Norris photographed when he was an officer in Corcoran's Legion, most likely in 1862, when his regiment was organized.

Although the Union victory must have filled Norris with pride, the end of the war was more bitter than sweet for the Irishman. According to the *New York Tribune,* Norris "returned home to find that he had lost his wife through worse than death," an apparent reference to infidelity. Thomas and Ann quickly divorced (something exceedingly rare in that era), and the court awarded him sole custody of their four children. But his attempts to reenter business failed. Rather than go back to his needle and thread, Norris tried to parlay his military renown into a career as a saloonkeeper, opening the Corcoran Legion House in 1865 at 362 Cherry Street in the seedy East River waterfront neighborhood known as Corlears Hook. Yet a year later the business went belly-up. Norris had apparently put every penny he had into the bar because soon, the *Tribune* recounted, "he had not a cent in the world."

It was at this point that Norris turned to peddling apples from a stand outside Castle Garden in Battery Park, "and with the pennies he made," reported the *Tribune,* "he managed to secure bread" for himself and his children. Due to the lingering effects of his wartime wounds, strenuous work like day labor on construction sites was not an option. By 1870, Norris had moved his family from New York City to Morrisania, located just across the Harlem River from Manhattan in what is now the south Bronx but was then Westchester County. There, where rents were far cheaper than in Manhattan, he worked as a lowly "paper dealer," a euphemism for someone who rooted through other people's garbage collecting discarded paper and rags to be sold to paper manufacturers. Norris's seventeen-year-old daughter, Mary Anne, cared for her three younger siblings and cooked the family meals.

Slowly, however, Norris improved his circumstances. He became active in the local Democratic Party organization and eventually began working as a real estate agent. He was doing well enough by 1875 that he ventured to lower Manhattan to open an account at the Emigrant Savings Bank. That Norris chose this bank, located many miles from his home, much farther from Morrisania than other banks he could have chosen, indicates the degree of loyalty many Famine immigrants felt toward this institution created by and for Irish Americans. A year later, he left the real estate business and began selling insurance. However, these commission sales jobs did not give Norris the income or job security he desired.

Ironically, it was getting arrested in 1879 that set Norris back on the path to prosperity. That summer, a "revenue officer" detained Norris for buying untaxed cigars from a street peddler. When brought before a magistrate, Norris pleaded for leniency, describing how he had sacrificed his body, his business, and his marriage for the cause of the Union and been unable since the war to find steady work due to his continuing medical issues. Norris even produced for the court a letter of reference from 1865 written by Horace Greeley, publisher of the *Tribune* and one of the most famous men in America back then, recommending Norris for a government clerkship because his injuries rendered him incapable of doing more strenuous work. Yet with thousands of disabled veterans seeking such posts, Norris had been unable to secure such a position.

All that changed after his court appearance. Reporters from both the *Tribune* and the *Herald* published accounts of Norris's woeful tale. Suddenly, he was offered a job in the New York County Clerk's office, a prize patronage plum that paid a whopping $1,500 per year. This abrupt change in fortune apparently emboldened Norris to seek a more active role in New York's Irish American community. In the fall of 1880, he began making appearances at the New York Philo-Celtic School, which taught Irish language classes on weeknights and Saturdays at its headquarters on the Bowery. Soon he joined its board and became its corresponding secretary.

Norris also started visiting schools with large numbers of Irish American students and singing to the children in Irish, then commonly referred to as Gaelic. He began contributing regular columns to the *Irish-American* as well, written in both English and Irish, to help Irish-born New Yorkers learn or improve their ability to read and write in their native tongue. He became so renowned in this regard that at Grover Cleveland's inauguration as president in 1885, Norris delivered a congratulatory address in Irish to the new president on behalf of New York City's Democrats. Meanwhile, Norris had also become active in the Irish Land League (which raised money to empower tenant farmers in Ireland and provide famine relief) and in New York's Civil War veterans' organizations. And in 1892, the sixty-five-year-old Norris finally remarried, wedding a New York–born daughter of Irish immigrants, Anna O'Sullivan, who at twenty-nine years of age was younger than all four of Thomas's children.

At various points, as the mayoralty changed hands, the new chief magistrates tried to replace Norris with their own favorites, but the Irish American press would kick up a fuss, condemning the "ingratitude" of those who would turn out "our gallant and patriotic friend." As a result, he would manage to win reinstatement. Norris eventually moved to a federal position as "storekeeper" (at $1,400 per year) in the custom service's bonded warehouse at 40 Water Street, just around the corner from where he had operated his clothing shop on South Street nearly forty years earlier.

Norris in 1894, near the end of his life.

CAPTAIN T. D. NORRIS.

In 1897, just a few months shy of his seventieth birthday, Norris lost his custom house position when Republicans took control of the White House. Norris decided to retire and moved to the eastern edge of Brooklyn. A few years later his health began to fail, and he died in January 1900 at age seventy-two of heart disease at a Greenwich, Connecticut, "sanitarium." Anna must have at least been happy to tell Thomas, shortly before he passed away, that she was pregnant. But six months later the baby, a little girl and the first she had managed to carry to term, died from "asphyxia" during delivery.

While Anna was grieving this loss, she was forced to fight with her stepchildren over Thomas's estate. That was because he bequeathed thousands of dollars to Anna but left just five dollars to his eldest daughter, Mary Anne, who had run their household as a teenager while he was in such dire straits and was now a widow herself and, she claimed, utterly "destitute." Mary Anne did not win any more of her father's estate in court, but she probably got some satisfaction by reporting Anna to the authorities when she learned that her stepmother was continuing to collect Thomas's Civil War pension after his death, even though she was not entitled to do so.

While all this family acrimony would have undoubtedly pained Thomas, who was known for his congeniality, he would have been pleased with the glowing tributes that appeared in New York's Irish press (and even in a few newspapers in Ireland) at the time of his death. They praised his brave and patriotic service to his adopted homeland during the Civil War and his extraordinary efforts to preserve the Irish language in the years since. "His simplicity and good nature endeared him to all," noted the *Irish World,* while the *Irish-American* offered perhaps the highest praise possible. "He was," wrote its editors, "a true Irishman in every respect."

———

Hundreds of thousands of struggling Irish Famine refugees like Thomas D. Norris managed to overcome incredible hardships to create comfortable middle-class lives for themselves in America. Yet anyone familiar with the typical depiction of the Famine immigrants would imagine that Norris's story must be an anomaly. From the time of the Famine all the way to recent Hollywood blockbusters like *Gangs of New York,* popular culture has presented these immigrants as locked in abject poverty, which they could escape only through larceny, violence, political corruption, or some combination of the three. Whether depicted by late-nineteenth-century novelists or by Leonardo DiCaprio and Cameron Diaz, the Famine immigrants had little money, even less education, and no opportunity to advance unless they were ferocious fighters or crafty criminals. About the only "honest" jobs that might provide a path out of privation in these portrayals were those of policeman and saloonkeeper. The Famine immigrants' dearest hope, according to the prevailing view, was that their American-born children would stay in school and out of trouble so they might have the opportunities that their parents lacked.

Typically, academics take issue with Hollywood depictions of history. In the case of the Famine immigrants, however, historians have actually bolstered the popular stereotype. One of the founders of the field of American immigration history, Oscar Handlin of Harvard University, was among the first to study the Famine immigrants. Handlin concluded that in Boston "the absence of other opportunities forced the vast majority into the ranks of an unemployed resourceless proletariat.... It is difficult to know precisely how they managed to exist." An "exceptional Irishman," Handlin admitted, might find "satisfactory employment," but that "failed to mitigate the abject circumstances of the group as a whole."

Handlin's book is eighty years old, but modern historical scholarship on the Famine Irish has emphasized the same themes. Kerby Miller, the most respected and widely cited contemporary historian of the Irish diaspora in America, echoed Handlin's conclusions. "The great majority of Famine emigrants—semi- and unskilled laborers and servants—seldom rose from the bottom of American urban society," he wrote. According to Miller, prejudice and a lack of education and capital meant that "upward occupational mobility" for the Famine Irish "was usually slight, even for those who remained settled in one locale for several decades, and the frequent necessity of sending children to work at early ages often precluded *their* chances to advance much beyond their parents' status." Overall, Miller concluded, the Famine immigrants led "gloomy" lives "of poverty and hardship or, at best, gradual and painfully achieved improvement."

These and other accounts have suggested that the Irish had hardly any control over their destinies. Their lack of education was irreparable. Their dearth of capital was insoluble. The prejudice they faced was insurmountable. They lacked virtually any agency whatsoever. The inevitability of the Famine immigrants' supposedly sorry fate suffuses the literature of Irish American history. "In the two decades before the Civil War," noted a scholar summarizing the prevailing view among historians, "the success of German and English immigrants stood in stark contrast with the dire poverty of the famine Irish."

That is the story of the Famine immigrants we've been told for generations. But why is it, then, that so many Irish immigrants' own accounts of their lives in America paint such a different picture? Every meal in America, they bragged, was like Christmas dinner in Ireland. "The worst table in New York is as good as the general run of tables of the Irish gentry," wrote one. "Any man or woman," argued another, "are fools that would not venture and Come to this plentyful Country where no man or woman ever Hungered or ever will and where you will not be Seen Naked," a reference to the embarrassing lack of clothing for so many in Ireland. The United States was, they mostly agreed, "the best country in the world."

These are not the words of gloomy people, and the stories they tell are not ones of "deprivation" or "helplessness." What accounts for the disparity between our impression of the Famine immigrants and their own view of themselves? If they could narrate their own stories, what tales would they tell?

———

Some of the difference between our image of the Famine immigrants and the accounts in their letters relates to the preconceived notions historians bring to their work: exploited, downtrodden immigrants are what they expect to find. Some of the contrast also results from a desire of Irish Americans to convince others that their forebearers suffered just as much as (or even more than) other immigrant groups. But probably the biggest reason that the Famine immigrants have been portrayed this way, despite their optimistic letters, is that it has been impossible to reliably trace the life stories of enough of them to determine which viewpoint is more accurate.

Say you wanted to discover what became of Peter Lynch, who you know stepped ashore in New York in 1846 in the first year of the Famine. Until recently, the task was simply impossible. The records that would answer the question were spread across fifty states. It would take years of travel and searching to examine the lives of all the Peter Lynches, and even then, there would be no way of knowing which Peter was the right one. That's because you would have found 123 natives of Ireland named Peter Lynch living in the United States in 1860, and dozens of them were born in about the same year as the Peter Lynch in question. And one couldn't narrow the possibilities any further by considering only the several Peter Lynches who were exactly fourteen years older in 1860 than the age stated on Peter's ship manifest in 1846, because census enumerators in the mid-nineteenth century were permitted to approximate ages, and the harried first mates who drew up the ship manifests usually guessed at their passengers' ages as well. The task was therefore impossible — and even more so if you were looking for a Murphy or a Sullivan or a Kelly.

Impossible, that is, until now.

INTRODUCTION

There were two prerequisites for turning the dream of tracing the lives of the Famine immigrants into a reality — the digital revolution and a fortuitous crossing of the corner of Fifth Avenue and Forty-Second Street in New York. The importance of the digital revolution is probably self-evident. Once those millions of pages of census records were digitized, the Internet made them easily accessible to almost any American. Thanks to affiliates of the Church of Jesus Christ of Latter-Day Saints, the half billion entries in those records were soon indexed. Websites like Ancestry.com, which made the records available to the public, were so popular with amateur genealogists that soon the companies that ran them agreed to digitize more federal and state records in return for the right to sell access to them. As a result, not only are federal census records available online, but also state censuses, naturalization documents, military records, wills, and ship manifests. So, too, are nongovernmental records like old newspapers and city directories.

These websites are a godsend for anyone who wants to search backward in time to fill in blank spaces on their family trees. If you know your grandparents' names, you can find records showing them as youngsters with *their parents* and thus learn the names of your great-grandparents. Find *those* ancestors when they were young, and you've uncovered the names of your great-great grandparents, and so on.

Yet these sites aren't nearly as useful for following people from the mid-nineteenth century *forward* in time. Give even a professional genealogist a Famine-immigrant ship manifest, which includes the name and approximate age of each newcomer, and the genealogist would be hard-pressed to tell you where 5 percent of them were living or what jobs they had twenty years later. Thus, even with the digital revolution, tracing the lives of the Famine immigrants would not have been possible but for one bank's incredibly obsessive recordkeeping — and that fateful trip across Fifth Avenue.

INTRODUCTION

When Thomas Norris patronized the Emigrant Savings Bank, it was located behind New York's City Hall at 51 Chambers Street. The bank had been founded in 1850 by the Irish Emigrant Society to encourage Famine refugees to save money in their adopted homeland, and many of these immigrants leaped at the chance to open accounts at a bank run by and for Irish Americans. In the bank's first twenty-five years of operation (when it was located in the portion of lower Manhattan most heavily populated by Irish immigrants), more than 110,000 accounts were opened. But in the twentieth century, with the locus of New York City life moving inexorably uptown, the bank relocated its headquarters to the northeast corner of Fifth Avenue and Forty-Second Street, in the heart of Midtown Manhattan.

The Emigrant Bank required customers such as Norris to provide an unusual amount of biographical information to its clerks when opening an account. In that era, banks typically asked for only three pieces of information from their customers: name, address, and occupation. Yet the Emigrant Bank also required depositors to disclose their precise birth town, parish, and county in Ireland, the name of the ship that brought them to America and the date that it landed, the names and whereabouts of their parents (including their mother's maiden name), and the names and locations of their siblings and children. The bank periodically updated this information, noting new addresses and occupations, spousal deaths, remarriages, and the like. Bank clerks logged all this information in large leather-bound volumes known as "test books," so called because they used them to ask "test" questions meant to expose (in an era before the invention of government-issued photo identification) thieves trying to impersonate depositors. In fact, the Emigrant Savings Bank was apparently the first business ever to use the maiden names of customers' mothers as a security question.

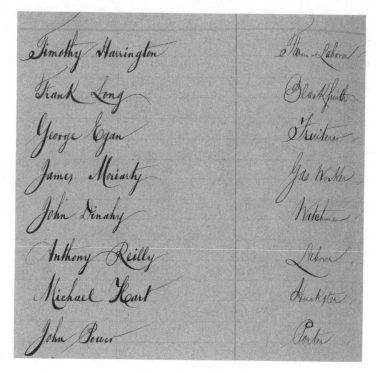

Depositors' names and occupations in the Emigrant Savings Bank test books.

Most American banks eventually discarded their century-old records to save space, not stopping to wonder if historians might find them valuable. As late as the 1960s, depositor records for what had been the biggest savings bank in mid-nineteenth-century New York, the New York Bank for Savings, were still housed in its headquarters. But after that bank changed hands several times during the savings and loan crisis, its old records disappeared. They are probably moldering deep below the surface of some city landfill.

Luckily, the Emigrant Savings Bank remained solvent during the savings and loan crisis, and the historical significance of its test books remained part of its institutional lore. So, when it came time for the Emigrant Bank to move from its expensive Midtown location and dispose of no-longer-needed old records, the bank's executives knew not to toss the old ledgers into a dumpster. Instead, in

1995, bank staff took them diagonally across the street from the northeast to the southwest corner of Fifth Avenue and Forty-Second Street, up the steps past the marble lions, and into the New York Public Library Special Collections department.

———

Most Irish Americans with ancestors who immigrated to America during the Great Famine don't know from where in Ireland those forebearers came. As family stories were passed down from generation to generation, such details were lost. The Emigrant Savings Bank records are thus a gold mine for Irish Americans whose precise ancestral home is uncertain and whose ancestors spent at least a little while in New York City. The usually quiet manuscripts reading room at the New York Public Library was soon overrun with Irish Americans hoping to discover their exact Irish origins. It wasn't long before the harried librarians decided to allow Ancestry.com to digitize and index the collection and place it online to meet the demand.

The information in the Emigrant Savings Bank test books enables historians to track the Famine immigrants to an extent never before possible. That is why virtually every immigrant whose story is recounted in the chapters that follow was at some point a customer of the bank. Each test book entry is a historical skeleton key, unlocking stories — unprecedented in their texture and detail — that might otherwise have remained hidden forever, or at best known to only a dwindling number of family members.

Take day laborer Peter Lynch, whose trail went cold after his arrival in New York because there were too many Peter Lynches for a researcher to choose from. In the Emigrant Bank test book entry for the account he opened in 1851, Lynch listed his brother as James and his sisters, from oldest to youngest, as Ann, Mary, Jane, and Ellen. While there are dozens of Peter Lynches of about the right age from this era in census records, there is only one who lived with siblings James, Ann, Mary, Jane, and Ellen Lynch, and that is the

Peter Lynch found in the town of Faxon, Minnesota, in that state's 1885 census. That clue led to additional research which confirmed that he was, in fact, the same Peter Lynch who landed in America in 1846 and opened a bank account in New York in 1851. He had moved to Minnesota in 1857, bought eighty acres of land for a hundred dollars, and farmed there until his death in 1891. Peter's probate records are online too, showing that he died a prosperous farmer with plenty of assets and not a single outstanding debt.

Biographical details on the life of Thomas D. Norris from his entry in the Emigrant Savings Bank test books.

Without the digitization of so many genealogical records *and* the deposit of the Emigrant Savings Bank test books at the New York Public Library, there would be no way to know that Peter the lowly day laborer in New York had become Peter the prosperous prairie farmer in Minnesota. When the thread of Peter Lynch's story is woven together with hundreds of others discovered in the same manner, they create the rich tapestry that is the Famine Irish saga in America.

The unparalleled detail of the immigrants' stories in this book makes it unique among accounts of the Famine Irish. Another unique feature is how the story is organized. From the moment they arrived in the United States, the Famine immigrants were obsessed with work. After all, unemployment and underemployment had been a defining feature for so many of them in Ireland. Consequently, as soon as they arrived in America, the immigrants immediately sought a job. For most of the men, this meant becoming laborers, longshoremen, porters, gardeners, carpenters, tailors, or shoemakers. Unmarried women primarily took jobs as domestic servants, but many married women worked for pay too, as seamstresses, laundresses, or taking in boarders.

That's where the typical history of the Famine immigrants' working lives ends. But the newcomers were determined to move up the American socioeconomic ladder, and huge numbers of them, like Thomas D. Norris and Peter Lynch, managed to climb to higher rungs of that ladder. *Plentiful Country* is organized to highlight this previously unrecognized part of the Famine immigrants' story. After a short opening section that explores what the immigrants' lives had been like before they left Ireland and began the process of settling in New York City, Part II mimics a climb up the socioeconomic ladder that the newcomers worked so hard to ascend. We start on the bottom rung with day laborers and domestics, then move one rung higher to look at peddlers and street vendors, and then another step up to examine tradesmen like carpenters and shoemakers, and so on until we reach the highest realistic goal for the Famine immigrants—the rung occupied by saloonkeepers. Doctors, lawyers, and priests stood at the pinnacle of the Irish American hierarchy, but so few of the Famine Irish could reach that lofty level that their stories are sprinkled throughout the other chapters rather than being given one of their own.

Several important themes unify these stories of ambition and striving. First, despite the common depiction of the Famine Irish as immigrants locked in gloomy lives of poverty, they actually found — or made — many opportunities for socioeconomic advancement. For example, 41 percent of the male Famine immigrants who began their lives in America in unskilled occupations like day laborer and were tracked for ten or more years finished their careers higher up the socioeconomic ladder. In fact, nearly half of all male Famine immigrants who came to the United States as adults ended their lives in white-collar occupations — many as clerical workers or civil servants, many more as saloonkeepers, grocers, and other kinds of shopkeepers, and a few (two out of every one hundred) as doctors and lawyers. Two-thirds of the immigrants who eventually ran businesses started out in the United States doing sweaty, dirty work that today would be called blue collar. Thus, the prevailing belief that the Famine immigrants "seldom rose from the bottom of American urban society" is simply not true. Only a quarter of the male Famine immigrants tracked for ten years or more spent their whole lives in America on the bottom rung of the socioeconomic ladder.

A second theme that recurs in these newly recovered stories is the avid entrepreneurship of many Famine immigrants. Leaving aside those who died in their first years in America, about one out of every three Famine immigrants in New York ended his career operating a business (mostly small) of one kind or another, and about half as many more tried doing so before returning to wage work. Others with an entrepreneurial bent supported themselves (as Norris did for a while) as peddlers, whose savings accounts reveal that peddling was a very profitable vocation. Many Irish entrepreneurs purchased income-generating real estate with their profits, supporting themselves late in life as landlords, another line of work that contradicts the prevailing impression of them as hapless, helpless victims of poverty and prejudice.

Third, the striving of the Famine Irish in New York profoundly shaped all of Irish America. Of the 1.3 million Irish immigrants who came to the United States in the decade after the onset of the potato blight in 1845, some 960,000 of them landed in New York. On many of the ships carrying the immigrants to New York, the mate compiling the passenger manifest asked each newcomer exactly where in the United States they planned to settle, and about half of the Irish said New York City. Yet by 1860, only about 200,000 Irish immigrants were living there. Many of the Famine immigrants had died before that date, but it seems that for every

Irish New Yorker remaining in the city in 1860, another had decided that they could do better elsewhere in the United States. Those ex–New Yorkers, such as Peter Lynch, took what they had learned in their months and years in Manhattan — about networking, saving money, starting a business, and so on — and applied those lessons in every corner of the United States.

Finally, in New York and elsewhere, the Famine migration to the United States fundamentally changed how Americans viewed immigrants and the American Dream. Before the Great Famine, few immigrants to the United States were fleeing lives of poverty. Only those with significant savings or assistance could afford the ship ticket, the large supply of food one had to bring on board for the five-week journey, and the several months of unemployment that could not be avoided in the transoceanic immigration process. The Famine changed all that. Many of its refugees were part of Ireland's lower middle class, but hundreds of thousands more had been impoverished by the catastrophe, and they comprised America's first "poor...huddled masses yearning to breathe free." Americans steeped in the Protestant work ethic believed that the Famine refugees couldn't possibly succeed in America — the newcomers were supposedly too uneducated, too unskilled, too poor, too Catholic, and too unaccustomed to hard work. They would inevitably become dependent on government handouts for support.

Some of the Famine Irish did struggle, of course, as had Thomas Norris. But overall, the Famine immigrants proved the naysayers wrong, demonstrating that the nation could uplift newcomers no matter how poor and uneducated they might be, and that such immigrants would eventually make the country a better place — stronger, wealthier, freer. The Famine immigrants showed that any group could succeed in America, and in doing so they transformed how Americans defined both their nation and its lofty ideals.

PART I

CHAPTER ONE

"Enough to Sicken the Heart"

Ireland, Famine, Flight

As he trudged down the gangplank from the sailing ship *West Point* and first set foot in New York in March 1851, Cornelius Sullivan must have felt a combination of exhaustion, exhilaration, and disorientation. Until a few weeks earlier, when he left his birthplace of Tuosist in the southwest corner of Ireland, the forty-seven-year-old had probably never seen a town of 5,000, much less one of 500,000 like New York. Cornelius, his wife, Honora (nicknamed Norry), and their four children (seventeen-year-old Mary, fifteen-year-old Timothy, ten-year-old Norry, and seven-year-old Daniel) had probably spent their entire lives in the vicinity of Tuosist, a remote, bucolic parish of green mountain peaks in County Kerry. There, the Sullivans had eked out a livelihood on the estate of an English landlord, the Marquis of Lansdowne, whose twelve thousand tenants were—even before the onset in 1845 of the potato blight that led to the Great Irish Famine—some of the most destitute, ill-clad, and decrepitly housed residents of Ireland.

Lansdowne rarely set foot in Ireland to see how his lessees lived on his 105-square-mile property. He divided his time between his palatial country estate in southwest England and his art-filled home in London, where he held a succession of high-profile positions in the British government, including stints as home secretary and chancellor of the exchequer. An Englishman who did visit Lansdowne's Irish estate a few years before the Famine, however, reported that Lansdowne's tenants "are nearly half naked, and are but half fed." Reverend John O'Sullivan, Catholic archdeacon of the estate's only town, Kenmare (pop. 1,300 in 1841), called his parishioners "the most wretched people upon the face of the globe."

The Famine made the already miserable conditions on the Lansdowne estate truly catastrophic. "Nothing more usual than to find four or five bodies in the street every morning" in Kenmare, wrote O'Sullivan in his diary in 1847. "The cries of starving hundreds that besiege me" are so incessant, he told a government official in London, that they "ring in my ears during the night." The situation was especially bad in isolated Tuosist. As the death toll there rose, and thousands of others were reduced by malnutrition to walking skeletons, a journalist characterized the parish as a "living tomb."

The British government sought to pass the responsibility for helping the Famine's victims to local Irish taxpayers. This meant that the cost of emergency food imports, public works programs, soup kitchens, and the operation of the poorhouse in Kenmare fell primarily on the shoulders of local farmers and landlords, and especially on Lansdowne as the area's primary landowner. The fiscal burden of the unprecedented crisis was too much for taxpayers other than Lansdowne, and soon the local relief board that arranged assistance to the poor and ran the Kenmare almshouse was on the verge of bankruptcy, as were its counterparts all across Ireland. As a consequence, assistance for those affected by the Famine was grossly inadequate.

At least a thousand of Lansdowne's tenants died of starvation or starvation-related diseases from 1847 to 1850—collapsing on the roads, in their one-room, mud-walled huts, and in Kenmare's overcrowded and disease-ridden poorhouse. Lansdowne's tenants there-

24

fore rejoiced when his estate agent announced, at the end of 1850, that the marquis would pay for the emigration of nearly two thousand of his poorest tenants. That winter, Sullivan and his wife and children, along with hundreds of other Lansdowne tenants, were taken to Cork, where they boarded steam-powered ferries to England and then transatlantic sailing vessels for the monthlong voyage to New York.

This replica of a Famine-era cabin, photographed in 2019, sits in the parish of Tuosist, where Cornelius Sullivan was born and lived until the Marquis of Lansdowne paid for him and his family to immigrate to New York in 1851. This black-and-white rendering makes the area look dry and barren, but in fact the landscape is composed of countless different shades of green.

Superficially at least, Sullivan's birthplace and his newly adopted home shared some characteristics on the eve of the Famine. The inhabitants of both Ireland and the United States lived overwhelmingly in rural areas or small towns. What little industry each country had was concentrated in the northeast, while the south and west were more rustic and isolated. And in every region of both Ireland and the United States, the vast majority of breadwinners worked on farms.

The biggest cities of the two countries also had some common features. New York and Dublin were each more than twice as populous as their closest domestic rivals and prospered both as financial centers and by collecting finished goods and raw materials produced in the hinterlands and shipping them to buyers across the sea. Both cities also contained shocking contrasts of wealth and poverty. Leading merchants, bankers, and lawyers in Dublin and New York ostentatiously displayed their wealth by building pricey mansions in the best neighborhoods, while a middle class of clerks and small shopkeepers aspired to join their ranks. Each city also had a large Irish-born underclass — of day laborers and longshoremen, scullery maids and seamstresses — often just scraping by but striving to save enough money to improve their lives and no longer worry about how they would pay the rent or feed their families.

Those surface similarities, however, were far outweighed by the nations' stark contrasts. The twenty-six United States in 1840 covered about 900,000 square miles (1.7 million square miles if one includes American territory that had not yet become states), but by the height of the Famine in 1847, it had grown to 2.9 million square miles. Ireland, in contrast, at 32,000 square miles, is only about the size of South Carolina or Maine. Yet Ireland was far more densely populated (at 262 people per square mile) than the United States or any of its individual states — five times more densely populated than New York State, three times more than Massachusetts, and two and a half times more than Rhode Island, the most crowded American state of that era. In fact, Ireland in 1841 had half the population of the twenty-six United States in just one-fortieth the space. The United States still had plenty of room to grow, while Ireland was bursting at the seams.

In the realm of politics, too, the status of the typical Irishman and American could not have been more different. While women in

Ireland in the Era of the Great Famine

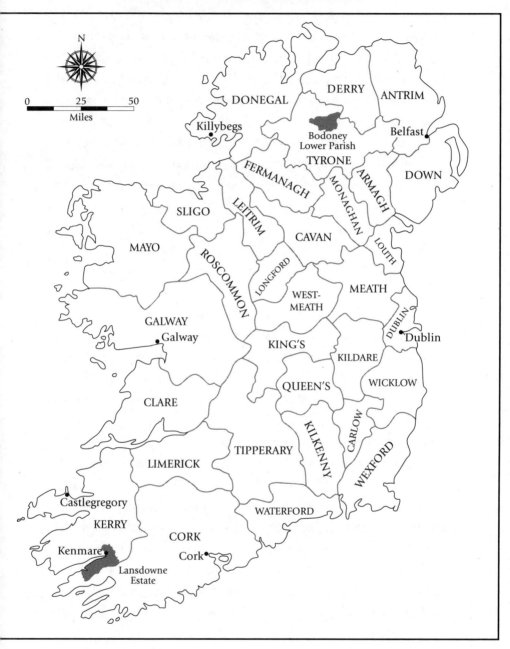

both countries were disenfranchised, all white men in the United States enjoyed the right to vote and all other political and civil privileges as well. In Ireland, however, the majority of men could not vote because they lacked the property that qualified them to do so. The disenfranchised Irish resented their lack of a political voice and their colonial status within the United Kingdom, whose leaders wielded ultimate control of their political destinies. Americans, in contrast, relished their freedom, independence, and political autonomy.

The economies of the United States and Ireland were also a study in contrasts. In the early nineteenth century, the American economy was a dynamo. Opportunity abounded, especially in the west, and as a result median family income in the United States was the highest of any nation in the world. Ireland's economy, however, was fairly stagnant other than in the northeast, which was undergoing an industrial revolution similar to that taking place in the northeastern United States. In most of Ireland, the contrast between well-to-do farmers and the rest of the rural population was shocking. A member of a surveying team sent northwest of Dublin in 1836 to County Meath, one of the wealthier farming districts in Ireland at the time, reported that "you see rich meadows and luxuriant fields of potatoes[,] wheat and oats in every direction and still the people are starving—'starving' they say 'in the midst of plenty.'"

Ireland's colonial status played a major role in hampering its economic growth. Absentee landlords, some of them English, owned a huge proportion of Irish real estate and were content to send their agents to collect rent payments from their tenants rather than make investments to improve their properties to stimulate economic activity. The rental income was often spent in Britain or elsewhere in Ireland, draining capital from the Irish countryside and further retarding growth. As a result, perhaps half the Irish population lived in abject poverty.

Tourists in Ireland, constantly accosted by beggars, were shocked at the widespread destitution. Johann Kohl, a German who had visited

Bosnians and Serbs, Hungarians and Russians, Latvians and Lithuanians, and even American Indians, insisted that none of those groups was worse off than the Irish. "Greater physical privations are endured by the Irish, than by the people of any other country," Kohl reported in 1844. "Look in whatever direction we may for a comparison, the Irishman stands alone, and his misery is without an equal." A Frenchman named Gustave de Beaumont, visiting Ireland a few years earlier, used strikingly similar terms. "Misery, naked and famishing, that misery which is vagrant, idle, and mendicant, covers the entire country," wrote de Beaumont. "[I]t shows itself everywhere, and at every hour of the day; it is the first thing you see when you land on the Irish coast, and from that moment it ceases not to be present to your view; sometimes under the aspect of the diseased displaying his sores, sometimes under the form of the pauper scarcely covered by his rags; it follows you everywhere, and besieges you incessantly; you hear its groans and cries in the distance; and if the voice does not excite profound pity, it importunes and terrifies you."

The Irish poor did not view their situation all that differently. "We are worked harder and worse treated than the slaves in the colonies," testified James McMahon in County Clare in remote southwest Ireland before a committee investigating "the destitute classes" in the mid-1830s. "I understand that they are taken care of by their masters when they are sick or old. When we are sick, we must die on the road, if the neighbours do not help us. When we are old, we must go out to beg, if the young ones cannot help us, and that will soon happen with us all; we are getting worse and worse every day." White Americans, even those on the bottom rungs of the socioeconomic ladder, were typically full of optimism about the future, but Irishmen like McMahon dreaded what the years ahead might bring.

———

A closer look at life in Ireland in the first half of the nineteenth century reveals why that pessimism was so pervasive. In the United

States, especially in rural areas, landownership was fairly wide-spread, and most farms were owned by the men and women who cultivated them. In Ireland, however, half the country was owned by just 750 wealthy families — many of them viscounts, marquises, and nobility of other ranks who lived primarily in England. Other large landowners (some whose real estate portfolios placed them among those 750, others with slightly smaller holdings) were members of what might be called the Anglo-Irish aristocracy. These were Irish-men (usually Protestants) whose ancestors had been granted land by English monarchs in the seventeenth century as a reward for loyal service to the crown, often rendered in the conquest of Ireland itself. Some of these landlords lived in England too, but most remained in Ireland, sometimes living in big cities like Dublin, but in other cases inhabiting grand residences on their Irish estates. Even if members of the Anglo-Irish elite could not boast noble titles like Ireland's biggest landowners, members of both groups could enjoy lives of leisure, supporting themselves in grand style solely on the rents they collected from those who leased plots on their vast, inherited estates.

The rung below these wealthy landowners in the rural Irish social hierarchy was occupied by "middlemen" and prosperous farmers (typically, those who owned roughly fifty or more acres of good land). Middlemen were residents of Ireland who supported themselves primarily by renting large tracts from the richest land-owners and then subdividing and subleasing that property to farmers. Some of these middlemen collected the rent (usually due twice a year) themselves, while others were absentees and hired agents to do so. In some cases, middlemen held leases that ran for ninety-nine years, while others ran for two or three "lives" (those of the original leaseholder and perhaps two of his children). In such cases, middlemen could become fairly wealthy themselves, paying a relatively low rent to the landowner and then charging a much higher price to the farmers to whom they sublet acreage as the population boom in Ireland drove rental prices much higher during the first half of the nineteenth century. Farmers lucky enough to have acquired leases to relatively large tracts of property often functioned as de facto middlemen too, farming some of the land themselves while subletting portions of their holdings to less fortunate folk who, as the century progressed, had to bid higher and higher sums in order to secure enough farmland to feed their families. By the 1830s, middlemen and large farmers in Cork could sublet their land for two to as much as twelve times what they were paying for it.

One level lower on the farming hierarchy were middling farmers, who occupied from five to twenty or thirty acres of land that was arable or good for grazing. They could grow enough to feed their families, sell a portion of their crop to pay their rent, and (if they had more than five or six acres) use the proceeds from the sale of the rest of their harvests to set aside some savings. Like the larger farmers, they tended to own livestock or pigs as well. Sometimes farmers would sell their cows' milk, while in other instances they would churn it to create firkins of Ireland's famous butter to be consumed in urban areas or in England. These farmers also sold steers to cattle traders who shipped them live to Britain for slaughter. Middling farmers acted as middlemen of sorts too. They typically rented small pieces of their land to agricultural laborers, who paid them not in cash but by working several days per week for the farmer, the number of days varying depending on the amount of land being rented and whether or not the farmer supplied manure from his animals to fertilize the plot.

These agricultural laborers, along with "small farmers" (also known as "smallholders") who tilled plots of less than five acres, comprised the bottom rungs of the rural Irish socioeconomic ladder. These were very crowded rungs. The large and middling farmers and their families made up only about 15 percent of 5.25 million men, women, and children who resided on farmland in pre-Famine Ireland. The remaining 85 percent were these smallholders and farm laborers.

In the United States, the distinction between a farmer and a farm laborer was clear—a farmer invariably worked land that he owned, while a farm laborer was a farmer's hired hand who typically toiled in return for room, board, and a monthly wage. In Ireland, however, those lines blurred. A smallholder with a wife and four children who leased only four acres could not, after selling a portion of his crop to pay his rent, feed his family on the yield of his remaining acreage. He likely had to hire himself out as a laborer to a large farmer or a road construction crew as well, and due to the oversupply of such workers he would earn just pennies a day, though he could make two to three times the normal rate in harvest season. Sometimes he might find such employment in the surrounding countryside, but in other cases he might tramp ten, twenty, or one hundred miles away—or even to England—to secure such work, typically doing so in the period between the date in the spring when his potato crop was planted and the date in late summer when it was time to begin the harvest. The agricultural laborer, in turn, usually could not adequately feed his family with the potatoes he grew on the plot he got from the farmer for whom he agreed to labor, so he too would rent additional pieces of arable land from other farmers to grow more potatoes. Thus, both smallholders and agricultural laborers supported themselves through a combination of raising crops for their families to eat and laboring for others.

Men were not the only ones doing farmwork in these families. Women toiled in the fields at planting- and harvesttime. The *Times* of London reported that in the west of Ireland, it was common to see barefooted women carrying "sea weed and shell-sand...in hampers on their backs great distances" to fertilize their potato plots. Women also contributed to the family income of smallholders and laborers by taking charge of feeding or grazing the family pig or cow and also, particularly in the north, spinning flax into linen, though this textile work was disappearing in the 1840s as manufacturers came to prefer machine-made linen to homespun.

This photo of women planting potatoes in northeast Ireland dates from the late nineteenth century rather than the Famine era, but it conveys a sense of the work involved.

In the mid-1830s, when Parliament decided to investigate the living conditions of the poor in Ireland, commissioners convened hearings around the country and asked local leaders how smallholders and laborers lived. When the questioning turned to housing, the witnesses used one word more than any other to describe these homes: "wretched." The laborers' cabins are "of the most wretched description," the investigators were told in Galway, Kildare, and Kilkenny. "Wretched beyond description" came the response in Meath. "Wretched beyond imagination" in Clare. "Most wretched" in Mayo and Longford. "Very poor and wretched" in County Sligo. "Indescribably wretched" in County Limerick, and "universally wretched" in County Cork. Only in the northeast and in the area around Dublin was this not the common refrain.

What made these cabins so terrible? They had just one room, mud and stone walls, and dirt floors that were always damp and often muddy. Many cabins had no windows at all; others had a tiny hole in the wall (perhaps one foot square) where a window might go, but there was rarely glass in that opening. The doorway, likewise, seldom contained a door. Cabins had no ceilings and "the thatch [of the roof] is in general very bad, and in heavy rain hardly ever keeps out the wet, which often pours through in twenty places; it is usually of straw, though often, in the most miserable, of sods, rushes, or potato stalks; and the rafters are bent, broken, and propped up in all directions." Most cabins did at least have stone hearths with chimneys above them, but they often did a poor job venting the smoke from the laborers' turf fires. As a result, smoke was commonly "seen rolling in volumes through the door." Forty-four percent of rural Irish families lived in such "fourth-class" cabins in 1841, but that proportion grew to as high as 75 or even 85 percent in the poorest parts of western Ireland.

The contents of a poor Irishman's home were no better than the cabin itself. "To speak of furniture is almost ridiculous," reported a wealthy Catholic landowner of the situation in Meath, while observers elsewhere agreed that what the typical laborer called "furniture" — consisting of "a stool, a pot, a sort of table," and nothing more — was "so wretched as not to deserve the name." This situation created unpleasant living conditions by day, but truly miserable ones at night. "Comfortable bedding, it is a thing almost unknown in a labourer's cabin," testified a priest in west Cork. Few laborers and smallholders had beds at all. The family typically slept on straw or hay on the wet dirt floor, though most placed "a few sticks, by way of bedstead, to keep the straw from the ground," usually "in the corner next [to] the fire." Cabin dwellers wore to bed the clothing that had covered them during the day, because they didn't have much else with which to cover themselves. "Blankets very scarce," ran a typical report, and "bed-clothes" (what Americans today would call sheets), if they had any at all, were "wretched and squalid." To cap it all off, the family pig slept in the same corner of the cabin as the rest of the family. "It is enough," concluded that wealthy Meath landowner, "to sicken the heart."

The diets of rural laborers and smallholders were just as inadequate as their housing and bedding. As the Irish poor were forced to feed themselves from crops grown on ever smaller plots, they came to rely more and more upon the potato as the centerpiece of their diet, because an acre of potatoes could feed one for many more days than an acre of oats, corn, wheat, or vegetables. And unlike those other foods, potatoes alone could sustain a person indefinitely. If an Irishman ate enough potatoes, he could get all the vitamin B and C he needed, as well as plenty of iron, potassium, and magnesium. Potatoes provided sufficient carbohydrates for a day working in the fields and, in adequate quantities, even enough calcium. With arable land at such a premium, millions of Irishmen, including a large majority of laborers and smallholders, had little to eat by the 1830s but potatoes. "Labourers never, and small farmers but very seldom, consume meat, eggs, or fish," read a typical report. Exceptions were made for Christmas and Easter, when even the poorest family would try to buy a cheap cut of meat for the holiday meal. But otherwise, they ate potatoes for breakfast, potatoes for dinner (the midday meal), and potatoes for supper, day after day after day. "It is historically unique," notes one expert, "that a single foodstuff, other than a storable grain, should dominate the diet of a people living in a temperate climate." But the extraordinary poverty found in Ireland forced its inhabitants to extraordinary measures.

The potatoes the Irish ate were not the envy of gourmets—no fingerlings or Yukon golds. Many grew and ate "the very worst" Irish potato, a mealy, coarse variety known as the "lumper," chosen for its high yield per acre. Nor could laborers or smallholders vary the way in which they cooked them—ovens were an unthinkable luxury, as was oil or animal fat for frying. If these country folk were lucky enough to have a cow, they boiled their potatoes in buttermilk, the slightly milky water left over after milk was churned into butter. If buttermilk was not available, they might cook the potatoes in sour milk given to them by the farmer for whom they worked. Otherwise, they would have to boil their potatoes in water, though in some places roasting them over a fire was more common. The only seasoning widely available to add flavor to the potatoes was salt.

While a poor Irishman's diet might have been unimaginably monotonous, it was at least filling. When potatoes were plentiful, the typical laborer ate one stone (fourteen pounds) of potatoes per day. "It was agreed on all hands," wrote a visitor examining the Irish dependence on the potato, "that a man could not subsist upon less than one stone of potatoes in the day." Women and children ate less, but the average Irish family of six still needed thirty-five to forty pounds of potatoes per day—even more if the children were teenagers. But by midsummer, typical laborers and small farmers began to run out of potatoes. July and August were known in Ireland as the "hungry months" or the "waiting months" as the poor awaited the first potatoes of the new crop to be ready to consume. If they had money, they might buy corn or cabbage, or collect nettles or seaweed to supplement their dwindling potato supply, and the cook of the family would serve only two meals a day, and in dire situations only one. As a result, by the 1830s a large proportion of the rural Irish population experienced terrible hunger each and every summer.

Not everyone in the Irish countryside suffered this way. There was much more poverty in the west of Ireland than the east. In the northeast and southeast, Ireland's "oatmeal zones," even many of the poor would have eaten oatmeal for breakfast much of the year. And middling and large farmers, who lived in comfortable housing with multiple rooms and well-stocked kitchens, would have eaten eggs, milk, oatmeal, bread, butter, and meat or fish every day. But even these relatively well-off people, notes a historian of Irish foodways, ate "a diet with a strong potato profile." As the population of

the Irish countryside skyrocketed over the course of the early nineteenth century, the middling farmers were forced to pay ever higher
rents to their landlords, cutting severely into their profit margins
and pushing them to eat more potatoes to stay afloat. They had less
to eat each July and August as well.

The rhythm of life in Ireland's large towns and cities differed
from that of the countryside, but even in urban areas poverty was
widespread. The inhabitants of Irish towns, like their counterparts
in the United States, ran the gamut from well-to-do doctors, lawyers, bankers, merchants, and small retailers to unskilled and
underemployed day laborers. But the pay for the unskilled in Ireland was just a fraction of that in the United States, especially outside of planting- and harvesttime. In those periods of slack rural
employment, laborers from the countryside might walk to urban
areas and compete for such jobs with townsfolk. Artisans could do
well if they had a specialty such as watchmaking or cabinetry that
was in short supply, but those in other trades, such as carpentry,
shoemaking, and tailoring, might not earn a whole lot more than
rural laborers. These poor city dwellers were nearly as dependent
on cheap potatoes to feed their families as were agricultural laborers and smallholders. Some rented land just outside of town to
grow potatoes for their families; others had to use their meager
incomes to buy them. It was harder than in the past for their wives
to contribute to the family finances because textile industry jobs in
Ireland were becoming scarce and the domestic service positions
that were so abundant in America were much harder to find in Irish
towns. Housing conditions for the urban poor could be just as bad
as those in the countryside. In Dublin, landlords converted what
had once been single-family homes into tenements housing four,
six, or eight families in squalid conditions. In many smaller Irish
cities, poor families lived in alleyways in windowless mud-walled
huts with dirt floors similar to those in rural areas. The main difference was that dozens of these cabins might be crammed into a city

block or two, meaning that their residents suffered all the housing problems that plagued rural residents plus the noise and unsanitary conditions that resulted from squeezing together so many homes that lacked toilet facilities of any kind. With so many town and country folk alike living in such terrible conditions, no wonder Ireland struck de Beaumont as "an entire nation of paupers."

Given these conditions, it is hardly surprising that in the decades after the Napoleonic Wars concluded in 1815, tens of thousands of Irishmen and -women chose to emigrate, and their preferred destination was the United States. Already by this point, "America" had gained renown in Ireland as a land of unprecedented economic opportunity. "The young men of Ireland who wish to be free and happy should leave it and come here as soon as possible," wrote one satisfied immigrant, for "there is no place in the world where a man meets so rich a reward for good conduct and industry as in America." Irish immigration to the United States also increased in these years because Irish Catholics were more willing to move there once it was no longer a British colony. By going to war with and defeating their English oppressors, Americans took on an exalted status in the eyes of Irish Catholics. One who became a schoolteacher in New York City described his adopted home as "a land of peace and plenty" and "a happy asylum for the banished children of oppression." This widower was paid so much better in New York than in northern Ireland, he boasted to his Irish parish priest, that he had saved "a handsome fortune for each of my children."

Such letters inspired additional emigration. Remittances sent by those who had already moved to the United States enabled still more Irishmen and -women to depart for America, as each successive immigrant would save to fund the migration of several more. As a result, emigration from Ireland to the United States increased sixfold from the early 1820s to the early 1830s and threefold more from the early thirties to the early forties, when, according to official data, it reached an average of about thirty-three thousand per year. The true number was probably about a third higher. Many Irish emigrants bought the cheaper tickets to British North America (as Canada was then known), worked in New Brunswick, Quebec, or Ontario for a while to accumulate savings, and then used that cash to buy transportation to the United States. Those who settled in the United States after living in Canada, no matter where they originated, were rarely counted in the official immigration records of this period.

━━━━━━━

For the millions of men and women remaining in Ireland and living in poverty, even a small reduction in their meager supply of food was bound to cause terrible hardship. So when a blight devastated the Irish potato crop in 1845, and continued to do so for several years thereafter, the result was a famine of historic proportions. The disease that destroyed so much of Ireland's potato crop was caused by a fungus-like organism that infested the tiny "seed potatoes" that farmers planted to grow their crops. That organism probably originated in the Andes and may have traveled to the United States in the Peruvian guano that American farmers used to fertilize their potato crops. When Americans sold their seed potatoes to Europeans, the organism made the trip across the Atlantic with them. North Americans barely noticed the disease on their potato crops — it did not thrive in America's hot, relatively dry summers. But Ireland's cool, cloudy, damp climate was a perfect breeding ground for the infestation. Just before harvesttime in 1845, seemingly healthy potato plants suddenly began to wither and die across Ireland. The damage varied from place to place, ranging from about 30 percent crop loss in some counties, like Cork in the south, to about 50 percent in Clare in the west.

Given the utter dependence of so much of the Irish population on the potato, any decrease in the harvest was sure to be catastrophic. In response to the crisis, the British government purchased thousands of tons of American cornmeal, which it then resold to the needy in Ireland. In May 1846 alone, the government depot in the city of Cork dispensed three hundred tons of cornmeal per week and the depot in the city of Limerick sold five hundred tons per week, even though no one customer was allowed to buy more than seven pounds in any seven-day period. One pound of cornmeal was hardly an adequate substitute for fourteen pounds of potatoes, and getting even that one pound of cornmeal was difficult for those who lived far from the cities where it was sold. By the summer of 1846, therefore, remote County Tyrone in the north of Ireland was "in a great state of destitution," according to a relief official there. Similar reports emanated from much of Ireland. Yet between the government assistance and help from better-off friends, family, and neighbors, most people managed to scrape by. Nonetheless, everyone anxiously awaited the end of the summer of 1846, when the next crop of potatoes would be ready for harvest and those teetering on the brink of starvation might finally have enough to eat.

Throughout that summer, the Irish potato crop appeared healthy and bountiful. Father Theobald Mathew, famous for his efforts to get the Irish to give up alcohol, rode across southeast Ireland from Cork to Dublin on July 27 and found, along the entire 150-mile route, fields of potatoes blooming "in all the luxuriance of an abundant harvest." Right around August 1, however, farmers began reporting a sickening "stench" emanating from their potato fields. A day or two later, the leaves of the potato plants turned dry and gray. The stalks did so a day or two after that, sure signs that the "potato cholera" had returned. Traveling the same road back to Cork on August 3, Mathew now found "one wide waste of putrefying vegetation." Farmers rushed to take the potatoes out of the ground, hoping they might not rot if separated from the diseased stalks and leaves. But the blight had already infected the tubers, and within a few days they too began to decay, quickly becoming "so putrefied and rotten" that even pigs refused to eat them.

Over the next two weeks of that late summer of 1846, the blight spread from one Irish valley and mountainside to the next until potato crops in nearly every corner of the country had been devastated. From the far north in County Donegal came reports of a "general and total failure of the potato crop"; it was wiped out in "every field and garden." From the far south came similarly dire news. "The state of the potato crops is throughout my district now fearfully awful," wrote a constable in County Kerry. Twenty miles away, a newspaper correspondent sent word that "the potato fields in this locality are a scene of desolation." The news was the same wherever in Ireland one turned. "No man now living ever witnessed such a sight," said one Kerry resident. "A nation's food is lost."

Further cornmeal sales could not alleviate a crisis of this magnitude. The government sold it at market price, but that rate skyrocketed with the failure of the potato crop. Besides, those most in need had no money left after the potato shortages from the 1845 harvest, so they could not buy cornmeal no matter the price. Not knowing where their next meal might come from, hundreds of thousands of Irish men, women, and children sought admission in the country's workhouses, set up a decade earlier as a last resort for the indigent who could not support themselves or feed their families. The Edenderry workhouse in King's County (now known as County Offaly) in central Ireland, built to hold 600 inmates, took in 1,800 "wretched souls." In County Cork, the Fermoy and Kanturk workhouses, designed to house 800, each also eventually held 1,800, while the one farther west in Skibbereen, also built to hold 800, contained 2,800. For every starving individual that officials accommodated, they turned away many more.

Those who ran Ireland's workhouses purposely underfed their "inmates" in order to discourage the poor from partaking of their services. As a result of this policy, and because so many of the new workhouse inmates were already sick or malnourished, thousands of those lucky enough to secure refuge in a workhouse nonetheless died there soon after arriving. A Catholic priest in County Leitrim in north central Ireland condemned the heartlessness of this policy, complaining that "the mortality in the poor house…was allowed to increase until the house literally emptied itself into the graveyard." In the city of Cork, a priest visiting the workhouse was likewise shocked to find dozens at death's door. "As rapidly as I could I gave Absolution and anointed these poor creatures before they died."

Every workhouse had a sick ward, but these infirmaries did not have enough space for all the ill inmates, who were sometimes forced to share beds with men, women, and children who had not yet become sick. Fearing they would succumb to their bedmates' diseases (many of which were spread by body lice or diarrhea), and coming to believe they might obtain more food begging or gleaning, thousands eventually chose to give up their coveted places in the workhouses. Others, having lost all hope, volunteered to leave because, as a relief official in Donegal observed, they preferred "to die in their own hovels rather than in the poor house." Tens of thousands suffered tragic, needless deaths in Ireland's workhouses during the Famine.

Knowing that the Irish workhouse system could not handle all those who needed help, and believing it was necessary to make the indigent work for their assistance, even in a time of crisis, the British government set up a massive public works program as the main strategy for averting famine. Beginning in October 1846, hundreds of thousands of starving Irishmen were hired to build or improve roads and carry out drainage projects to prevent flooding in the perpetually rainy nation. At its peak in March 1847, public works employed 714,000 Irishmen. Because each worker, on average, supported four or five family members, about half the Irish population was being sustained at that point by this public works program.

While the huge public works scheme, to that point one of the biggest ever instituted for unemployment relief, provided income that helped many families survive the crisis, the aid was too little and too late for hundreds of thousands more. In order to discourage the Irish from taking these temporary jobs if private-sector employment was available, the government set the pay well below the prevailing rate, which itself had fallen to rock-bottom levels because of the crisis. So with food prices skyrocketing due to the potato shortage, the eight pence a day typically paid to the public works employees would not buy enough food to keep them and their already famished wives and children alive. As a result, many of those employed by the public works got thinner, weaker, and sicker each week they held those jobs. In Leitrim, a father of seven ate just one meal every other day so that he could give more to his children.

As autumn turned to winter, the situation deteriorated, and continual undernourishment took its gruesome toll. "On one road, on which I have 300 men employed, the deaths are three each day," reported an official in Kenmare in February 1847 about the neighboring parish of Tuosist, Cornelius Sullivan's birthplace. The dependents whom these workers struggled to support were suffering too. In Leitrim, their children were "worn to skeletons, their features sharpened with hunger, and their limbs wasted almost to the bone." They were dying as well but did so hidden in their cabins rather than out on the roads. Thousands of Irishmen, and thousands more of their family members, perished from malnutrition, diseases brought on by malnutrition, or starvation itself while employed at public works jobs meant to save their lives.

To make matters worse, the winter of 1846–47 was unusually cold and harsh. Snow was usually rare in Ireland, but not that winter. "The snow falling thick and the wind blowing strong at daylight," reported one relief official in late November. Two weeks later, "snow...falling and now upwards of six inches deep and in many places much more." Snow closed public works sites across much of Ireland at various points that winter, and government officials, following the letter of the law, did not pay their starving employees if they did not work. As a resident of Kerry's Dingle Peninsula put it in a letter to a local paper, "with the price of provisions so high, the rate of wages so low, and the weather so bad...what are we to do?"

The situation was even more desperate for those unlucky souls who could not get a public works job, lost one they already had, or were too sick to take or keep one. Starving Irishmen had pawned or sold their coats and other decent clothing in order to buy food, and as a result they were not properly dressed to work outdoors during a particularly cold and snowy winter. "The poor people go literally half naked to their work," reported a doctor in County Clare, "and sleep at night without changing their clothes, having no other night covering." In some locales, those too ill to continue working were told they could stay home and receive half pay, but with their families already starving, few were willing to accept a pay cut, so these unfortunates actually worked themselves to death trying to earn a few extra pence for their families. As the winter wore on and the death toll mounted, some localities announced that their relief budgets were running out and that they would have to cut their workforces. At a jobsite in County Cavan in south Ulster, lots were drawn to decide which famished workers would lose their positions. "The wretched creatures on whom the lots fell raised a cry that still rings in my ears," wrote their supervisor. "It was like a death sentence to them."

By the middle of that winter of 1846–47, men, women, and children all over Ireland were dying each week by the thousands of hunger or hunger-related diseases. While Ulster in the northeast suffered the least, the situation there was still grim. "Famine, disease and premature death" were "prevailing in some degree everywhere," reported a Belfast newspaper. "Accounts multiply of destitution and suffering and death in their most appalling forms." The elderly and the infirm were said to be suffering the most. In County Armagh, for example, children were discovered "so emaciated as to be unable to either stand or move a limb." A teenaged boy was found in a cabin there "without a single vestige of clothing, the eyes sunk, the mouth wide open, the flesh shrivelled up, the bones all visible, so small around the waist that I could span him with my hand." A relief official in the far north of County Antrim called it "a famine unparalled [sic] in the annals of human suffering."

The crisis was even worse in west Ulster, especially in southwest Donegal. The inhabitants there were so poor, even before the potato blight broke out, that according to a Derry newspaper report in 1844, "there is scarcely a parish in which there are not hundreds of families who are writhing in the agonies of famine." In and around the fishing village of Killybegs (pop. 800), in particular, "the acme of misery has been reached." After the blight struck for a second time, in 1846, the situation there became still worse. "At least 10,000 people have no provisions at all," wrote a local land agent late in 1846 of the parishes around the seaport. "The potatoes are entirely gone." By February 1847, a visitor to Killybegs found that "the destitution is frightful; two or three funerals pass by my window every morning, arising of course from want of food, which produces, first, diarrhoea, then prostration, low typhus fever, and death." A few months later, wrote a local Catholic priest, the death toll was accelerating: "Every day adds new horrors to the scene around us — we are hourly sinking into a deeper abyss of misery."

In central Ireland, the Famine was just as deadly as in the north. "Our town is becoming one entire Bazaar of Beggars," stated a newspaper correspondent in Kells, County Meath. "Scores of famished women and children [are] prowling about from morning until night, from door to door shivering with cold — attacking every individual that may chance to come into the town on any business whatever, with wailings for relief to save them from perishing." Farther west in County Leitrim, "fever is very prevalent and the poor are dying every day," stated a minister. "The dead are buried by the dying." In neighboring County Roscommon, "deaths by famine are so prevalent that whole families who retire at night are corpses in the morning." By the time these Famine victims could be discovered, hungry dogs and rats had often gnawed their bodies, sometimes severing and dragging off whole limbs. Such was the scale of the catastrophe, wrote one observer in King's County in central Ireland, "that even the crows have been reduced to skeletons."

Bad as things were in the Irish midlands, they were even worse on the west coast. When the British government assessed the severity of the Famine in each part of Ireland to determine which districts needed extra funding for relief programs, every district that qualified for such aid lay in the western half of Ireland, and nearly all of them were on the Atlantic coast. In Mayo, the only county in which every parish was deemed "distressed," an English visitor found countless dying Famine victims "moaning piteously" in their hovels, "pale and ghastly," a "heart-rending spectacle." In County Clare, the Famine was just as severe. In December 1846, a relief official reported to his superiors that "although a man not easily moved, I confess myself unmanned by the extent and intensity of suffering that I witnessed, more especially amongst the women and little children, crowds of whom were to be seen scattered over the turnip fields, like a flock of famishing crows, devouring the raw turnips, mothers half naked, shivering in the snow and sleet, uttering exclamations of despair, whilst their children were screaming with hunger." Just south of there, in north Kerry, the situation was no better. "Hourly destitution is becoming—not more extensive, for that is impossible—but more tortuous, more fatal," reported a newspaper in Tralee. "Hundreds are dying and the living are but crawling skeletons."

An English Quaker who made deliveries of emergency food supplies up and down the west coast of Ireland in 1847 wrote that terrible as the suffering might be in the northwest counties, it got "worse as you travel south," and that in far western County Cork "the very climax of misery finds its resting place." The locale in southwest Cork that became internationally synonymous with Famine suffering was Skibbereen, a market town of about forty-seven hundred inhabitants forty-five miles southwest of the city of Cork. A sketch artist sent there by the *Illustrated London News* imagined that the initial horrific reports from the town had to be exaggerations, but witnessing the scene himself, he insisted that "neither pen nor pencil ever could portray the misery and horror." An American visiting the poorest part of the town was repulsed by "the wretchedness of this little mud city....In every hovel we entered, we found the dying or the dead." All around him he saw signs of famine edema (what contemporaries called dropsy), in which the starving, with emaciated, skeletal limbs, had grossly swollen bellies due to the pooling of bodily fluids that would be evenly distributed in those who were healthy. About a quarter of the inhabitants of Skibbereen and many of the towns farther west died in just the first few months of 1847 alone. As a result of this calamitous death toll, in west Cork and all over Ireland, this year became known in Irish history as "Black '47."

BOY AND GIRL AT CAHERA.

A Victorian sense of propriety and the inadequacy of woodcut illustration technology prevented the world from seeing realistic images of the Irish Famine's victims. Compare the woodcut on the left of boys near Skibbereen by the sketch artist of the *Illustrated London News*, who admitted that "neither pen nor pencil ever could portray the misery and horror" of the Famine's victims, to the photo on the right from a famine in another British colony, India, in 1877. These are the "walking skeletons" that aid workers described in their efforts to convey the horrors of the Irish Famine to the outside world.

The situation in Irish cities was somewhat better than in the countryside. In Dublin, the relatively small number of Famine deaths occurred primarily among famished people who had come to town from the surrounding countryside looking for work, charity, or a place in the city's workhouses. In Belfast, where the linen industry was suffering a severe recession, destitution and suffering were more common but starvation was still rare. Cities in the south and west, however, faced greater challenges. An American ship captain who arrived in Cork in April 1847 with a cargo hold full of cornmeal toured the city and in one of its impoverished quarters saw "the valley of death and pestilence itself!" A Galway newspaper in February likewise detailed "the ghastly suffering of the poor destitutes of this city. On every side nothing but cries of destitution and starvation are heard. The poor are literally dropping on the public highways from hunger." In these places, too, the most critically ill were often desperate residents of the countryside who had walked to these cities in a last-ditch attempt to fend off starvation.

—————

Why did the British government not do more to prevent the Famine that all observers knew was inevitable after the crop failure of 1846? The inadequate English response resulted in part from prejudice. Many in Great Britain believed that the Irish were habitually lazy and that too much Famine aid would make them even more indolent. A brush with starvation, however, might induce Catholic Ireland to adopt a Protestant work ethic. The English officials tasked with Famine relief were also excessively concerned that their efforts might harm "private enterprise." As a result, they sold emergency food supplies rather than giving them away and set the price too high for many Famine victims to afford. Such overzealous (and selective) adherence to the tenets of laissez-faire economics enraged the Irish. "Can it be that our countrymen are indeed to be reduced to living skeletons, rather than that our statesmen should swerve from their stern principles of so-called political economy," asked a newspaper in County Clare. "Surely it is disgraceful to a powerful empire like Great Britain to have recourse to such a mean, niggardly system of relief."

Part of the problem was that many British leaders doubted that they ought to be helping the Irish at all. These Englishmen thought Ireland was overpopulated and that the Famine was how "an all-wise Providence" had decided to remedy the situation. Besides, wrote Charles Trevelyan, the British official in charge of Famine relief, "it forms no part of the functions of government to provide supplies of food" to the hungry. The Famine was part of God's plan, he believed, and he hoped that "we may rightly perform our part and not turn into a curse what was intended for a blessing." With that kind of attitude, no wonder Famine relief fell so miserably short. Many Irishmen were not surprised by the government's inadequate response. Who could expect more from the English, wrote an Irish nationalist, given that England had spent the previous several centuries "robbing, ravishing, murdering, exterminating, exiling, torturing, starving, and brutalizing the Irish."

Nonetheless, international indignation as the Famine death toll rose finally forced the British to do more. In February 1847, Parliament authorized the creation of government-financed soup kitchens to feed the hungry, and in the months that followed they began operation. By July, three million individuals were receiving daily rations of soup — in some locales in the south and west as much as 80 or 90 percent of the population was fed each day. Still, the obsessive fear that the Irish would become lazy if they received too much aid shaped even the soup kitchen program. Each quart, the daily allotment, contained just a half ounce of meat, one ounce each of barley and flour, and three ounces of onion. An American who sampled the soup insisted that it "would be refused by well bred pigs" in the United States. But the desperate Irish did not refuse it. People poured in from the surrounding countryside to the towns where the government located the soup kitchens. The relief station in little Castlegregory (pop. 500) on the Dingle Peninsula in Kerry, for example, distributed 498,000 quarts of soup in the six months after it opened. With the advent of the soup kitchen program, starvation in Ireland came to a halt. It was enough to keep the indigent alive, albeit just barely.

By this point, after two disastrous potato harvests and the government's callous response, many Irishmen concluded that emigration was the best means of escaping the Famine. "In the memory of the oldest inhabitant in this part of the country," reported the *Meath Herald* late in 1846, "the spirit of emigration was never known to have arrived at the height it is at present. Numbers who can muster sufficient funds are wending their way towards the shipping ports for America." News that the populace was "flying to America" emanated from across Ireland. "Emigration from all parts of this country is now taking place to a most unprecedented extent," announced the *Clare Journal* in March 1847, while in County Cork it was said that "any persons fortunate enough to have reserved a little means, are making preparations to emigrate by the spring ships." Customs reports from the emigrants' destinations substantiated these observations. The number of Irish emigrants arriving at American ports nearly doubled from 1845 to 1847, reaching 107,000 in the latter year. About the same number landed in Canada (a ticket there was cheaper than one to the United States in 1847), and perhaps twice as many (those who could not afford the fare to North America) migrated to England.

Most of those emigrating were not at death's door. The steerage fare to the United States was £4 to £5 (equal to roughly $750 to $1,000 today), and most passengers also had to bring their own food onboard for the five-week journey. The famished thus could not afford to immigrate to America—they were spending any money they had on food to keep themselves alive. Instead, it was members of the lower-middle ranks—not the long-term poor—who were filling the steerage compartments of ships headed for the United States. The emigrants from Galway, according to a newspaper there, were "well-dressed, healthful, and, we may add, cheerful." Most of the emigrants from Leitrim, too, "are comfortable farmers," stated a paper there. Irish Americans recognized this trend as well. "The pith and marrow of Ireland, with money and value," were the ones who had been coming to America over the past two years, noted the New York *Irish-American* in 1849. That the Irish who immigrated to America during the Famine were disproportionately middle class is also reflected in the fact that adult Irish immigrants in New York in the 1850s were three times more likely to be able to read and write than the adult population of Ireland.

Why would Irishmen who could dip into their savings to pay the rent due on their farmsteads and buy food for their families leave for America? Some did so from "dread of fever," worrying they would catch the Famine-related diseases that had stricken their starving neighbors. But most emigrated because they worried that with successive years of potato blight and no apparent remedy on the horizon, they might eventually exhaust their savings and join the ranks of the starving. They left while they could still afford to do so. They did not want to suffer the fate of one minister's starving parishioners in County Cork, who did not have the money for emigration to the New World and so instead undertook, as he put it, "emigration to the Next World."

Those who decided to emigrate might indeed have joined their countrymen in the "Next World" had they stayed in Ireland — because the Famine did not end in 1847. There were not many reports of blight in the fall of that year, but so few Irishmen had had the means to buy seed potatoes or confidence that planting them was worth the investment that the potato harvest yielded only a tiny fraction (in some places as little as 10 percent) of pre-Famine levels. Yet seeing no blighted potatoes, the government closed most of its soup kitchens, and as a result, reports of starvation, which had all but ceased once the soup stations opened, began to appear once again. In the meantime, the British had instituted a new system under which Irish landowners would be taxed to support those who could not adequately feed themselves. But with so many of their tenants unable to pay their rents, many landlords did not pay the new tax, and as a result relief measures once again fell short. "Imagination can scarcely conceive the state of our poor," wrote a priest in northwest Kerry in the spring of 1848. "They have neither employment, nor clothing nor food. At almost every step one meets on the roads the hideous spectacle of human beings in the agony of hunger, walking in a living death."

With the potato disease apparently waning, farmers planted them in abundance in 1848, yet the mysterious blight again destroyed almost the entire crop in the south and west, as well as in several counties elsewhere, such as Cavan. News dispatches coming from the poorest parts of Ireland in the winter and spring of 1849 soon began to resemble those from Black '47. "Human tongue and human pen are utterly inadequate to convey an idea of the horrors which abound," insisted the *Cork Examiner,* while a minister in coastal Mayo reported that "the sandbanks around me are studded with bodies of the dead."

The more isolated and impoverished the locale, the more likely its residents were to suffer grievously as the Famine entered its third and fourth years. One such place was Lansdowne's estate in southwest Kerry, birthplace of Cornelius and Honora Sullivan. Already renowned for its poverty before the Famine, the property became especially notorious for its grisly death toll once the potato blight struck. "I was shocked in Skibbereen, Dunmanway, Bantry," wrote a visitor to Kenmare in early 1849 who had just come from those infamously destitute west Cork towns, "but they were as nothing to what was now before me....Bad as the Bantry paupers were they were 'pampered rogues' in comparison to these poor creatures...

Spectres from the grave could not present a more ghastly, unearthly appearance....The very thought of them to this moment sickens me." By the end of 1849, between a thousand and seventeen hundred of Lansdowne's twelve thousand tenants had died during the Famine of starvation or related diseases. Thousands more were barely hanging on.

In Kerry and elsewhere, those with relatives in the United States wrote letters to their kin begging them to send passage money so they too could escape the Famine. Very few of these letters survive, but those that do convey the continuing hardships of the later Famine years. A Mrs. Nolan in County Kilkenny wrote to her son Pat in Rhode Island that she could no longer attend church because she had pawned her coat and petticoat in order to buy food. She had also pawned her bed, blankets, and her shoes. She and "little dickey" (either her son or an orphaned nephew) had been periodically homeless until they got the thirty shillings (about $7.50) Pat had sent by mail. But that money had all been spent and now "we are without a bit to eat and I wood Be Dead long go only for two Nebours that ofen gives me a Bit" of sustenance. Mrs. Nolan believed that Pat would be sending more assistance but for "Mary," probably Pat's wife. "Tell Mary that this is the poorest prospect of a winter that ever I had sence I began the world...without house Nor home...fire Nor candlelight...freind Nor fellow No[r] a Bit of food to eat....So tell her thats my prosspects." In case reason was not getting her point across, Mrs. Nolan tried guilt as well. "For god Sake," she declared, "you promised to [send money to] take me and little dickey out" of Ireland.

What Mrs. Nolan had been promised was that Pat and Mary would engage in a favorite Irish practice now known as "chain migration." Under this immigration strategy, a family that could afford only (or had received only) a single transatlantic fare would send to America the person thought to have the best chance to quickly land a job and save money. That person would economize obsessively and save every penny until they could afford to buy a ship ticket for a second family member. The first immigrant would help the second find work, and the two of them would then pool their savings until they could purchase a ship ticket for another kinsman. The process would be repeated until everyone in the family who wanted to emigrate had done so. Then, if the kinsmen were so inclined, they might finance the emigration of a niece, nephew, or cousin, and the whole process would begin again. In this manner, a remittance that was only large enough to finance one ticket might serve as a springboard to enable an entire family of six or more to eventually emigrate.

The Cain family from Ardstraw parish in County Tyrone was one of many that employed chain migration to finance its emigration. Jane left first, at age nineteen at the very beginning of the crop failures, and most likely worked in New York as a domestic. Not until 1850 had she saved enough to bring over brother John, a twenty-six-year-old bricklayer. A year later came another brother, seventeen-year-old James, a wheelwright, and then in 1853 sixteen-year-old Bernard, another bricklayer. Finally, in 1854, the siblings brought over their seventy-one-year-old father, Patrick. It did not usually take Irish families so many years and so many voyages to reunite in America, but stories like the Cains' were not uncommon.

"Each American mail brings remittances to a large amount of persons in this neighborhood" intending to emigrate, reported the *Leitrim Journal* in commenting on the popularity of chain migration, which it called "sibling emigration." "Never before...have so many left this neighborhood for the land of the Stars and Stripes." Yet for those who were starving—who had been reduced to skin and bones and nothing more—the wait for the next remittance from across the sea seemed interminable. Their pleas are heartbreaking even 175 years later. "For God's sake," wrote Mary Rush from County Sligo, "take us out of poverty, and don't let us die of the hunger."

CHAPTER TWO

"The Best Country in the World"

Coming to New York

LIKE MARY RUSH and Mrs. Nolan, most victims of the Famine relied on family members to pay their way to America. But a small proportion, somewhere between 3 and 10 percent, emigrated thanks to landlord, government, or charitable assistance.

One of these subsidized immigrants was Cornelius Sullivan (whom we met at the beginning of chapter 1) from bucolic Tuosist on the Lansdowne estate in County Kerry. Even in a metropolis like New York, teeming with one hundred thousand Famine refugees by 1851, Sullivan and the other Lansdowne immigrants stood out. Most of the Famine immigrants, especially those who arrived in 1846 and 1847 when remittances were scarce and chain migration had not yet brought many poorer Irishmen to America, came from the middle to lower-middle ranks of Irish society. New Yorkers did not grasp this fact until they laid eyes on Lansdowne's gaunt, penniless exiles. The *Evening Post* lamented that they had been shamefully dumped on the docks "in a starving condition." The *Sun* called them "the most miserable looking creatures that we have ever seen landed upon our shores."

As a result of both their disorientation and their poverty,

Cornelius Sullivan and many of his Lansdowne compatriots initially had to live at the charity boardinghouse run by the New York Commissioners of Emigration on Canal Street. Cornelius and his son Daniel were still lodging there (or had returned there) five weeks after their arrival in New York, while his wife, Honora, and their three other children had to take refuge at the city almshouse on Blackwells Island in the East River. Cornelius and Daniel were far from the only Lansdowne immigrants at the charity rooming house. "It is a remarkable fact, that in one night there were no less than 196 Sullivans and 95 Shays [Sheas] in the Canal street lodging house," remarked one newspaper. (Sullivan and Shea were the two most common surnames in and around Kenmare.) "They were all tenants of the Marquis of Lansdowne."

Given his precarious circumstances, after five weeks in New York, Cornelius Sullivan did something that might surprise us — he opened a bank account. When he walked into the Emigrant Savings Bank on Chambers Street behind City Hall, he placed $5 (nearly a week's wages for a day laborer, and equal to about $200 today*) on the counter as his first deposit. The bank secretary asked Sullivan exactly where in Ireland he had been born, the date he had arrived in America, the name of the ship on which he had traveled, where he was living, and his occupation (Sullivan said "farmer").

Life must have been incredibly difficult for the Sullivans. Their ten-year-old daughter, Norry, died sometime during the family's first six weeks in America. Soon, Cornelius moved the rest of his family out of the almshouse and into a dilapidated apartment among brothels and bawdy basement dance halls on Little Water

---

* Determining what a dollar from the 1850s is worth today is very difficult, and economists use a variety of methods to make such estimates. Here and in the pages that follow, I have used the most conservative method (in other words, the smallest multiplier) for estimating what dollar amounts from the past would equate to in 2023, when this book went to press. My rationale for choosing the most conservative option, and descriptions of the other methods available for making such estimates, is described in "A Note on the Value of a Dollar," page 415.

Street, one of the seediest blocks in Five Points, a notoriously over-crowded, run-down, impoverished neighborhood a half mile north-east of City Hall, which was home to more Irish immigrants than any other part of New York. Scraping by was difficult. Three months after Sullivan opened his account, he withdrew his $5 and closed it.

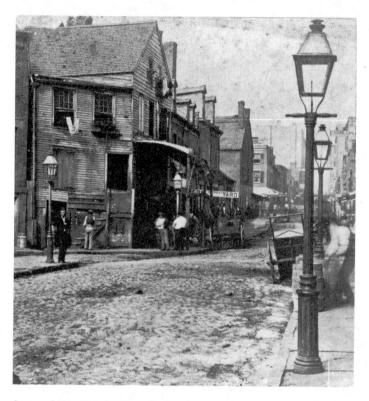

This photo of Five Points dates from about 1870, but the view in the 1850s was virtually identical. It shows Anthony Street (renamed Worth in the mid-1850s) looking west, with the corner of Little Water Street (renamed Mission Place at the same time) on the left. The doorway at the left (behind the man standing next to the gaslight) was the entrance to 7 Little Water Street, where Cornelius and Honora Sullivan lived soon after arriving in America.

Even though most of the Famine immigrants had never set foot in a bank before they arrived in America, they understood the importance of saving. A year before the Sullivans landed in New

York, Irish journalist Thomas Mooney, who lived in America for most of the Famine era before ultimately returning to Ireland, noted that many of the immigrants "who have had the prudence to save their money have put up a little; still I am sorry to say there are too many in New York who live from hand to mouth." The Sullivans were in that latter group in 1851, but would not be for much longer. A year later, Cornelius opened a new bank account, and in it over the course of the ensuing decade he and Honora saved $367, the equivalent of $13,000 today.

Much of that savings was amassed in the final year or two of their first decade in America, when Sullivan decided to supplement the income from his low-risk, low-reward employment as a day laborer with riskier but potentially more remunerative work as a peddler. Almost anything one could buy in a brick-and-mortar shop in nineteenth-century New York could be purchased for a bit less from a street peddler—food and clothing were especially popular items to hawk on the city's streets. But Sullivan decided to try a relatively unusual product line and invested some of his hard-earned savings in a supply of corks.

Cork peddling might not seem like a lucrative line of work. After all, how often did one need to buy a bottle stopper? Yet peddling almost anything could be profitable for a savvy negotiator with a winning personality. And in an era before plastics in a city in which empty glass bottles were ubiquitous, there was apparently a steady demand for replacement bottle corks. It may have also helped that this was a line of peddling in which there were very few Irishmen, giving Sullivan a sales advantage with a huge portion of the city's population. Sullivan did so well peddling corks that he soon made it his full-time vocation, and the decision paid off handsomely. By the middle of 1865, the Sullivans had tripled their bank balance to a whopping $1,173 (equal to more than $22,000 today), a veritable fortune for a destitute family on the brink of starvation in the "living tomb" of Tuosist fourteen years earlier.

We don't know what became of Cornelius and Honora Sullivan after 1865. They may have moved; they may have died. With more than one hundred Irish-born Cornelius Sullivans and nearly seventy-five Honora Sullivans of about the right age living in the United States in 1870, it's impossible to be sure. But even the story of their first fourteen years in America is rich with meaning. Like the Sullivans, many of the Famine Irish may have started out dirt poor in the United States, but it was possible to escape that poverty. They were not hapless or helpless. And even those Famine refugees who were utterly lacking in the educational and vocational skills most sought after in America brought with them other traits — ambition, perseverance, ingenuity — that perfectly suited their new homeland.

———

The voyage to America taken by the Sullivans and the other 1.3 million Irish immigrants who came to the United States in the decade after the onset of the potato blight was harrowing in every respect. Most of the Famine emigrants began their emigration journey by walking dozens of miles to an Irish port town. Almost all the sojourners then boarded a steam-powered ferry and traveled from these ports (most often Dublin, Cork, or Belfast) 150 to 300 miles eastward (*away from* the United States) to Liverpool, then the hub for most travel to North America. There, they would typically have to wait several days (and sometimes longer) before their transatlantic vessels were ready. In those days, ships did not typically depart on a schedule, but instead set sail when their owners decided that they had taken on enough passengers and cargo to make the trip sufficiently profitable. As a result, the Irish in Liverpool with a little money to spare had to spend some of that precious savings on space in a boardinghouse, where in most cases they would share beds with total strangers. Those who could not afford that "luxury" would sleep on the streets until their ship was ready to sail.

The vessels that carried the Famine immigrants across the Atlantic were tiny compared with modern-day cruise ships. While today's behemoths average 1,000 feet in length, the typical ship plying the route from Liverpool to New York was only 150 feet from stem to stern, and none were longer than 200 feet. These ships, which before the Famine might have brought 150 to 200 passengers per voyage, now crammed 300 to 500 on board.

This image of a ship leaving Liverpool filled to capacity (and perhaps a bit beyond) with Irish emigrants at the height of the Famine in 1850 conveys a sense of the overcrowding on transatlantic vessels in this era. Almost all of these passengers would have been required to squeeze into the steerage compartment at night and during storms.

Those passengers were divided into two or three classes, depending on the ship. The first- and second-class voyagers were known as cabin passengers. If there were both first- and second-class cabins, families in first class had a room to themselves, while those in second class had to share a cabin with other passengers but were guaranteed not to have to sleep in beds with strangers. The average ship carried fifteen to twenty cabin passengers.

The rest of the emigrants were housed in the steerage, large rooms in the bowels of the ship whose walls were lined with triple-tiered bunk beds, each of which measured six by six feet, the dimensions of a king-size mattress today. Four adults (or two adults and four children) were expected to share each of these bunks. As a result, most steerage passengers shared their beds with total strangers, with each adult allotted eighteen inches of space per bunk. For most of the Famine migration, men, women, and children — married and unmarried — were all crammed together like sardines into a single steerage area. In 1852, Parliament enacted legislation mandating that each ship create a separate steerage compartment for single men. However, this still meant that women had to undress and even use their chamber pots in front of dozens of *married* men. (There were privies on deck but these quickly became so foul due to overuse that women avoided them at all costs.) Only *after* the Famine era were shipping companies required to give women and their young children a separate steerage area.

When their vessels finally headed out to sea, many emigrants were overwhelmed with emotions. Some mourned the thought that they would never again set foot in their beloved homeland. "Oh thou spot of earth, endeared by a thousand tende[r] ties and fond recollections," wrote one Famine emigrant in his journal in a maudlin but heartfelt attempt to express these feelings, "your receding form but little knows with what sad feelings your unhappy exile bids you his last farewell!!" Others lamented that they had quite possibly laid eyes on their parents, siblings, spouses, or even children for the last time, because even if they intended to send remittances to allow those loved ones to join them, there was no way to be sure those family members would survive the ongoing Famine long enough to make that reunion possible.

Right around the time those tears of sadness might finally dry, seasickness would overcome the passengers, especially at night when the immigrants were expected to vacate the deck and stay in their windowless, cramped steerage compartment. Quickly the steerage began to reek of acidic vomit, which would befoul the floors when the sick could not make it up to the deck to wretch. The odor from all those unwashed bodies wearing all that sweat-soaked clothing made the smell of the steerage even worse, as did the inevitable spillage from chamber pots tossed to and fro as the ship was undulated in the Atlantic swells. The steerage contained, a ship inspector recalled years later, "the foulest stench that can be conceived of."

To make matters worse, the voyage was inconceivably slow and mind-numbingly boring. Sailing against the prevailing winds, it took the emigrant sailing ships thirty-five days, on average, to traverse the thirty-three hundred miles of ocean that separated Liverpool from New York. That meant that the ships were progressing toward New York at a speed of just four miles per hour.

The trip was made even more excruciating by how little food and water the emigrants received during the voyage. Cabin passengers were fed by the ship's crew, but the immigrants in steerage were expected to bring their own food to supplement the meager rations that the ship provided. Each steerage passenger was given a pound of bread, "biscuit" (similar to hardtack), or cornmeal per day, as well as three quarts of water for cooking, washing, and drinking. If the food ration was bread, it was not fresh baked, but rock hard, and like the biscuit had to be soaked in the precious supply of water to be made edible. If the ration was given as flour or cornmeal, then the steerage passengers were expected to mix it with their water and cook the resulting batter as pancakes in the communal cooking space on deck.

Henry Johnson, a relatively well-off Famine emigrant from County Antrim, made the voyage to America in 1848 and brought food with him as he had been advised. But when he opened his trunk after a week at sea, he found the ham he had packed "alive with maggots," so he threw it overboard. The crew provided

Johnson with five pounds of biscuit and two of flour each week, but the biscuit he received was so foul, he reported to his wife back in Ireland, that even the pigs on board refused to eat it. After the rest of the food Johnson brought with him ran out, he tried to beg sustenance from other passengers to supplement his flour pancakes, "but it was every man for himself." As a result, "for the remainder of the passage I got a right good starving." So, too, did tens of thousands of other Famine immigrants.

Besides worrying about getting enough to eat, the immigrants also feared catching a deadly disease on board their ships. Many steerage passengers suffered from severe diarrhea, due to their terrible diets during the sea voyage or intestinal infections resulting from contaminated food or water. Some emigrants died of these ailments before reaching America, especially if they were already frail from years of famine. Steerage passengers more commonly perished from typhus (known popularly as "ship fever"), a bacterial infection spread through the feces of the body lice that commonly infested cramped steerage quarters. When the lice's human hosts scratched their itchy skin, they created microabrasions that allowed the typhus bacteria to infect themselves. During the Famine years, an average of 1.5 out of every 100 would-be Irish New Yorkers died of such ailments before reaching America.

That death rate did not qualify these New York–bound vessels as "coffin ships," those that arrived in port having lost dozens of passengers to illness and which loom large in Irish American remembrance of the Famine. In the initial years of the potato blight, the fare to what is now Canada cost only half that to New York; as a result, the poorest, most famished emigrants booked passage on ships to Quebec, New Brunswick, or even Newfoundland. At the height of Black '47, a dozen ships headed for British North America suffered death rates of 15 to 30 percent, ten to twenty times that of the typical voyage to New York. *These* were the "coffin ships" whose passengers suffered so terribly. Their tragic, preventable fates are etched into the cultural memories of

Irish Americans, even though their ancestors who came to New York never set foot on one of these infamous vessels. After the debacle of the coffin ships in 1847, Canadians imposed a head tax on Irish immigrants to try to deter so many penniless immigrants from landing in their ports. That action and others raised the fare to Canada so that it matched that to the United States, and from then on nearly all the Irish who emigrated bought tickets to New York.

After five weeks at sea, when their transatlantic vessels finally entered New York Harbor, the immigrants were overcome with joy. "No words can describe it," reminisced an immigrant who had arrived in New York in 1847. "To the nearly-emaciated, forlorn emigrant, [it] is about the happiest moment of his life." Tears flowed for many, and some knelt on the deck and gave thanks to God or their favorite saint for allowing them to survive the perilous journey. In those days, there was no Statue of Liberty waiting to greet the immigrants, nor tall skyscrapers for them to gawk at — just a mass of red-brick warehouses, workshops, and tenements punctuated by the occasional tall church steeple.

For the Famine immigrants, unlike so many generations of refugees that followed them, the difficult journey to America had a relatively easy, almost anticlimactic ending. To enter and settle in the United States, they went through no formal process whatsoever. Other than a cursory medical examination looking for signs of typhus while they passed through the Narrows off the coast of South Brooklyn, not a single American official would greet them, inspect them, or even record their arrival. No passport, visa, or document of any kind was required to enter the United States — either temporarily or permanently. Ellis Island, with its rigorous inspections, would not open until 1892. Instead, once their ships docked at one of the piers at the southern end of the East River, the immigrants simply gathered their belongings, trudged exhaustedly down the gangplanks, and set immediately to work building their new lives in New York.

Nothing they had ever experienced could have prepared the Famine immigrants for the sights and sounds that overwhelmed them
once they set foot on Manhattan Island. Upon arrival, Thomas
Mooney told prospective immigrants, "all will be apparently Baby-
lonian confusion—such rattling of omnibuses, carriages, trucks—
such helter skelter—that coming as *you* have from a quiet inert
place like Ireland you will think the people all crazy." Liverpool
was nearly as populous as New York, and its port was just as busy,
but Liverpudlians seemed to move in slow motion compared with
Manhattan's frenetic inhabitants. Immigrants from this era who
recorded their first impressions of New Yorkers never failed to men-
tion how rapidly they walked and how quickly they talked.

New York at the start of the Famine was already, by far, the
most populous city in the United States.* In 1845 it had a population of 371,000, making it three times larger than its closest American rivals, Baltimore and New Orleans. (Dublin at that point had
about 240,000 inhabitants, while Cork and Belfast each had about
80,000.) Yet geographically, New York was tiny. Nearly all those
371,000 inhabitants resided in the six square miles of Manhattan
Island south of Thirty-Fourth Street. A few New Yorkers lived north
of that area, in the villages of Yorkville (now known as the Upper
East Side), Harlem, and Washington Heights. There was even a predominantly African American community known as Seneca Village, consisting of several hundred inhabitants occupying shacks
and cabins in the area stretching from West Eighty-Second to West
Eighty-Ninth Streets. Dozens of Famine immigrants would settle in

---

* Note that New York City in the era of the Great Irish Famine consisted only of Manhattan Island, Blackwells (now Roosevelt) Island, and Governors Island. New York City
added parts of southern Westchester County (which became known as the Bronx) to its
territory in 1874 and 1895. Only in 1898 did New York City expand to its current bor-
ders by annexing the previously independent city of Brooklyn, as well as Queens
County on Long Island and Staten Island.

Seneca Village before city officials evicted all its residents around 1860 to make way for the construction of Central Park. But other than small settlements like these, Manhattan north of Thirty-Fourth Street was uninhabited in 1845. Some of it was still being used as farmland.

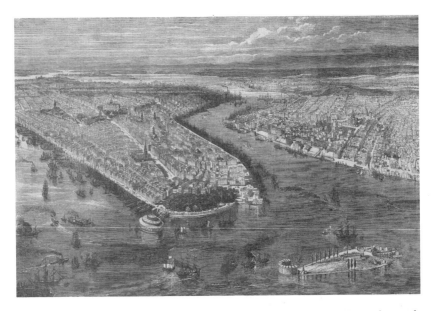

A bird's-eye view of New York City looking northeast in about 1850. The Hudson River is on the left and the East River on the right. To the right of the East River is Brooklyn, then a separate municipality and, with 100,000 residents in 1850, the seventh most populous city in the United States.

Even in 1845, New York was already a city of immigrants. Thirty-seven percent of New York's inhabitants at that point were foreign-born, about the same percentage as in 2023. About half of those immigrants had come from Ireland; nearly a quarter were from England and Scotland; one-sixth hailed from the German states; while the remaining 10 percent, befitting one of the world's busiest ports, came from nearly every other corner of the globe.

For most of New York's history to that point, there had not been particular neighborhoods where immigrants concentrated. In the two hundred years after the city's founding in 1624, rich and poor, black and white, natives and newcomers had all lived together in truly diverse neighborhoods. But that began to change in the 1830s as wealthier New Yorkers decided they no longer wanted to reside so close to their rowdier, poorer employees and neighbors. As a result, by the time the Famine immigrants began arriving, New York City neighborhoods had become more economically and ethnically homogeneous, with the wealthy (primarily Protestants of Dutch and English descent) choosing to live near Fifth Avenue and Broadway midway between the East and Hudson Rivers, while the poor (primarily Catholic and Irish by 1845) inhabited neighborhoods close to the waterfront. New York's large middle class filled the spaces in between.

By 1845, immigrants tended to live on the East Side, with the Irish especially numerous in Wards One, Four, Six, and Seven, while Germans also concentrated on the East Side but inland from the East River in Wards Ten and Seventeen. (For the location of these wards, see the map on page ix.) As a result, the East Side became the home of most of New York's Catholic inhabitants, while the West Side in the pre–Civil War years remained predominantly Protestant. Yet so many Irish immigrants arrived in New York during the Famine years that they could no longer be housed primarily in four wards. From 1845 to 1855, the Irish-born population of New York tripled, to 175,000. In that latter year, New York's population reached 630,000, of whom 51 percent were immigrants. With the city's traditionally Irish neighborhoods able to accommodate only a fraction of the Famine influx, the new arrivals had to find homes in every nook and cranny of the city. As a result, by 1855 Irish-born adults outnumbered native-born adults in nearly all the city's twenty-two wards.

It was no small task to house all these newcomers. Since the beginning of the eighteenth century, immigrants had typically rented space in the homes of more prosperous New Yorkers—in most cases, their employers. But in the fifteen or so years before the Famine, as employers started moving to more fashionable neighborhoods, the owners of wooden single-family homes on the East Side began subdividing them into apartments and renting them out to immigrants and other less wealthy New Yorkers. At first, Manhattanites called this new type of habitation a "tenant house," but by the eve of the Famine they had become known as tenements.

Thus, as the Famine began, most New York tenements were not the iconic five- to six-story brick buildings we associate with the term today, but two-and-a-half-story wooden structures that usually measured only 20 to 25 feet square. These tenements typically contained four to six apartments, depending on whether some of the space was rented out to retailers. But the flood of Famine immigrants changed all that. "The little low wooden houses [are] coming down," noted Mooney soon after the start of the Famine, "and five and six story...brick and stone houses ascending in their stead." Property owners hired immigrant labor (primarily Irish) to build these new 25-by-50-foot, five-story brick tenements, which sprouted up both in lower Manhattan on lots where wooden tenements had once sat and uptown on empty lots located north of Twenty-Third Street.

Whether constructed uptown or downtown, these brick tenements typically contained eighteen to twenty apartments (four per floor) and could command higher rents than flats in frame tenements because they were both newer and less drafty in the winter. The greediest landlords often built a second, 25-by-25-foot, five-story brick tenement directly behind the larger one, to squeeze another ten rents out of the standard 25-by-100-foot Manhattan lot. The apartments in these rear tenements rented for a bit less (and thus tended to house the poorest immigrants) because their only windows faced the malodorous outhouses that filled the tiny yards between the two buildings. Six of these "privies" might be utilized by upward of one hundred tenants.

Each apartment in these typical brick tenements provided inhabitants with just 225 square feet of living space divided into two
rooms. Shoehorning an Irish family of six or more into one of these
tiny apartments might seem like a hardship, but the cabins they
had inhabited in Ireland had not been much larger. In fact, with a
floor made of wood rather than damp dirt, and a solid ceiling above
their heads rather than a leaky, bug-infested thatch roof, New York's
tenement apartments might have seemed almost luxurious to the
Famine refugees. Even so, after the Civil War, real estate developers

There are no photographs of tenement apartment interiors from the Famine
era, but this is one of those same standard two-room apartments photographed around 1900, when many of New York's old Irish neighborhoods like
Five Points had become predominantly Italian. The front room where all
seven of this apartment's inhabitants are posed measured just twelve feet
square. The back room, usually measuring just six by eight feet, was only
barely big enough to fit a bed. When the Irish lived in these apartments, there
would have been a solid wall — rather than a window — next to the doorway
separating the front from the back room.

(some of them successful Famine immigrants) decided to give immigrants more space, and made three-room, 325-square-foot tenement apartments the new norm.

To help them find their first place to live, the newly arrived Famine immigrants utilized their preexisting social networks. The first people to whom newcomers would turn were kinsmen who had preceded them. Friends were another option in case the immigrants had no relatives in New York or were the first in their families to emigrate. And as a last resort, the Famine refugees would rely on advice from other immigrants who had been born in the same village, parish, or town. Some of these folks might have arrived in New York just months before those seeking their assistance. Others had immigrated years earlier—perhaps before the Famine—and had already established secure footholds in American society. Even for the newly arrived immigrant from the most isolated part of Ireland, there was always someone who knew another someone who could help find at least a temporary place to lodge and some kind of work for the newcomer.

The impact of this networking is apparent in the particular areas of New York in which the new immigrants chose to live. The Irish, in fact, often settled in the same neighborhoods where others from their particular part of Ireland had already begun to concentrate. Most of Cornelius Sullivan's compatriots from the Lansdowne estate chose to live where he did in the portion of the Five Points neighborhood where Anthony (now Worth) and Orange (now Baxter) Streets intersected. The Famine refugees who fled the contiguous County Sligo estates of Lord Palmerston (then the British secretary of state for foreign affairs) and Sir Robert Gore-Booth concentrated a few blocks north of the Lansdowners near the intersection of Orange and Canal. And immigrants from the Sperrin Mountains in County Tyrone in northern Ireland clustered along a stretch of the East River near Corlears Hook that straddled the boundary between Wards Seven and Thirteen.

Five Points

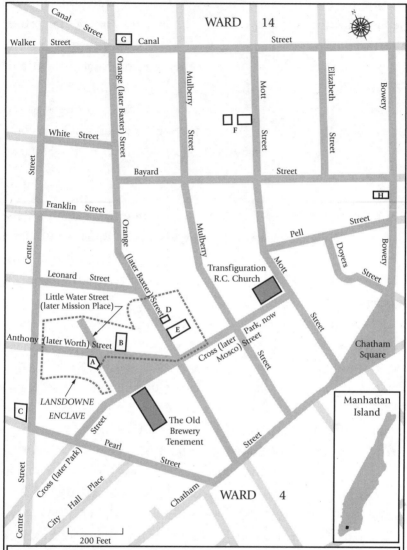

A: Cornelius Sullivan's first New York home at 7 Little Water Street; B: 153 Anthony Street, where Bartholomew O'Donnell moved when the Old Brewery tenement closed; C: Monroe Hall, the saloon Walter Roche took over when Matthew Brennan was elected police justice; D: 35 Baxter Street, location of "Mrs. Sandy Sullivan's genteel lodging-house"; E: 31 Baxter Street, location of John Lane's first saloon; F: 65 Mott Street, the oldest tenement still standing in New York; G: Mark and Mary Ann Driscoll's brothel; H: 28 Bowery, where Jonathan Dillon worked on watches both before and after his stint repairing timepieces (including Abraham Lincoln's) in Washington, D.C.

Yet not all Irish immigrants concentrated in this manner. The Famine refugees from Ireland's biggest cities — Dublin, Cork, and Belfast — settled all over New York. Perhaps these immigrants, already accustomed to city life, did not feel as disoriented as those from the countryside and therefore felt less need for the sense of security and familiarity that an enclave might offer. Still, in the post–Civil War years, as immigrants from Ireland continued to settle in New York, more wards and neighborhoods would become known as centers for newcomers from particular parts of Ireland.

Even if immigrants did not initially live with others from the same part of Ireland, their network of friends and kinsmen would help them land their first American jobs. Like Cornelius Sullivan, most of the male Famine immigrants had supported themselves as potato farmers and they would have to find new occupations in New York City. But even many of those who had not worked as farmers in Ireland — and might have expected to continue in their old vocations in America — found upon arrival that they had to take different, lower-status jobs than they had held previously. Drapery maker Martin Dwyer had to work in the laundry room of the St. Nicholas Hotel on Broadway after he arrived in New York in 1853. Carpenter John Connolly from County Monaghan became a day laborer, as did grocer Michael J. Dunn from Kildare. Blacksmith George Branagan became a waiter, while carriage maker Michael Brady, shoemaker Patrick Coffey, clerk Laurence Collins, bookkeeper Edward A. Kelly, and watchmaker Martin O'Brien all initially found work as porters.

There were several reasons that so many immigrants had to start out in worse jobs in America than they had had in Ireland. Friends and family members who had arrived in New York before them and helped the newcomers find jobs often did not have connections in the right fields to help them transition to their desired occupation. Even when an immigrant with vocational training other than farming got connected to a sympathetic employer, that boss might find the immigrant unqualified. An Irish carpenter might not know American building techniques, or an Irish-trained baker might not have the know-how to prepare the cakes and breads that New York's bakeshops sold. Some desperate employers were willing to allow these immigrants to learn such things on the job, but others were not so accommodating.

In many instances, however, Irish immigrants' inability to land jobs in fields in which they had already trained must have resulted from discrimination. New York employers, who were mostly native-born and Protestant, stereotyped the Irish (and, in particular, Irish Catholics) as "slothful and lazy," and therefore not the kinds of employees they wanted in their workplaces. Business owners who sought to avoid hiring Irish immigrants could easily do so without asking where a job applicant had been born. Even if a Famine immigrant had managed to Americanize his wardrobe, his accent was sure to reveal his ancestry.

The laziest of these bigoted employers did not want to be bothered by any Irish applicants at all and placed help-wanted ads in newspapers that laid bare their prejudice. Most newspapers in this era refused to run ads that explicitly said, "No Irish need apply," but advertisers found other terms — such as "must be Protestant" or "English, French, or German" preferred — to get their points across. Such advertisements enraged Irish Catholics and convinced many of them that their inability to find work in their chosen vocations resulted from anti-Irish and anti-Catholic prejudice.

Most of this prejudice against the Irish grew out of the centuries-old antagonism between Protestantism and Catholicism. At the dawn of the Famine migration, more than 90 percent of Americans were Protestants, and most of them believed that Protestantism was what made America great. Americans enjoyed unprecedented levels of political freedom, went this line of argument,

Three of the first four ads in the help-wanted column on the front page of the *New York Tribune* on May 14, 1852, made it clear that Irish Catholics would not be hired, even though only the first used the phrase "No Irish need apply."

because Protestantism preached self-determination. American prosperity was said to result from Protestantism's encouragement of scientific discovery, in contrast to Catholicism's punishment of great scientific thinkers like Galileo who questioned church orthodoxy. Catholic leaders, according to their Protestant detractors, discouraged all but the most rudimentary education for their followers because "superstition and ignorance" were essential to perpetuating the Catholic faith. Finally, said many Americans, Catholicism encouraged acceptance of one's fate, even if that fate was abject poverty, while Protestantism taught that people could change their destinies through virtuous living and sustained effort.

Another reason Irish Catholics could not succeed, many Americans believed, was that they lacked a Protestant work ethic. Although Max Weber would not coin that phrase for another half century, Americans in 1850 were intimately familiar with the concept. Irish Catholic immigrants were doomed to lives of poverty and menial drudgery, most Americans thought, because these newcomers lacked the educational, spiritual, and entrepreneurial tools that Weber would eventually encapsulate in his famous phrase.

As the Famine immigrants flooded into the United States, the American press was filled with comments that reflected these prejudiced views. Irishmen "idle about our Atlantic cities," complained a New York magazine, rather than strive to get ahead. The immigrants from the Lansdowne estate in County Kerry were "hapless beings," agreed the *New York Herald*, so beaten down by years of "misery, disease and want" that "to earn a day's living," much less climb America's socioeconomic ladder, seemed impossible.

What especially prevented the Famine refugees from improving their status, most Americans believed, was that the Irish could not even *imagine* doing so. Through colonial oppression and their devotion to Roman Catholicism, the Irish had been "rendered lazy and lounging," insisted a newspaper correspondent quoted in the New York *Irish-American*. It was impossible to rid the Famine immigrants of "their habits of squalor and indolence," said this columnist, because they "have no plan, and no energy to form one." This noxious belief—that the Famine immigrants could not prosper because they were incapable of even envisioning a strategy for improving their circumstances—was widely held. "When they arrive they have no plans for the future, and no enterprise to quicken their perceptions," argued a Connecticut newspaper in 1855. "They stop at the first practicable or impracticable dwelling place. New York is America and they don't dream that America is anywhere but New York. So there they stop, and beg, and steal, and starve."

The rise of the Know Nothing Party at the tail end of the Famine migration was the culmination of this groundswell of prejudice against the Irish. This group had its origins in a secret society called the Order of the Star Spangled Banner, which was founded by New York City nativists around 1850. If a member was asked about the fraternal order, they were required to feign ignorance and say that they knew nothing about it. By 1853, so many New Yorkers were giving this response when asked about the group that the *New York Tribune* dubbed it the "Know-Nothing organization." The name stuck, even though members eventually called themselves the American Party in a bid to be taken more seriously. The Irish, however, refused to stop calling them Know Nothings.

The Know Nothings demanded that immigrants in general, and Irish Catholics in particular, should have less political power. To that end, the Know Nothings proposed lengthening the waiting period before immigrants could become citizens and vote from five to twenty-one years, a move that would disenfranchise all the Famine immigrants. Know Nothings also wanted to ban immigrants from holding elective or appointed government offices. In addition, the Know Nothings attempted to limit the impact of Irish immigrants on American schools. With the influx of so many Famine immigrants, Catholic leaders had been asking for changes to the curricula of public schools, where students were often required to read the Protestant King James Bible and textbooks were tinged with anti-Catholicism. Know Nothings, however, insisted that Americans should make no curricular concessions to the newcomers.

This platform — a twenty-one-year wait until immigrants could become citizens and vote; no immigrants in government jobs; and no changes to the public schools to accommodate Catholics — appealed to many Americans. In 1854 and 1855, Know Nothings in the northeast and midwest elected eight governors, more than one hundred congressmen, and thousands of local officials, including the mayors of Boston and Chicago. Even though Know Nothing candidates did not win any contests in New York City, where so much of the electorate was foreign-born, Manhattan's Famine immigrants viewed the organization's success elsewhere as a provocation, an insult, and a threat to their dreams of a better life in the United States.

Despite the xenophobic forces that would give rise to the Know Nothings, the Famine immigrants found that most—but not all— aspects of their lives in America were much better than they had been in Ireland. "It is easy making money in this Country," wrote Eliza Quin, who had emigrated in 1847 from County Sligo to New York. James Cullinane, living in Detroit, informed his daughter Mary in west Cork that he was earning ten times the wage he had made back home. John Flood, a native of Leitrim, sent word from Philadelphia that he was paid six times more. Even poorly compensated Irish-born domestic servants in America, Flood marveled, earned "more wages than a working man at home" in Ireland and received free room and board as well.

Because they were paid so much more and unemployed so much less, the Famine immigrants' diet was also far better in New York than in Ireland. We "can eat good beef, and pork, and butter, and eggs, and bread—not so at home in the old country," wrote Five Points resident Michael Coogan in a letter to the editor of the *Irish-American*. Domestic servant Bridget Rooney, a former tenant of Lord Palmerston, boasted that in America we "are fed everyday like on Christmas at home." No wonder Quin called the United States "the best Country in the world."

Yet while the immigrants' incomes and diets were far better in New York than they had been in Ireland, other aspects of their lives remained very difficult. Death, for example, was ever present in their lives. Having resided primarily in the countryside before coming to the United States, the Famine immigrants had not been exposed to many of the communicable diseases that were so common in urban Ireland and America. Squeezed so closely together in steerage compartments and then in tenements and crowded urban saloons, large numbers of the Famine immigrants contracted diseases like typhus, pneumonia, and tuberculosis after arriving in

New York. So many of the Lansdowne immigrants got seriously ill after landing that a section of New York Hospital, the medical facility closest to their Five Points enclave, was supposedly known as the "Lansdowne Ward." In an era before antibiotics and antiviral drugs, when brandy was still the most likely "medicine" to be prescribed for many ailments, the immigrants were most often discharged from that ward, noted a Dublin magazine ruefully, "in their coffins."

Even for Famine immigrants who did live to a ripe old age in New York, their American-born offspring often led tragically short lives. The average married Famine immigrant who survived her childbearing years (by no means a foregone conclusion) gave birth to eight children over the course of her lifetime, but on average only four of those eight children survived to adulthood. Yet the Irish American childhood mortality rate was about the same as that for native-born Americans. In the era before vaccinations, young children perished from a huge variety of ailments; the most common were lung infections (caused by influenza, tuberculosis, or whooping cough) and gastrointestinal maladies that led to uncontrollable diarrhea. Even for those who survived childhood, the average life expectancy in this era (for immigrant and native alike) was only about forty years.

Yet childhood mortality did not hit all Famine immigrants equally. Nora and James Deasy, a laborer who eventually opened a New York junk shop and then a Long Island beer garden and hotel, had ten children, of whom nine were still living in 1900. Nine of the ten children born to Anna O'Shea and her husband, Patrick, a bookstore clerk who eventually became a publisher of Catholic religious tracts, also survived to the twentieth century. At the other extreme, day laborer Lawrence Grimes and his wife, Ann, from the Palmerston estate in Sligo, lost nine of their twelve children; gashouse laborer Maurice Spillane and his wife, Catherine, from Castlegregory in County Kerry, also lost nine of their twelve sons and daughters; and piano maker Anthony Abberton from Galway and his wife, Mary Ann, outlived eleven of their twelve offspring. That Anthony did so was somewhat miraculous. In 1871, he was so viciously attacked with a meat cleaver about the head and neck that newspapers reported he had been "chopped to death." Yet he recovered and lived another thirty years.

Having grown up with their own siblings dying frequently, one might imagine that the Famine immigrants would have been prepared for the deaths of their children. But many immigrants found the loss of so many innocent lives excruciatingly hard to bear. Some undoubtedly relied on their Catholic faith to get them through such heartache. Others tried different means to ease their pain. Rosanna and Michael J. J. Kavanagh, for example, natives of Wicklow, lost nine of their ten children, and it seems that after most of these deaths they hoped that a change of scenery would help them cope. The Kavanaghs tried Albany, then Milwaukee, then Madison, Wisconsin, then Lenox, Massachusetts, after which they returned to New York City, where they ran a succession of candy and stationery stores. Finally, in 1880, when they were both about fifty years old, Michael and Rosanna took their one surviving child (fifteen-year-old Michael J. Kavanagh) and made their biggest move yet, to the wide-open spaces of Pottawatomie County, Kansas, where they became farmers.

In some cases, Irish Americans relied on alcohol to deaden their pain when overwhelmed with grief over the loss of their children. As police arrested Maurice Mariga for public drunkenness in 1881, he told the officers that "he had been drinking heavily for the past three weeks to drown his sorrow," reported the *New York Herald*. "His grief was due to [all] four of his children having died within a short time." Mariga was thrown in jail, where he tore out his hair, begged for more liquor, and wailed repeatedly that "I loved my darlings, and God took them from me!" The next morning he was found dead in his cell, having apparently died from alcohol poisoning.

Alcoholism was a problem for the Famine Irish in America well beyond cases of grief like Mariga's. Back in Ireland, alcohol addiction had not been common among the future emigrants because spirits were in short supply and too expensive for most of Ireland's inhabitants, who might go an entire year without seeing much, if any, cash. In New York, however, alcohol was cheap, abundant, and omnipresent, and even the lowliest day laborer was paid in cash every Saturday evening. Furthermore, in New York's most Irish neighborhoods, immigrants did not even have to leave the house to buy booze, because in these locales most tenements contained a saloon, liquor store, or grocery that sold alcohol for as little as a penny a glass (many groceries had bars in the back). In Five Points, a single address might contain two or even three saloons — one in each of the two retail spaces in the front tenement and a third dram shop in the rear building.

BACKGROUNDS OF CIVILIZATION.—MRS. CROWN'S FIVE POINTS BAR-ROOM, ON CROWN'S CORNER, WORTH AND CROSS STREETS.—See page 229.

This was the bar at the back of Crown's Grocery in Five Points. Saloons admitted only men, but women were expected to patronize groceries. That Irish American women would drink in public at the bars in their neighborhood groceries seemed particularly appalling to native-born American sensibilities.

It is difficult to determine how much of a problem alcoholism was to the Famine immigrants because so often its impact went unrecorded or was not ascribed to alcohol when it should have been. But the signs of alcohol's destructive power were everywhere: the wife telling the Emigrant Savings Bank not to let her husband withdraw any money because he was on a bender; the teenage son having to quit school and take over the family business because his father was usually too drunk to operate it; the woman who called the police after her brother-in-law, a liquor store operator, broke a piece of crockery over her sister's head; the Irishman in Brooklyn whose cause of death could not be determined with certainty because it was not clear if the internal bleeding in his head had begun a month earlier when he fell off a train platform while drunk or a few weeks later when he injured his skull on a curbstone while being thrown out of a saloon for excessive inebriation; or the fourteen-year-old girl who was left an orphan because her widowed father staggered onto a wharf while drunk, fell into the water, and drowned. That the Famine Irish could afford to drink to excess was a sign that their economic circumstances had markedly improved since their arrival in America. Yet that fact was cold comfort to the thousands of Irish Americans whose parents or spouses were physically abusive, or unable to support them, or suffered premature, needless deaths because of alcohol addiction.

With the temptation of whiskey and gin all around them, and the specter of discrimination apparently blocking so many paths to upward mobility, the lives of the Famine immigrants could have easily followed the trajectory that nativists predicted. Men who arrived in New York without any vocational skills useful in a big city might have spent the rest of their lives doing day labor for a dollar a day, content to earn for such work far more than they had in Ireland. Likewise, the Irish carpenters, tailors, and shoemakers who came to America could have been satisfied toiling as employees in those same vocations in New York, also bringing in much more than they had earned at their trades in Ireland. All this assumed, of course, that these "slothful and lazy" immigrants bothered to work at all, rather than support themselves, as the nativists predicted, at government expense by taking refuge at the city almshouse.

Yet the Famine immigrants did not usually end their lives in America in the same occupations in which they began them. The newcomers may have initially been amazed at how much American employers paid for a day's work, but they were also incredibly ambitious. Coming of age in Ireland, whose colonial status (and resulting economic stagnation) made significant upward mobility rare, the Famine immigrants leaped at the myriad opportunities for advancement they saw all around them in America. The English looked at the poverty that dominated Ireland and concluded that the Irish were lazy. But in fact, Irishmen's ambition and drive were merely suppressed, weighed down by the political and economic shackles that the British had placed upon them. Relocating to New York revived the immigrants' long dormant determination to achieve not just self-sufficiency, but prosperity.

In bank ledgers, census records, and city directories, the ambition of the Famine immigrants is palpable. Porters become policemen, shoemakers become saloonkeepers, and gardeners become grocers. Such examples of upward mobility bring to mind that classic image from any freshman sociology or economics class: the socioeconomic ladder, on which each higher rung marks progress away from bare subsistence toward ever-increasing levels of prosperity, security, and status. Indeed, the Irish determination to climb the American socioeconomic ladder, and the benefits that would accrue to both them and their children by doing so, was the focus — the very organizing principle — of the Famine immigrants' lives.

That ladder had six basic levels for men in mid-nineteenth-century New York. The bottom rung was occupied by those whose jobs required little or no previous training. Two-thirds of the men in this category did "day labor"—digging and hauling on construction sites and road crews. The next most common jobs for the Irish in the unskilled category were porter, coachman, waiter, cartman, boat hand, stable hand, bartender, watchman, and longshoreman.

One rung up the socioeconomic ladder, in the second position, were peddlers of one kind or another—who sometimes also referred to themselves as "hucksters" (the term did not carry negative connotations in those days) or "vendors." They were not considered superior to day laborers in terms of social status, but they made a lot more money than the unskilled wage workers and thus deserve their own rung in the immigrant occupational hierarchy.

A step higher, on the third rung, stood the skilled artisans. In the Irish immigrant community, tailors, carpenters, and shoemakers dominated this category. But bakers and blacksmiths, hatters and harness makers, masons and machinists, plasterers and printers, as well as weavers and watchmakers, were also quite numerous.

The fourth rung from the bottom, resting one above the skilled workers, held the lower-level white-collar workers—primarily office and store clerks, but also agents, salesmen, and civil servants. These employees often earned less than those positioned below them, but clerks worked shorter hours (typically having to report to work at 9:00 rather than 7:00 a.m.) and enjoyed much more upward mobility.

On the fifth step, very near the top of the occupational ladder, sat the Irish-born business owners. Theirs were mostly small enterprises—family-run saloons and groceries were the most common businesses they operated. But New York's Irish shopkeepers might specialize in almost any item imaginable—beef, poultry, milk, fruits and vegetables, pickles, cigars, soda water, ice, fabric (known as dry goods), clothes, hats, undergarments (known as fancy goods), hardware, or hay. Edward A. Kelly, the Irish bookkeeper turned New York porter, eventually operated a Manhattan shop that sold nothing but spyglasses.

Finally, at the pinnacle of the ladder, on the sixth and highest rung, stood the professionals—primarily doctors, lawyers, and clergymen. But most Famine immigrants could not dream of reaching that lofty occupational category. For the vast majority, ascending to the ranks of the business owners (and in particular, to become a saloonkeeper) was their highest aspiration.

Up until now, it has been impossible to determine exactly where on the socioeconomic ladder the Famine immigrants started when they arrived in America. Census records tell us the occupations of every resident of the United States every ten years, but those records for the nineteenth century do not differentiate an immigrant who was fresh off the boat (to use modern parlance) from one who had already lived in the United States for many years. But the Emigrant Savings Bank records, which contain the precise date of arrival for tens of thousands of Famine refugees, enable us to discover, for the very first time, what kinds of jobs these immigrants secured upon arrival.

Occupations Within One Year of Arrival of Male Irish Immigrants in New York and Brooklyn, 1850–1858, Compared with Those of Native-Born New Yorkers in 1860

	FAMINE IRISH NEW YORKERS	U.S.-BORN NEW YORKERS	MOST COMMON IRISH JOBS IN CATEGORY
Professionals	0.7%	4%	Lawyer, doctor, clergyman
Business Owners	5%	15%	Saloonkeeper, grocer, shopkeeper
Lower White-collar	11%	29%	Clerk, civil servant, agent
Skilled Workers	33%	35%	Tailor, carpenter, shoemaker
Peddlers	5%	0.7%	Peddler, huckster, vendor
Unskilled Workers	46%	16%	Laborer, porter, waiter

As one might imagine, the Famine immigrants started overwhelmingly on the bottom half of the socioeconomic ladder. About half the men initially occupied the very lowest rung, a category made up primarily of day laborers. Given the stereotype of the Famine Irish in that era as lazy and unambitious, however, it is surprising that *only* half the Irishmen began their lives in America in unskilled occupations. Fully a third of them started out in New York as skilled tradesmen, something that is also not well-known, even by scholars of Irish America. Historians would not be surprised that only about 15 percent of the Famine immigrants immediately found some kind of white-collar employment. Indeed, that figure is probably higher than scholars would have expected.

Given the belief of native-born Americans at the time that the Famine Irish were "lazy," "hapless," "indolent," and utterly lacking in ambition, and the long-held view of modern historians that these immigrants could not advance due to a lack of education, skills, and acceptance, the astonishing rates of upward mobility for the Famine immigrants from their initial American occupations come as a great surprise. After twenty years in America, the Famine Irish had moved impressively up the socioeconomic ladder.

Comparison of First and Final Occupations of Male Famine Immigrants Who Initially Lived in New York City*

	OCCUPATION WITHIN ONE YEAR OF ARRIVAL	FINAL KNOWN OCCUPATION OF THOSE TRACKED 20 OR MORE YEARS
Professionals	0.7%	2.4%
Business owners	5%	31%
Lower white-collar	11%	11%
Skilled workers	33%	28%
Peddlers	5%	3%
Unskilled workers	46%	25%

* For evidence that Emigrant Savings Bank customers, from whom these data are derived, are fairly representative of the entire Famine immigrant population, see "A Note on Sources," page 415.

Nearly *half* the male Famine immigrants had ended their careers in white-collar occupations. The proportion doing unskilled work had dropped to only 25 percent, while the ranks of the business owners had increased by more than 600 percent. In fact, after twenty years in America, a higher proportion of the Famine immigrants ran their own businesses than did native-born New Yorkers aged forty or higher. Yet very few outside the Irish American community noticed these accomplishments. And until now, most scholars have been unaware of them as well.

In the chapters that follow, we will see how the Famine Irish managed to achieve so much despite starting with so little. We will climb the socioeconomic ladder with them, starting at the bottom and working our way to the very top. On each rung, we'll encounter irrepressible immigrants successfully ascending the socioeconomic hierarchy and others striving to rise but prevented from doing so by poor health, poor luck, or poor business plans. Still others will manage to reach the very pinnacle of the ladder only to suffer setbacks (some beyond their control, others of their own making) and fall back down to where they started. But overall, our ascent up the socioeconomic ladder will mirror the overall trajectory of the Famine immigrants themselves. That the Famine Irish accomplished so much, despite facing what their contemporaries imagined were insurmountable obstacles, escaped the attention of most of their non-Irish contemporaries. But the few who did notice were astounded. "This Celtic success," admitted one, "is truly miraculous."

PART II

Doctors & Lawyers
Business Owners
Clerks, Civil Servants
Artisans
Peddlers
Unskilled Workers

CHAPTER THREE

"All the Rude and Heavy Work"

Day Laborers, Domestics, and Other Unskilled Workers

Bartholomew O'Donnell was walking in circles, but he was not lost. He knew exactly where he was — in Coakley Hall at the corner of Pacific and Clinton Streets near the Brooklyn waterfront, just across the East River from the southern tip of Manhattan, where he had arrived as an immigrant in January 1849. Now it was February 1879, and the same drive and determination that had enabled him to escape the Great Famine was propelling him around a 160-foot indoor sawdust track, for five hours, ten hours, twenty hours, until he had completed more than twenty-four hundred laps. Yet no matter how hard he tried, no matter to what lengths he pushed himself, the prize he was seeking — both in Coakley Hall on that February night and in America itself — somehow always remained tantalizingly just beyond his grasp.

Bartholomew, known to his friends and family as Bartley, had been born in the city of Limerick in southwest Ireland and had set sail from there, down the River Shannon and out into the Atlantic, at the end of 1848 on the four-masted bark *Heather Bell* headed for

New York. He was accompanied by his widowed mother, Mary, and his younger siblings John and Catherine. Also traveling with them was an infant, Cornelius O'Donnell. The baby might have been born to Catherine out of wedlock. But given that the O'Donnells left Limerick at the height of the Great Famine, Cornelius may have been an orphan, perhaps a nephew or cousin.

That they arrived in New York in early January indicates just how desperate the O'Donnells' circumstances must have been. Even the least worldly men and women in a port city like Limerick knew that the beginning of the year was the worst possible time to immigrate to America. New York construction sites, the main source of employment for unskilled immigrants like O'Donnell, lay dormant in January and February due to the cold, ice, and snow. Thousands of unemployed New York construction workers tramped the streets each winter begging for a job — any job — to help pay the rent and put food on the table until the building industry revived in the spring. In the winter, many immigrant New Yorkers ventured south to warmer climes searching for work. Having only disembarked from the *Heather Bell* on January 8, and no doubt feeling weak and ill after a hungry, thirsty, and frigid month at sea, Bartholomew probably did not leave New York to find employment during his first months in America.

Another indication of the O'Donnells' desperate situation was where in New York they decided to live. Not only did they settle in Five Points, but they chose to reside at 61 Cross Street (later Park, and now Mosco), in its dirtiest, unhealthiest, most lawless, most infamous tenement — the Old Brewery. As the name implied, the Old Brewery had once been a manufacturing facility, turning out barrels of lager for thirsty New Yorkers using water drawn from the same underground source that had once fed the nearby Collect Pond, early Manhattan's largest freshwater lake. As the population of the city expanded northward toward the lake, municipal authorities decided to fill it in and allow developers to build housing over it, forcing the tanners, rope makers, and ceramics manufacturers who depended on the lake's water to relocate. The brewery eventually closed as well, and in about 1837 its owners converted the structure into a huge tenement.

Few residential buildings in New York in this period were even half the size of the Old Brewery. Because the edifice had been designed for manufacturing, no amount of renovation could really make it suitable for habitation. The tenement was full of window-less interior apartments and pitch-black, labyrinthine hallways, making it an ideal hideout for thieves, drunks, and sex workers. "No language can exaggerate its filth or the degradation of its inmates," insisted Methodist missionaries who worked with the poor in Five Points. A newspaper called the Old Brewery "the wick-edest house on the wickedest street that ever existed in New York, yes, and in all the country and possibly all the world." Given its reputation, only the poorest of the poor, those who could afford nothing else, would choose to live in the Old Brewery. The O'Don-nells must have fit that description, because soon after their arrival in New York they moved into the teeming tenement.

The O'Donnells did their best to adapt to life in New York. Bar-tholomew found employment in the line of work that supported more Irish immigrant families than any other — day labor. In an era before construction cranes and mechanical excavators, thousands of day laborers used pickaxes and shovels to dig the cellars of tenements, town houses, and commercial buildings and then tediously carried the broken-up dirt and rocks to waiting horse-drawn carts. In subsequent weeks, those same laborers hauled V-shaped, shoulder-borne troughs known as "hods" full of bricks and mortar up rickety wooden ladders perched precariously on scaffolding to the masons who built the exte-rior, load-bearing walls of these buildings. (Those masons, skilled craftsmen, sat two rungs higher on the socioeconomic ladder than day laborers.) After that work was done, laborers hoisted the beams, joists, two-by-fours, stair treads, banisters, door and window frames, lath, and nails up those same ladders to the carpenters (also considered skilled craftsmen) who constructed the interiors of the structures.

Building sites weren't the only places in New York to find work as a laborer. Foundries hired laborers to move tons of iron and brass around shop floors. Shipyards employed them to transfer raw materials from docks and delivery wagons to shipbuilders. Streetcar companies used laborers to help maintain their tracks. Yet eight out of every ten New York laborers would have spent their days toiling on construction sites.

While day-labor jobs were much more plentiful in New York than in Ireland, and paid far better, food and rent were much more expensive in America, even if one lived in the decrepit Old Brewery. After three years in New York, the O'Donnells had not saved much more than twenty dollars, the amount Bartley deposited when he opened an account at the Emigrant Savings Bank on January 14, 1852. This was not a paltry sum (it was equal to almost a month's wages for a day laborer at the time), yet it was less than a laborer would ideally have on hand to help make ends meet during the winter when work was scarce. By 1852, Bartley had not only a widowed mother to support but a wife as well. Sometime after arriving in New York, but before he opened his bank account, he married Jane Riley from County Cavan in Ulster. With all these dependents, and winter employment opportunities scarce, Bartholomew left New York looking for work right after he opened his account. His brother John, who remained in New York with their mother and Bartholomew's new wife, reported a month later that his brother was in South Dover, probably referring to a town eighty miles north of Manhattan near Poughkeepsie. Yet investing in a train or steamer ticket out of town did not always pay dividends. Apparently finding scant work upstate, Bartley returned to New York in mid-February, withdrew the twenty dollars he had placed in the bank for safekeeping, and closed his account.*

---

* Americans opened and closed savings accounts much more frequently in the nineteenth century than they do today. One reason they might close an account was that they needed to withdraw every penny they had, and banks typically required

This print of the Old Brewery depicts that infamous tenement in about 1850, when Bartholomew O'Donnell lived there with his mother and brother. The numbers in the first-story doorways identify particularly notorious parts of the building, such as "Murderer's Alley" (number 1) and the "Den of Thieves" (3, 4, and 5). The Methodists who ran the Five Points Mission bought the building in 1850; two years later, they evicted the tenants, tore the building down, and constructed a headquarters for their charity work in its place.

Making ends meet became even harder for O'Donnell in 1853, for by then his wife, Jane, had given birth to a daughter, Margaret, and they had moved across the street to the two-and-a-half-story wooden tenement at 153 Anthony Street. The move may not have been voluntary. The Old Brewery had been bought by Methodists who operated a charitable organization known as the Five Points Mission. In the middle of 1852, they evicted the building's tenants, tore the tenement down, and built a headquarters for their

customers to maintain a minimum balance of one dollar to keep an account open. More often, however, customers closed their accounts in this era because, in the days before deposit insurance, the slightest rumor of a bank having financial difficulties caused depositors to withdraw their hard-earned savings rather than chance losing it. Once the rumors abated, New Yorkers who coveted the 6 or 7 percent interest rate that savings banks typically paid in this era would open new accounts.

operations, which included food and clothing distribution, job training, and aggressive proselytizing among the predominantly Catholic residents of Five Points. The demolished tenement may have been squalid and dangerous, but for people living on the margins such as the O'Donnells, the loss of even such wretched shelter brought expenses and risks that they would have preferred to avoid.

Nonetheless, Bartley opened another Emigrant Savings Bank account in 1853, though he could manage an opening deposit of only ten dollars at that point. Paying the bills was clearly still a challenge, as only a month later he withdrew his entire balance and again closed his account. By 1855, still working as a day laborer, he had not saved enough to make it worth opening another one.

Bartley and Jane are difficult to trace over the next few years. He reappears in the city directory in 1863 operating a junk shop out of his home in the rear tenement at 21 Atlantic Avenue in Brooklyn near the waterfront. Neighborhoods like that one, inhabited primarily by the poor, were ideal for junk dealers, since scavengers (both adult and juvenile) brought a steady supply of found (or stolen) scrap metal, salvaged (or stolen) machine and vehicle parts, and discarded (or stolen) furniture to their neighborhood junk dealers. Those selling such goods in Five Points or near the Brooklyn docks were not likely to drive a hard bargain so long as the junk dealer did not ask many questions about the origins of the goods. Operating a shop was definitely several steps up the Irish American socioeconomic ladder from day labor, but a junk shop was the most precarious business an Irish immigrant could open. Indeed, Bartley did not last long in the junk business and soon had to return to day labor.

We don't know Bartley and Jane's financial situation at this point because they no longer had an account at the Emigrant Bank. Some of its customers kept their accounts even after they moved to Brooklyn, but the O'Donnells were not among them. It is conceivable that the O'Donnells patronized a Brooklyn financial institution at this point, but it is also possible that they lacked the savings to make an account worthwhile. The precariousness of their situation is reflected in the fact that they were constantly on the move. It was common for working-class New Yorkers to relocate frequently. The first of May was known as "Moving Day" in New York. Almost every residential lease in the city expired on that day, and as a result perhaps half the city's tenants moved on that date each year. They did not typically go far, but they did move often, looking for a slightly better apartment, a lower rent, or a shorter commute to work. But as New Yorkers — even immigrant New Yorkers — got older, they tended to settle down and relocate less frequently.

MAY-DAY IN THE CITY.

This image of Moving Day, May 1, conveys a sense of the chaos that ensued as half the population of New York changed addresses on this single day each year.

The O'Donnells, however, never settled down. In not one instance after they left the Old Brewery can they be documented as living at the same address in consecutive years. They lived in Brooklyn at two different addresses on Atlantic Avenue, then 114 Butler, then 513 Court, then 193 Luquer, then the rear house at 422 Baltic, then 398 Bond, then 180 Partition (now Coffey), then 143 Conover, and so on, and so on.

Bartley's appearance on that sawdust track in the winter of 1879 was further evidence of his precarious circumstances. Under a headline reading "Unsuccessful: A Plucky Old Man on the Track," the *Brooklyn Daily Eagle* explained that "Bartholomew O'Donnell, the octogenarian pedestrian," had set out at 10:30 p.m. on Friday, February 21, in an attempt to walk seventy-five miles in twenty-four hours on an indoor track measuring thirty-three laps to the mile. O'Donnell was attempting to profit from the sporting craze of the day: marathon race-walking, known as "pedestrianism." In the most famous marathon walking events, which drew competitors from around the world, thousands would pay to enter America's biggest sporting arenas to see who could walk the farthest in twenty-four, forty-eight, or, in the case of the sport's most coveted prize, the Astley Cup, seventy-two hours.

O'Donnell was not vying for one of the huge purses offered in pedestrian contests at Madison Square Garden (which would host such events when it opened a few months later), and he wasn't attempting the feat simply because he enjoyed a challenge. O'Donnell was trying, in an extraordinarily taxing way, to earn money for his family, doing so by renting a venue and hoping that the entrance fees charged to curious onlookers would exceed his outlay. "Although strictly temperate and industrious in his habits," reported the *Eagle* in explaining O'Donnell's motivations, "he never made muc[h] headway in securing a competence, and he looked forward anxiously to his big walk as a means for providing him with a few dollars to carry him through the Winter, without being obliged to do whatever odd jobs he could pick up." It was undoubtedly difficult to secure work as a day laborer at an advanced age, and today's sources of income for the elderly like Social Security and 401(k) plans had not yet been invented. Those who could do so saved a portion of their earnings so they would not need to work for their entire lives. Others expected to rely on their children to support them in their dotage.

Bartholomew and Jane had only that one child, Margaret, and he and Jane did eventually move in with her and her husband, Massachusetts-born cooper William Cowan. The four of them lived, along with the Cowans' children, in close quarters in a Brooklyn tenement in the latter half of the 1870s. Bartholomew was clearly expected to contribute money for food and rent and did so any way he could. "In Summer time," the *Eagle* noted, O'Donnell was "a constant visitor to picnics," such as those held by the various Irish county societies, "where he engages in athletic sports and dancing" and often took home the modest prize money offered in such contests. "But in Winter," the newspaper explained, "he has to depend for his support on being employed to shovel snow or put in coal," and it was his desire to avoid these arduous tasks that led "the octogenarian pedestrian" to attempt his newsworthy feat.

There was just one problem. Bartley was not in his eighties when he took to the track at Coakley Hall. He was not even in his seventies. He was actually in his early sixties. It was common for New Yorkers to *subtract* years from their actual age as they got older, but after he moved to Brooklyn, O'Donnell did something very unusual—he *added* fifteen or twenty years to his. Perhaps living through the Famine and the Old Brewery had prematurely aged his features and he hoped to take advantage of that fact to make some money. After all, Brooklynites were more likely to pay to watch a self-professed eighty-year-old walk for twenty-four hours than someone twenty years younger.

But while he might fool Brooklynites about his age, he could not fake how many laps he had walked around the sawdust track at Coakley Hall. By 8:45 p.m., he had completed only 2,046 laps, leaving him thirteen miles to walk in just 105 minutes, "a matter of impossibility," observed the *Eagle*'s correspondent. O'Donnell's friends convinced him that rather than risk his health, "it was better for him to give up, which he did with much regret and much against his will," the *Eagle* reported. "For the old man's sake it is to be regretted that he did not meet with more success in his...undertaking, for the receipts will fall short of the outlay."

Bartholomew O'Donnell was certainly not a typical Famine immigrant. Most did not make headlines. Most could not boast of having survived the Old Brewery — "famed in song and story," as one contemporary account put it. And most did not partake in the pedestrian craze. But in more mundane ways, O'Donnell's story reflected that of hundreds of thousands of other Famine immigrants. Like so many of them, O'Donnell began at the bottom of the American socioeconomic ladder working as a day laborer. Like many, he found it difficult to accumulate savings to safeguard his family should he become unable to support them. Like so many of his compatriots, O'Donnell tried to improve his family's fortunes by starting a business. And like many of the Famine immigrants, he failed in his business venture and struggled thereafter to make ends meet doing arduous manual labor for the rest of his life. O'Donnell probably did not regret having come to America, but he learned that the obstacles to upward mobility for the Famine immigrants were more numerous and more difficult to overcome than most Irishmen and -women had imagined. Tens of thousands would manage to surmount these impediments. But thousands more, like Bartley O'Donnell, never would.

When Dublin-born journalist Thomas Mooney visited New York in the early years of the Famine, he found that Irish immigrants were already doing "almost all the rude and heavy work" in the city. For most unskilled Irish immigrants, that meant day labor. In the late 1840s and early 1850s, New York was basically one giant construction site, as real estate developers built more than a thousand tenements and commercial structures each year. Still, not every day laborer did construction work. Mooney noted that the New York Irish also dominated the crews that were "blasting rocks up town, mending the streets, digging sewers, and laying water or gas pipes." Unskilled Irishmen could also be found "plying on the river, as [steam engine] firemen and boatmen, [and] in the thousand canal and steam boats that flit too and fro on the Hudson and 'East River.'" Nonetheless, in the decade after the commencement of the Famine, eight out of every ten Irish day laborers in New York City would have found themselves digging, hauling, or heaving on a building site somewhere below Fifty-Ninth Street.

Before the invention of hard hats and safety goggles, construction work was even more dangerous than it is today. Falls were especially common. Dominick Follis, for example, arrived in New York on July 4, 1852, from Thomastown, Kilkenny, settled on Frankfort Street in Ward Four, and found employment as a day laborer on a construction site in his neighborhood. A few weeks after his arrival, while he was up on scaffolding in front of the tenement he was helping to build, the platform "suddenly gave way," according to the *Times*, "precipitating the men at work upon it into the cellar beneath." Follis fractured his collarbone while another laborer broke both legs and a mason badly injured his arm and hand.

There were other, more insidious dangers as well. Employers sometimes pushed day laborers to the brink of exhaustion or beyond. Twenty-two-year-old laborer Richard Fitzgerald from Kenmare, for example, who had arrived in New York in 1852 and lived in the Lansdowne enclave in Five Points, died of sunstroke in 1855 after a day of hard work during an unusual June heat wave.

A coffin being taken in 1865 from the Five Points tenement at 31 Baxter Street to a waiting hearse. This was the very tenement in which laborer Richard Fitzgerald resided when he died of heatstroke in 1855.

The dangers of a laborer's life were exemplified by two workplace incidents from a single day in 1850, when Famine immigration was approaching its zenith. On Monday, April 29, workers were tearing down the old headquarters of the Chemical Bank on Broadway just north of Fulton Street when the floor of the highest remaining level, the third, collapsed, causing it and the floors below to pancake down into the cellar. Most of the demolition workers, with Irish surnames such as Brady, Hughes, Kane, McIlaven, and O'Connor, escaped without life-threatening injuries, but Martin Kehen "was seriously hurt, and when taken from under the rubbish with which he was covered, he presented a frightful spectacle." Another survivor "lost his reason temporarily," according to the *Herald*, "either from a blow on the head or from terror."

A more tragic incident occurred the same day at a warehouse at 35 Water Street just north of the Battery. Five days earlier, the building at 33 Water had been destroyed by fire. The side wall of that structure had collapsed during the blaze, and once it came down the adjoining wall of 35 Water Street began to bulge out and occasionally "swayed to and fro in a most frightful manner." The city's chief engineer initially declared 35 Water unsafe and sought to have the leaning wall torn down, even though doing so might result in the collapse of the entire building and the loss of the tons of goods stored inside. The building's owner, Stephen Whitney (the city's third-wealthiest resident, behind only John Jacob Astor and Cornelius Vanderbilt), convinced officials that the structure could be saved and repaired if the contents were removed. The mayor, fearing a lawsuit from the deep-pocketed Whitney if the city went ahead with the demolition, overruled the engineer and allowed Whitney to hire workers to empty the building. On Saturday the twenty-seventh, men could not be found willing—for the typical day laborer's wage of eighty-five cents to one dollar per day—to enter the "tottering" warehouse to haul out the 250-pound barrels of flour and 500-pound bales of cotton. By Monday morning, however, enough supplemental inducements had been offered that a dozen or so Irish immigrants living along the East River waterfront began the dangerous work.

It was not long before the city engineer's worst fears came true. Around 10:00 a.m., the shifting of the building's weighty contents sent the bulging wall tumbling down "with a tremendous crash," according to the *Herald*, "burying at least eight under the ruins." When rescue workers managed to reach the lifeless bodies, reported the *Evening Post*, "a frightful spectacle was presented." In one hole they found "four poor fellows who had been literally smashed together." According to the *Herald*, one victim's "head and face were made perfectly flat" by the crush of falling brick, timber, and flour barrels, while the flour and debris on top of another dead worker,

John Hayes, were so weighty that his face "was rendered as white as if it were painted, the flour having been imbedded into it." William Pratt from County Cork was also "crushed and mangled beneath casks of flour." Once word of the calamity spread, kin began converging upon the warehouse to learn the fate of their loved ones. "The agonised mothers, and wives, and sisters, and daughters," noted the *Herald*, "exhibited a scene that we feel utterly unable to describe."

Today, the families of workers killed on the job in New York City are reimbursed up to $12,500 for burial expenses through the workman's compensation insurance fund supervised by the state. If the deceased are survived by spouses, they receive two-thirds of the victim's predeath pay for the rest of their lives (or until they remarry, if they do so) from the same fund. Surviving family members today also receive Social Security benefits if a breadwinner dies on the job. But laws mandating such compensation date only from the early twentieth century. Before that, injured employees or their surviving kin had to rely primarily on the generosity of employers to compensate them in cases of disability or death resulting from workplace accidents.

Stephen Whitney, the third-wealthiest man in the wealthiest city in the United States, could certainly have afforded to be generous. He must have felt *some* pangs of guilt, having pushed the mayor to allow workmen into his building over the objection of the city engineer. And while Whitney did eventually compensate the families of the victims, he did not do so generously. The two lawyers hired by the eight widows demanded $5,000 per family, the equivalent of nearly twenty years of a day laborer's wages, to compensate for Whitney's negligence. Whitney somehow persuaded the attorneys instead to take just $250 per victim, yet eight months after the tragedy each widow had received less than $100. The women then had to sue their attorneys, who claimed that their expenses in the case had been very high and that the widows were entitled to nothing more. A judge assigned yet another lawyer to investigate the matter, and the examiner found that the widows had been overcharged by the attorneys and together were owed another $1,168.

The result of all this double-dealing and evasion was that Mary Hourigan, a thirty-five-year-old native of County Cork with three children, received for the death of her spouse a total of about $225 — what her husband would have made in ten months of day labor. Twenty-eight-year-old Joanna Hayes from Limerick, with four children to care for, received about the same. Bridget Pratt with one child, Catherine Larvey with three children (including one she was carrying when her husband, John, died), Susan Barry with two small children, and Lucy McShane, twenty years old and the only widow with no children, also received about $225. From one of the wealthiest men in America, with assets worth the equivalent of about $350 million today, this was all the compensation the Irish day laborers' widows and their children would get.

———

There were alternatives to day labor for unskilled immigrants, but some were barely safer than construction work. Hundreds of Famine immigrants living in Ward Eighteen, above Fourteenth Street on the East Side, for example, took jobs as gasmen, toiling at the hulking New York Gas Works that occupied the entire city block northeast of the corner of First Avenue and East Twenty-First Street. These immigrants spent their days shoveling tons of coal into huge furnaces known as retorts, in which the coal was heated to 1,500 degrees Fahrenheit. The gas produced at that temperature was channeled into condensing and purifying units before being stored in gigantic aboveground tanks, among the largest structures in the city. The tanks supplied fuel to the city's thousands of gaslights. Once the gas-making process was complete, the gasmen had to shovel out the coal ash that remained in the retorts before starting the process all over again.

This image of gasmen stoking retorts in an English gasworks in 1821 conveys a sense of the intense heat and heavy smoke that such workers had to endure each day. It is hardly surprising that Famine immigrants did not typically make a career of gashouse work.

Gasmen could count on year-round employment, unlike day laborers, who were typically unable to find work for most of January and February, when construction sites shut down. But in most cases, even Famine immigrants did not consider the reliability of gashouse work adequate compensation for its hellishness. Gashouse labor was noxious and exhausting, especially in the summer when temperatures inside the facility rose to extraordinary levels. As a result, gashouse turnover was high. Only one of the sixteen Emigrant Bank customers who worked in a gashouse from 1850 to 1858 was still employed there in 1860. All the rest had moved on to other work, though in almost every case that meant day labor. Maurice

Spillane, for example, spent a couple of years as a gashouse employee and then most of the following half century as a Manhattan day laborer. By 1910, Maurice had finally given up day labor for a job as a watchman. He passed away in 1914, a few days after his eightieth birthday.

While a job at the gashouse was one alternative to digging and hauling on a construction site, unskilled Irishmen in New York who rejected day labor most often became porters. There were two kinds of porters—those who toiled for wages for a business owner (moving crates in a hardware store or furniture and guests' trunks in a hotel) and those who were self-employed and sought work in public places such as railway stations and ferry terminals. These "public porters" had to buy a one-dollar license and agree to charge standard fees set by the city council for each trunk, crate, or valise they carried, but many worked as porters without the required certification.

Not just anyone could succeed as a public porter. When fewer passengers requiring assistance arrived at a ferry terminal than there were porters to greet them, only the most aggressive men with the best sales pitches would win customers. Over the course of a long workday, this meant the difference between thriving or barely surviving.

In an era when visiting tourists and businessmen were more likely to pack their belongings in trunks than suitcases, making it all but impossible for travelers to carry them by themselves, work for porters was plentiful. But it was far from easy. Porters placed coiled ropes on their backs between their shirts and the trunks and crates they carried to protect their skin and clothing. And while on a construction site there was often less strenuous work that could be reserved for older day laborers, that was not the case for porters, for whom hoisting and carrying heavy things on their backs was a daily necessity.

This advertisement contains a rare depiction of a mid-nineteenth-century porter at work.

Despite these difficulties, porters made significantly more money than day laborers. The median porter saved 25 percent more in his Emigrant Savings Bank account than the median day laborer. Consequently, many day laborers tried their luck as porters, though given how physically demanding the work could be, few remained in that occupation for their entire lives. Timothy Cleary from County Tipperary, however, was a porter in New York for more than a quarter century. So were William Cornwall from Clare and William Follis from Kilkenny. Yet there was far less demand for porters than day laborers. For every Irish-born porter working in New York in 1855, there were a dozen Irish day laborers.

Unskilled immigrants who sought to escape the backbreaking work of porters and day laborers as they got older often became coachmen. Few immigrants could get these jobs immediately upon arrival in America because they did not know their way around the city well enough, but eventually the Famine immigrants began to secure these positions. Drivers earned more than laborers but less than porters, though at least the pay was predictable. A coachman could also derive psychological satisfaction if he worked for a notable employer. Patrick Brennan from County Kildare, for example, arrived in New York at about age nineteen in 1851 and two years later was lucky enough to find work on the large household staff of former congressman John A. King, an attorney who also had a sizable family farm in what is now the New York City borough of Queens. At some point in the 1850s, Brennan became the family coachman, though it is not clear whether the immigrant assumed that post before or after King was elected governor of New York in 1856. King died in 1867 but Brennan remained in the family's employ until at least 1880, when King's son Louis committed suicide with a pistol and Brennan found the body.

Coachmen could save significant sums. Brennan, a lifelong bachelor who received room and board from his employer, had by 1869 amassed $1,339, the equivalent of about $31,000 today. Yet Alex McConnerty amassed far more. McConnerty was a teenager when he emigrated in 1851 and he spent his first decade in New York as a hostler, mucking out stables for a livery company. But he eventually worked his way up to a job driving the stable's horse-drawn carriages. McConnerty and his wife, Bridget, who was a domestic servant before they married, managed to save $536 by 1865 and in the 1870s they moved to the northern outskirts of Brooklyn and bought themselves a modest frame home (still standing) at 1073 Lorimer Street in the Greenpoint neighborhood. Alex remained a carriage driver until at least 1900, but that real estate investment was just as valuable as his wages. When Alex and Bridget died a few months apart in 1917, they left behind an estate worth $15,000, equivalent to roughly $350,000 today. Alex and Bridget outlived all six of their children, however, so their estate passed to four nieces, a nephew, and a cousin.

Most coachmen toiled for hourly wages or a fixed salary. In

contrast, Irish immigrants who worked as cartmen (another step up from laborer within the unskilled category) were largely entrepreneurs. Cartmen bought or rented a horse and cart and then sold their carting services to fellow New Yorkers. Like porters, cartmen had to buy a license from the city and agree to charge set rates for their services. Yet there were several gradations among the city's five thousand or so cartmen. "The most profitable branch of the business," noted the *Tribune*, was hauling dry and clean items such as bales of cotton, barrels of flour, as well as construction materials such as timber, bricks, and stone; carting dirt, other construction rubble, and ash was considered a step down (and required a cheaper license); and carting "night soil" (also covered by the dirt-cart license), the euphemism Americans used for feces and urine, was considered the worst job of all. Virtually none of New York was connected to sewer lines in 1850, so the human waste that collected in New Yorkers' chamber pots and privies had to be loaded into barrels and hauled away so it could be dumped at sea. For most of the city's history up until the Famine, immigrants had been banned

A New York cartman circa 1840, by Nicolino Calyo.

by law from the highest-paying, most desirable carting and were granted only dirt-carting licenses. But this restriction had been repealed by the time the Famine Irish began streaming into New York. Nonetheless, the start-up costs for cartmen (the horse, the cart, the fodder, the stable, the license) were high and as a result, it took the Famine immigrants a while to break into the carting field. By 1860, however, the ranks of the Irish-born cartmen had grown to equal those of the native-born.

Cartmen made good livings. While porters were able to save 25 percent more than day laborers, cartmen saved 35 percent more than porters in their Emigrant Bank accounts. In fact, cartmen accumulated more in their savings accounts than most Irish-born artisans. Robert Wilson from County Down, for example, arrived in New York in 1846 and saved nearly $750 over the next eleven years working primarily as a porter. He used his savings to acquire a horse and cart and by 1870 had doubled his net worth, to $1,500. Not everyone thrived as a cartman, of course. John McSweegan from County Tyrone left the business for a less strenuous job as a clerk, while John Hanlon from King's County gave up carting to take a job as a coachman. But most Famine immigrants who managed to become cartmen remained in the lucrative business.

While carting was the highest-paying unskilled occupation for New York's Irish immigrants, waiting tables paid the least. Before the Irish arrived in New York in large numbers, African Americans did much of the table waiting in New York, and restaurateurs could get away with paying Black New Yorkers near-starvation wages. As a result, the Irish who took jobs waiting tables had to accept some of the lowest pay in the city. New York waiters were not highly trained like many of their European counterparts. They "plop down before you," observed Mooney, "a platefull of meat, potatoes, bread, knife and fork" with a carelessness that would prompt outrage in England but was the norm in New York. Furthermore, Americans would not begin to tip their waiters until the end of the nineteenth century.

Even in fancy hotels catering to wealthy tourists, Mooney noted, waiters "do not, as in the Old Country, get any *vails*, or gifts, from travellers." Consequently, Irish-born food servers accumulated less in their Emigrant Savings Bank accounts than any other unskilled male workers.

All of this meant that, while there were many Irish waiters, few Irishmen made a career of it. Waiter John Brogan soon became a fireman (shoveling coal into the fireboxes of steam engines), while Terrence Connelly moved to Massachusetts and there became a successful barrel dealer. Those who did stick to their jobs in food service tended to work in hotels. Thomas McCabe emigrated from County Meath in 1855 and waited tables in a New York hotel for a quarter century. Thereafter he supervised the establishment's younger waiters as the dining room steward, holding that job for another twenty years, until his death at age seventy-six in 1902.

Like McCabe, about half of all male Famine immigrants initially worked in New York in unskilled occupations. Of these, 88 percent held jobs as day laborers, porters, waiters, coachmen, or cartmen. The rest primarily tended bars, cared for horses in the city's hundreds of stables, served as deckhands on the boats and ferries that plied the city's waterways, worked along the shores of those rivers loading and unloading those vessels, and guarded the city's docks, warehouses, and stores as watchmen.

Yet even lifelong unskilled workers were by no means stuck in a single line of work. Some moved from one unskilled occupation to another, often many times over. John Duffy from Dublin was a driver as a twenty-year-old in 1856, a fireman in the 1860s, a deckhand in 1880, and a day laborer when he died in Brooklyn in 1909. Likewise, Newell McMurray from Armagh was employed as a porter in 1855, a laborer in 1860, a porter again in 1864, and a cartman from the late 1860s to the early 1880s when he retired. Some, however, remained a laborer or a porter or a driver—year after year, decade after decade.

There were just as many Irish-born women employed as domestic servants in New York in the 1850s as there were Irish-born men who worked as day laborers. In fact, domestic service was an even more common occupation for Irishwomen than was day labor for Irishmen. About a third of adult male Famine immigrants in New York did day labor in 1855, while fully two-thirds of working Irishwomen toiled as domestics. In fact, 70 percent of the city's domestic service jobs were filled by Irish-born women.

With so many indigent kinsmen in Ireland to support and possibly bring over to America, Irish immigrant women were much more likely to seek work outside the home than other white New Yorkers. Three-eighths of all adult Irish-born women in New York were employed in this period, compared with only 20 percent of German-born women and 15 percent of white American-born women. Poverty was the main factor driving women to work in this era. Within New York's African American community — the only one less well-off than Irish Americans — two-thirds of women were employed, also primarily as domestics. Both groups found the marketplace for their services full of prejudice. Some employers refused to hire Black women because of their race, while others turned away Irish Catholic applicants because of their religion. Women from both groups were forced into domestic service in part because they were not welcome in other fields — such as nursing — that paid better. On the other hand, there was far more demand for domestic servants in New York than there were women willing to do such work. As a result, Irish domestics did not experience the seasonal unemployment that plagued most Irishmen.

The working conditions for the typical Irish domestic were as onerous, if perhaps not as dangerous, as those for any day laborer. Domestics usually lived where they worked in order to be at their employers' beck and call both day and night. The "servant girl," whose median age was twenty-four, would rise well before anyone else in the house to empty chamber pots, light the fires, and have a hearty breakfast ready when the family awoke. The rest of the day involved cooking; cleaning pots, pans, and dishes; carrying wood in from the backyard, coal up from the cellar for fires, and buckets of water in from the yard for cooking, bathing, and cleaning; polishing silverware; washing, ironing, and starching clothes; fire tending; taking out garbage; childcare; drawing baths (and bathing the children); cleaning the outdoor privies; and scrubbing floors on hands and knees to remove the mud and horse manure tracked inside from New York's filthy streets. Only after everyone else in the household had gone to sleep did the domestic's breathless workday finally come to an end, allowing her to slip upstairs to her attic garret for a short, but well-deserved, night of rest.

DECEMBER 7, 1867.]   HARPER'S WEEKLY.

EGGS-CEEDINGLY CLEVER.
MISTRESS.—"Bridget, I told you to Boil the Eggs soft—and they're quite Hard!"
BRIDGET.—"Soft is it, Mem? Why I've been Bilin' 'em this hour, and the Water won't get 'em Soft anyhow!"

Employers often ridiculed the cooking skills of Irish servants, who had very little experience preparing anything besides potatoes before they came to America. The caption of this image of an Irish domestic makes fun of her belief that eggs, like potatoes, would get softer the longer one cooked them.

For all this work, domestics were paid shockingly little. Inexperienced servants in the 1850s got four to eight dollars *per month* (which employers justified on the grounds that they were also providing room and board), a pittance by any standard and paltry even in comparison to the dollar a day that most day laborers earned. But those with experience, good references from American employers, and impressive cooking skills could earn double those amounts. Still, domestics worked not only more hours per day than male wage workers, but also more days per week. The typical household servant was only off duty every other Sunday, and sometimes they even had to work half days on their days "off." Yet with few alternatives, female Famine immigrants who were desperate for money to help support their kin back in Ireland or to pay for their emigration flocked to these arduous jobs.

Given how difficult domestic service could be, few Irish immigrants aspired to remain household servants their whole lives. "The relationship between the servant girl and her employer," observed one contemporary, "is nearly the same as that of master and slave." Marriage was the surest way out of domestic service. Mary Dougherty, for example, emigrated from County Roscommon as a teenager in 1847 and soon found a job as a domestic in Brooklyn. There she met and married laborer Luke Clark, and shortly thereafter the couple moved to Will County, Illinois, where they became farmers and raised seven children. Margaret Barry from Killarney also worked for several years as a domestic in Brooklyn before marrying English-born baker Sanford Clay. Her sister, Mary, likewise went "out to service" (as she put it to the Emigrant Bank clerk) before she became Mary Barry Murphy. A third sister, Ellen, told the bank she worked as a "washer," perhaps focusing on this task alone in a household with multiple servants, until she married printer Denis Noonan. A fourth Barry sister, Catherine, who undoubtedly worked a stint as a domestic as well, wed house painter Richard Clay, Margaret's brother-in-law, and they also moved to Brooklyn. There they eventually managed to rent a spacious (for the period) thousand-square-foot apartment at 300 Hewes Street in South Williamsburg in a three-story building that's still standing. Richard and Catherine needed every inch of that space to house their ten children and an orphaned niece as well.

Even those domestics who did not marry would have typically tried to move into a different line of work, one that paid more, had better hours, and was less demanding and demeaning. Nonetheless, some Famine immigrants were employed as domestics for their entire adult lives. Mary Bradley from County Tyrone, for example, arrived in New York in 1852 and by age eighteen, in 1855, was already working as a domestic servant for sixty-seven-year-old Herbert Lawrence, a wealthy shipbuilder, his wife, Sarah, and their unmarried adult son at 267 Henry Street, a few blocks from the East River shipyards near Corlears Hook. Twenty-five years later, Sarah still kept house for the three Lawrences at the same address, though by that point Mary had persuaded them to add her older sister Ann to the household staff. Margaret Heslin from County Leitrim also worked for more than thirty years as a domestic, in her case for a prosperous Brooklyn shoe merchant.

Despite the drudgery of their daily lives, some domestics became quite fond of their employers. Mary Ann Booth arrived in New York in about 1846 and found work as a servant in the home of an Irish-born Wall Street stockbroker, John Maxwell, his Massachusetts-born wife, Caroline Mulligan Maxwell, and their four children. The Maxwells became quite wealthy and remained so even after John's death in 1872. Three years later, the six remaining family members—Caroline, two of her children, two sons-in-law (one a widower), and one grandchild—were attended by four live-in servants who were supervised by a fifth, Mary Ann Booth. When Booth died at age seventy-five, she bequeathed more money to the Maxwells' children and grandchildren than to her own kin. The Maxwells repaid the compliment by interring Mary Ann in the

Maxwell family plot in Brooklyn's Green-Wood Cemetery, the only one of the family's many servants so honored.

Domestics like Booth who worked in the homes of particularly wealthy or famous New Yorkers must have viewed their status as superior to that of the servants of more ordinary New Yorkers. Ellen Cummiskey, for example, who arrived in the United States in 1834 at age twenty-two, worked as a servant for Joseph Stuart, a Presbyterian Irish immigrant from County Armagh who founded a successful dry goods import business. In 1850, Ellen was one of three Irish servants living in Stuart's lower Manhattan home along with his wife, Anna, and their four children. Stuart was so successful that in the early 1850s he left the dry goods trade and opened his own private banking firm. And in 1854, he became president of the Emigrant Savings Bank—the very institution whose careful record-keeping would one day enable us to know just as much about Stuart's servant as about the banker himself. Stuart soon moved his family and household staff to a swankier address befitting a bank president, 11 East Thirty-Sixth Street, in a neighborhood full of rich merchants and other notables. After his relocation uptown, Stuart hired a fourth live-in servant, Ellen's little sister Susan, who was more than twenty-five years younger than Ellen and had immigrated to New York by herself at age fifteen in 1855. Susan stopped working for Stuart in the second half of 1870, when she married a day laborer. They moved to Meriden, Connecticut, where they eventually ran a grocery and had four children. But Ellen was still serving the Stuart family as late as 1880, when she was sixty-eight years old. If she was disappointed that she had remained a domestic her whole life, she must have at least taken pride in the fact she had lived in such an upscale neighborhood and worked for one of the city's most prominent Irish-born inhabitants. Sometime after Anna Stuart died in a carriage accident in 1881, Ellen left the Stuart household and moved in with her little sister in Meriden. She resided there until her death in 1892.

Service to the wealthy could bring more than a psychological payoff. Rose Bray from County Louth, just north of Dublin, came to New York in 1854 at age twenty-one and after stints working as a domestic in the homes of an insurance broker and a chemist, she found employment in the household of Charles O'Conor, the American-born son of an Irish immigrant and one of the most prominent attorneys in the city. Around the time Bray began working for O'Conor, he became notorious for agreeing to represent Jefferson Davis after the Confederate president was charged with treason at the end of the Civil War. O'Conor repaired his reputation to some extent a few years later by serving for several years, pro bono, on the team that prosecuted New York City's corrupt Democratic boss, William Tweed. In 1875, when the seventy-one-year-old O'Conor was thought to be near death, the *Herald* noted that the widower was being nursed back to health by his nephew "and his faithful attendant, Rose Bray," then in her early forties. In 1880, Bray headed a household staff of seven that cared for O'Conor's family of six. They lived at his country estate in Fort Washington, now known as Washington Heights, in upper Manhattan. When O'Conor wrote his will, he did not forget his loyal servant — at his death in 1884, O'Conor left Rose $10,000, equal to more than $310,000 today.

Irish domestics were renowned for their frugality and could save surprisingly large sums from their meager wages even if they were not rewarded as extravagantly as Rose Bray. Ellen Cummiskey had saved $200 before her little sister arrived in New York in 1855, and in the ensuing decade the pair increased their nest egg to $775 (about $14,500 today). Bridget White from Clare accumulated $1,025 (about $24,000 today) in fifteen years of work as a domestic in New York and Brooklyn, while Sarah Corrigan from Fermanagh put away $1,069 in fifteen years of employment as a servant at the Washington Hotel at 1 Broadway at the southern tip of Manhattan.

Yet such accumulations were exceptional. It is impossible to determine the precise average savings of domestics because many kept their accounts open after they got married, meaning one cannot tell whether the savings of someone who was a domestic when she opened an account was all accrued through household service, or instead through the earnings of a husband as well. But the median peak bank balance for servants whose occupations could be verified for at least ten years was about $160 (approximately $6,000 today), precisely the same as that for Irish-born day laborers.

NEW YORK CITY.—IRISH DEPOSITORS OF THE EMIGRANT SAVINGS BANK WITHDRAWING MONEY TO SEND TO THEIR SUFFERING RELATIVES IN THE OLD COUNTRY.—SEE PAGE 27.

Female customers (many undoubtedly domestics) of the Emigrant Savings Bank sending money to their relatives in Ireland in 1880. Aside from the clothing, the scene in the bank would not have looked much different in the Famine era.

Many unskilled Famine immigrants were probably content with their American jobs, given that they were paid so much better and employed so much more steadily than in Ireland. Thousands who took employment as day laborers when they arrived in New York

117

did such work for decades without ever trying another vocation. Michael Connell from County Cork, for example, came to New York in 1849, settled at the south end of Cherry Street two blocks from the East River waterfront with his wife, Mary, and three kids, and became a day laborer. Thirty-one years later, at age seventy, Michael and Mary still lived on the same block, and he was still working as a day laborer. Yet other Famine immigrants were not satisfied with the pay and status that unskilled work offered. They sought to use their initial occupations as springboards to jobs that offered higher pay, less danger, more prestige, and perhaps a chance to pass a skill or business on to their children.

And many of them succeeded. By the ends of their careers, 41 percent of the Famine Irish who emigrated as adults and started in New York in the ranks of the unskilled had managed to move up the socioeconomic ladder, a much higher proportion than anyone familiar with the reputation of the Famine Irish would have guessed. We have already encountered several examples of these upwardly mobile immigrants. Cornelius Sullivan from the Lansdowne estate, for instance, transitioned from day labor to peddler and made a killing selling corks. Domestic Mary Dougherty Clark and her day laborer husband, Luke, moved to Illinois and became farmers and later Chicago landlords. More of these social climbers will appear in the chapters to come, as we follow the Famine immigrants' progress up the socioeconomic hierarchy.

One of the biggest surprises is how far up many of these social climbers managed to move. More than two-thirds of those who advanced upward from the unskilled category moved into white-collar jobs — some as clerks and agents, but most operating their own businesses. A quarter of these retail establishments run by onetime unskilled workers were saloons, while grocery stores were the second most popular option (16 percent of all businesses opened by the unskilled). Patrick Wallace from County Louth, for example, immigrated to America at age thirty-three in 1846. He

Occupational Mobility of Male Famine Immigrant Unskilled Workers*

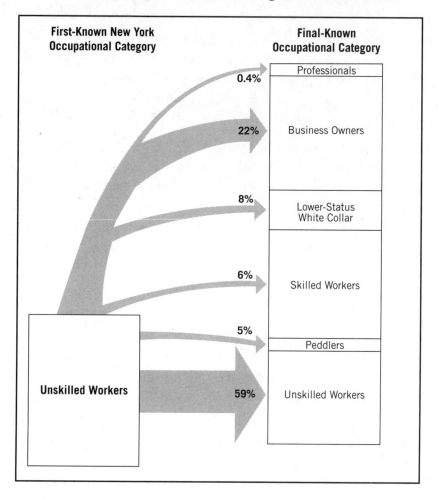

worked as a day laborer for most of his first decade in New York before opening a grocery on West Twenty-Fifth Street in 1856. He remained in business on that same street for the next quarter century, until his death at age sixty-nine in 1882. The third most common choice for unskilled workers who became business owners

---

* NOTE: Percentages may not total 100 due to rounding and refer only to immigrants whose occupations could be tracked for at least ten years.

was to leave New York City altogether and buy a farm in the midwest, like Mary and Luke Clark—this was the business venture of about one in eight unskilled workers who became self-employed.*

One unskilled immigrant who became a business owner, John McMahon, pulled himself up from the ranks of the unskilled by creating a business that found work for other unskilled immigrants. McMahon had emigrated from northwest Kerry at age twenty-four in 1851, leaving four brothers and a widowed father behind in Ireland. After working for several years as a day laborer, John married Margaret James (also from north Kerry) and the two of them set up a boardinghouse in the Kerry enclave near the Hudson River in Ward One. That business failed, as did another boardinghouse on the Upper East Side. John eventually landed a position as a clerk, but by 1863 had returned to day labor.

At several points in the 1850s John was not listed in the city directory, and in those years he may have sought work outside the city. Perhaps in doing so he noticed that while Manhattan was sometimes overflowing with underemployed laborers, positions for day labor in the countryside often went unfilled due to a lack of applicants. Hoping to capitalize on that imbalance, in 1864 John went into the employment "intelligence" business, setting up an office at 16 Greenwich Street (just steps from the immigration depot at Castle Garden) and promising to match unemployed laborers with far-flung employers at no cost to the workers; McMahon received commissions from the companies that hired his recruits. When foot traffic at his office did not bring him enough customers, McMahon advertised. "50 Laborers Wanted for a Railroad in Pennsylvania," stated a newspaper ad he placed in July 1866. "Wages $2 per day." A year later, McMahon ran an ad seeking fifty laborers to do track maintenance in upstate New York and

---

* I've counted those who left New York and bought farms as business owners because, like opening a shop, farming involved the investment of capital and the risk of its loss.

twenty-five more for railroad construction in northern New Jersey, both at a rate of $1.75 for a ten-hour day, significantly more than day labor paid in Manhattan. Those interested did not have much time to consider their options. McMahon's recruits had to leave for the jobsites (accompanied by McMahon or one of his employees) the same day—and sometimes the very morning—that the ads appeared.

McMahon also found employment for women seeking jobs in domestic service and he eventually narrowed his focus to specialize in that field alone, from new offices that he opened on both Washington Street and Broadway. He did well enough in the intelligence business that in 1875 he was able to purchase, for $10,650, a three-story brick building at 240 Henry Street on the Lower East Side. It was big enough to hold the McMahons and several other families, to whom John and Margaret rented apartments. Margaret died at age fifty-two in 1884, about the time John retired, but he continued to live in his rental property with three of his adult children and an unmarried niece until his death at age eighty-three in 1907.

Not every Famine immigrant who left an unskilled occupation for a higher-status job succeeded in their new line of work. Domestic Mary Dunahoe, for example, married porter Patrick Winters in the early 1850s and they soon opened a grocery just east of Tompkins Square Park in Ward Eleven. But the business closed in the early years of the Civil War and Patrick spent most of the next twenty years as a day laborer, notwithstanding a brief, second failed attempt to operate a grocery. In the 1880s he became a carriage driver and was so employed when he died in 1887 at age fifty-eight.

Like Patrick Winters, most unskilled workers who failed in bids to climb the socioeconomic ladder fell back to the bottom rung fairly quickly. But for those who spent years in the middle (or even upper-middle) class, the descent back to the level at which they had started must have been embarrassing, perhaps even humiliating.

Such was the case for Dennis O'Keefe and his wife, Ellen Dwyer O'Keefe.

A native of Fermoy in County Cork, Ellen moved to New York at about age twenty in 1851 and quickly married Dennis, whom she had apparently known back in Ireland. They settled in Ward One, and Dennis took work as a laborer. By the time Ellen opened an account at the Emigrant Savings Bank in 1856, the couple had accumulated $50. Even after becoming customers of the bank, the O'Keefes did not save much — $20 the first year, $65 the second year, and $60 in the third. But in 1860, by which point they had moved to Brooklyn, their rate of savings began to increase, perhaps because Dennis was now working as a porter. Their balance rose from $200 at the beginning of 1860 to $800 three years later. Soon, their deposits grew even more dramatically in size and number. The O'Keefes added $800 to their account in 1863, $2,400 more in 1864 (equal to about $47,000 today), and another $1,000 in 1865. By the beginning of 1867, they had accrued $6,000, which, even with wartime inflation, was the equivalent of nearly $125,000 today — an astounding sum for a Famine refugee who still claimed to be a porter.

How had the O'Keefe family made so much money? It appears that Dennis was hiding his true vocation. During the Civil War, the United States levied its first income tax, and O'Keefe may have been one of the many New Yorkers who balked at handing over a portion of his earnings to pay for a conflict he may not have even supported. In the war years, O'Keefe apparently began supplying New Yorkers with tobacco, perhaps shipped illicitly from the Confederacy. In the 1870s, to judge by the city directory, he was a tobacco dealer and then a cotton broker, and he must have begun speculating in tobacco during the war. In 1872 O'Keefe's nephew told the *New York Herald* that his uncle owned a "tobacco factory" in Brooklyn. "He's pretty well off and owns two houses," the teenager divulged, implying that tobacco was not a brand-new business for

Dennis. This likely explains the O'Keefes' bulging bank account, which contained more money than all but about a dozen of the more than fifteen thousand accounts opened by Irish immigrants at the Emigrant Bank in the 1850s.

Those involved in speculative businesses like tobacco or cotton often exposed themselves to huge financial risks should demand suddenly decline, and that was precisely what happened during the depression that followed the Panic of 1873. This financial crisis may explain why O'Keefe's fortunes plummeted as quickly as they had risen. By the time the depression began to recede in 1878, O'Keefe was no longer in business, reporting instead that he worked as a clerk. In 1879, he was employed as a foreman. And in 1880, he landed back pretty much where he had started, toiling once again as a porter. He made one more unsuccessful foray into the tobacco business but mostly bounced around between jobs as a foreman and porter until he died of a cerebral hemorrhage at about age sixty in 1884.

Dennis and Ellen's nephew John O'Keefe, the one quoted in the *Herald*, experienced a similarly spectacular rise and fall, made all the more exhilarating (and then excruciating) because both his ascent and descent made headlines from coast to coast. John's parents, Timothy (Dennis's brother) and Catherine O'Keefe, had first emigrated from Ireland to England, where Johnny was born in about 1857. They came to America soon after that, eventually moving into the same building that Dennis and Ellen occupied at 107 Washington Street in Ward One, where Johnny grew up. This Hudson River "wharf rat," who hawked newspapers before and after school to earn spending money, attracted the attention of reporters in 1872 because he had the audacity to appear, said the *Herald*, in a "collarless shirt, sieve-like shoes, coarse, dirty clothes and unkempt hair" at an examination to choose a single resident of New York City to become a cadet at the United States Naval Academy at Annapolis. The teens who attended the competition were grilled on math, spelling, geography, and grammar, and in the end, to the amazement of nearly all in attendance, the "saucy, overgrown newsboy" received the highest score and the coveted nomination. The *Herald* ran a two-column profile of the lad it would dub "the Newsboy Admiral," who told the press that he loved diving off ships docked at the Hudson River piers and swimming under the hulking vessels — he did so three times a week to keep clean. "Rough diamond though he be," predicted the *Herald*'s reporter, O'Keefe "will prove himself to be a worthy representative of the district." The Irish American press glowed with pride at the young man's achievement, and the amazing story of Admiral Johnny, the collarless cadet, soon spread across the nation.

Johnny's luck, however, like his uncle's, soon ran out. In those days, the first year at the Naval Academy ended with exams that determined whether the "freshies" would continue and become "midshipmen" or instead be "bilged" and sent home in embarrassment. O'Keefe was one of the unfortunates who failed his exams. To make matters worse, on the day in June 1873 when the navy announced the test scores, O'Keefe and a half dozen of his friends who had also been bilged took their frustrations out on James Conyers — their lone African American classmate and the first ever admitted to the academy — who had also flunked out. Feeling free to intensify their hazing of Conyers now that they would all be leaving Annapolis, O'Keefe and his buddies attacked Conyers with a fusillade of stones, and when the South Carolinian fled into an academy bathhouse for protection, O'Keefe and his friends locked him in it. The navy jailed and court-martialed O'Keefe and the others for the assault before sending them home, and the incident made front-page news across the nation, adding to the embarrassment that came with flunking out of the academy. O'Keefe, "from whom [so] much was expected," returned to Ward One in disgrace. Seven years later, at age twenty-three, O'Keefe still lived at 107 Washington Street and was employed as a day laborer, supporting his widowed mother and three sisters. Given how many John O'Keefes there were in New York, it is impossible to determine what became of him after that.

Of course, we've already met another Famine immigrant whose failed attempt to raise his social status made news. Bartholomew O'Donnell's fifteen minutes of fame, however, did not end with that unsuccessful attempt to fund his retirement by walking seventy-five miles in twenty-four hours. Like most Famine immigrants, the O'Donnells could usually depend on their network of friends and countrymen for help if they fell upon hard times. When word of O'Donnell's failed pedestrian feat reached Brooklyn's broader Irish community, it sprang to his aid. Philip Casey offered O'Donnell use of his own Brooklyn social hall, free of charge midweek, so O'Donnell might try again and recoup his losses.

This time, even the Manhattan press was in attendance. "The start was made in the presence of a fair number of spectators who cheered the aged pedestrian heartily," announced the *Times*, whose correspondent found O'Donnell's approach to the task a bit unorthodox. "Contrary to all rules of training," wrote the reporter, O'Donnell "smoked a short, black pipe at intervals, and appeared to derive much comfort from the indulgence." The *Times* also found it odd that O'Donnell did not fortify himself with alcoholic stimulants, instead drinking "large quantities of tea," boiling hot, which his wife brewed fresh at trackside. This time O'Donnell reached his goal, completing 2,240 laps of the indoor track with energy to spare. "After leaving the track he danced an Irish reel," reported the *Times*, "stepping as lightly as if he were 40 years younger."

Nonetheless, O'Donnell's pedestrian feat and the fleeting celebrity that accompanied it did not produce the windfall he sought. O'Donnell continued to live with his only child, Margaret O'Donnell Cowan, for ten years, until he passed away in 1889 at age seventy-four. He clearly did not leave much of a bequest to Margaret. Eleven years later, in January 1900, she was a single mother trying unsuccessfully to make ends meet as a laundress. Her eldest, a son, had already married, left home, and joined the navy. The two next eldest, fifteen-year-old Joseph and thirteen-year-old Edwin, were living with her, probably because they were old enough to earn some money. But her three youngest — eleven-year-old Loretta, nine-year-old Willie, and eight-year-old Viola — were residents of the Brooklyn Home for Destitute Children, along with 350 other unfortunate waifs. And five more of Margaret's children were dead, an unusually high number for this era and one that probably reflected, at least in part, the impoverished circumstances into which they had been born.

As we've seen, about half of Famine Irishmen who arrived in New York, and most of the Irishwomen who worked, started out on the bottom rung of America's socioeconomic ladder as day laborers, domestics, and the like. Of those men, four in ten managed to improve their standing in the socioeconomic hierarchy over the course of their lifetimes. The O'Donnells, however, could never quite do so. Most day laborers and domestics, waiters and washers, longshoremen and laundresses did not live as precariously as the O'Donnells did decades after arriving in New York. Those who remained in the ranks of the unskilled rarely struck it rich, but most *could* secure the "competence" that eluded the O'Donnells, allowing them to pay doctor's bills if there was a major illness and to weather even fairly long stretches of unemployment. Yet there were some, like the O'Donnells, who never reached that level of economic security and spent their entire lives in America barely scraping by, racing in circles toward a prize they could never quite reach.

CHAPTER FOUR

"Too Often Seen to Need Description"

Peddlers, Hawkers, and Vendors

Americans do not associate Irish immigrants with peddling. The image of the immigrant peddler that comes to mind tends to be a southern or eastern European immigrant, perhaps with a pushcart, hawking goods in New York's Little Italy or Lower East Side at the turn of the twentieth century. But thousands of the Famine Irish — particularly those with an entrepreneurial bent — tried their hand at this trade. In fact, looking at Irish immigrants' occupations within a year of arrival in the United States, there were as many peddlers as there were carpenters or shoemakers, and nearly as many as tailors or porters. Most Famine immigrants tended to leave peddling after they became better established in their new homeland, but others remained street hawkers for their entire lives if they enjoyed being their own boss or were especially successful.

Yet such success, even when one's peddling proceeds were safely squirreled away in the vaults of the Emigrant Savings Bank, did not guarantee long-term financial security. Take the case of John Griffin, who at age twenty-three had left the town of Killarney in County Kerry and arrived in New York in February 1851. John's younger brother Michael, like John a bachelor, made the journey three months

127

later. When Michael landed, he found that his brother had become a peddler and had settled near the East River waterfront in Ward Four.

Ward Four was not as well-known as Ward Six, home of the infamous Five Points neighborhood — but it was nearly as bad. Its tenements were almost as crowded and run-down, its inhabitants were almost as poor, and it had almost as much prostitution, crime, and homelessness. Ward Four also had the second-highest concentration of Irish immigrants in the city — trailing only Ward Six. Ward Four was pretty much Ward Six on the waterfront, but without the notoriety. Still, thousands of Irish immigrants living in Ward Four opened accounts at the Emigrant Savings Bank — their numbers exceeded only by residents of Five Points.

John Griffin rented an apartment in a huge brick tenement at 20 Roosevelt Street in the northeast part of the ward. It wasn't one of the worst blocks in the district (those were on Cherry and Water Streets), but it wasn't one of the ward's nicer blocks either. The defining feature of this stretch of Roosevelt Street was the gashouse that belched putrid black coal dust into the air each day while producing fuel for city gaslights. Griffin's apartment was just two doors down from, and on the same side of the street as, the gashouse. Nonetheless, Michael moved into the soot-filled apartment with his brother and became a peddler as well.

Soon the brothers found spouses and went their separate ways. Michael wed Bridget McCarthy, from remote western Kerry, who had come to America in 1852. She gave birth to their first child at the beginning of 1855, and immediately thereafter they moved just across the Hudson River to Jersey City, where Bridget and Michael lived for the rest of their lives. John, in contrast, stayed in Ward Four and married Mary McMahon, a native of County Clare who, on her frigid voyage to America in December 1848, had shared the steerage cabin of the *Heather Bell* with future marathon race walker Bartholomew O'Donnell. John and Mary had four children — Jeremiah in 1854, Johanna in 1856, John Jr. in 1858, and Josephene in 1861.

Ward Four in the 1850s

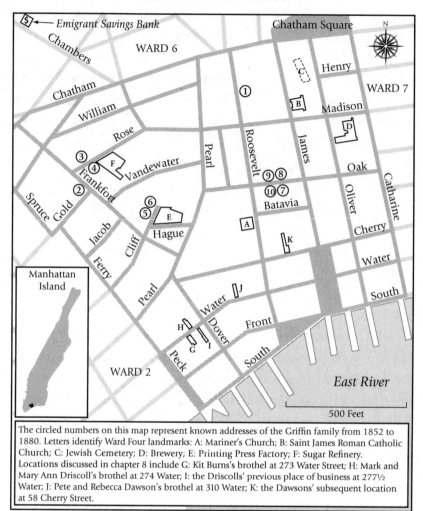

The circled numbers on this map represent known addresses of the Griffin family from 1852 to 1880. Letters identify Ward Four landmarks: A: Mariner's Church; B: Saint James Roman Catholic Church; C: Jewish Cemetery; D: Brewery; E: Printing Press Factory; F: Sugar Refinery. Locations discussed in chapter 8 include G: Kit Burns's brothel at 273 Water Street; H: Mark and Mary Ann Driscoll's brothel at 274 Water; I: the Driscolls' previous place of business at 277½ Water; J: Pete and Rebecca Dawson's brothel at 310 Water; K: the Dawsons' subsequent location at 58 Cherry Street.

Peddling might seem like a precarious enterprise. Historians have usually imagined it to be a vocation of last resort — one taken up out of desperation by those who could not find or hold steady wage work. But the Emigrant Savings Bank records prove otherwise. Irish immigrants who began their American working careers as peddlers saved more money on average than any other Irishmen except doctors, lawyers, and saloonkeepers. And John Griffin fared even better than average. He and Mary were determined, regimented savers. Starting with an initial deposit of $50 in 1852, they increased their nest egg to $250 in 1853, $350 in 1854, $500 in 1855, and $600 in 1856. Their savings continued to grow at that pace so that on New Year's Day 1860, their balance reached exactly $1,000, the equivalent of nearly $37,000 today—an extraordinary sum for Famine refugees who could not write their own names. John did not earn every cent of this nest egg as a peddler. He worked occasionally as a day laborer and a cartman. Mary brought in some income as well, running a modest boardinghouse for at least a while in 1857. But most of their savings came from John's peddling.

We don't know what John Griffin peddled. Some Irish traders carried a cornucopia of items in heavy packs—one on their chest and one on their back for balance—hoping to stock any item a tenement dweller might need at a given moment. Other peddlers specialized in a single commodity. Cornelius Sullivan, we have seen, made a good living selling nothing but corks. Other hucksters focused on fruit or fish, while still others sold only firewood, kindling, or charcoal. John Gallery from Clare peddled nothing but "chamois skins," specially cured leather cloths used for drying and polishing fine objects. Secondhand clothing was an especially popular item to carry door to door—peddlers might buy a dead man's garments from his grieving widow in one tenement and unload them minutes later to a greenhorn in the building next door. Housewives were especially fond of those vending needles, pins, and thread, as these hawkers might agree to tiny sales that brick-and-mortar shopkeepers would never consider.

Some hucksters changed their stock depending on the season. Hot corn on the cob was a favorite street food in early autumn, the same time of year that apples became ubiquitous. Both were sold primarily by women. Come winter, peddlers hawked lozenges and hot chestnuts on New York's sidewalks. Most peddlers tramped the streets looking for customers, but some set up their wares on tables or stands in a favorable location and waited for passersby to discover them. In either case, hucksters loudly announced their inventory to drum up business: "My clams I want to sell to-day; the best of clams from Rock-away," called one Irish peddler, while another simply cried, extending the two syllables as long as possible, "Fresh sha-a-d!"

"OLD HAT" MAN.   UMBRELLA DEALER.

New York street peddlers as depicted in *Harper's Weekly* in 1868.

Whatever it was that John Griffin peddled, his fortunes declined dramatically after he and Mary reached that thousand-dollar threshold. In the spring of 1860, their second child, who went by "Hannah," died at the age of four, and the medical bills and burial expenses took a significant bite out of their savings. John may have fallen ill and been unable to work for long stretches as well, because while the family had made lots of deposits and few withdrawals from its bank account before Hannah's death, now they made frequent withdrawals and no deposits at all for the ensuing decade. The Griffins' balance fell from $900 after Hannah's death to $800 at the beginning of 1861 (when Josephene was born), $750 at the beginning of 1862, and $650 at the beginning of 1863. John was clearly unable to work by that point: he was no longer listed in the city directories as having an occupation, and the family began consistently making $20 monthly withdrawals. Their declining status was reflected in the fact that they moved from one of Ward Four's more pleasant thoroughfares, Rose Street, to the bleak, dead-end block of Cliff Street, where their dark tenement faced a printing press factory. By fall, John must have been very ill — Mary began withdrawing $50 or more each month as the doctors' bills presumably piled up.

He never did recover. John Griffin died at age thirty-five on November 11, 1863, and the following day Mary withdrew $100 from their bank account, probably to cover John's final medical bills and funeral expenses. A good chunk of that sum was spent erecting an ornate black marble tombstone (in the shape of a Celtic cross) that is still standing in Calvary Cemetery in what is now Queens. That expenditure left Mary and the kids with just $220 (equal to about $5,400 today), quite a precipitous fall from their flush times just three years earlier.

Mary now took over as the family breadwinner and she too became a peddler, running a vegetable stand to support herself and Jerry (now age nine), John Jr. (age five), and Josephene (age two). Mary managed to make ends meet, but just barely. Perhaps her brother-in-law in Jersey City helped. Mary surely could have used some assistance because in September 1869, when the Emigrant Bank switched to a new set of ledgers that are no longer extant, her account held just $61. Mary probably spent much of that meager sum in the next few weeks because John Jr. fell ill and died, at age eleven, in late October.

By that point, at least, John and Mary's son Jerry was able to help support the family. He stopped going to school and took a job as a messenger. By 1875, at about age twenty-one and entrepreneurial just like his parents, Jerry opened a pork shop on the ground floor of the huge tenement that the family, still in Ward Four, lived in at 27 Oak Street. He continued in the meat business (with a brief, unsuccessful detour into saloonkeeping) until 1880, when he landed a coveted position as a policeman, delivering the steady income and guaranteed pension that a potentially profitable but always precarious occupation like peddling could never provide.

———

Of the 275,000 or so employed New Yorkers in 1860, about 5,000 worked as street peddlers of one kind or another. Immigrants dominated the peddlers' ranks, but in this era there were actually more German than Irish-born peddlers in New York City. Yet the language barrier restricted most German peddlers to the part of Manhattan where Germans concentrated—Wards Ten, Eleven, Thirteen, and Seventeen—which would soon become known as the Lower East Side but was then referred to as Klein Deutschland, "Little Germany." That language barrier left the city's Irish peddlers, vendors, and hawkers almost free rein in the city's other eighteen wards.

Who were New York's Irish peddlers? They were not all men—about one out of every five Irish street vendors was a woman. They were also recent immigrants to the United States. Those in their first decade in America were twice as likely to peddle as those who had come to America twenty or more years before. And like some other occupations, peddling involved networking and particularly attracted immigrants from certain parts of Ireland.

New York's Irish peddlers originated, in particular, in the rocky, windswept northwest Irish county of Donegal. Immigrants from Donegal made up only about 3 percent of New York's Irish population in the 1850s but they accounted for approximately a quarter of the city's Irish peddlers. The Donegal peddlers originated almost exclusively in just one part of that large county—the fishing village of Killybegs and its immediate surroundings, constituting three of the county's fifty-two parishes. Three-quarters of Manhattan's Donegal peddlers came from this tiny portion of Ireland's northwesternmost county.

How did this concentration of Killybegs men in New York peddling begin? We can't say for sure, but it definitely developed in the pre-Famine years and is likely connected with the emigration in 1824 of James Cunningham, one of the first emigrants from Killybegs to arrive in New York. Cunningham sailed to North America at about age twenty, and it is not clear what he did in the United States until the late 1840s, when he reported that he made note cards and resided on Elizabeth Street in Ward Fourteen. In the early 1850s, Cunningham told the clerk at the Emigrant Savings Bank that he had switched to pencil making, a somewhat ironic occupation for a man who could not write his own name. By that point Cunningham's family had spread out far and wide. Brother Hugh lived in Tennessee, sister Sarah had settled in Glasgow, and two other brothers remained in Ireland.

But the apparently modest vocations that Cunningham had reported to census takers and bank clerks did not tell the whole story. He was not making cards and pencils as an employee but as a small business owner and wholesaler. This fact explains how, by 1855, Cunningham had amassed more than $2,500 in the Emigrant Bank, the equivalent of about $95,000 today and an amount that made him one of that institution's wealthiest depositors. Nor was that the entirety of Cunningham's wealth. Sometime in the early 1850s, he had purchased the two tenements at 233 Mulberry Street in Ward Fourteen. The rents he collected from his tenants help explain why his savings could increase so quickly. Cunningham was not even the first Killybegs native to purchase property on that block. The tenement next door at 231 Mulberry had been owned since at least 1850 by James McGill, who had emigrated from Killybegs in 1835, become a peddler, and plowed his peddling profits into that 25-by-100-foot rectangle of Manhattan real estate.

McGill, Cunningham, and their tenements became the locus of New York's sizable Killybegs emigrant community. Anyone coming from the fishing village or its environs in the Famine years brought with them McGill or Cunningham's name and address and knew that they could find lodging and perhaps even a job from these trailblazers. James Bresland, for example, arrived in New York in 1847, moved into McGill's tenement, and became a peddler. Bresland's brother John eventually did so as well. McGill likely showed them the ropes and perhaps even connected them with a wholesaler from whom to purchase their first stocks of goods. McGill might have even lent the greenhorns money to make these first purchases. Perhaps the Breslands sold Cunningham's note cards and pencils. In 1850, the Bresland brothers boarded with McGill, his wife, Marjorie, their three small children, and a third Killybegs peddler. But by 1855, each brother was renting his own apartment from McGill. Now married, each shared a flat with a wife and baby. A third brother, Charles, who arrived in New York in 1851, eventually moved into the building too.

This process repeated over and over, as more and more inhabitants of the Killybegs area made the trek to America. In 1848, Alexander Watson left the seaport for New York, moved in with McGill, and became, in his own words, a "travelling merchant." In 1849, Thomas Rolston arrived in New York, took lodging with McGill, and tried peddling as well, as did James McShane in 1851. Killybegs natives James Dowd, Joseph Brogan, and James Burns chose apartments across the street, perhaps because McGill's and Cunningham's tenements were already overflowing with their countrymen (Cunningham eventually dealt with this problem by buying 232 and 235 Mulberry as well). Even before he expanded his real estate portfolio, Cunningham rented space to a plethora of Killybegs kinsmen. John Haffey, who emigrated in 1852, became a peddler, while Ann and Mary Cunningham (not sisters but perhaps nieces or cousins of James), who left Ireland in 1851 and 1853 respectively, took jobs at the "card factory" that James had started or purchased sometime in the 1850s. Killybegs peddlers undoubtedly sold Cunningham's stationery all around town and, quite possibly, throughout the northeastern United States.

This intense networking paid handsome dividends for the Killybegs peddlers. The median savings of peddlers who emigrated from Killybegs in the Famine years was $570, more than double that of Irish peddlers born in other parts of Ireland. This success may stem from the fact that the Killybegs peddlers spent most of their earnings within their tight-knit community. They paid their rent to landsmen like McGill. They bought their food from grocers like Killybegs native Isabella McGonegal. They purchased their peddling supplies from wholesalers like Cunningham. And they spent their leisure time in saloons such as the one run by Killybegs emigrant John Freel. Patronizing the businesses of community leaders allowed those same leaders to help even more residents of the Killybegs area make the voyage to America and become safely and profitably situated in New York after they arrived.

Being able to rely on this network made remaining in New York an attractive proposition for immigrants from Killybegs. Yet many of them eventually left New York to settle elsewhere in the United States. Some used their peddling proceeds to purchase farms. John Haffey and his wife, Margaret Cunningham Haffey, moved to Wayne County in northeast Ohio. John worked there as a peddler until at least 1870, but then bought a seventeen-acre farm on which he and Margaret raised their seven children. Joseph Brogan left New York in the late 1850s and acquired a farm in northwestern Arkansas, which he cultivated with a brother and a cousin. Yet Joseph apparently found farming there unappealing. In the 1860s, he moved to Fort Smith and opened a general store, which the lifelong bachelor ran until his death, at age fifty-three, in 1873.

Most Killybegs peddlers who left New York moved not to the countryside, but to other cities. Thomas Rolston, for example, withdrew his $450 in savings from the Emigrant Savings Bank and ventured south, where his older brother Walter, who had also previously worked as a peddler in New York, was plying the same trade in Baltimore and living in a small home he had bought with his wife, Mary Hamilton Rolston. Thomas lived with Walter, Mary, and their growing family until Thomas married a Mary of his own, Irish-born Mary Young from Philadelphia, in 1868. Although Thomas had a short stint as a bookkeeper, and Walter held a position as a police officer for nearly a decade, they worked primarily as peddlers until Walter died at about age seventy in 1896; Thomas passed away eight years later.

The most successful Killybegs traveling salesman of all, however, made a fortune by remaining in New York City and becoming a supplier to peddlers. Andrew Brice arrived in New York at age fifteen in 1853 with his mother, older sister, and three younger siblings. There they joined Andrew's father, Michael, who had emigrated a year earlier and had, of course, become a peddler. By age seventeen, Andrew was a huckster as well. Like many peddlers, he eventually opened a brick-and-mortar shop. His Broome Street emporium sold imported linens, many undoubtedly from Ireland, in partnership with another Killybegs peddler, James Johnson. Brice and Johnson sold primarily to peddlers, outfitting them with both dry goods and the "notions" (like buttons, needles, and thread) that were such an important part of the huckster's trade. Brice's peddler-supply business was so successful that he eventually opened branches in Cincinnati and Nashville to outfit traveling salesmen in those regions. When he died in his Upper East Side brownstone in 1913, Brice left his two surviving children an estate (primarily in the form of blue-chip stocks like Union Pacific, U.S.

Steel, and Amalgamated Copper) worth $148,000, equal to about $4.5 million today.

———

At its heart, peddling was a speculative venture. Vendors bought their goods as cheaply as possible and then hoped to resell them at the highest price the market would bear. Many bought damaged or imperfect products at wholesale auctions on Pearl Street in lower Manhattan and then peddled them uptown to unsuspecting buyers "at a good retail profit." Peddlers might take on debt to purchase their stock, and the interest rate on the loan affected their bottom lines. Hucksters who sold goods like fruit or fish, which would eventually spoil, could have a difficult time determining how much to buy. Purchase too much, and they might lose money if their goods rotted before they could be sold. Acquire too little, and the peddler might curse himself for all the potential profits he had lost when customers asked for a product he no longer had in stock. Even nonperishable items carried risk. A certain hat might go out of style. A particularly dry summer might mean meager umbrella sales. Wielding a shovel as a day laborer paid only a dollar a day, but at least at the end of that day you knew you would have that dollar. A peddler might make many dollars in a day, or none at all. It was a high-risk, high-reward vocation — not one for the faint of heart.

We know that peddlers were keenly aware of the speculative nature of their trade because they sometimes referred to themselves as "speculators." Patrick Barrett, for example, arrived in New York from County Kilkenny at age twenty-seven in 1850 and was peddling and living in Five Points when he opened an Emigrant Savings Bank account in 1855. A year later, he told the bank that he was a "fruiterer" and in 1859 he called himself a "speculator," a term he also used to describe his vocation in 1863. In the summer of 1875, he again told a census taker that he was a "speculator," but when the enumerator demanded more detail, Barrett told him that his speculation involved "produce," implying that Barrett was still a peddler of some kind. Whatever the case, this vocation had allowed Patrick and his wife, Ann, to buy a home, albeit a modest one, at 128 Eighteenth Street, in what is now the South Slope neighborhood of Brooklyn, for themselves and their eight children. Even so, being self-employed meant that Barrett's future income was far from secure. In 1878, he was working as a watchman. The following year, he reported that he was a "merchant," while in 1880 he once again called himself a speculator. By the late 1880s, however, Barrett was once again working as a watchman, his occupation when, according to a news account in 1893, he "dropped dead" unexpectedly at age seventy while waiting for a train on an elevated platform in lower Manhattan.

Some peddlers engaged in a variety of speculative ventures. Andrew Brosnan, for example, left Castleisland in County Kerry in 1847. There was not much reason for the twenty-nine-year-old to stay in his homeland. His parents were dead, and he had no surviving siblings. After six years in America, Brosnan was a peddler and had saved $75. By then, he had married another Brosnan, Margaret (also from Castleisland), they had an infant daughter named Mary, and the three of them were living in what is now the Financial District of lower Manhattan in Ward Two.

Andrew eventually specialized in fruit peddling and found it a profitable trade—by 1858 he had amassed savings of more than $570. Just after the Civil War, the Brosnans (now with five children) moved to South Brooklyn, renting an apartment at 67 Union Street on a block with many other Brosnans, perhaps Andrew and Margaret's kinsmen. According to the Brooklyn city directories of the late 1860s, however, Andrew had given up peddling for day labor. He also suffered the loss of Margaret in 1868, after what the family termed "a long and tedious illness." Andrew was left with five children to care for, ranging in age from two to fifteen, but he never remarried. His eldest child, Mary, became the family housekeeper.

Perhaps Margaret's death rekindled Andrew's entrepreneurial drive. In 1870, he told the compiler of the Brooklyn city directory that he was now a "speculator," although his speculative activities included not only peddling but also the purchase of the tenement at 10 Union Place in that borough. Brosnan eventually sold that property and invested the proceeds in another tenement around the corner at 72 Union Street, all the while continuing to alternate between day labor and fruit peddling. He and all five of his children still lived at 72 Union in 1880. A year later, when Brosnan died at about age sixty-three, he bequeathed the tenement (owned "free and clear," he boasted in his will) to his five children. Four of them eventually sold their shares to the fifth, Patrick, who as late as 1896 still lived there and collected rents while working a day job as a driver. His brother Andrew Jr. joined the fire department while another, Timothy, operated a grocery for a while just down the street from the three-story brick tenement, which still stands just steps from the South Brooklyn waterfront.

Some peddlers tried to reduce the amount of cash they risked in their speculations by manufacturing the very items they sold. Widow Anastasia Mullen made men's "drawers" and then sold them herself to support her six children. Bernard Hanratty from Dundalk in County Louth made and peddled corks. Like Cornelius Sullivan, Hanratty found the cork trade very profitable. He had accumulated $1,000 in his bank account by 1860 and had $9,000 in assets when he died in 1865 at age sixty, allowing his widow to buy a home in Jersey City for herself and their three surviving daughters.

Peddlers of umbrellas also manufactured them in their tenement apartments when the weather was good and then hawked them on rainy days. Thomas Field from Dublin, for instance, tried peddling secondhand clothes in Manhattan but eventually moved with his wife, Anne, to Brooklyn, where he first worked as a house painter but then started making and peddling umbrellas. Thomas's younger brother Timothy, who came to America three years after Thomas, moved in around the corner from his brother and took up the same vocation. By the late 1850s, when Thomas's eldest son, Edward, became a teenager, the boy began helping to make the umbrellas. In 1859, however, Anne died at age thirty-six. Thomas passed away just four years later, at age forty, of what the coroner characterized as "exhaustion of the brain." By then, luckily, Thomas's eldest child, Catherine, was twenty-one and old enough to keep house for her younger siblings while Edward now supported the family peddling umbrellas.

The Field children's young cousin Timothy Jr., who lived around the corner, was less fortunate. When both his parents died in the late 1850s, tiny Tim was placed in the city-run orphanage on Randalls Island in the East River. It is not clear what became of him, but his cousin Edward Field did land on his feet. A lifelong Brooklynite, he married Jane Cooms and worked at various times as a coachman, a peddler (hawking clothing rather than umbrellas), a day laborer, a cabinetmaker, and an upholsterer before his heart gave out, at age eighty-nine, in 1935.

―――――

Even though it was considered a bit scandalous for women to interact with male strangers, many of New York's Irish peddlers were women. What kinds of women would risk their reputations and become street vendors? They were overwhelmingly women who were or had once been married. Of the female Irish-born peddlers who had accounts at the Emigrant Savings Bank, about 45 percent were married, another 45 percent were widows, while only the remaining tenth had never been wed. Women with small children also avoided peddling because it took them away from their families. If mothers with young children needed a job, they tended to work as seamstresses (even though such work paid less than any other employment) because needlewomen could do their sewing at home. But for widows or married women whose children did not need constant attention, peddling was a viable option.

By far the most popular item for women to hawk on the streets was fruit. Three-quarters of all female peddlers operated sidewalk fruit stands. In fact, they far outnumbered men in this pursuit. Widow Catherine Norris from Tipperary sold fruit in the early 1850s to support two teenage children. Honora Hickey from Limerick did so too even though her husband, Dennis, a shoemaker, was still alive. The additional income must have been welcome to help support their eight kids. Initially Honora operated a "notions stand," but that apparently did not pay well, so she switched to fruit peddling and remained in that vocation from 1853 to at least 1859, when Dennis died. By then her eldest children could take jobs to help support their mother and younger siblings. Honora's son John, a shoemaker like his father, could not help his mother for very long. He came home to his Roosevelt Street tenement one day in 1869 to find two of the female tenants fighting. While trying to break up the quarrel, Hickey was kicked in the groin with such force by one of the women — also an Irish immigrant — that the blow ruptured his bladder and killed him.

The reasons that married women took up peddling are harder to determine. Some husbands could not find employment due to illness or disability, and in such cases a wife might become a street vendor to compensate. Ann Quigley's husband, Patrick, could not work at all for some reason, so Ann supported them and their four sons as a fruit seller in the 1850s. She eventually saved enough from that work to open a grocery. Likewise, William Mooney could not generate enough income on his own to provide for his wife, Teresa, and their six-year-old daughter, Rebecca. A year after their arrival in New York, they could only afford squalid lodging in an unfinished tenement basement in Ward Seventeen. To help improve their situation, Teresa peddled glassware from a sidewalk stand, perhaps with Rebecca in tow.

In other cases, women peddled even though their husbands had steady employment. These families may have wanted extra income in order to quickly accumulate enough money to bring starving family members to America, support indigent kinsmen who remained in Ireland, or start a brick-and-mortar business in New York. Jane McShane from County Longford, for example, ran a fruit stand in 1857 even though her husband, Anthony, worked as a laborer and she cared for three sons, aged seven, ten, and thirteen. Perhaps her profits were what allowed Anthony to open a crockery shop by 1860. Their two eldest sons had jobs by that point as well. Nonetheless, Jane remained in the fruit business until at least 1862. Catherine Murphy from County Cork also ran a fruit stand in the early 1850s while her husband, Daniel, worked as a laborer. Her business must have been quite profitable because by 1860, Daniel had abandoned day labor and taken over the fruit stand.

The business know-how gained in peddling also sometimes helped women start other enterprises. Jane McShane eventually operated a "toy store." Catherine O'Connell, who like McShane was married, peddled fruit briefly before becoming a boardinghouse keeper. She remained in that business until at least 1868. Catherine Dowd from Queen's County (now Laois) peddled fruit in the second half of the 1850s while she was married. When her husband, John, died in 1867 following what the family characterized as "a long and painful illness," Catherine moved to New Jersey with her daughters Julia and Katie and supported them operating a "home saloon" in the house she bought there. By 1880 she had converted her retail space into a small grocery.

In only a single instance could I determine why one of the Emigrant Bank's never married female customers took up peddling rather than domestic service. Honora Shea, born in Tuosist parish on the Marquis of Lansdowne's estate in southwest Kerry, was about forty when, in 1851, she took advantage of Lansdowne's offer of free passage to America. But Honora was not your typical unwed Irish immigrant. Making the journey with her on the *American Eagle* were her children Ellen and William, then about twelve and four years old, who were born out of wedlock and had different fathers. Honora might have hoped that coming to America and settling among the multitudes in Manhattan would allow her to escape her tarnished reputation and start over with a clean slate, but that was not the case. When she walked to the Emigrant Bank in 1853 with Patrick Murphy and widow Barbara Sullivan, both also from Tuosist, to open a savings account for herself and daughter Ellen, the bank clerk wrote in his ledger that Ellen Harrington was Honora's "illegitimate" daughter. Two years later, when Honora established an account for son William Hearly, the clerk used the same term to describe the boy's parentage.

There's no way to know why the scribe felt obligated to record this detail, nor how Honora felt about the stigma under which she and her children clearly labored. But whatever the obstacles, Shea was determined to provide a decent life for her children. She worked tirelessly as a fruit peddler and managed to save about $275 in those two accounts (equal to about $10,500 today), 70 percent more than the average Famine immigrant saved and nearly three times what the median female peddler squirreled away. It's not clear what became of Shea or her children, but even a "fallen woman" like Honora could count on help from at least some inhabitants of the Lansdowne enclave if she or her children ever needed it.

In their quests to climb America's socioeconomic ladder, Irish-born peddlers did surprisingly well. Of New York's male Famine immigrants who could be tracked for ten years or more and worked initially in America as a peddler, 42 percent ended their careers in white-collar vocations. Two-thirds of those former peddlers became business owners, while the other third moved to lower-status white-collar jobs—primarily as clerks. Peddler Peter Bryson, for example, worked as a dry goods clerk in the 1870s, as did former peddler Hugh Conaghan, who like Bryson was from Donegal. Of the 58 percent of peddlers who did not end up in white-collar jobs, about half remained peddlers, while most of the rest ended their work lives in unskilled positions like day laborer or watchman.

In some cases, the downwardly mobile peddlers lived very difficult lives. Thomas McClafferty, for example, was born a mile from Killybegs and came to New York in 1852 with his wife and young daughter, both named Susan. Thomas became a peddler, but after a few years the family returned to Ireland. A decade later, now with five children, the McClaffertys emigrated again, but this time they settled 250 miles northwest of Manhattan, in the town of Waterloo, New York, where Thomas again became a "pack peddler." He and Susan even managed to buy a cheap home (worth $450 in 1870), which they could afford in part because the younger Susan worked in a local woolen mill.

Thomas's income from peddling must not have been very reliable—by the mid-1870s he had switched to day labor. We don't know what happened to the family over the next quarter century, but Thomas clearly did not enjoy the financial success of other Donegal peddlers, at least not over the long term. Perhaps he used up his savings. Or maybe he had mistakenly counted on his children to care for him in his old age. Thomas outlived both his wife and all of his children but one, who either could not or would not care for him. As a result, though McClafferty still owned his own home as late as 1900, in May 1902 the seventy-seven-year-old had to seek refuge in the Seneca County Poor House. He passed away three months later.

McClafferty's story of downward mobility is tragic—but it was not typical, something that becomes clear when considering another measure of how peddlers fared in New York: their savings. For women, peddling was no better an occupation than other jobs they might take as far as wealth accumulation was concerned. The median savings of a female peddler was $100, just a few dollars less than all other employed women managed to accumulate. For men, however, peddling was far more lucrative than most other employment options. The median savings of Irishmen whose first-known job in New York was peddling was $300, versus $176 for all other men. These peddlers accumulated twice as much as skilled workers, 75 percent more than those whose first jobs in the United States were unskilled, and 50 percent more than men who began working in New York as clerks and other lower-status white-collar jobs. In fact, peddlers accumulated no less in savings than men whose first-known American occupation involved running brick-and-mortar businesses.

What do these numbers tell us? First, they show that despite their low social standing, peddlers earned more than all but a handful of other Irish immigrants. Their working conditions might be terrible—having to suffer through rain and snow, heat and cold to sell one's wares—but the payoff for enduring these indignities was substantial. Second, they remind us that when judging immigrants, looks can be deceiving. Images from this period depicting peddlers show, without exception, shabby-looking men and women who seem to be barely earning a living. Yet their bank accounts tell a different story. Third, the amount of money peddlers were able to squirrel away in their savings accounts indicates that, in New York at least, peddling was not a vocation of last resort, but one that paid very well for those with entrepreneurial acumen. That acumen need not have come from a formal education. A third of New York's Irish peddlers could not even write their own names, and the bank balances of illiterate peddlers were no smaller than those of their literate counterparts.

Finally, the economic success of Irish peddlers reminds us that in nineteenth-century America, entrepreneurship was the fastest route to financial advancement. The dollar a day earned by day laborers enabled many of them to do little more than scrape by. In contrast, while the payoff for peddlers was uncertain, the risk involved in peddling was usually accompanied by a substantial reward.

Those potential rewards, even for lifelong peddlers, are evident in the story of the next-biggest cohort of Irish peddlers in Civil War–era New York after that from Killybegs. Emigrants from Donegal's neighbor to the east, County Tyrone, also created a peddling network in Manhattan. But whereas the Donegal peddlers sold whatever wares they found profitable, the Tyrone hucksters developed a single peddling specialty—charcoal. In fact, men from Tyrone nearly monopolized that trade by the late 1850s. All twenty-five charcoal peddlers who opened accounts at the Emigrant Savings Bank in that decade were born in Tyrone. Furthermore, just as Donegal peddlers were mainly from Killybegs, more than three-quarters of the Tyrone charcoal dealers originated in just one of that county's forty-three parishes, Bodoney Lower.

While the lives of those born in Killybegs were inexorably shaped by the sea, most inhabitants of Bodoney had never even seen an ocean before they packed up their meager belongings and journeyed to Derry or Belfast to set sail for America. Nestled in the verdant Sperrin Mountains fifty miles east of Killybegs, the tiny hamlets that made up Bodoney Lower parish lay perched on the tall hillsides of a small valley bisected by the headwaters of the Owenkillew River. At its source in Bodoney Lower parish, the river is just a stream, too shallow for even the tiniest watercraft but deep enough to support "trouts in abundance" (as a local minister put it) all year round and salmon during the summer spawning season. Small farms dotted the lower halves of each mountainside while sheep grazed in the green pastures above that reached almost to the very tops of the highest peaks. The mountainsides thrusting up from either bank of the river are not very tall—hardly more than a thousand feet—but they are steep and close to both the north and south sides of the river, increasing the sense of isolation the residents of this beautiful but "cold dreary region" felt from the outside world.

Bodoney Lower Parish on the Eve of the Famine

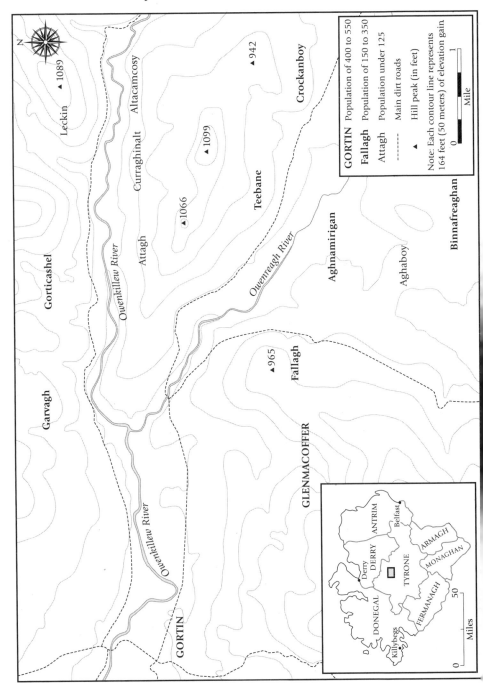

As had been the case with the Killybegs peddlers, an early emigrant from Bodoney seems to have blazed the trail into the New York charcoal business. Daniel Kane from the hamlet of Curraghinalt (pop. 96) arrived in New York in 1837. At least two siblings, brother Henry and sister Sarah, had ventured to America a couple of years before him. By the early 1840s, they were living in the easternmost part of the Lower East Side in Ward Thirteen, near the point of land jutting into the East River known as Corlears Hook. Daniel's other three sisters, Mary, Susan, and Catharine, and his mother, Rose, eventually made it to New York as well. Henry worked as a road paver. Sarah, and undoubtedly her sisters as well, took jobs as domestic servants. But somehow, by the early 1840s, Daniel had become a charcoal peddler.

Through most of that decade, Kane worked as a charcoal vendor and lived at 55 Cannon Street with his wife, Ann, and her son from a previous marriage. Joining him in the building (and perhaps initially sharing an apartment) was another Bodoney-born charcoal peddler, Patrick Moss. Moss had come to New York with his wife, Mary, and their children, Ellen and John, in 1839. From this nucleus, a community of several hundred Bodoney natives—with most of the men peddling charcoal—sprouted in the Corlears Hook neighborhood.

Corlears Hook was not as infamous as Five Points, but it was an equally inhospitable district. Whereas Five Points was renowned for its run-down, overcrowded tenements, Corlears Hook was unpleasant to live in primarily because its residences were scattered among many of the city's most noxious commercial enterprises. The waterfront neighborhood was home, for example, to a sugar refinery, a "fire brick manufactory," a distillery, and a tobacco warehouse. Even worse for the air quality of the district were the two oil refineries. Both processed sperm-whale oil for the making of candles, medicinal ointments, and cosmetic creams, while one also produced linseed oil from flaxseeds for the manufacturing of paints, varnishes, and lacquers. Then there were the neighborhood's many foundries, making copper, brass, and iron products of all shapes and sizes and spewing huge amounts of smoke from their coal-fired furnaces. Several small factories produced finished products using the output of these metalworks. One made Singer sewing machines, but the biggest was Allaire's Iron Works, at one point the nation's largest manufacturer of steam engines. The huge Allaire plant—with a footprint the size of a football field—covered most of the block bounded by Corlears, Cherry, Walnut, and Monroe Streets.

Corlears Hook in the 1850s

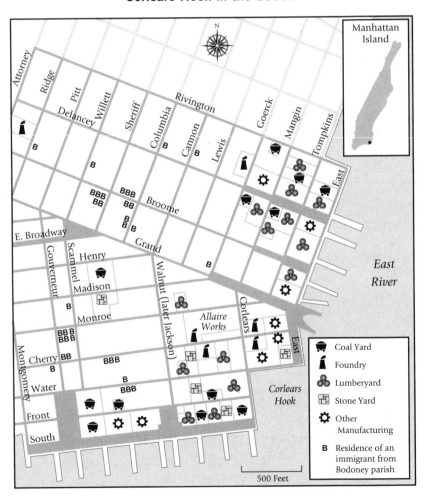

That was not all. The neighborhood also had a half dozen stone yards and several dozen lumberyards, each featuring steam-powered cutting, sawing, and planing equipment that sprayed smoke, stone dust, and sawdust throughout the area. One was a spar yard, transforming raw timber into finished ship masts for use in East River shipyards. To power all this commercial enterprise, Corlears Hook featured several dozen coal yards, some of which were wholesalers of charcoal as well. This last fact—plus the cheap rents charged by the landlords for space in the neighborhood's typical two-story wooden tenements suffused with filthy air—is probably what induced most of the Bodoney emigrants to settle in Corlears Hook.

While charcoal is light, it is also bulky, so charcoal peddlers could not carry their stock on their backs. Instead, charcoal dealers did business from covered horse-drawn carts. Some worked alone; others employed a driver so the peddler could focus on rounding up business and haggling with customers. By the 1850s, charcoal

Nicolino Calyo's depiction of an Irish American charcoal peddler in New York dates from the 1840s.

vendors and their wagons became so ubiquitous that a journalist writing a magazine piece about New York's street peddlers could devote just a single sentence to the "charcoal-vender" on the grounds that he was "a character too well known and too often seen to need description."

Daniel Kane, that pathbreaking Bodoney charcoal peddler, had already established a foothold in the business by the time the Famine struck—but once it did, the exodus from Bodoney accelerated dramatically. Kane's mother-in-law, niece, and nephew arrived in 1850 and moved in with the Kanes, who by that point had relocated across the neighborhood to Gouverneur Street. The Mosses moved to the same building. Other early Bodoney emigrants took in their kin once the Famine struck. Patrick Devlin from the hamlet of Fallagh emigrated in 1845 and within a decade six of his cousins, all Devlins and all from Fallagh, had made the journey as well—all but one became charcoal peddlers. The six Devlin charcoal dealers clearly wanted to live as close to one another in New York as they had in Ireland, given that Patrick and his cousins James, James, John, Michael, and Patrick ended up residing in the late 1850s at the southern end of Corlears Hook, at 658, 655, 640, 647, 651, and 652 Water Street, respectively.

Other Bodoney families followed suit. Charles and Francis McConnell from Glenmacoffer, also cousins, left Tyrone six months apart in 1848 but reunited in New York and took an apartment in Corlears Hook at 17 Sheriff Street, where they boarded with another cousin, charcoal dealer Alexander Fisher, born at the other end of the valley in Teebane. He had lived in New York since 1840. In 1850, Fisher's incredibly cramped apartment housed his wife, Ellen, his five-year-old daughter, Bridget, the two McConnells, four other Bodoney charcoal peddlers (some of whom were nephews and cousins of the Fishers), and three other boarders—twelve inhabitants in all. Five years later, the three Fishers were still renting space to eight boarders—an assortment of aunts, uncles, cousins, and former Bodoney neighbors. All but the Fishers had come to New York after the start of the Famine. The inconvenience of cramming so many people into such close quarters eventually paid off for the Fishers. By 1860 they had saved enough money to purchase 17 Sheriff Street (which they bought for about $2,500) and could now collect rent rather than pay it.

Because they networked so assiduously, the Bodoney charcoal peddlers fared far better than the average Irish peddler, and even better than the Killybegs street vendors. After ten years in America, the post-1845 migrants from Bodoney had a median savings of nearly $700 (equal to about $26,000 today), more than double the median for all other peddlers. That was quite a feat considering that they probably arrived in America with very little money at all and many (including Fisher) were illiterate. Even those from Bodoney who were not charcoal peddlers seemed to benefit from the group's tight-knit ways. The median savings of male non-peddlers from Bodoney was nearly double that of all male Irish immigrants.

In many cases, the Bodoney immigrants eventually used their peddling profits to bankroll other ventures. Peter Devlin moved to Staten Island, where he bought a house and eventually became a saloonkeeper. One of the James Devlins from Fallagh, after years of hard work peddling, opened his own coal yard in the 1880s at the eastern end of the Corlears Hook neighborhood, bought a small tenement (in which he lived) on Monroe Street near the corner of Corlears Street, and by the mid-1890s had purchased a larger brick tenement at 410 Cherry Street, which he immediately tore down so he could erect an even bigger, more profitable one. The other James Devlin and his brother Michael eventually moved to Jersey City, where James opened a "charcoal factory" to supply other peddlers. (In 1895, James's wife, Ann Clarke Devlin, "became suddenly insane," a Jersey City newspaper reported, "from excessive religious devotion." A judge committed her to a state asylum, but she was back home by the time James died in 1899.) In his will, James left his widow and children an estate worth, in today's dollars, about $400,000; Michael's estate when he died in 1890 was worth at least two-thirds of that amount. Charles McConnell took the $2,700 he had saved as a charcoal peddler and relocated to Brooklyn, where he tried his hand as a merchant and speculated in real estate in what is now the Clinton Hill neighborhood, increasing his net worth to about $22,000 (equal to about $500,000 today) by the time he died in 1871 at age forty-four. Fisher and McGill (the two peddlers turned tenement owners mentioned at the beginning of the chapter) were the executors of his will.

Other Bodoney immigrants did not move up the socioeconomic ladder. John Conway remained a charcoal peddler in Corlears Hook for thirty years. The two Patrick Devlins from Fallagh stuck to peddling as well. So did Charles Clarke, who emigrated from Fallagh in 1851, and Edward Fox, who arrived in New York from Bodoney in 1847 (accompanied by yet another Devlin). But they still saved surprisingly large sums. Conway's bank balance peaked at $539. His wife, Bridget, brought in some of that income early in their marriage by taking in paid boarders (including several Devlins) until, after giving birth to six children, that was no longer feasible. Of the remaining Devlins, one Patrick Devlin saved about the same amount as Conway, while the other accumulated nearly $1,500 in just his first five years in New York. After a decade in Manhattan, Fox reached and maintained exactly $1,000 in savings, while Clarke reached precisely $1,500 in the same time frame.

Yet, as John Griffin's story demonstrated, no amount of savings could guarantee an easy or long life in this era. A pair of Edward and Rose Fox's children, aged one and two, died on the same January day in 1858. And in 1869, the five surviving Fox children became orphans. Rose passed away in the early 1860s, while Edward perished "after a short but severe illness, of inflammation of the bowels," in November 1869. The orphans, aged seven to sixteen, moved in with their aunt, Alice Fox Clark, her husband,

Michael Clark, Alice and Michael's five children, and their servant. The uncle, Michael, had come to America from Tyrone in 1840 and worked for twenty years as a shoemaker before becoming a successful Corlears Hook saloonkeeper on East Broadway. By the time the Fox kids moved in, Clark had bought the tenement that his family lived in as well as several more. The presence of so many Bodoney natives in Corlears Hook meant that when tragedy struck, as it so often did in this era, there were plenty of kinsmen nearby who could lend a hand.

In the late twentieth century, a large multinational mining company discovered gold — three billion dollars worth — far below ground in the same little valley where these Bodoney charcoal peddlers were born and raised. It was, the company boasted, "one of the best gold projects on the planet." As of 2023, the project was in limbo due to local opposition. Residents insist that the company's plan to extract and process fifteen hundred tons of rock per day can't be accomplished without polluting and ultimately destroying the valley's bucolic landscape, despite the company's promises to the contrary. Should mining eventually begin, many of the valley's residents may wish that their own Famine-era ancestors had joined the exodus from Bodoney to New York 175 years ago. Those immigrants didn't find streets paved with gold, but they did discover that by cornering the Manhattan market for another valuable commodity — black, sooty charcoal — they could build sizable bank balances, which could be withdrawn in the form of ten- and twenty-dollar gold pieces. The prosperity these Famine immigrants achieved as peddlers would have been unattainable had they remained subsistence potato farmers in the mountains of Tyrone.

CHAPTER FIVE

"I Was Never Out of Work for Twenty-Four Hours"

Artisans

M ICHAEL QUINN WAS born in 1817 in the small city of Waterford in southeast Ireland and began serving an apprenticeship as a printer there at age thirteen. After completing his training, Quinn moved to London and found work setting type for the city's best-known newspaper, the *Times*. He must have been a fast compositor, because he bragged decades later that the paper's production team entrusted him to set the type for the story of the century: Queen Victoria's wedding to Prince Albert in 1840. A few years after that, Quinn married Bridget Buckley, also a native of Waterford; her brother Daniel was a printer as well. Daniel immigrated to New York in 1850 and clearly sent positive reports about the city to Bridget and Michael because in 1851 they sailed to New York to join him. For some reason, all three of them returned to Europe soon afterward. At the end of the summer of 1855, however, the three-some went to Liverpool once again and boarded the S.S. *Yorkshire* for the voyage back to New York, this time for good.

Upon landing, Michael, his wife, and his brother-in-law moved in together in Ward Ten on the Lower East Side. Daniel and Michael readily found work as printers in New York's bustling publishing industry. Michael took a position as a compositor at the *New York Evening Post*, founded by Alexander Hamilton and today the United States' oldest continuously published newspaper. By August 1857, Buckley and the Quinns had both accumulated $100 in savings, which they deposited at the Emigrant Savings Bank in accounts they opened a few days apart.

Bridget's brother managed to add only another $100 to his account—perhaps because he became too ill to work. He died of "consumption" (today known as tuberculosis, a bacterial lung infection) at age twenty-eight in February 1859. The Quinns probably had their own medical issues, reflected in the fact that they never had any children, something quite rare for Irish immigrants in that era.

But the Quinns did succeed at saving money. Michael and Bridget were regimented, methodical savers, almost always visiting the bank on Mondays, which makes sense given that Michael would have been paid on Saturdays by the *Post*. The Quinns usually waited until they had four or five dollars to deposit before they made the trip to Chambers Street to visit the bank. Sometimes they could make only one deposit a month, but more often they made two, and occasionally they could afford a deposit every Monday in a month. Over the course of four years, they made fifty deposits and only a single withdrawal, so that by July 1861 they had increased their balance to $514, an emergency fund equal to about eighteen months of a printer's wages.

Still, the Quinns must have chafed at how hard it was to put away money on a printer's wage. As skilled workers, printers occupied a higher rung on the socioeconomic ladder than peddlers or day laborers. Yet printers earned far less than the royalty of the artisanal ranks—the high-demand, short-supply tradesmen like jewelers, gunsmiths, boilermakers, shipwrights, and leather dressers.

Detail from the deposit ledger for the Emigrant Savings Bank account of Bridget and Michael Quinn. The letter "B" to the right of a date indicates a deposit, "T" denotes a withdrawal, and "I" is an interest payment.

New York printers also made less than artisans in the building trades such as masons, carpenters, bricklayers, and plasterers, and less also than machinists, blacksmiths, carriage makers, and cabinetmakers. Printers badly trailed even the lowliest of skilled workers—the shoemakers and tailors—whose crafts were being "bastardized" by mechanization, allowing the goods artisans made painstakingly by hand to be produced cheaply and shoddily by semiskilled or unskilled workers (many of them women) aided by machines. And while New York might be the publishing capital of the Americas, it was full of immigrant printers, sharply reducing the wages they could command.

All this may explain why, in September 1861, the Quinns moved to Erie, Pennsylvania, where rents were far lower than in New York and a dearth of printers meant that men like Quinn could command a good wage. Michael became a compositor for the *Erie Dispatch*, and soon the couple purchased a modest home at 153 East Fourth Street, which they appraised at $1,000 in 1870. Around 1880, after working nearly twenty years at the *Dispatch*, Quinn took a job with its rival, the *Erie Herald*. By 1884, at age sixty-seven, "Father Quinn" (as he was known to his younger colleagues) was still setting type and doing so without eyeglasses.

Quinn was a well-known figure in Erie by 1884, but that summer he became the best-known printer in America. At midyear, newspapers around the country carried the story of a compositor in California who, if one included his apprenticeship, had been setting type for fifty years. The Erie correspondent of the *Cleveland Herald* countered with a profile of Quinn, boasting that the Irishman had been "at the case" (cases were the trays holding the typesetter's letters) for several more years than the Californian. Quinn told the reporter that in his heyday, he could set 10,000 "ems" of type per day but that now he could manage only 5,000. The newsman, who clearly had a mathematical bent, calculated that if Quinn had averaged 7,500 pieces of type per day, six days a week, for fifty-two years, then over that span he had set more than 119 million pieces of type, weighing nearly ninety-four tons. The columns of print that Quinn had set, "string" in printer's parlance, would have stretched, if laid end to end, 158 miles. Quinn attributed his longevity and fitness to being both a teetotaler and a devout Catholic who "observes all the fast days." Editors across the nation found Quinn's story irresistible. It was reprinted in newspapers from Ann Arbor to Atlanta and Kalamazoo to California, and still attracted attention a year after it was first published.

Quinn continued working as a typesetter after his brush with fame, retiring at about age seventy-five. In his last few years as a printer, the energetic Irishman held a second job as an "emigration agent," working to lure new immigrants to Erie. After Quinn became a widower in 1892, he moved to St. Mary's "Old People's Home," where he died a few days before Christmas in 1899 at age eighty-two.

––––––––––

When Michael Quinn arrived in New York in 1855, he became one of the city's approximately one hundred thousand artisans — workers whose jobs required manual labor and extensive training. A few of these occupations, such as house painting, might be learned in months, but most took years of apprenticeship to fully master. Nonetheless, upon arrival in New York, about a third of male Famine immigrants immediately took jobs in these trades.

There were three levels to the trades, and recognizing them is important for understanding the status and earning power of Irish immigrant artisans. On the bottom level of the craftsman's hierarchy stood the apprentices, boys in their teens training to learn a given occupation. A "master" tradesman who needed help in his shop would take in a promising teen and commit to teaching him all the skills and customs of his craft. The teen, in return, committed to working for the master for nothing but room and board for an agreed-upon period (typically five years), even though he would have fully learned the trade in about half that time. Those who completed their apprenticeships ascended to the middle level of the artisanal hierarchy and became "journeymen" who were paid daily wages. A journeyman with entrepreneurial acumen might open his own shop and become a "master," the summit of the artisanal hierarchy. Master tradesmen typically spent little time at a workbench and instead devoted their days to soliciting and serving customers (either wholesale or retail), hiring and supervising journeymen, tracking their business's finances, and training apprentices. As a result, those who ascended to the status of master tradesmen were no longer thought of as artisans, but as business owners, a couple of steps up the socioeconomic ladder.

The printing, carpentry, and painting businesses shown here in about 1865 at the foot of Hudson Street in Ward Three would have definitely employed journeymen (such as the man in the apron and traditional tradesman's cap standing on the balcony in the very center of the photo) and perhaps apprentices as well.

Most Irish immigrants served their apprenticeships before they came to America. James W. Pratt, for example, trained as a printer in Queen's County, Ireland. He worked in that vocation in New York, then in Philadelphia, and finally in Brooklyn until his death there in 1896. Edward Butler also learned his trade in Ireland. He apprenticed as a watchmaker in Clonmel (pop. 13,500 in 1841), the largest town in County Tipperary, before coming to New York in 1848 at age thirty-eight with his wife, Mary, and their eldest child (age eighteen) and youngest (age six). Two more children made it to New York in 1849, and the last arrived in 1850. Butler had probably been a master watchmaker in Clonmel, and by 1851 he had reached this same status in New York, operating his own watchmaking shop in Ward Four. He trained all three of his sons in his craft and soon made the eldest, John, a business partner. Edward eventually decided to leave the New York business to John and moved with Mary twenty miles north to the Westchester County village of Dobbs Ferry, where he ran another watchmaker's shop until he passed away in 1877.

Despite the obstacles to doing so, some Famine immigrants learned their trades in New York. In most cases, these American-trained artisans acquired their new skills on the job at their initial workplaces. Henry Martin, for example, arrived in New York in 1850 and took a job in a foundry as a laborer hauling the heavy raw materials used by the ironworkers. By 1860, however, he had moved up the shop hierarchy and become an iron smelter. A decade later, he had climbed higher still and become an iron molder, a more prestigious, higher-paying job. Likewise, James Dowling immigrated to New York in his early twenties in September 1848 without any occupational training and initially became a day laborer. It was probably while working at a construction site that a short-handed contractor offered Dowling the chance to wield a hammer and nails. By 1854, Dowling was calling himself a carpenter and he continued to do so until his death at age forty-two in 1868.

Some Irish immigrants acquired trade skills in America by other means. Timothy Carr, a native of County Kerry, came to New York in 1851, took work as a day laborer, and married Mary Shanahan a year later. In the late 1850s, he worked as a cartman. Carr also joined the Sixty-Ninth New York Militia Regiment, an all-Irish organization. Militia units were the equivalent of today's National Guard, training once a month to be ready to take up arms in case of invasion or insurrection, and many Irish immigrants joined militia units hoping that the training they received could

While this image of iron molders is from Australia, it is one of the few that survives showing foundry employees at work in the era of the Great Famine. It was common for tradesmen to march in parades in this period behind banners like this one that depicted their work.

one day be used to help liberate Ireland. When the Civil War began in 1861, the unit was activated and sent to Washington as part of the so-called Irish Brigade to help put down the Southern insurrection. Carr fought at the Battle of Bull Run, the very first of the Civil War, at which he was both wounded and captured. Carr was said to have been the very first soldier injured in the battle. He was eventually exchanged in a prisoner swap, returned to action, and remained with his unit through the Battle of Fredericksburg in December 1862, by which point he had been promoted to corporal.

Carr then moved back to New York and in 1864 was running a saloon in the Kerry enclave at the southern end of Washington

Street in Ward One. When that venture failed, around the time that the Confederacy surrendered, Carr was able to fall back on skills he had learned in the army. Now that the Sixty-Ninth had returned to New York, it needed an armorer, a weaponry expert whose responsibilities included organizing, maintaining, and making simple repairs to the unit's weapons, which in peacetime were stored in its headquarters above the Essex Market at the corner of Grand and Essex Streets on Manhattan's Lower East Side. Carr got the coveted job, which came with free lodging in the market complex for him and his family of seven. He held the armorer's post for most of the succeeding thirty-five years.

Carr's winning personality must have helped him keep the position for so long. Even a quarter century after the war, he could "foot it with the best" at regimental dances, especially after the band went home and the music was provided by the unit's veterans. One would pull out a fiddle, another would grab his Irish flute, while a third provided percussion on a set of bones. It was then that Carr "lost control" and wowed the younger members of the regiment by dancing jigs late into the night. Carr was equally adept at handling the New York press. Newsmen on deadline could rely on him to provide column upon column of colorful, quotable reminiscences about each Civil War battle in which the "Fighting Sixty-Ninth" had participated, even those at which Carr had not actually been present.

At one point around 1880, Carr must have had a falling-out with the regiment's commanders because he lost the armorer's position and had to take a job as a janitor at the market. But he regained the armorer's post a few years later and remained in it until his death at about age seventy-five in 1901. Carr did well enough in the position that he was able to leave three of his daughters each $1,000 (the equivalent of about $36,000 today) and divided another $700 and his gold watch and chain among another daughter and his two sons.

Timothy Carr, wearing his prized gold watch and chain, in an undated family photo.

For some immigrants who acquired their skills only in America, it is harder to determine how they obtained their training. Felix Toole from County Carlow worked two decades in New York as a laborer, cartman, and junk dealer before becoming a "house carpenter." John Riordan toiled as a day laborer and a porter for about ten years after his arrival in New York until he started working as an upholsterer. Daniel Cunningham from rural County Limerick was also a day laborer in his first decade in America before somehow becoming a butcher. Friends or kinsmen must have helped these Irishmen acquire their skills.

In some instances, communities of Famine immigrants made concerted efforts to train their compatriots in certain trades after they arrived in America. That is the only apparent explanation for how morocco dressing, the tanning of goat hides with sumac to produce faux leather used to make cheap furniture, purses, and bookbindings, came to be dominated in New York by immigrants from Donegal — and in particular from the parish of Stranorlar. Six of every ten morocco dressers with accounts at the Emigrant

Savings Bank were from Donegal, and half of these Donegal men hailed from Stranorlar, even though there was no tradition of goat-skin processing in that part of northwest Ireland. Morocco dressing was considered a semiskilled trade, one that could be learned more quickly than higher-prestige crafts like cabinet- or watchmaking. Pre-Famine immigrants who picked up morocco dressing in New York taught it to many of the subsequent arrivals and in that manner developed the specialty. In the 1850s, almost all of New York's Irish-born morocco dressers lived on the block in Ward Four bounded by Jacob, Frankfort, Cliff, and Ferry Streets—a locale known as "the Swamp" that was home to most of the city's leather wholesalers. As was the case for gasmen from Castlegregory and charcoal peddlers from Bodoney, there was a financial reward for living in a geographic enclave with an occupational niche. The median savings of morocco dressers from Donegal was $505, a full 83 percent higher than the savings of others doing the same work.

The image on the left depicts a morocco dresser preparing a goat hide, while that on the right shows the skins floating in the sumac solution that dyes them.

There were well over one hundred artisanal trades followed by New Yorkers, and the Irish could be found in every one of them, from auger maker and awning maker to wire drawer and wood turner. Yet about 40 percent of Famine Irish artisans were concentrated in just four of these trades: tailoring, shoemaking, carpentry, and masonry. That these were the most popular trades is understandable, given that all New Yorkers needed homes to live in, clothes on their backs, and shoes on their feet. They needed to eat as well, and the two most popular food trades, butchering and baking, were not much further down the list.

Tailors, who accounted for about one in every eight Famine Irish artisans in New York, were among the worst-paid skilled workers. Clothing once made entirely by one male tailor was by 1850 increasingly manufactured by women (each doing one part of the job) who received a fraction of the wage tailors had commanded. To retain business, male tailors had to accept lower and lower prices for their services as the decades passed. The advent of the sewing machine around the time of the Civil War further degraded tailors' incomes. Nonetheless, tailors stuck doggedly to their trade, hoping to one day become retailers like the Brooks brothers, who sold suits and coats from their huge emporium on the Lower East Side. While the Brooks siblings were native-born Americans, the second-biggest clothing retailer in New York in the 1850s was Daniel Devlin & Company, started by an immigrant from Donegal who had come to America in 1833. Already trained as a tailor by the time he arrived, over the following decades Devlin built a nationwide retail and wholesale clothing empire that by 1860 had made him the wealthiest Irish immigrant in New York—and one of the half dozen wealthiest Irishmen in America—with a net worth in that year of $600,000, equal to $22 million today.

It was probably harder for Famine refugees to make the leap from journeyman to merchant tailor than it had been for the earlier generation of Irish immigrants such as Devlin. About one in five Famine immigrants who were journeymen tailors when they opened an Emigrant Savings Bank account in the 1850s managed to eventually make that transition. The best-known was George P. Fox, who was born in Dungannon, County Tyrone, in about 1814. After marrying Mary Rowley, an Englishwoman, George and his new bride moved to England, where he began working as a tailor and she had five children in quick succession. It appears that George came to New York without his family around 1846 and worked as a journeyman tailor while living just north of the Corlears Hook neighborhood in Ward Eleven. After learning the lay of the New York retail landscape, he returned to Ireland, retrieved Mary and their children, and set sail with them from Derry to New York, arriving in January 1848. By the end of that year, he had set up his own clothing shop at 65 Chambers Street, facing the back of City Hall and just a few doors down from where the Emigrant Savings Bank would open two years later.

Fox was a master of self-promotion. In an era when most newspaper advertisements were tiny, Fox ran huge, splashy ads that dwarfed those of his competitors. At first, he placed them in New York's cheaper, less popular papers, aiming to entice customers of modest means by emphasizing his "exceedingly moderate charges" and "cheap stock." But Fox eventually realized that he could make more money if he could sell expensive clothing with a higher profit margin to a wealthier clientele, so he began running ads in newspapers that reached more prosperous Manhattanites, moved his shop to a choice corner storefront on Broadway, and began to promote his business as the "New York Bazaar Fashionable Tailoring Establishment."

Perhaps just as important for growing his business, Fox ventured to Washington and blanketed the capital's newspapers with ads inviting members of Congress, military officers, and representatives of foreign legations for fittings at a pop-up shop he opened temporarily in the Willard Hotel. Fox knew that one famous Washington client might bring him fifty additional customers, so in his first forays to the capital he sent gifts of fine cloth to eminent Washingtonians and then, according to a later press account, "offered to make it up into garments gratis." This strategy paid off. Secretary of State Daniel Webster ordered a "chaste, but richly made blue dress coat" that he chose to be adorned in after his death, both for lying in state in the Capitol Rotunda and for his burial, which took place in the fall of 1852. A few months later, Fox made the suit of clothes that President-Elect Franklin Pierce wore to his inauguration. Before long, the Irishman could claim former president Millard Fillmore, General Winfield Scott, Commodore Matthew Perry, and even Ireland's most famous priest, Father Theobald Mathew, among his clients.

Fox gushed about his famous customers in his newspaper ads, but he also reminded shoppers that his humble beginnings meant he understood the needs of up-and-coming New Yorkers. That was why he charged as little as two dollars for vests, four dollars for

PERFECT FITTING COAT, VEST, AND
PANTALOONS!!!
NEW YORK BAZAAR FASHIONABLE
TAILORING ESTABLISHMENT.
GEORGE P. FOX,
[Late of 65 Chambers street, opposite the Park,]
PROFESSED PANTALOON MAKER AND LEADER
OF FASHION,
333 Broadway, corner of Anthony street,
Opposite the Theatre and Hotel de Paris.
CLOTHING.
FALL AND WINTER IMPORTATIONS.
The advantages of this establishment are the following :—
1st. ☞ Buying cheap, the proprietor invariably pays cash for all his goods when purchased, at auction or on importation.
2d. ☞ No goods will be offered but the best and most fashionable articles, from the looms of England, Scotland, France and Germany.
3d. ☞ None but scientific cutters, and the best practical workmen shall be employed, capable of fitting all ranks and professions.
4th. ☞ The prices for ready made Clothing and those made to order are on the lowest possible scale, for cash only.
5th. ☞ No article is considered as delivered till the purchaser has expressed his entire satisfaction with it.
6th. ☞ References can be given here and in Europe to the Rev. Clergy as to capability of making correctly Soutanes, Cassocks, &c. &c.
7th. ☞ Every order receives the personal superintendence of Mr. GEORGE F. FOX,
Military Tailor, who has had a most extensive practical experience in the manufacture of Cloths—and, in addition, twenty-one years in both the wholesale and retail departments of this trade, and can guarantee perfect fitting fashionable garments.
Liet of Cash Prices.
PERFECT FITTING COATS.
Milled Cloth and Tweed Travelling Overcoat $8 00 to 17 00
Fine Pilot Cloth Frock Surtout and Sac Coat   10 00 to 19 00
Boys' and Youths' Overcoats, Cloth or Beaver   6 00 to 13 00
Devonshire Kersey Milled and Beaver Overcoats   15 00 to 28 00
Double and Treble Milled Cloth and Beaver Overcoats 20 00 to 35 00
Superfine Cloth Sack Coats and Frock, any shade or color. $6 00 to 14 00
French Cloth Dress Coat, Frock, Sack or Riding, do 9 00 to 16 00
Extra quality do, Biolli's, Simoni's, Nicoli's, &c. do 15 00 to 20 00
English or French (the best that can be produced) do 25 00 to 28 00
PERFECT FITTING VESTS.
Black and Colored French and English Cassimere Vests $2 00 to 4 75
Silk Figured, Wool Velvet, Cashmere, Dress, Fancy do 2 50 to 5 00
Rich Silk, Plain New Style and Figured French Satin do 3 00 to 5 50
Marseilles Figured and Plain Dress Evening   2 75 to 4 0
Silk Velvet, Satin and Embroidered Cassimere   do 5 00 to 7 00
PERFECT FITTING PANTALOONS.
Superfine Doeskin Cassimere Pants, (any shade or color) $4 00 to 7 50
Extra fine manufactured French Black Cassimere Pants 5 50 to 9 50
Bonjean's, Simon's, Nellison's Fancy Doeskin   do 4 75 to 8 00
French and English Fancy New Style Cassimere   do 5 09 to 10 00
☞ NOTE MY ADDRESS—
333 BROADWAY, Corner of Anthony street.
BEWARE OF MISTAKE—NO CONNECTION WITH ANY
STORE OF SIMILAR NAME IN THIS CITY.   au31

One of George P. Fox's early newspaper ads from 1850.

"perfect fitting pantaloons," and eight dollars for "milled cloth and tweed traveling overcoats." Through this strategy, Fox declared in 1855 that he had "progressively rise[n] from the humble rank of selling one vest pattern in Wall street a few years ago" to become "THE GEORGE P. FOX," "l'Inventeur des Modes" and the "United States Leader of Fashions."

Like many successful immigrants, Fox bought rent-generating real estate with his profits. By 1870, he and his sons Joseph, Robert, and Charles (who took over the business after Fox retired in the mid-1860s) claimed to have non-real-estate assets worth $13,000 (the equivalent of more than $300,000 today). Yet this last, self-reported figure needs to be taken with a healthy dose of skepticism. In 1852, an employee of the Mercantile Agency, the forerunner of R. G. Dun & Company (the firm that evaluated the creditworthiness of Civil War–era business operators), called Fox "a great brag" who was prone to exaggeration. He is "all bubbles" and "no soap... all sail, no ballast." Some considered his braggadocio an eccentricity, but others "think him a little deranged at times." Yet by the mid-1850s, the agency admitted that the "tricky" Irishman was "doing a considerable business." He "gets up a fashionable and tasty garment" that is "popular in...style."

While it's hard to determine the true size of Fox's profits, his influence in the men's fashion industry clearly stretched far and wide—a Cincinnati newspaper called him "the Beau Brummel of the nineteenth century." In his retirement, Fox kept busy and in 1871 published *Fashion: The Power That Influences the World* to spread his belief that "fashion is and has been and will be, through all ages, the outward form through which the mind speaks to the material universe." Yet the fashion world eventually moved on, and the press took little notice when Fox passed away, at age seventy-one, in 1885.

Few Irish-born tailors could match Fox's notoriety. Most remained journeymen their whole lives. A more typical Irish tailor was

Thomas Bannon. He and his brother John emigrated at about age twenty from Galway, where they had apparently learned the tailor's trade. Both were employed as journeymen in Ward Eight soon after their arrival in New York in the early 1850s. In 1855, Thomas married Bridget Devaney, a Ward Four shirtmaker who was also from Galway. She continued working as a "tailoress" until the couple had their first child in 1859. Yet like most journeyman tailors, Bannon had great difficulty saving money. The most the couple's Emigrant Savings Bank account ever held was $44, and in the summer of 1863, with their balance down to just $10.75, Bridget withdrew every last cent and closed the account.

That the Bannons were out of money in the middle of 1863 probably explains why, at the end of the summer, Thomas volunteered to serve in the Union army. (His brother John had moved to Massachusetts and enlisted in an infantry regiment there in 1862.) By 1863, the military was so desperate for volunteers to fill its depleted ranks that the bounties and bonuses being offered for enlistees had grown enormous — $500 or more — equal to nearly two years pay for a tailor like Bannon. The army sent Thomas to the front lines in Virginia as a member of the Army of the Potomac and his unit saw action in all the major battles — the Wilderness, Cold Harbor, Petersburg, and Appomattox — that occurred after General Ulysses S. Grant took command of those troops. Remarkably, Bannon escaped these bloody engagements physically unscathed and returned home to Bridget and their son, Peter. The couple had at least three more children after the war.

Life never got much easier for the Bannons. After Bridget died in 1886, Thomas had no surviving offspring either willing or able to care for him. Nor, apparently, would brother John, who was prospering in Massachusetts and had bought a small tenement (in which he also lived) in East Boston. As a result, Thomas, who was suffering from debilitating rheumatism and struggling to support himself on the Civil War pension of eight dollars per month, which he began receiving in 1890, decided a year later to check himself into the Togus National Home for Disabled Soldiers in chilly Chelsea, Maine. With Bannon's health declining still further a few years later, doctors transferred him from that sprawling facility to the affiliated one in Hampton, Virginia, where the warmer weather might ease his symptoms. By that point Thomas had only twenty-five cents to his name. He died at that old soldiers' home, of an inflammation of the lungs known as pleurisy, in 1897 at age sixty-four.

Other tailors struggled due to different kinds of problems. Michael Flanagan from County Clare landed with his wife, Mary Qualy Flanagan, in Quebec in 1849 at about age twenty-seven. They returned to Ireland not long after but then re-emigrated — this time to New York and for good — in the mid-1850s. By the eve of the Civil War, they had saved $373 in their Emigrant Savings Bank account, an above-average emergency fund for a journeyman tailor who worked all day, and often long into the night, sewing coats, vests, and pantaloons for the likes of Brooks Brothers, Devlin & Company, and George P. Fox. But not long after their ninth child was born in 1869, Michael's alcohol abuse became a serious problem, so much so that Mary took the embarrassing step of going to the bank and instructing its employees that Michael should "get no money" because of his "drinking." That Mary in 1865 had opened a second family bank account — in her name only — suggests that Michael's alcoholism predated the bender that led her to confide Michael's problem to the bank's employees. Michael's drinking must not have kept him out of work for long periods of time, or perhaps the Flanagans increasingly relied on the wages earned by their children (five of whom, by 1880, were working outside the home while continuing to live with their parents). However they managed it, the Flanagans kept moving to incrementally nicer neighborhoods — from Five Points to Ward Fourteen to Ward Seventeen to Ward Eighteen — until Michael passed away at age sixty-four in 1887, one year after Mary's death.

Tailors saved, on average, less than any other Irish-born New York tradesmen in their bank accounts, though their median savings was slightly higher than printers'. In fact, the median Irish-born tailor saved 40 percent less than even the median day laborer. In part, that is because while day laborers often transitioned to better-paying jobs, tailors almost always stuck stubbornly to their trade. Of the sixty-one tailors who opened accounts at the Emigrant Bank in the 1850s and could be tracked for ten or more years thereafter, only two did not end their careers in the garment trade. The rest continued to ply needle and thread even though life for the typical Irish journeyman tailor in New York was one of struggle and hardship.

Irish shoemakers who emigrated during the Famine fared significantly better in New York than tailors. The median shoemaker saved 60 percent more in his Emigrant Savings Bank account than the median tailor, primarily because lowly paid women were not competing with men for shoemaking jobs as they were for needlework. But shoemakers also saved more than tailors because they were 50 percent more likely to become wholesalers or retailers as "master" shoemakers. Twenty-nine percent of journeymen shoemakers who opened accounts at the Emigrant Bank ended their careers as shoe retailers, while only 17 percent of tailors finished their lives as clothing merchants. Even considering only those who never rose above the rank of journeyman, shoemakers saved a third more than tailors.

Like tailors, shoemakers were devoted to their trade. Patrick Costello from the city of Galway immigrated to New York in 1846 and continued as a journeyman cobbler on lower Seventh Avenue for thirty-five years. Andrew Delany learned shoemaking in the town of Mountmellick in Queen's County and departed for America at age twenty-nine in 1848. He worked as a journeyman cobbler until he retired in the early 1880s. Jeremiah Crowley from County Cork, who left Ireland at age twenty-two in 1852, spent nearly a half century as a journeyman shoemaker—the first fifteen in New York and the remaining thirty-five in Cambridge, Massachusetts, where even on a journeyman's wages he could afford to purchase a modest home.

A journeyman shoemaker could not afford real estate in Manhattan, but putting aside a significant nest egg was not unrealistic. John Burke from rural County Limerick, for example, arrived in New York via Quebec at about age forty-two in 1847 with his wife, Johanna, and several children and settled near the East River. He remained a journeyman shoemaker, yet by 1861 he and Johanna had managed to save $500. Patrick Costello accumulated $429 by 1855 and Andrew Delany had socked away $444 by 1865. The savings account of John Cleary from Cashel in Tipperary, who worked for thirty years as a journeyman shoemaker on the East Side of Manhattan, was more typical. His bank balance peaked at $299 in 1869, equal to about $6,700 today.

There were advantages to remaining a journeyman. It might take years to accumulate enough savings to start a business, savings that could be lost in a matter of months if fire destroyed one's uninsured inventory or if one of the nineteenth century's periodic financial panics struck, causing consumer demand to suddenly collapse and suppliers to require immediate repayment of outstanding debts. Many workers were content to labor for decades as journeymen and leave the risks and stress of business ownership to others.

Many artisans, however, yearned to be their own bosses and were willing to gamble their accumulated capital for the potential rewards of entrepreneurial success. A second cobbler named John Burke, this one from County Westmeath, arrived in New York at about age twenty-eight in 1847 just weeks before his namesake from Limerick. A few years after his arrival, he married Hester McCarthy from Dublin and a few years after that, the ambitious young man began operating a shoe store. Burke's first shop was located on Sixth Avenue near Washington Square in Ward Fifteen, but he soon tried pricier locations on Broadway, initially in Ward Eight and then in Ward Fourteen. Those apparently did not suit him either, and Burke finally decided to focus his business in the Wall Street area, where he sold shoes from the mid-1870s (by which point he and Hester had nine children) until his death in 1892.

It's impossible to say with certainty how many journeymen shoemakers tried but failed to become shoe retailers, because in many cases no documentary trail of those efforts remains 175 years after the fact. But some of these unsuccessful efforts can be uncovered. James Cassidy from County Donegal, for example, arrived in New York in 1846 already trained as a shoemaker, settled on Hudson Street in Ward Eight, and began plying his trade. He worked as a journeyman there for nearly two decades before opening his own boot and shoe shop at 407 Hudson Street. After four years of struggle running his own business, however, Cassidy closed it and in 1868 became a journeyman once again. He died two years later, at age fifty-two.

While journeyman tailors who sought to escape their station almost always opened tailoring or clothing shops (making them "master" artisans), shoemakers often chanced entrepreneurial efforts outside of their craft. One who succeeded handsomely was John Kernan, who was trained as a shoemaker in Granard, the largest town in County Longford, before he emigrated in 1846 at about age twenty-one. He initially made shoes in New York, but eventually opened a saloon in the Flatlands neighborhood of Brooklyn and remained in the liquor business there until he retired at about age sixty-five in 1890. Kernan died in 1896, leaving his wife and daughters an estate of $25,000, equal to more than $900,000 today.

Yet many who tried to leave shoemaking failed at their new endeavors. Arthur Thompson lasted only a year as a grocer before returning to his cobbler's bench to support his wife and ten kids.

Richard Daly attempted to make the transition from shoemaker to farmer, but struggled at that, had to become a day laborer, and was back to shoemaking by 1880. John Wharton from County Carlow worked for more than a decade in New York as a shoemaker before snaring a coveted position on the city police force. Yet he lost his plum post after six or seven years and had to return to shoemaking. After his four kids grew up and left home and his wife, Ann, passed away in 1890, John (now in his late fifties and living in Brooklyn) found it increasingly difficult to find and keep a job. He was in and out of the Kings County Almshouse several times in the first decade of the twentieth century before he passed away, at age seventy-four, in 1908.

―――――

Despite the difficulties of men like Wharton, there were clearly opportunities for journeymen tailors and shoemakers to move up America's socioeconomic ladder, and that was true for other trades-men as well. Of Famine immigrants whose first-known employment in America was as journeymen and who can be traced ten or more years, 27 percent ended their careers in a higher-status vocation. That figure increases to 35 percent for those whose occupations can be traced for twenty or more years.

Some journeymen moved just one rung up the ladder to lower-status white-collar positions — clerkships, sales, supervisory, or civil service positions. Robert George Wilson from Kerry, for example, spent decades making gold pens but eventually became a real estate agent. Shoemaker Bernard Morrissey found a job as a clerk, as did stonemason Michael Daly. Cobbler John McMahon became a teacher. Cloth finisher Robert Benson was hired as a church sexton. But most of the tradesmen who ascended to this occupational category took civil service jobs. Gunmaker Richard Ormsby became a custom house inspector, while marble cutter John McEvoy from Kildare and engineer Thomas Pearson from

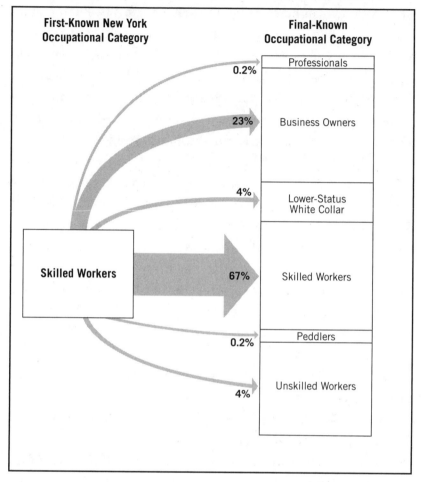

Occupational Mobility of Male Famine Immigrant Tradesmen*

Kilkenny were just two of the many Irish immigrants who became policemen.

For every journeyman tradesman who transitioned to these jobs, however, there were six who moved still higher, to the business owners' ranks. About half of these men moved into a business related to their trade. Shoemakers and tailors opened shoe and clothing shops. Carpenters and masons became contractors and

---

* Percentages do not add up to 100 due to rounding.

177

builders. Blacksmiths opened their own horseshoeing businesses, while journeyman butchers became meat purveyors. But the other half started businesses wholly unrelated to their craft training. Most became saloonkeepers and grocers, but the variety of possibilities was almost endless. Baker William Sheehan opened a variety store. Shoemaker James Regan started a candle shop, while cobbler Joseph Ismay became a stationer. Bookbinder Patrick Shanahan started a successful business selling "undertakers' trimmings."

Of course, some skilled workers climbed the socioeconomic ladder into the ranks of New York's business community, only to fall back down again and end their careers back where they had started. Paul J. Hurley from Dublin worked as a silversmith in New York for more than a decade, then ran a "bar room" on the Lower East Side for another decade before returning to making silver forks and spoons until his death in 1893. Wheelwright William Barry from Tipperary did not succeed as a grocer and became a journeyman once again, as did mason Thomas Kelly from Cavan after he failed as a builder. Because the typical New York journeyman earned much less than the average Manhattan shopkeeper, the artisans who failed at business would have felt chagrined, and in some cases ashamed, of their inability to succeed in business.

Even tradesmen who remained journeymen their whole lives could suffer significant setbacks, indicating that their lives were far from stable. Some, for example, managed to join the ranks of homeowners, only to have that status slip away later. Mason John Carey from Fermanagh, who arrived in New York in 1852 and settled in Ward Seventeen, managed by 1860 to buy a modest home (worth $600) in Greenpoint in northern Brooklyn. A decade later, however, John and his wife, Mary, had somehow lost their home. They were still living in Greenpoint, but they and their seven children (ranging in age from two to seventeen) were now renting an apartment from another Irish-born stonemason, Patrick Leonard.

In 1875 they had moved around the corner and were leasing from yet another Irish-born artisan, machinist Anthony Kelly.

While home ownership for tradesmen was rare in New York City, it was fairly common in cheaper nearby locales such as Brooklyn and Jersey City. Moving away from New York City not only increased the Famine immigrants' likelihood of owning their own home but also improved their chances of enjoying upward occupational mobility. About a third of journeymen with accounts at the Emigrant Savings Bank who left New York City ended their careers on a higher rung of the socioeconomic ladder, versus only about a quarter of those who remained in Manhattan.

For some artisans, this improvement in occupational standing meant a position as a foreman overseeing the work of other tradesmen. Machinist Francis C. Graves, for example, left Brooklyn at the end of the Civil War to take a job at an envelope factory in Hartford. He worked as a machinist there for more than twenty years but proved his worth to his employer by inventing several ways to modify the factory's equipment to make the business more profitable—Graves and the company patented these innovations beginning in 1883. The Meath native and active Methodist was rewarded for his ingenuity with a promotion to foreman in 1888 and to superintendent (in effect, the supervisor of the foremen) about fifteen years later.

John Sinnamon from County Armagh was another machinist who left New York City. Initially he tried to set up his own machine shop in Oswego, New York, where his brother William (also a machinist) was already living. But when that did not pan out, John took work maintaining equipment at the Ames Iron Works there, a huge factory that was famous for its engine on wheels which farmers' horses pulled through fields to power mechanical threshers. Like Graves, Sinnamon secured several patents for improvements he made to his employer's products and was also eventually promoted to foreman and superintendent. He held that last post in several manufacturing facilities—including one in Oregon for about a year—before setting up a successful machinery business of his own back in upstate New York in the late 1880s. Soon thereafter he retired and was on a grand tour of England, Ireland, Scotland, and Germany with his twenty-eight-year-old daughter, Caroline, a teacher, in 1894 when he died of a heart attack at age sixty-seven "in a disreputable house" in the "slums of Glasgow."

The "Improved Threshing Engine" was the bestselling product of the Ames Iron Works, where John Sinnamon worked for about a quarter century, progressing from machinist to foreman to superintendent. The engine powered mechanical threshing machines that farmers used to harvest crops throughout the late nineteenth century. Horses pulled both the engines and the threshers through the fields.

Journeymen aspiring to become retailers were also more likely to succeed if they left New York. Francis Brady spent nearly a decade in New York and Brooklyn as a journeyman tailor before heading west and becoming "a pioneer merchant tailor" of Fremont, Ohio. Shoemaker Richard Sharkey may have gotten a sense of the possibilities that lay outside New York when he volunteered for the army during the Civil War. When peace returned, he and his wife, Mary Ann, moved to gold country deep in the California mountains between Sacramento and Reno, where they supplied miners with boots and shoes and raised ten children.

William Stapleton from County Tipperary was another journeyman shoemaker who became his own boss once he left New York. In 1850, three years after emigrating, the twenty-nine-year-old Stapleton was one of seven journeyman shoemakers employed by a German-born shoe manufacturer in Ward Five. That was about the time he married Ann Comey. Five years later, they had three kids and only $103 in savings, so that spring William and Ann packed up their kids and their meager belongings and moved eight hundred miles due west to Joliet, Illinois. William may have initially worked in Joliet as a journeyman, but by 1861 he owned a modest home there at the north end of town and was running a small shoe business from it. Initially, Stapleton ran the shop entirely on his own, waiting on customers, doing all the repairs, and making new shoes and boots to order. By 1862, the credit agency Dun & Company reported that Stapleton was "doing a good bus[iness]" (enough that he had to hire "one or two hands" to keep up) and praised him as "honest and hardworking." Stapleton also benefited from Joliet's affordable real estate market. The house he bought there for about $500 in the late 1850s was worth five times that by 1866, the Dun agent noted. A small town like Joliet also offered opportunities for political advancement that would have been unavailable to a shoemaker in New York. Stapleton was able to supplement his shoemaking income with a stint as the Joliet "city collector," and was able to quit shoemaking altogether after thirty-five years at his cobbler's bench when Democrats in 1885 chose him, "one of the best men in the city," to be a justice of the peace. He served for four years and passed away a few years later, at age seventy-one, in 1892.

In rare cases, immigrant tradesmen could move to the very pinnacle of the Irish occupational hierarchy and become doctors or lawyers. Patrick Keady, for example, arrived in New York at age nineteen in 1851 from County Roscommon with his widowed mother and for the next decade worked as a house painter. Keady taught himself proper penmanship and grammar after arriving in America and around 1862 he managed to parlay those skills into a job as a stenographer for the *New York Evening News*. Soon after that, the editors promoted him to a position as a reporter. Keady was also active in the city's workingman's rights movement, giving speeches at several outdoor rallies. This notoriety helped Keady, who like most of his fellow Irish immigrants had joined the Democratic Party, win election in 1866 representing Brooklyn in the New York State Assembly, where he won praise for his advocacy of tenement reform and an eight-hour workday. Like Abraham Lincoln, Keady manifested an interest in becoming an attorney only after his experience serving as a legislator. To achieve that goal, he read law while clerking at a Brooklyn attorney's office and was admitted to the bar in about 1870. Keady married soon thereafter and practiced law in Brooklyn for the next few decades. In 1898, New York's mayor appointed Keady to a judgeship, which the onetime house painter held until his death in 1908.

Most journeymen, of course, failed to move to a higher-status occupational category, and this was the case even if they left New York City. Michael Smee continued to work as a cooper after he relocated to the Hudson River Valley and remained in that trade until his death in 1884. Richard Casey remained a journeyman carpenter after moving to San Francisco until he died in 1888. Robert

Edgeworth relocated to Jersey City but continued to toil as a journeyman plasterer there until 1896.

Some who left New York decided that they had made a mistake and returned to Manhattan, sometimes even giving up the autonomy they had gained by moving. William M. Dowling and his wife, Alicia, for example, emigrated in 1849 from Queen's County, Ireland, to New York. There he took work as a cloth cutter, preparing the fabric that would be sewn together by less skilled needleworkers. With only twenty-seven dollars in savings in 1863, the Dowlings closed their Emigrant Bank account and moved to Lansing, Michigan. William initially worked as a journeyman tailor there in a German immigrant's shop, but a few years later he became a merchant tailor and bought a modest home.

Yet something about New York pulled the Dowlings back. Perhaps they had family there. Perhaps they missed the more vibrant Irish social scene. Or perhaps William hated the stress of keeping a small business afloat. Whatever the cause, in 1882 the Dowlings sold their shop and moved back to New York, where William resumed work as a journeyman cloth cutter in the city's ever-expanding garment industry. Three years later, however, still not satisfied, the Dowlings moved to New Jersey. William became a cutter for one of the largest clothing manufacturers in Newark while buying a home in the leafy suburb of Clifton. When the devout Catholic passed away at age sixty-five in 1895, a local newspaper wrote that "a man of more honesty, piety and faith in God would be hard to find."

———

A surprising number of immigrants returned to New York after relocating elsewhere. Most had gone only as far as Long Island or New Jersey, but others came back from as far away as New Orleans or California. One of these wandering souls was Jonathan Dillon. He was born in August 1822 in the town of Waterford and was trained in watchmaking there by his kinsmen, who ran a jewelry shop that had been in the family since 1750. Jonathan was apparently not in line to take over the family business, which in any event was saddled with debt, so in 1845 he left for America with his elder brother Edward (also a watchmaker) and two other relatives.

Both Dillons took jobs as journeymen watchmakers in New York. They may have initially been employed by their elder half brother Joseph Dillon, who had come to Manhattan in 1836 and by 1845 was operating a watch shop in Ward Two. By 1850, however, Jonathan apparently worked at the Five Points jewelry shop of William Tarbell at 28 Bowery. As was often the case for journeymen in those days, Jonathan rented accommodations from his employer. Luckily for Dillon, Tarbell let the Irishman pack his quarters to the brim. In August 1850, Dillon's apartment contained him, his wife, Isabella Martin Dillon (who had emigrated from Ireland in 1846 and married Jonathan in 1848), their eleven-month-old baby, Frances, three other Dillon kinsmen, and two women in their twenties who were probably related to the Dillons or acquaintances from Waterford. Isabella had been a well-regarded opera singer before she got married, but she stopped performing professionally after she gave birth to Frances who, like her seven younger siblings, was baptized in the Episcopal Church.

Epitomizing the term "journeyman," Dillon never stayed in one job or residence for very long. In 1852 he opened his own watch shop on Carmine Street in Ward Nine, but by 1853 he was out of business and working for wages once again. Luckily, the demand for watchmakers—unlike tailors and day laborers—was constant in a wealthy city like New York. "I was never out of work for twenty-four hours at a time until I retired," boasted Dillon years later. He spent most of the next thirty years working as a journeyman and moved to stay close to (or possibly live with) whichever jeweler employed him. In 1855, Jonathan and Isabella were residing on the far Upper East Side with their children and two boarders. A year later, they moved to Corlears Hook. Twelve months after that, they lived near Union Square.

When the Panic of 1857 brought business to a virtual halt in New York, Dillon relocated his family to Washington, D.C., where money still flowed from government coffers into the hands of federal officeholders. Dillon immediately found work at a pricey Pennsylvania Avenue jewelry store that counted among its clients many of the nation's most prominent statesmen. He was still employed there in the spring of 1861 as the secession crisis built toward a climax. Shop talk concerning sectional hostilities must have become especially tense for the Irishman because Dillon's employer, Mathew W. Galt, was a Virginian and, as Dillon recalled, "I was the only Union sympathizer working in the shop." Perhaps that was why, when the pocket watch of the newly inaugurated president, Abraham Lincoln, was brought in for repairs, Dillon was given the job.

Days later, on April 13, Dillon was reassembling the president's timepiece, which he described as "a gold, hunting case, English lever watch," when Galt came rushing upstairs to the workshop from the retail space below, "very much excited, and gasped: 'Dillon, war has begun, the first shot has been fired.'" Word had just reached Washington of South Carolinians' bombardment of Fort Sumter and the federal army's valiant effort to defend it.

Dillon immediately decided that this historic moment and his support for Lincoln and the Union — in a shop full of Southern nationalists — had to somehow be recorded for posterity. Once Galt departed, Dillon removed the watch dial and with a sharp instrument wrote in tiny cursive letters on the brass innards of the watch the date, the news from Fort Sumter, and the words "thank God we have a government," a phrase commonly used in those days to express support for Lincoln in contrast to the administration of his predecessor, Democrat James Buchanan, who Republicans felt had done nothing to prevent secession. Dillon then etched his signature onto the brass, reassembled the watch, and brought it downstairs to be returned to Lincoln, who never saw the Irishman's words of support.

A couple of years later, the Dillons moved back to New York, where Jonathan worked as a watchmaker for the next quarter century, and in those decades Americans tried to put the trauma of the Civil War behind them. A taciturn workman might have told the story of his brush with the Great Emancipator to no more than a few shop mates and family members. But Dillon was a garrulous fellow who relished an audience, perhaps even more so after he reluctantly left shop life behind in his late sixties and retired. Thus, in April 1906, when at age eighty-four Dillon received a jury duty summons, he did not claim the automatic exemption granted to anyone over age seventy. Instead, he took the long walk from his apartment in central Harlem to the subway and rode it all the way to lower Manhattan to the New York County courthouse (now known as the Tweed Courthouse), which sat on Chambers Street directly across from the Emigrant Savings Bank. There on his old stomping ground near Five Points and his Bowery jewelry shop, Dillon happily regaled both jurors and courthouse reporters with his tales. The account of Dillon's secret message to Lincoln seemed so extraordinary that even the *New York Times* found it fit to print. Over the weeks that followed, dozens of newspapers across the country reprinted the *Times* story, making Jonathan Dillon the most famous watchmaker in America, as well-known as printer Michael Quinn had become twenty-two years earlier.

Among the hundreds of thousands who read Dillon's reminiscence was Chicagoan Robert Todd Lincoln, the president's only living child. Dillon's story piqued the curiosity of Lincoln, who still owned the watch in question. He brought it to a Chicago jeweler, who opened it up and confirmed Dillon's account. Yet while the *Times* coverage of Dillon's story made headlines from coast to coast, no wire service took note of the Chicago denouement. As a result,

Jonathan and Isabella Dillon in undated photographs.

few besides the president's son and his jeweler knew that Dillon's story had been verified.

Jonathan Dillon had passed the tale of the secret message to his eight children and their children, who conveyed it to subsequent generations of family members. One of those descendants — Douglas Stiles, an Illinois attorney, appropriately enough — yearned to know whether the story was more than an ancestor's boast, especially after he found the century-old *Times* account online. On the two hundredth anniversary of Lincoln's birth, February 12, 2009, Stiles called the Smithsonian Institution's National Museum of American History, which had acquired the watch in the 1950s, and asked if the curators would consider opening it to see whether the tale was true. A curator finishing work on an exhibition about Lincoln could not resist the free publicity that examining the timepiece would bring. A month later, in a room packed with reporters, television crews, a makeshift workbench, and a jeweler who specialized in antique watches, it was opened for the second time since

Abraham Lincoln's death, now for the whole world to see. The event received international coverage and Jonathan Dillon became famous yet again, this time to a worldwide audience.

There was one final twist revealed at the Smithsonian that had been known to — but was concealed by — Lincoln's son. At the end of the summer of 1864, when the Union cause was looking especially bleak, the president again brought his timepiece to Galt for repair. Dillon had already moved back to New York, so the watch was entrusted to another journeyman watchmaker, Louis E. Gross. Unlike Dillon, Gross sympathized with the Confederate cause. When he opened Lincoln's watch and saw what Dillon had written, Gross spitefully etched into the brass, in larger letters than Dillon's, the name of the Confederate president, "Jeff Davis." Lincoln would have found it amusing that even the innards of his pocket watch became contested ground as Americans fought their civil war.

Irish watchmaker Jonathan Dillon scrawled pro-Union messages on the inside of Abraham Lincoln's timepiece in 1861, while another jeweler spitefully scratched the name of the Confederate president into the brass three years later.

After the Dillons returned to New York, they continued to move frequently—to Brooklyn, then back to Ward Nine in Manhattan just after the war concluded, then to Ward Fifteen, then back to Brooklyn, then to Harlem, then Ward Eighteen, then the Upper East Side, and then to what is now known as Midtown. Like many journeymen, Jonathan spent several years late in his career as a "master" watchmaker running his own retail shops—in two different locations near Wall Street in the early 1870s and then in the mid-1880s back at 28 Bowery, where he took over the storefront in which he had done watch repairs as a young journeyman thirty-five years earlier. That was apparently Jonathan's last job before, after more than four decades as a watchmaker, he retired in 1888 and moved north with his wife to one of the new suburban villages of Westchester County. Yet after Isabella died from throat cancer in 1896, Jonathan apparently found the suburbs too quiet and moved back to Manhattan, where a jury summons that he could not resist briefly made Dillon, in two different centuries, the most famous watchmaker in America.

Given the fame they achieved, watchmaker Jonathan Dillon and printer Michael Quinn might seem atypical. But their experiences reflected those of most Irish-born New York tradesmen in the Famine era. Like the majority of their skilled compatriots, Dillon and Quinn learned their trades before coming to America. Dillon, like most foreign-born artisans, never owned his own home, but might have been able to afford one had he been willing to leave New York permanently as Quinn had. Like Quinn, most journeymen never managed to run their own businesses, but about a quarter of them ended their careers, like Dillon, higher up the socioeconomic ladder (mostly, like the watchmaker, as retailers of the goods they had once made for other shopkeepers). Like virtually all artisans, Dillon and Quinn remained devoted to their crafts even though many Famine immigrants with no occupational training were earning more than them as saloonkeepers, grocers, peddlers, and even cartmen. Finally, like most tradesmen other than perhaps journeymen tailors, Dillon and Quinn were not trapped in financial precarity. Artisans' lives were often difficult, but they could (and frequently did) move from job to job, neighborhood to neighborhood, and even city to city to take advantage of better wages, lower housing costs, and greater opportunities. While a few, like John Wharton, might end their lives in an almshouse, most were moderately successful. And no matter how they had fared financially, each one took great pride in his craft and the social status it conferred within the Irish American community.

CHAPTER SIX

"Never Was There a Brighter Brain"

Clerks, Agents, and Civil Servants

STANDING JUST FIVE feet five inches tall with blue eyes and light-brown hair, James Cavanagh from Carrick-on-Suir in County Tipperary came to New York in 1851 at age twenty-five. Trained in his hometown of eight thousand residents as a carpenter, Cavanagh readily found work as a journeyman in that trade when he settled in Manhattan. But like so many of the Famine immigrants, James and his wife, Alice Lonergan Ryan Cavanagh, were determined to improve their status in America. Alice had come to America before the Famine, gotten married, and had several children with her husband Daniel Ryan, who kept a grocery/liquor shop in a small wooden tenement on Cedar Street in Ward One. When Daniel died, Alice took over the shop and continued to run it after she married Cavanagh, even though she still had two sons to care for from her first marriage and soon had a child with James as well. James eventually devoted more of his time to running the grocery and less to carpentry.

James also tried to satisfy his ambitious nature outside the workplace. Like many ardent Irish nationalists, Cavanagh volunteered for the Irish-dominated Sixty-Ninth Regiment of the New

York State Militia, becoming one of the unit's officers. When the Civil War broke out and the regiment was sent to the front lines, Captain Cavanagh was designated the third highest-ranking officer in the unit. He led his company of about one hundred men, which included future armorer Timothy Carr, up Henry House Hill in the Union's losing effort at the Battle of Bull Run in 1861. The following year, Cavanagh rose to second in command of the Sixty-Ninth during the intense firefight at Malvern Hill, the climactic battle of General George McClellan's ill-fated Peninsula campaign. There Cavanagh (now a major) led a successful counterattack against the oncoming Confederates despite having his horse shot out from under him.

During Robert E. Lee's invasion of Maryland a few months later, Cavanagh took charge of the entire Sixty-Ninth after the regiment's commanding officer was shot in the face during the deadliest hour of the deadliest engagement on the deadliest day of armed conflict in all of American history — the fight for the Sunken Road running through a cornfield in Sharpsburg, Maryland, at the Battle of Antietam on September 17, 1862. Knowing that to have their position overrun might very well mean the loss of the entire war, Cavanagh rallied his troops time and again even though their comrades were dropping all around them with gruesome injuries. During a lull in the fighting, General Winfield Scott Hancock rode up to Cavanagh's position and, seeing only about a hundred men left where the entire Irish Brigade (the Sixty-Ninth plus several other Irish-dominated regiments) had once stood, asked how long they could hold that key portion of the field. "That depends, General," Cavanagh replied, "on how long it will take to kill every man of us," at which his men gave a cheer. By the time another regiment could be found to take their place, 60 percent of the soldiers in the Sixty-Ninth had been killed or injured, one of the highest casualty rates of any unit in any battle in the entire war. "It was certainly the most awful sight that I ever witnessed," wrote an Irish-born soldier afterward as he watched the surgeons saw off the mangled limbs of those shot in their arms and legs, "and may God forbid I shall ever witness another of the same sort."

Three months later at Fredericksburg, Cavanagh cemented his legacy as the "Fighting Little Major." Although Confederates occupied an impregnable position atop Marye's Heights, on the thirteenth of December General Ambrose Burnside sent wave after wave of Union soldiers up toward their position — "a perfect slaughter-pen," according to an Irish immigrant journalist who covered the battle — in a futile effort to dislodge them. After several failed assaults by other units, Burnside ordered the Sixty-Ninth into the breach. Despite understanding that victory was all but impossible, Cavanagh led the regiment up the sloping hill, stepping over the corpses and bleeding bodies of moaning Union soldiers who had fallen earlier that day. As Cavanagh and his men fought their way across barren cornfields on that cold December day and approached within a hundred yards of the stone wall that Confederate infantrymen were using for cover, the Northerners were (according to the same reporter) "greeted by a murderous fire" from both artillery and rifles that mowed many of them down. Nonetheless, Cavanagh urged his men to ignore the blizzard of lead flying at them. "Blaze away and stand it, boys!" he shouted, leading his men almost to the stone wall itself. Seconds later, however, Cavanagh was "severely wounded" by a shot to the hip and soon thereafter the Irishmen retreated, carrying their commander to safety so he could be treated by Dr. William O'Meagher, another Famine immigrant from Tipperary. General Thomas Francis Meagher, the famed Irish revolutionary who had escaped banishment to Tasmania by the British and become the commander of the Irish Brigade after Michael Corcoran was captured, wrote of Cavanagh's performance at Fredericksburg: "never was there a truer heart; never was there a bolder arm; never was there a brighter brain" than those displayed by Cavanagh on that fateful day.

Cavanagh eventually recovered, although he never again engaged in a major battle. Instead, the army assigned him the task of recruiting soldiers in New York. Despite Cavanagh's notoriety and promotions, money must have still been tight for the family. James tried to become a "builder" while simultaneously doing his recruiting work but was not successful. Perhaps as a result, Alice advertised in the *New York Herald* in 1864 seeking a position as a wet nurse to earn extra cash.

After the war, the Cavanaghs moved to Brooklyn and James — despite his national renown — once again became a lowly journeyman carpenter. He did continue serving part-time as an officer in the Sixty-Ninth, which had become a militia unit again, yet Cavanagh clearly aspired to a station in life that seemed commensurate with his military fame. He ran as a Republican for the state legislature in 1870 and 1875 but was defeated both times (in the latter case after initially being announced the winner). Around 1880, he opened his own carpentry business in Brooklyn, but that failed as well, forcing him to become a journeyman yet again. He briefly went back into business as a builder at the end of the 1880s but was again unsuccessful.

Cavanagh's postwar challenges would not defeat him, however, for he had many friends and admirers among Irish nationalists and Civil War veterans in Brooklyn. Seeing Cavanagh struggling, in 1892 they secured him an appointment to a custom house position overseeing the workers on the Brooklyn docks who moved and appraised imports for the Department of the Treasury. Cavanagh retained that post until just before his death, from acute bronchitis, in January 1901.

James Cavanagh was a revered figure in the Irish American community, and even though it had been more than thirty-five years since the Fighting Little Major had last made headlines, the Irish American press gave him a hero's send-off at his death. The *Irish World*, for example, called Cavanagh's "record of honorable service" in the army one "rarely equalled in [the] military annals" of any nation. Yet beyond Cavanagh's military accomplishments, his story also reminds us that while the stereotypical Famine immigrant wielded a shovel or a hammer in a blue-collar occupation, many of these folks, like Cavanagh, eventually transitioned into jobs as clerks, salesmen, teachers, or civil servants. These white-collar Irish immigrants played an important yet underappreciated role in the making of Irish New York.

THE LATE BREVET BRIGADIER-GENERAL JAMES CAVANAGH.

When James Cavanagh died in 1901, the New York *Irish-American* honored the Fighting Little Major with this large, front-page commemorative portrait, which many Irish immigrants, especially Civil War veterans, would have cut out and displayed proudly in their homes.

It is not well-known that there were many Famine immigrants like James Cavanagh who held jobs that we might call lower-status white-collar. These were occupations that did not make one dirty or sweaty and did not pay as well as high-status white-collar work in the medical or legal professions. Not every Famine refugee could aspire to such jobs, however, because they usually required literacy, good penmanship and grammar, and in most cases decent math skills as well.

This occupational category was the most transitory of all the rungs on the Irish American socioeconomic ladder. More than half the Famine refugees who started out in America as clerks and the like managed to end their careers as business owners or doctors and lawyers. And more than half of those whose last job before retirement or death was lower-status white-collar had begun further down the occupational hierarchy. An Irish immigrant journalist explained the high rate of movement in and out of this employment category. Those with experience working in Ireland as either clerks or shopkeepers, he noted, "have very poor chances of getting 'situations' in New York" like those they had held in Ireland. "They must take some secondary work to support them, and bide their time, before they can find the place for which they are suited." As a result, those who had been employed in Ireland as clerks often had to start out in New York doing manual labor, while small Irish shopkeepers after emigrating usually began their American careers as store clerks. Thus, while only about one in eleven Famine immigrants found a lower-status white-collar job immediately upon arrival in America, about one in six held such a job at some point in their lifetime. Less than a quarter of the Famine immigrants who worked in these jobs were people who held them from the very beginning to the very end of their American careers.

About 70 percent of the Famine immigrants who worked in lower-status white-collar occupations described themselves as clerks. This term could describe a store clerk, but most New York clerks worked behind the scenes at the businesses that employed them. In the days before typewriters and word processing, calculators and computer spreadsheets, New Yorkers employed thousands of clerks to write out and duplicate correspondence with suppliers and business customers, track and tally income and expenditures, oversee shipments and financial transactions, and even negotiate purchases and sales of raw materials, wholesale goods, and retail products.

Clerks who could demonstrate experience and aptitude in

Occupational Mobility of Male Famine Immigrant Lower-Status White-Collar Workers*

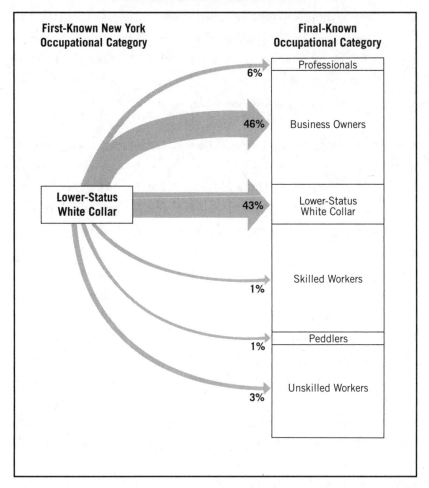

First-Known New York Occupational Category

Final-Known Occupational Category

Lower-Status White Collar

Professionals — 6%

Business Owners — 46%

Lower-Status White Collar — 43%

Skilled Workers — 1%

Peddlers — 1%

Unskilled Workers — 3%

several of these areas could command high salaries. Robert Lewis from Dublin, for example, arrived in New York at age fifteen in 1851 and developed a lucrative specialty as a dry goods clerk. His responsibilities eventually included buying lace for the dry goods firm that employed him, a task that required shrewd negotiating

---

* Percentages may not total 100 due to rounding. These figures refer to immigrants whose occupations could be tracked for at least ten years.

skills and the ability to distinguish fine lace from run-of-the-mill product. Lewis was well enough compensated that by the 1860s he could buy a three-story brick town house (still standing) at 449 East 118th Street in Harlem, worth about $5,000 in 1870. Lewis had $5,000 in other assets by that point as well. Other than a brief and unsuccessful effort to go into the lace business on his own, Lewis remained a dry goods buyer for the rest of his life.

Other dry goods clerks also prospered. John Devins from Carrick-on-Shannon in County Leitrim arrived in New York in 1849 at age eighteen, having already worked as a grocer's assistant in Ireland. In New York, though, he took a job as a dry goods clerk. By 1853, he had saved just $20 in his account at the Emigrant Savings Bank, perhaps because he was sending money back to Ireland to pay for the emigration of other family members. But by 1856 he had saved $200, and two years later his bank balance had climbed to $430. Unlike Lewis, Devins never tried to go into business for himself. But he was a well-paid clerk—he must have known his kersey from his corduroy and been able to distinguish among a dozen different types of cotton and cashmere. He made enough money as a dry goods clerk to eventually buy his family a home in Brooklyn.

Not every clerk thrived, of course. William Durack from County Galway started out in America as a clerk, saved enough to open his own grocery, but failed in that pursuit and ended his career as a night watchman in Chicago. Widower Alexander Furlong arrived in New York in 1851 at age forty-four, having already lost his wife and their two children. He worked in New York as a clerk for several years, but nonetheless died in 1857 in the city almshouse on Blackwells Island.

Clerks were far less likely than tradesmen or unskilled workers to face financial ruin if their business ventures failed, because so long as their health was good and their reputations were intact, they could return to their relatively high-paying clerical positions.

John Brown, a farmer in County Derry, immigrated to New York in 1848 at about age twenty-five. Seven years later, he was working as a shoe store clerk and living in Ward Nine, a favorite locale of Irish-born Protestants. Brown was a determined saver. By 1860 he had accumulated nearly $500 in his account and reported to the census taker that his net worth was $3,000. Brown used that nest egg to become a shoe dealer. He did well initially—he reported owning $16,000 in real estate in 1870—probably a reference to the stately four-story brownstone that he, his wife, Mary, and their four children inhabited facing Fort Greene Park in Brooklyn. But Brown's business did not succeed in the long run, perhaps a casualty of the depression that followed the Panic of 1873. By 1880, Brown was an employee once again, working as a shoe buyer for H. B. Claflin & Company, the nation's largest dry goods wholesaler. The family had not lost its home, however. The Browns still lived in their brownstone facing Fort Greene Park when John died in 1882 and were inhabiting the same residence when Mary passed away eleven years later.

Clerks' salaries varied quite a bit depending on their experience and area of expertise, but were generally well above those of skilled and unskilled workers. Precise figures are difficult to come by for the pre–Civil War years, but after Tweed Ring corruption was exposed in the early 1870s, New York City began publishing the salaries of its municipal employees, making it possible to track clerks' pay and compare it with that of other workers. Clerks employed by the city in 1874 made from $1,200 to $3,000 per year, with the highest salaries going to clerks with legal and financial acumen. In contrast, day laborers and porters employed by the federal government in New York at that point were paid $720 per year, messengers were paid $840, and watchmen drew salaries of $1,000.

One of the clerks at the lower end of the occupation's pay scale was Richard Oulahan. Born in Dublin in about 1827, Oulahan became active in the Irish independence movement and especially well-known for the poetry he contributed to nationalist publications. When the English began jailing those advocating Irish independence in 1848, Oulahan fled to New York, arriving the following year. He worked throughout the 1850s as a clerk and bookkeeper and on December 19, 1862, became a lieutenant in one of the city's Irish regiments, whose ranks had been decimated six days before by the Union defeat at the Battle of Fredericksburg, where James Cavanagh had been so badly injured.

Like many Irish officers, Oulahan opened a saloon upon leaving the army, but the venture quickly fizzled. Needing a reliable income to support his wife, Mary, and their five children, Oulahan parlayed the political connections he had forged in the army into an appointment as a clerk in the Department of the Treasury in Washington. After seven years on the job, Oulahan's salary was $1,400, not the lowest in the office of the Third Auditor, but $100 below the average. Twenty years later, the pay scale in that office had not changed, but Oulahan's salary had been reduced to $1,200, a fact he must have found vexing. Nonetheless, Oulahan remained in the same post in the same Treasury Department office until his death in 1895.

For every immigrant like Oulahan who began and ended their American working lives as clerks, there was another who successfully used a clerical position as a stepping-stone up the socioeconomic ladder. Many advanced remarkably quickly from clerkships to business ownership. Thomas E. Foran from Dublin, for example, emigrated in 1855 at age twenty-four and worked as a clerk in his first couple of years in New York, but by 1858 had become a saloonkeeper on the Lower East Side. Foran remained in that business until 1869, when he left the liquor trade to open a real estate agency farther uptown. Yet Foran apparently found the profits reaped by those who built homes more appealing than the commissions of the agents who sold them. In 1873, he closed his real estate agency and became a builder on the West Side. Foran's timing was terrible, as the housing market collapsed following the Panic of 1873. But he managed to remain a builder until he retired in 1887, four years before his death.

James Goodwin from County Kildare was another clerk who quickly moved up New York's occupational hierarchy. Goodwin emigrated in 1854 at age twenty-one and became a clerk for the paper brokers Beebe, Hall & Sands while boarding with the family of his older brother Henry, who operated a paper store in lower Manhattan and had been in America since at least 1846. In 1856, James started his own paper business, but it failed and he had to return to clerking. By 1861, however, James was back in the paper trade, this time for good.

Unlike Henry, who was a paper retailer, James focused on the wholesale business, supplying primarily book and newspaper publishers. He "made a g[oo]d deal of money" in the 1860s, reported the Dun & Company credit rating agency, which at the end of the decade estimated Goodwin's net worth at $20,000 to $25,000 (about half a million dollars today). Seeking to further increase his profit margins, however, in the early 1870s Goodwin invested in paper mills in the Berkshire Mountains of Massachusetts. His timing was unfortunate, too, as the Panic depressed demand for paper and Goodwin's mills became insolvent. But Goodwin was a "tricky" and "cunning" businessman, as his employees learned to their chagrin. He broke many pledges to his mill hands, some of whom worked for a year without compensation as their repeatedly promised pay never appeared. He eventually declared the mills bankrupt and gave the workers only half of what they were owed. By 1880, however, Goodwin had maneuvered his business out of bankruptcy and managed to revive his manufacturing enterprise, albeit on a smaller scale. He moved his family to the Berkshires for a while so he could nurse the operation back to health. Goodwin soon returned to New York and remained in the wholesale paper business (although never again reaping the windfall profits he had enjoyed in the 1860s) until his death in 1911.

GOODWIN, COBB & CO.,

COMMISSION

PAPER WAREHOUSE,

IMPORTERS AND DEALERS IN

BLEACHING POWDER, SODA ASH,

ULTRAMARINE,

Felts, Rags, Gunny & Kentucky Bagging,

MANILLA AND HEMP ROPE,

Paper and Paper Stock of all kinds,

AND

MANUFACTURERS' MATERIALS OF EVERY DESCRIPTION.

Book, News & Printing Paper Manufactured to Order, on Shortest Notice.

16 and 18 READE STREET,

JAMES GOODWIN,
A. H. COBB,
F. D. HODGEMAN,

NEW YORK.

A trade journal advertisement from 1871 for James Goodwin's paper business.

Peter McCullough was another Famine immigrant who quickly used a clerkship as a springboard into business. Better educated than the typical emigrant from the Bodoney parishes in Tyrone (most of whose emigrants became charcoal peddlers), McCullough arrived in New York in 1849 at about age eighteen and rapidly found employment as a clerk. By 1853 he was operating a grocery, but it didn't last even a year. McCullough returned to clerking, yet late in 1855 the ambitious Irishman managed to open a saloon, perhaps with advice from the saloonkeeper with whom he boarded.

The location Peter chose for his watering hole, a sparsely populated intersection at what was then the very northern extremity of

Seventh Avenue, might have seemed curious to some, but McCullough knew what he was doing. Soon Longacre Square, the confluence of Seventh Avenue and Broadway where McCullough established his saloon, became a bustling hub, and thirsty workers crowded into his establishment. By 1860, McCullough had accumulated $1,122 in his Emigrant Savings Bank accounts, and his net worth grew even more rapidly in the ensuing decade as he began investing some of his profits in Seventh Avenue real estate. He was so successful that by 1870, at age thirty-nine, McCullough declared himself "retired," something he and his wife, Delia (daughter of that saloon-keeper with whom Peter had boarded), could afford in part because they never had any children. The McCulloughs lived off the rents they collected from their tenement properties until his death in 1904, the year one of the city's leading newspapers moved its head-quarters to that same intersection where Peter had located his saloon and the city renamed Longacre Square as Times Square. At his death, McCullough's estate was valued at $40,000, the equiva-lent of at least $1.5 million today.

McCullough's unusually detailed will forestalled a battle among his heirs over its terms, but that did not prevent them from fighting over the burial expenses of the rich old man. Peter's widow, Kate, (whom Peter had married after Delia died in 1896) asked Peter's nephew Joseph McCullough, a cotton broker, to arrange his uncle's wake. Joseph spared no expense, ordering a case of whiskey, four cases of beer, one bottle each of port and sherry, two hundred cigars, and candy cigars for the children. Joseph also purchased twenty-six pounds of ham, ten pounds of corned beef, a variety of "steaks and other meats," and plenty of fixings to turn those items into sandwiches. He then presented a bill for $71.25 (about $2,500 today) to Peter's executors. These were usually spouses, chil-dren, or siblings, but Peter apparently did not trust his kinsmen with his money. He had chosen a local notary and a priest as his executors.

They refused to reimburse Joseph, claiming that wakes were "immoral" and not a necessary part of a Catholic burial. Undaunted, Joseph sued the executors to recover his costs. A municipal court ruled against McCullough, but he would not admit defeat and appealed the decision to a state tribunal. McCullough's lawyer quoted from the Bible, Virgil, Sir Walter Scott, and Shakespeare's *Hamlet* to demonstrate that catered celebrations of a dead man's life were a centuries-old tradition. Besides, he contended, it would be embarrassing for a rich man to have a cheap wake. These arguments swayed the appeals court, which ruled in 1907 that wakes were a "racial custom" of the Irish and that in preparing for them, "expenditures...for certain items, delicatessen in their nature," as well as alcohol and tobacco, were appropriate and therefore could be charged to the estate. The executors appealed this decision but were unsuccessful and eventually had to pay for the wake and Joseph's legal fees. Peter, a frugal Famine refugee, might have considered all those ten-cent cigars and bottles of whiskey an extravagance, but he probably would have applauded his nephew's audacity and determination.

Other Famine immigrants who started out as clerks in New York moved on to careers in medicine or the law. George Hargan, a Roman Catholic from the town of Derry, managed to quickly climb New York's socioeconomic ladder. He arrived in New York in 1847 at about age seventeen, having already worked as a teacher in Ireland. In New York he found employment as a bookkeeper and probably helped finance the subsequent emigration of his parents and seven siblings, who came to New York one, two, three, five, and seven years after him. Meanwhile, in 1850, Hargan identified an attorney willing to take him on as a clerk and tutor him in the law. He passed his bar exam in 1853 and initially took a civil service job as New York's commissioner of deeds. But by 1855, Hargan had joined the Wall Street law firm of a wealthy ex-congressman, Francis B. Cutting. In 1858, Hargan left to start his own practice, but he did not prosper. That may have been because Hargan had a gratingly disputatious temperament, even for an attorney. He had public spats with groups as diverse as his ward school board and the New York Academy of Music, and his legal career apparently suffered as a result. Few tears were shed, outside of his own family, when Hargan died suddenly in 1863 at age thirty-three.

Even some immigrant doctors started out in America as clerks. William O'Meagher, for example, the physician who treated James Cavanagh's wounds at Fredericksburg, came to America in 1852, having already attended a year of college in both Galway and Cork, passed the Dublin apothecary exam, and interned for a London physician. He served as the medical officer on his emigrant ship in exchange for complimentary passage. (The medical officers on such vessels did not, in most cases, actually have medical degrees.) O'Meagher initially worked in New York as a drugstore clerk, but by 1855 he had opened his own pharmacy and around the same time began taking classes in medicine at New York University, from which he graduated in 1857. He then opened his own medical practice on the most upscale block in Five Points.

Dr. O'Meagher could have made a comfortable living treating patients there, but he apparently did not find such a career satisfying. In 1859, he took a staff position at St. Vincent's Hospital while simultaneously founding and editing the *New-York Medical Press*, the first weekly medical journal published in the United States. The journal was a joint project with his brother-in-law, another Famine immigrant who had worked as a druggist en route to a medical degree. The duo suspended publication in 1861, however, when O'Meagher volunteered to serve as surgeon for an Irish American regiment heading south to suppress the Confederate rebellion. He eventually became the Irish Brigade's surgeon in chief, though not before being captured on three separate occasions when he remained on battlefields to treat the wounded after Union armies withdrew following the Second Battle of Bull Run in 1862, the Battle of Chancellorsville in 1863, and the Battle of the Wilderness in 1864. After the war, William and his wife, Cecilia Kiernan O'Meagher, moved to Harlem, and William continued to prefer appointed positions to private practice. He served as a pension examiner for Civil War veterans, sanitary inspector of Staten Island, chief medical officer of the Sixty-Ninth Regiment, deputy city coroner, and eventually coroner of the city of New York, a position he held from January 1895 until his death thirteen months later.

———

Another career alternative for those who sought to escape their clerical jobs was to teach. Henry Madden, for example, emigrated in 1849 at age twenty-seven and after working for several years as a clerk in New York, he joined other family members in Albany, where he became a "well known schoolmaster." Madden was "in the habit of reading in bed almost every night," reported the *Albany Argus*, as if that was an eccentricity. Yet it did turn into a tragedy. Madden fell asleep on a Sunday night in November 1870 while reading by the light of a kerosene lamp, and when he woke up with a start, he knocked over the lamp. "The fatal kerosene exploded," wrote the *Argus*, "and he inhaled the flames while endeavoring to jump from the bed of fire." Madden was dead by the time firemen arrived on the scene.

Most Famine immigrants who worked as teachers did so in the public schools, but some found employment in the United States' expanding Catholic school system. Teenagers John and Stephen McMahon emigrated from County Mayo in 1848 with their father James (a shoemaker), their mother, and two sisters. Three younger siblings joined them in New York a year later. By 1850, John (then twenty), Stephen (eighteen), and their father all worked as journeyman shoemakers.

The typical Famine immigrant hoped to strike it rich in America, so what Stephen did in 1854 was unusual—he took a vow of *poverty*. Doing so was a prerequisite to being accepted into the Christian Brothers, a Catholic religious order that focused on teaching. John, who had dropped shoemaking for a clerkship, soon followed his brother into the order. John had a long career as a teacher. In 1900, he was working as an English teacher at the La Salle Academy, a Catholic high school in Manhattan. By 1910, at age eighty, he had joined the faculty of Manhattan College, a Christian Brothers university, and he taught there until he was nearly ninety.

Meanwhile, the Christian Brothers decided that Stephen had leadership skills that made him too valuable to be left in a classroom. After his teaching stints in Montreal, Quebec City, and Baltimore, the Christian Brothers began putting him in charge of entire schools—first in Utica and Baltimore and then in San Francisco. But even that was considered too narrow for Stephen's talents. "Brother Justin," as he was known within the order, had a "magnetic personality," recalled one acquaintance. "Quick in his talk, quick in his walk, quick in his perceptions," he had a gift for convincing everyone around him that any goal, no matter how lofty, could be achieved.

Brother Justin became a veritable Johnny Appleseed for Christian Brothers schools, spending a decade after the Civil War traveling the length of the Pacific coast to open high schools and colleges. Transferred back east, he was put in charge of the order's operations in the northeast United States and Canada, opening several dozen schools, orphanages, and teacher-training facilities from Ohio to Nova Scotia. In the early 1890s, Brother Justin spent four years in Ireland helping to reorganize its Catholic schools. When he returned to the United States, Justin began a relentless lobbying campaign to get a Catholic chapel added to the facilities at the United States Military Academy at West Point, something he finally achieved in 1899. After a falling-out with his order's leaders over his zealous (and ultimately unsuccessful) efforts to retain the teaching of Latin in all their schools, Brother Justin was demoted to more modest roles. Nonetheless, he was remembered as one of the "giants" of the order when he passed away in 1912.

Women worked as teachers too, but very few female Famine immigrants could get teaching jobs in the 1850s. The school board in each ward chose which teachers to hire, and in predominantly Irish wards the teachers were usually Irish Americans. Most had arrived in the United States as children and were educated in New York's schools before they taught in them. But a few women who fled the Famine as adults did manage to land teaching jobs. Josephine Cowen from Dublin, for example, found a position as a schoolteacher within a year of her arrival in 1853, and Josephine Gibbons from Clare secured one too.

It was easier for those who emigrated as adults to get work in the 1850s as music teachers. Emma Kingsbury, who arrived in New York from Antrim in 1848, was a music teacher in New York by 1855. Margaret Antisell, who emigrated from Dublin, taught music in Brooklyn from 1853 to at least 1880. Margaret Smithson from Dublin worked in Brooklyn as a music teacher too.

Men also sometimes found teaching jobs that did not involve working in a school. Michael J. Sause from Tipperary, for example, initially worked in New York in the same trade as his father, making "agricultural implements" such as plowshares and other groundbreaking devices. But Michael's passion lay elsewhere. In 1867 he gave up metalworking, rented space near Union Square, and became a ballroom dance teacher. Known as "Professor Judson Sause," he hid his Irish roots and became a nationally renowned instructor, teaching not only waltzes and two-steps but also quadrilles, English galops, and the latest French favorites. To increase his income, Sause leased entire Manhattan buildings that contained large ballrooms. Then he would give lessons on the dance floor, live in another part of the building, and rent out the rest of the space (some of it to other dance instructors) to earn additional income. Sause also threw masquerade balls and other dance parties— "the most select and enjoyable in the city," gushed one newspaper— where New York dance enthusiasts could pay to enjoy their favorite pastime with other devotees. Sause also published a guide to ballroom dance and etiquette that went through many printings.

By 1897, an Atlanta newspaper claimed that Sause "probably has taught more American dancers than any other living man." He was "one of the last of the old school of dancing teachers," noted the *New York Times* when Sause passed away in 1906, at age seventy-three, in his rooms at Lyric Hall on Sixth Avenue, "where almost every night in the week there is a dance of some kind....As the old teacher died he must have heard the waltz music below going to the shuf-shuf of the dancers' feet. He died happy."

Nearly half of the Famine immigrants who finished their careers as teachers had, like Sause, first worked lower on the socioeconomic ladder. But even teachers who managed to avoid manual labor in America sometimes took circuitous routes to the classroom. Anthony Geraghty, for instance, had grown up in the town of Westport in County Mayo and arrived in New York at about age twenty-three in 1851 with Thomas, his older brother. Thomas became a day laborer, but Anthony was able to land a less physically strenuous job as a clerk, which he held for most of the 1850s while living in Ward Three just a block north of Washington Market, a huge wholesale fruit and vegetable emporium on the Hudson River that took up an entire city block between Fulton and Vesey Streets. In about 1858, Anthony became a produce dealer at the market, but apparently that business did not suit him. In 1859, he opened several saloons but failed at the liquor trade too. These ventures took a terrible toll on his family's finances. His bank balance, $1,500 in 1857, had fallen to just $170 by the middle of 1860, about the time he shuttered his saloons.

Still in his early thirties, Geraghty found a new career to which he was apparently much better suited. Perhaps through the political connections he had made in the liquor trade, he landed a job in 1861 as a teacher at Grammar School No. 70 on the Upper East Side. He turned out to be a gifted teacher and remained at the school until he died of heart disease just shy of his sixtieth birthday. Geraghty was so beloved as a teacher that his death was noted not only in the *Irish-American* but also in the *New York Times*, which rarely paid much attention to the Irish American community at all, much less one of its public school instructors. The *Times* noted Geraghty's long service to the public schools and reported that he had been "painstaking, energetic, and...very popular with his pupils." This was surely an epitaph of which any teacher could be proud.

There were a variety of other modest white-collar jobs that Famine immigrants might secure with the right combination of education and ambition. Catholic church sextons, for example, had to not only read and write well but also be able to keep the church account books and have a thorough knowledge of Catholic ritual to assist priests officiating at masses, baptisms, and weddings. The sexton, who would typically wear a suit and tie to work, also ordered church supplies (both ordinary and sacramental) and worked closely with local undertakers to manage the funerals that were held in their church.

This last fact may explain why so many sextons became morticians. Two-thirds of the sextons who opened Emigrant Savings Bank accounts in the 1850s and could be traced ten or more years eventually became undertakers. Edward Delaney from King's County, for example, served as sexton of the Church of the Annunciation in west Harlem for about a decade before becoming an undertaker just around the corner from the church. He remained in business there until his death in 1883. Daniel Quinn from Tyrone also parlayed a job as a sexton (at St. Columba's Church on West

Twenty-Fourth Street) into a business as an undertaker, which he operated until at least 1880. Some immigrants, like Quinn, maximized their incomes by working simultaneously as both undertakers and sextons.

Journalism was another field to which Famine immigrants could aspire. Most labored in relative obscurity. Daniel D. McCarthy, who had been a clerk in County Cork, emigrated in 1848 at age nineteen with two older sisters and quickly found a clerical job in New York. But he wanted to be a journalist, and by 1857 he had secured a post at the *New York Tribune* writing business news. The job was high on prestige but paid terribly, so McCarthy supplemented his income by running a cigar shop in his tenement on Grand Street. Seeking still greater profits, McCarthy decided to launch his own newspaper, a Catholic weekly he called *The Nation*. The journal folded after a couple of years, so McCarthy took a position covering the Civil War for the *Tribune*. After Appomattox, McCarthy went to work for a dry goods trade journal, eventually becoming its editor. When that periodical folded in 1889, the publisher hired McCarthy to edit a new venture, a weekly guide to events taking place in New York City that was sold to tourists in hotel lobbies. These jobs paid well enough to allow McCarthy to buy a home on Mulberry Street and later, after he moved to Staten Island, donate a one-ton bell to his local Catholic church.

Not everyone who broke into journalism remained in the field, a fact exemplified by brothers Gerald and Richard Lalor, both very hard of hearing, who emigrated from County Kilkenny in 1850. Like Benjamin Franklin, the Lalor brothers used training as printers as a stepping-stone to white-collar newspaper work. Gerald, the younger of the two, was employed for most of the 1850s as a printer — lastly as compositor for the *Irish News*, a paper started by Thomas Francis Meagher in the late 1850s (before he became James Cavanagh's commanding officer in the Irish Brigade) to try to rally support in America for the Irish independence movement. Gerald became an office clerk for the *News* and then its assistant editor on the eve of the Civil War, when the paper shut down. Meagher then hired Gerald as his private secretary as Meagher helped organize the Irish Brigade. After Meagher took over the brigade, Gerald became an assistant editor of the *Irish-American*, New York's most successful publication aimed at the Famine immigrants, and he held that position for the rest of the decade. In 1870, with his health failing, Gerald found a less demanding position closer to his Brooklyn home as secretary to the commissioners of excise of that city. But his health continued to decline, and he succumbed to consumption at age forty in 1871.

Richard Lalor also ended his career in the lower white-collar ranks. After also starting out in New York as a printer, Richard became the business manager of the *Irish News* in 1856. When the *News* folded in 1861, Dick (as he was universally known) also assisted Meagher with the formation of the Irish Brigade and then for the first half of the war became the unit's sutler, the civilian authorized to sell soldiers goods like tobacco and alcohol that were not supplied by the army. After giving up his work as a sutler, Lalor returned to New York and opened a saloon, locating it on the same block of Ann Street where the *Irish News* had been founded. But in 1868, he left the retail liquor business and instead went to work for one of his beer suppliers as their Brooklyn agent. He still had that job when he died from stomach cancer at age fifty-six in 1884.

Some white-collar jobs involved supervising other workers, but it often took the Famine immigrants decades to climb the ranks to such positions. That was the case for John Irvine, born in County Fermanagh, who arrived in New York in 1850 with his wife, Margaret McNeely Irvine, and settled on Mulberry Street in Five Points. That a census taker recorded their surname as "Arwin" gives some sense of how they pronounced it. John soon found a job as a laborer in the pickling plant of Stephen H. Provost and John B. Wells on Front Street in Ward Two. There was certainly lots of moving and lifting to do in a wholesale pickling operation, so the proprietors must have kept John busy. The Irvines carefully saved as much of John's pay as they could. By December 1853, they had amassed $160 (equal to about $6,000 today) in their Emigrant Savings Bank account. At that point, they began saving at an even faster rate. In just eighteen more months, their balance tripled, to $500.

John now reported to the bank secretary that he was a "pickle maker." Perhaps Provost and Wells had trouble finding experienced preservers and decided to train him. Still saving at a prodigious pace, the Irvines accumulated another $500 by the fall of 1857. During the Civil War, they saved faster still, and by the end of the conflict had amassed about $2,500. Prosperous enough to leave Five Points, they moved first to Ward One and then just after the Civil War to Ward Seven, where the Irvines eventually bought two tenements.

It is not clear why the Irvines fared so well. John and Margaret never had any children, something that certainly made saving easier. Furthermore, the sectional conflict created an unprecedented demand for preserved foods of all kinds to feed members of the military, so business must have been extraordinarily brisk. John may have also created a bidding war for his services among the city's picklers. Irvine left Provost and Wells to take a job with one of the nation's largest makers of preserved foods, Kemp, Day & Company. There he rose from pickler to a less physically demanding job as clerk, and then higher still through the managerial ranks to (in 1870) superintendent of their vast food-processing complex, which was located near the Hudson River in Ward Three. Margaret did not get to enjoy the fruits of John's impressive supervisory position for very long. She passed away in 1872 at age forty-eight. John quickly found a new spouse, Lizzie Murphy, twenty-seven years his junior, and they had at least four children before she died in 1889. John had retired by then, but he continued to earn money renting out his tenement apartments on Rutgers Street. John passed away there, at age seventy-eight, in November 1900.

While some jobs, like superintendent of a manufacturing plant, were readily identifiable as white-collar, others were not. Consider the career of Peter J. Faye. Two years after his emigration in 1848 from Loughrea, a lakeside town in central Galway, Faye was among dozens of Irish immigrants living in and working sixteen-hour days as servants at the Washington Hotel facing Battery Park. Five years later, Faye had found a higher-status job as a clerk, perhaps owing to his beautiful handwriting, yet he soon gave up that employment for an apparently lowly position as a doorkeeper. Why? Because he was opening doors (in more ways than one) at the New York Stock Exchange, a dream job for an ambitious immigrant who was adept at networking.

The Washington Hotel at 1 Broadway, where Peter Faye worked as a "servant."

The term "doorkeeper" hardly did justice to Faye's duties. The Exchange had very few employees in those days, and as a result Faye, who wore a suit and tie to work rather than a doorman's uniform, "was the custodian of money, packages of securities, important messages and the like, for every member of the Exchange," reported the *Herald*. He tracked down members at their clubs and homes after hours with recently delivered letters or news flashes that might cost the traders dearly if they were missed or delayed. Faye was also "a natural-born statesman," according to the *New York World*, and seeing this, stockbrokers entrusted him to act as their middleman in sensitive financial transactions that required secrecy or tact. For this dedication to his employers, Faye was rewarded by the Exchange's leaders with thousands of dollars in gratuities. The brokers also "let him in on stock-exchange deals" that were "a sure thing." As a result, when Faye died in 1884, he purportedly left an estate valued at $100,000. Several Wall Street titans attended his funeral.

For many Irish immigrants, the most desirable white-collar positions were those offered by the federal, state, or municipal governments. Civil service jobs, as they eventually became known, were salaried positions that could be clerical, supervisory (inspectors and foremen), legal and judicial (court officers and justices of the peace), or even involve law enforcement (marshals, sheriffs and their many deputies, and policemen). Some of these posts were elective, but most were obtained through connections. In the 1850s and 1860s, well before the advent of the civil service exam, someone with political influence had to sponsor an aspirant to get him one of these positions. And if an immigrant's patron fell from favor or died, then the newcomer would usually lose his civil service job, no matter how good at it he might be.

Some Famine immigrants took civil service positions late in life, transitioning to them from occupations that were precarious or had become too strenuous. James Verdon, for example, arrived in New York from Louth in 1848 at about age forty-five with his wife, Ann, and five daughters and by 1850 had bought a farm in Warren,

New Jersey. With no sons to take over the farm, James decided, when he turned sixty, to rent out his land and take a less arduous job as the town's commissioner of deeds.

For others, government jobs provided supplemental income rather than a full-time occupation. That was the case for Michael Quigley. Born in rural County Clare in about 1834, Quigley came to New York in 1850 with his three younger brothers, doing so three years after his father, Patrick, had emigrated and one year after his mother, Ann, had left Ireland. (We encountered Ann in chapter 4, peddling fruit because Patrick was unable to work.) Michael immediately took a job as a day laborer upon arrival, but in the late 1850s he bought a seventeen-foot rowboat with forty dollars in savings and became a boatman, charging fees to row people and goods between the ships anchored in the harbor and a pier at the foot of Whitehall Street, the southernmost point of Manhattan Island. The job was a physically demanding one, but by this point Quigley was "a tall, stout man, weighing over two hundred pounds, and of immense strength." His personality was as big as his frame, and as a result he became a "famous" waterfront character, according to a journalist, "well known" to New Yorkers who frequented the Battery and to "all the sea captains who ever came to this port."

Quigley's imposing stature attracted the attention of the leading politicos in Ward One. Power brokers curried favor with men like Quigley, whose intimidating features might sway the results of a primary or general election. "In those days...politics ran to a high pitch and 'knocking out' was a distinct feature of every election," recalled the *Herald*, looking back on the Civil War era. The *Herald* was referring to the fact that ward politicos in that era stationed bruisers like Quigley at polling places to threaten or use violence to prevent their opponents from voting. "Quigley became a potent factor for the republican party," the *Herald* noted, "and many an incautious democrat has felt the force of his powerful arm and fist."

For rendering such service to the party, ward heelers compensated pugilists like Quigley with patronage, and this was the route through which Quigley entered the civil service. In the early 1860s he served two stints on the harbor police force. Quigley could draw that salary while simultaneously continuing his employment as a boatman because the harbor police job merely required him to remain on standby near the harbor should any trouble break out — something easy for Quigley to do since he worked at the Battery and lived a half block from it. A year after those harbor police gigs ended, Quigley was made a Ward One inspector of elections, an ironic assignment given his history of polling-place fisticuffs. Later, Quigley was appointed an officer of the Court of General Sessions, another part-time job that augmented his boatman's income. These supplements to Quigley's income enabled him, just after the end of the Civil War, to open a saloon and buy a home on State Street near the Battery. He left the liquor trade after several years, but could afford to start another business, a boat rental operation at the Whitehall Street piers for couples and families seeking some recreation and cool breezes on the waters of New York Harbor.

Yet Quigley's life soon began spiraling downward. By the mid-1870s, he had lost his home, perhaps because the bank called in his mortgage after the Panic of 1873. The death in 1874 of his wife, Catherine, at age thirty-five, must have been a terrible blow as well, though his eldest child, fourteen-year-old Mary Ellen, took over housekeeping duties and cared for her two younger brothers.

At this point Michael, always prone to heavy drinking, became a true alcoholic. Even Quigley's erstwhile political allies could no longer tolerate his increasingly frequent drunken sprees, with the *Times* complaining in 1877 that Quigley had in recent years been "charged with stabbing, assaults with blunt weapons," gouging the eyes of his "adversaries, and even with mayhem, but has escaped proper punishment" due to his political influence.

By 1880, Quigley's seventeen-year-old son, William, was helping to operate the boating station and soon he had to take it over
completely because his father became incapacitated by his alcoholism and the health problems it caused. When Michael died at age
forty-nine in 1883, the press tactfully ascribed his death to consumption, but the coroner, uninhibited by any need for decorum,
pronounced the cause as "cirrhosis of liver & kidneys."

Some Famine immigrants had to win elections to secure civil service jobs. Patrick Drury, for example, immigrated in 1851 and
worked for more than a quarter century as a shoemaker in New
York City, Westchester, and on the outskirts of Brooklyn before
securing the Democratic nomination there for one of five positions
as constable, which in his locale was a court officer who carried out
judges' bench warrants. He held that position for a dozen years,
until his death in 1892.

Occasionally, Famine immigrants won fairly prestigious government offices via election. One was James M. Brann, who emigrated from County Cork at age eighteen in 1850 and quickly found
work as the sexton of St. Peter's Church in Jersey City. A few years
later, when the church opened the first Catholic school in Hudson
County, Brann became a teacher there and soon thereafter its vice
principal. His younger brother Henry, who attended the school,
became a priest. James married Sarah McEvoy in 1858 and left
teaching for a higher-paying job at the McEvoy wholesale produce
firm, which sent Brann into the New Jersey countryside to negotiate
the purchase of grains and vegetables. Brann eventually started his
own wholesale produce business and traveled "in nearly all the
Western States...and Canada" buying potatoes, which he sold to
Manhattan retailers in New York's Washington Market.

Brann had trouble paying his creditors after the Panic of 1873
turned into a depression, so in 1874 he sold his produce business

and sought the Democratic nomination for Hudson County clerk. This might seem like a step down, but serving as county clerk was a position of prestige that paid well and that, in Hudson County, offered opportunities to supplement one's salary with bribes and kickbacks. Brann had spent the past several years laying the groundwork for his run by ingratiating himself with voters at Jersey City's Democratic clubs. His family's prominence in Jersey City's Catholic community also helped his cause, noted the *New York Herald*. Its reporter asserted that Brann "wielded more influence among his Countrymen in Hudson County than any other man."

Brann won the post and served six years in office, but not without controversy. In part this was because while Brann may have been influential, he was not very likable. Brann was argumentative and litigious, nursed grudges for years, and conveniently took to his sickbed rather than face problems or creditors. After instituting more than a dozen libel suits against his political enemies, Brann himself was sued in 1877 for libeling a Democratic rival and escaped punishment only when, at the conclusion of the trial as conviction seemed certain, his brother the priest came forward and dramatically declared himself to be the actual author of the libelous broadside. The *Herald* called it "the most remarkable case ever tried in the Hudson County courts."

A year later, while still serving as county clerk, Brann disappeared. Rumors swirled that he had "misappropriated" county funds and checked himself into "a lunatic asylum" in Manhattan to avoid punishment. Those rumors turned out to be true, and Brann only resurfaced two months later, by which point his allies had somehow managed to repay the missing funds. Yet it was hardly a surprise that voters did not reelect Brann when his term expired. Brann tried to return to the produce business, but his partners accused him of malfeasance there as well, so he left that trade and held a variety of clerkships in the Hudson County agencies that handled lucrative public works contracts until he retired in 1895 after severely injuring himself in a fall from a trolley.

Like Brann, James Buckley held both appointive and elective civil service positions. Born in the town of Kanturk in County Cork, Buckley emigrated in the early spring of 1851, just shy of his fourteenth birthday, with his siblings Timothy Buckley and Mary Buckley Twomey as well as her two children. Mary's husband, Edward, had preceded them to America and found work as a porter on the Brooklyn waterfront. By his late teens, James was working as a porter there too. James also became "an earnest worker in the Democratic ranks," according to a Brooklyn newspaper, joining a Democratic club, becoming a member of a volunteer fire company affiliated with the party, and working at election time for Democratic candidates.

In 1860, that activism helped the twenty-three-year-old Buckley land a job as the clerk of Kings County's First District Court. His boss was not a judge but a justice of the peace. In Brooklyn, this was only a quasi-judicial position; legal training was not a prerequisite even though the justices (as they were known) held legal hearings and disposed of simple matters like misdemeanors so that judges with legal training could focus on trials and more serious cases. After four years as clerk to one of Brooklyn's two justices of the peace, Buckley was selected by Democrats as their nominee for the other justice-of-the-peace position and he won election to a four-year term by a comfortable margin.

Justice Buckley's first term in office concluded without incident, but things began to change after he won reelection in 1868. One of his duties was to count the votes in his district when Brooklyn held elections. In response to complaints of electoral fraud lodged by Republicans in 1869, the Kings County district attorney indicted Buckley for not tabulating the ballots "in the presence of the citizens" as required by law. Buckley pled guilty, claiming he had done so out of convenience rather than to perpetrate fraud, but a judge nonetheless sentenced him to ten days in jail.

Buckley's legal troubles did not abate after his short stint behind bars. Lawyers who appeared before the justice had complained for some time that Buckley was often too inebriated to properly carry out his duties. His debility became so severe that in October 1872, a Brooklyn grand jury indicted him for "being in a gross state of intoxication while upon the bench" and for dereliction of his duties. Buckley's drinking apparently took a toll on his health as well. Or perhaps his erratic behavior resulted from a cause other than alcohol. Buckley took to bed after his indictment, claiming he was not feeling well, and three days later the thirty-five-year-old passed away. The coroner ascribed his death to "congestion of [the] brain."

Buckley's thirty-year-old widow, Mary McCauley Buckley, initially tried to support herself and her two surviving young daughters selling shoes, but Brooklyn's Democratic solons eventually gave her a more reliable income with a civil service job of her own. Mary was made matron of the women's ward of the Kings County Jail, a position that put her in charge of both the female prisoners and the kitchen staff that fed them. The job also came with a free apartment inside the detention center. When Republicans in the mid-1880s briefly took over the county government, they tried to remove Buckley, charging that she allowed rampant drunkenness among her female kitchen employees. But Buckley managed to retain her position until at least 1899, though by 1905 she had been demoted to a job as a cleaner. She accepted that post, however, because it still provided free housing for her and her orphaned grandchild, Mary Meade, whose mother, Julia, had succumbed to breast cancer. Mary Buckley died of acute bronchitis in 1907, at about age sixty-five, while still working at the jail.

———

For the majority of Famine immigrants, who did not have enough education to become a justice of the peace or a county clerk, the most sought-after civil service position was a place in the police department. The Irish found police work enticing for many reasons. After centuries of being denied positions of authority in Ireland, Irish Catholic immigrants found it especially gratifying to be entrusted with policing their adopted homeland. Furthermore, police work paid better than unskilled work and almost every kind of artisanal labor, and the income was far steadier too. Unlike manual workers, who regularly went weeks and sometimes even months without work (especially in the winter), the New York City policeman collected the same pay envelope (about twelve dollars per week in the mid-1850s) every week of the year, come rain or shine, heat or cold, boom or bust. That income reliability paid significant dividends when it came to savings. The average policeman saved more in his Emigrant Savings Bank account than not only the average day laborer, carpenter, porter, and mason, but also the average clerk, peddler, and grocer. Only immigrant doctors, lawyers, and saloonkeepers saved more. Furthermore, beginning after the Civil War, New York City policemen received a pension after twenty years of service — a measure of social security that Famine immigrants found fantastical given their near-death experiences in Ireland just a few years earlier.

Given the potential financial rewards of serving as a police officer, competition for the positions was fierce. There were no prerequisites for the job as there are today — no physical or mental tests to pass and no educational requirements. The trait that most successful police aspirants had in common was not toughness or fearlessness but political connections. These could be made working for the party at election time and augmented by currying favor with an influential neighborhood saloonkeeper. Marrying the barkeep's sister or daughter improved one's odds even more. And if a policeman's patron had a falling-out with the alderman or some other ward heeler, then the patrolman needed to start looking for a new job, no matter how talented an officer he might be.

Irish immigrants from almost every occupational background became policemen. Among the Emigrant Savings Bank customers who snagged a position on the police force were bartenders, chair makers, clerks, goat skinners, grocers, gunsmiths, iron molders, laborers, machinists, marble cutters, porters, and shoemakers. Even the occasional saloonkeeper gave up his place behind the bar for a patrolman's beat. One was Felix Hayes from Kerry, who lived across from Michael Quigley on State Street when he became a policeman in 1861. Eighteen years later, the *Times* lambasted Hayes for his "stupidity" in carelessly handling a prisoner in court. But Felix must have had a powerful patron in City Hall. He remained on the force for twenty-five years, long enough to collect an annual pension of $600 (half his final salary) from the date of his retirement in 1886 until his death at age sixty-two in 1893.

It was much more common for blue-collar workers to become policemen. Patrick Crinnion, for example, emigrated from Louth in 1857 at age twenty-three and immediately found work as a machinist, first at the Globe Iron Works in the Tenderloin district on West Thirty-Fourth Street and later for the Hudson River Railroad in the same locale. Crinnion "was looked upon as a good machinist," noted the *Herald*, "able to make good pay, but the life of a policeman, with its constant promise of promotion, looked tempting." So Crinnion rallied his politically connected friends, and they managed to get him appointed to the force in 1870 at the standard salary of $1,200 per year. Yet Crinnion found that those expected promotions were harder to come by than he had imagined. "Paddy the Horse" would patrol the same beat—Thirty-Eighth Street from Fourth to Seventh Avenues—for more than a quarter century. He retired at age sixty-five after twenty-nine years on the force, never having received a single promotion. But he enjoyed his well-earned $600-per-year pension until he passed away from heart disease in 1907.

Snaring the promotions that eluded Crinnion required a combination of leadership skills, tact, and political clout that most men lacked. John Mara, however, had all three. Born in rural County Limerick, Mara came to America at age twenty in 1848 and initially settled in Harrisburg, Pennsylvania. Apparently unhappy with his employment options there, in 1850 Mara joined the army and was sent to Fort Columbus on Governors Island in New York Harbor. In order to rise through the ranks more quickly, Mara quit the "regular" army when the Civil War broke out so he could enlist as an officer in one of the city's volunteer regiments, serving on the front lines in Virginia for almost two years, including in McClellan's Peninsula campaign with Meagher, O'Meagher, Cavanagh, and Carr, before returning to New York late in 1862 to become the captain of a unit of "veteran volunteers," injured soldiers who had recovered enough to continue their service as a home guard protecting the city from potential rearguard actions. That year Mara also married Rose McMahon and they had six children in quick succession, although only three of them survived to adulthood.

Immediately after the war, Mara became a policeman in Brooklyn. He certainly looked the part: at six feet tall, the hazel-eyed, sandy-haired Irishman had a military bearing and towered over most other New Yorkers. Unlike Hayes and Crinnion, Mara was also perceived to have leadership potential. After fifteen years as a patrolman, Mara was promoted to roundsman (now equivalent to a sergeant), and four years later, he became a sergeant (equal now to a lieutenant). Those promotions reflected the respect Mara commanded from his subordinates. "Mara is a big, powerful, close-mouthed fellow," reported the *Brooklyn Times*, and "has the general reputation of having always treated the policemen under him like white men."* Mara made enough money as a sergeant to be able to buy, in 1890, a modest three-story brownstone with a pretty bay

---

* Even forty years after the end of slavery, bigotry and discrimination against African Americans was so endemic all over America, including in New York, that the phrase "treated like a white man" was shorthand for being treated with respect, dignity, and fairness.

window at 620 Macon Street in the Brownsville neighborhood. Mara paid $6,800 (equal to about $225,000 today) for the house, which is still standing. He put down $2,800 in cash and secured the rest through a mortgage.

That Mara was a Republican in heavily Democratic Brooklyn might have prevented him from climbing higher in the ranks, but by the end of his career Mara benefited from the fact that his godson and cousin, John F. Carroll, had become the right-hand man of New York Democratic Party chieftain Richard Croker (himself an Irish immigrant who had worked as a machinist alongside Crinnion before gaining renown, like Quigley, for his political pugilism and moving on to a career in politics). As a result, Mara was promoted to captain at age seventy-one in 1900. He remained on the force three more years before retiring, and passed away at age seventy-nine in 1908.

John Mara in 1900, when he was promoted to captain in the police department.

John Mara.

One Famine migrant who joined New York's lower white-collar ranks probably touched the lives of more Irish immigrants—the lives of more immigrants from all over the world, in fact—than any individual in nineteenth-century America. His name was Hubert D. Glynn.

Born to a family of some means in County Galway, Glynn enrolled in college early in the Famine years "with the view of his studying for the Catholic priesthood." Yet feeling ambivalent about committing to that vocation, Glynn in 1851 decided to leave Ireland and start a new life in New York. In Manhattan, he was drawn to a vacant clerkship with the New York Commissioners of Emigration, a state entity that oversaw all regulation of immigration to New York before the federal government took over that responsibility in the 1890s. From their office in Ward Five, the commissioners ran a lodging house for indigent newcomers and a "labor exchange" that connected immigrants with employers. Many Irish immigrants in this era did not speak English, and the commissioners sought a clerk "as their special Irish supervisor" who could assist Irish speakers visiting the labor bureau and also aid with the commissioners' voluminous correspondence and recordkeeping. Glynn, with his impressive educational credentials and fluency in Irish, landed the job.

When Glynn had arrived in New York, there was no single place where immigrants landed. A doctor was ferried out on a pilot boat to meet each ship in the Narrows (the channel between Staten Island and Brooklyn that ships crossing the Atlantic traversed to reach New York Harbor) to check immigrants for contagious diseases. The pilot boat brought those thought to be infectious to the Quarantine Hospital on Staten Island to recover. The rest of the passengers continued to any one of dozens of Manhattan piers on either the East or Hudson River waterfront. The main problem with this system, as far as the Commissioners of Emigration were concerned, was that it left the newcomers unprotected from the hordes of con men and thieves, known collectively as immigrant "runners," who awaited each ship. Seeking to protect the immigrants from the runners, the commissioners decided a few years after Glynn's arrival to create a central location where all immigrants would step ashore, so that their entry into the United States could be supervised by agents employed by the commissioners (who could not afford to place personnel at every pier in Manhattan).

The spot the commissioners chose for their "Emigrant Landing Depot" was Castle Garden, a huge theater-in-the-round built atop the ruins of Castle Clinton, which sat on a man-made island just off the southwest tip of Manhattan and was connected to the mainland at this time via a footbridge. There the commission would sell the immigrants food as well as train and boat tickets, exchange their foreign currency, and help them locate temporary lodging before the runners could fleece them. The commissioners also moved their labor exchange to Castle Garden so immigrants might find work or at least know the going rate for labor before being duped by unscrupulous employers. Finally, to provide data that might benefit them in their role as regulators of immigration, the commissioners would station clerks at Castle Garden to record the name, age, birthplace, and occupation of each immigrant, how much money they brought with them, and where in the United States they intended to settle.

One might wonder why the commissioners collected such information, given that federal law required ship captains to convey to port officials a manifest containing the name, age, birthplace, occupation, and destination of each passenger they carried to America. These ship manifests, however, typically compiled by a harried first mate, were notoriously skimpy on details. Often name and age were the only things written down. Part of the reason the commissioners wanted its clerks to interview the head of each immigrant family was to collect a more accurate accounting of the immigrants. Furthermore, the ship manifests were the property of the U.S. secretary of state, and custom house officials quickly forwarded these documents to Washington. Only by compiling their own immigration data would the state's commissioners be able to have a record they could rely on and have at hand for future use.

The commissioners decided to put Glynn in charge of this huge information-gathering operation. Thus, when Castle Garden began processing immigrants in 1855, the *Irish-American* noted proudly, it was one of their own, "Hubert D. Glynn, [who] opened its gates to the first immigrants."

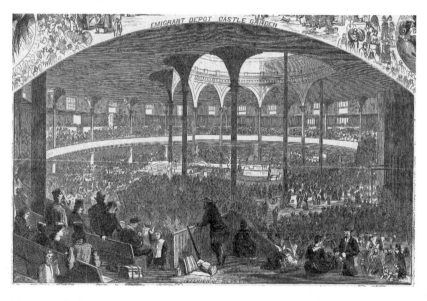

This was the scene on most days in Castle Garden, where Hubert D. Glynn supervised the clerks who recorded the names, occupations, and destinations of hundreds of thousands of immigrants each year.

Glynn must have enjoyed his work, because he held his position overseeing the compilation and archiving of Castle Garden immigration records for more than thirty years. He was a "genial" presence at the facility, noted one press account, and frequently helped indigent newcomers with money from his own "not over-inflated pocketbook, and many a heart warms with the memory of his kind deeds." In truth, Glynn was financially secure. When his wife,

Emilie, died in 1867, leaving him with four children aged six to twelve to care for, he could afford to hire a live-in housekeeper rather than remarry. But like so many Famine immigrants, Glynn lived unpretentiously and a few years after Emilie died, he bought his family a home in New Lots, a neighborhood that was then on the outskirts of southeast Brooklyn.

In July 1876, almost a decade after his wife died, Glynn suffered a different kind of heartache when a fire burned Castle Garden to the ground, destroying nearly all his previous twenty years' work. A few immigrant ledgers that happened to be off-site that day survived, and the process of compiling the record of each immigrant to land in New York resumed the following morning with the latest shiploads of arrivals (processed in temporary quarters down the street from the charred ruins of Castle Garden). Henceforth New York's immigration registers would be stored for safekeeping in fireproof vaults in Albany. All those records—the volumes that had escaped the flames in 1876 and those compiled thereafter—were transferred to Ellis Island at the insistence of federal authorities when that new immigration station opened on New Year's Day 1892. Yet every single one of *those* precious volumes was destroyed when the original Ellis Island immigrant reception facility—made entirely of Georgia pine—burned to the ground in 1897.

Glynn did not live to see that second calamity, having passed away in 1894 at age seventy-five. He had worked at Castle Garden until about age seventy and in his thirty-five years in charge of recordkeeping at Castle Garden had supervised the arrival of more than five million immigrants. While the Great Famine had ended by the time Castle Garden opened, the refugees who fled that catastrophe paid for the emigrations of hundreds of thousands of their kin in the subsequent decades, especially when another famine devastated Ireland in 1879. Tens of millions of Americans—including many, many Irish Americans—would know a lot more about their immigrant ancestors had Glynn's life's work survived.

CHAPTER SEVEN

"Getting On Very Well"

Business Owners

For every Irish-born clerk like Hubert Glynn who remained in that occupation for his entire American career, there was another who ended his working days running his own business. And there were even more Famine immigrants who ascended to the ranks of business ownership from much further down the socioeconomic ladder.

But no matter where one started, there were certain traits that helped these immigrants succeed in business. Arriving in New York with significant savings was the surest route to becoming an entrepreneur. Assistance from American kinsmen who already ran a commercial enterprise could also provide the guidance needed to establish a retail business. Even if an immigrant could not fall back on such help, a knack for negotiation, the capacity for shameless self-promotion (think George P. Fox), or a highly developed appetite for risk-taking might provide a springboard to success.

This last trait explains the accomplishments of Andrew Kerwin, who arrived in New York in 1847 at age fourteen with his mother, Elizabeth, and his two younger brothers. His father, John, had come to America the year before and found work as a plasterer, a trade he had probably learned in Ireland. Soon Andrew and his brothers, perhaps trained by their dad, became plasterers too.

Andrew's father and siblings continued to do plaster work, but Andrew had bigger ambitions. By 1860, he described himself as a "master mason," meaning that he bid on contracts to do the stone- and plasterwork on newly built structures, paid and supervised journeymen who did the work, and pocketed the difference. This was a profitable enterprise, especially for someone like Andrew with a winning personality and a reputation for reliability and good work. Still, Andrew was not satisfied. Why, he must have wondered, could he not reap the seemingly huge profits made by his customers, the builders? They bought cheap empty lots, hired Irish immigrants to construct tenements or town houses on the properties, and then sold them at big markups to upwardly mobile New Yorkers. Soon after the Civil War, Andrew became a builder himself.

Yet builders did their work primarily with borrowed money. If a sudden economic panic struck, a builder could be saddled with huge losses if his investments in land and materials did not begin producing income quickly enough to make the interest payments on his loans. Kerwin apparently suffered this fate during the depression that began in 1873 and lasted for the next half decade. His creditors began to hound him in the summer of 1876, and in 1878 Kerwin declared bankruptcy. His debts were staggering. He owed nearly $600,000 to the Goelet family (one of the richest in New York), $300,000 to the Germania Life Insurance Company, $80,000 to the city's Dutch Reformed Church, $40,000 to the New York Bank for Savings, and nearly $1 million more to sixty other creditors. His debt was the equivalent of about $67 million today.

Yet Kerwin somehow survived this liquidity crisis. Perhaps he used the threat of default to renegotiate the terms of his loans. In any case, before long his business was thriving again. By 1884, the credit rating agency Dun & Company was describing Kerwin as "a successful operator" who had "made considerable money." That was in part because he had made a shrewd judgment about the future of high-end New York City housing, focusing his building in increasingly desirable parts of the Upper East Side around Park and Madison Avenues, near Central Park.

A BARGAIN—SIX NEW FOUR STORY PRIVATE Dwellings, differing in design and finish; would cost $3,500 each to duplicate more than asking; best location in city, 92d st., between Madison and Park avs.; open every day. Builder, Andrew J. Kerwin.

An advertisement Andrew Kerwin placed in the *New York Herald* in 1886 for homes he had built on Manhattan's Upper East Side.

In another instance, Kerwin tried to turn an undesirable neighborhood into a more attractive one. Unlike today, when buyers pay a premium for river views, in the late nineteenth century well-to-do New Yorkers did not want to live near the waterfront, which was full of noxious industries as well as bars and brothels catering to sailors and dockworkers. Kerwin decided that with the right branding, he could make the riverfront attractive to affluent Manhattanites. Along with Anson Phelps Stokes and several other developers, Kerwin bought up land on Avenue A along the East River from East Fiftieth to East Fifty-Ninth Street and got the city to give the street a swankier name, Sutton Place. He also created a new street, right on the water's edge, that he dubbed Riverview Terrace. Prosperous New Yorkers did not initially gravitate to the development, so Kerwin moved into 1 Riverview Terrace himself. Eighty years later, an architecture critic called Kerwin's home there "the most perfect small house in the city." By that point, the neighborhood had acquired the cachet Kerwin had envisioned and socialites flocked to the area. Jack L. Warner, cofounder of the movie studio that bears his name, made 1 Riverview Terrace his New York home in the decades after World War II, and oil magnate Clint Murchison Jr. purchased it in 1972, a few years after he founded the Dallas Cowboys football team. Kerwin, who passed away at age sixty-eight in 1902, may not have lived to see the day when Sutton Place became one of New York's most fashionable

addresses, but he died a wealthy man and his family remained in the
real estate business well into the twentieth century.

———

Thousands of Famine immigrants like Andrew Kerwin dreamed of
leaving behind the drudgery of manual labor for the prestige and
higher income that they associated with owning their own businesses. With a shop of one's own, an Irish immigrant did not have
to worry about seasonal unemployment, layoffs due to sudden
downturns in the economy, being fired on a whim by an obnoxious
boss, or being groped by a lascivious employer. Street peddling was
one means of establishing economic independence, but those yearning for the greatest financial security would have aspired to own
and operate a brick-and-mortar enterprise.

The proportion of Famine immigrants who worked as business
owners varied over time. Few started businesses immediately after
arriving in America—only three or four out of every hundred adult
male Famine immigrants managed to open one within a year of
immigrating. But 29 percent of those who can be tracked ten years or
more finished their careers as business owners, and many others ran
a retail enterprise for at least a while before ending their lives in
another line of work. So, while the dream of presiding over the bar at
the corner tavern and enjoying the status and income that came with
it may have been out of reach for most, business ownership itself was
not a farfetched goal. The dream alone was enough to inspire many
immigrants to scrimp and save in the hopes that they might one day
join the ranks of New York's Irish business owners.

There were dozens of commercial ventures an immigrant might
start, ranging from apothecaries and auction houses to watch and
wine shops. Yet slightly more than half of all male Famine-era Irish
immigrants who became business owners in New York worked in
just two fields—liquor and food sales. (Liquor dealers played such
an oversized role in the Irish business community that they will be

233

treated separately in the next chapter.) The junk trade was the third most popular business for men (about one in ten Famine Irish business owners operated a junk shop), and running a boardinghouse ranked fourth. "Dry goods" broadly defined (draperies, cloth, thread, clothing, and footwear) rounded out the top five business pursuits. Included in this category are wholesalers and retailers of hats, "fancy goods" (bras, corsets, hosiery, scarves, and hair ornamentation), and "gentleman's furnishings" (including "underdrawers" and undershirts, neckties, gloves, and men's scarves).

Irishwomen became business owners too — one out of every six Famine immigrants who identified themselves to census takers as operators of a business was a woman. But this figure actually underestimates the number of women who ran businesses. It was somewhat embarrassing for immigrants to admit that the "man of the house" could not support his family on his own, so Irish immigrant women often told census takers and directory compilers that they were homemakers even when they were actually the primary proprietors of a business. Businesswomen, however, concentrated in different fields from men. They were much less likely than men to sell alcohol and much more likely to run boardinghouses and "fancy goods" shops. When women ran retail enterprises typically associated with men, they usually did so after a husband who had been the primary operator of the business had passed away. Still, there were Irish-born women managing virtually every kind of New York retail business. The thousands of enterprises run by New York's Famine Irish immigrants, men and women alike, soon became an integral part of the city's economic dynamism and eventually, as those Irish immigrants spread out across the United States, a key contributor to the unparalleled prosperity of the nation as a whole.

Most Famine immigrants who would eventually become business owners did not begin their new lives in America as retailers. They worked at lowlier vocations first, usually to earn enough money to start a business, but in some cases to learn the contours of the New York retail landscape before investing their precious savings in a business venture. It is impossible to identify what jobs every Emigrant Bank customer had in America before they started businesses, but it is known that at least three-quarters of the bank's male customers in the 1850s who eventually became business owners began on some lower level of New York's occupational hierarchy.

Occupational Origins of Male Famine Immigrants Who Ended Their Careers as Business Owners

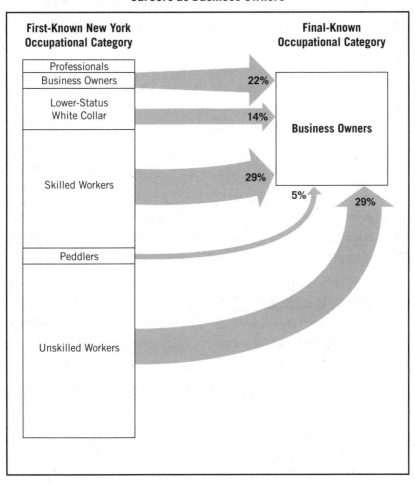

Of the New York Famine immigrants who ended their lives as business owners, 29 percent started out on the very bottom rung of the American socioeconomic ladder as laborers, porters, and the like. For most of the unskilled who ultimately ran businesses, there was no obvious link between their initial occupation in New York and the business they eventually operated. But in some cases, even a job requiring little or no training could prepare an immigrant to make the leap from wage worker to entrepreneur. Bernard Mulgrew, for instance, who arrived in New York at age fifty-three from County Tyrone, toiled as a waiter for several years before opening his own restaurant on Fourth Avenue in Ward Fifteen. Robert Yates from the town of Monaghan also worked his way up from waiter to restaurateur.

Another Famine immigrant whose early unskilled work experience prepared him to make the leap to business ownership was Edmund Butler from tiny Rathnagard (pop. 89) in hilly north central Cork. He arrived in New York at age twenty-four in May 1850 with his mother and two brothers, settled in Ward One at the southern tip of Manhattan, and found work as a day laborer. Living so close to the city's busiest piers, Butler would have sometimes taken jobs on the docks. As he hauled sacks, crates, and barrels on and off ships, Butler must have noticed that while in some months dock work was slow, in others the managers of the shipping lines were desperate to find enough longshoremen to offload and reload the vessels efficiently. He decided to become a stevedore — a waterfront labor contractor — striking agreements with shipping companies to supply labor on their docks at a certain price, hiring other Irish immigrants to do the work, and pocketing the difference. His company eventually became "one of the largest stevedoring firms in New York," noted a newspaper profile. It "employs over a hundred men, and does work for some of the heaviest shipping and warehousing concerns in New York and Brooklyn." Flush with success, in the mid-1860s Butler bought the gorgeous brick town house at

33 Willow Place on a leafy street in Brooklyn Heights, just two blocks from the waterfront, where he and his wife, Catherine, raised seven children. A decade later, he spent $40,000 on a country estate in Westchester County. The Brooklyn home, valued at $7,000 in 1870, is still standing, and today is worth about a thousand times what Butler paid for it.

Thomas Meagher (no relation to the general of the same name) also rose from an unskilled occupation to the ranks of the city's Irish American business community, but he had a much harder time making that leap than did Butler. Meagher was born in 1832 in County Tipperary in Thurlesbeg, which had a population of fewer than two hundred at the start of the Famine and only half that many by the time Meagher left Ireland in 1850. He arrived in New York that November, also settled at the southern tip of Manhattan, and began supporting himself as a porter. On New Year's Eve 1857, however, Meagher opened an Emigrant Savings Bank account and reported that he was now a "storekeeper," had married Kate Burke (born in the same place as Thomas), and already had one child.

Over the course of the ensuing decade, Meagher struggled to remain in business. In the late spring of 1860, he told the census enumerator that he was a porter, although a few months later he was again a storekeeper. He was still a retailer in mid-1861; then a porter in 1863; an "agent" in 1864 and 1865; and a cartman in 1866. Thomas and Kate's personal life was a struggle too. They had three children in quick succession in the late 1850s, but all three died before their tenth birthdays. Kate died at age thirty-four in 1869.

A year later, Thomas finally managed to achieve some semblance of stability for himself and his two surviving daughters, opening a grocery just north of the Battery in the tenement at 20 Greenwich Street, where the Meaghers had been living for the past fifteen years. At one point he transformed the space into a saloon, but two years later he reconverted it into a grocery, operating at that location until he died in 1882 — by which point, he had remarried (to another Kate), had more children, and moved his family to, of all places, a stately brick town house at 35 Willow Place in Brooklyn Heights, right next door to the Butlers. Meagher did not become nearly as wealthy as Edmund Butler, but when Meagher passed away at age fifty of paralysis and "softening of the brain" after a stroke, he left Kate and his four surviving children an estate worth about $6,500, far bigger than that of the typical Famine immigrant (and equivalent to about $200,000 today).

Another New York businessman who started off with very little, on the very bottom rung of the socioeconomic ladder, was Laurence J. Callanan. Callanan was born in Clonakilty, a market town of about four thousand people in County Cork, where his father was a successful grocer. As a teen, Callanan worked for the family business, albeit "under strict discipline and no favors." Such strict discipline, in fact, that after a fight with his father and the promise of a punishment when the seventeen-year-old returned from delivering goods to Cork, Laurence decided to run away. He used part of the proceeds from the transaction in Cork to buy himself a steerage ticket on a ship leaving imminently for America, mailed the rest of the money back to his father, and sailed for New York, arriving there on December 16, 1853.

In Manhattan, Callanan moved in with an aunt and took odd jobs over the winter until he managed to find steady work as a gardener in the spring. Figuring his retail experience ought to be worth something, Callanan inquired about positions as a grocer's clerk but discovered that there were so many young men in the city hoping to apprentice in that trade that it paid far less than gardening. Nonetheless, wanting to learn the American grocery business, Callanan eventually took a clerk's job with an Irish-born grocer in Brooklyn for just five dollars a month plus room and board. Hearing that experienced clerks earned more out west, Callanan sailed to New Orleans and worked there as a grocer's assistant for higher wages, but he disliked the South and in 1857 returned to New York, where he eventually secured a live-in clerkship in the wholesale grocery of another Irish immigrant, Peter Lynch, on Vesey Street in Ward Three (near where the World Trade Center would eventually stand).

When Callanan took the position with Lynch, four and a half years after arriving in America, the twenty-two-year-old had accumulated about $60, which he deposited at the Emigrant Savings Bank in March 1858. Determined to strike out on his own, Callanan began saving more diligently. By the end of the year, he had increased his balance to $150. That was all he needed, he later recalled, to open his own grocery, which he did in 1859 just a few blocks north of the Battery. Callanan enjoyed being his own boss, but business was slow at his shop on Rector Street, a commercial thoroughfare with few residents. Callanan was not losing money, but he was not making much either.

As a result, he was not displeased when Lynch visited his shop in 1862 with an offer. Lynch's recently deceased father-in-law had operated a large grocery on a densely populated block in Five Points. Would Callanan take over the shop and also the job of collecting the rents from the inhabitants of the property's two tenements? Callanan leaped at the chance. Six years later, still impressed with Callanan's drive and business savvy, Lynch asked Callanan to come back downtown and become his junior partner, which involved buying a share of Lynch's business. Callanan accepted that offer and moved his wife, Ellen (also from Clonakilty), and their first child into rooms above the wholesale emporium.

First with Lynch and his other partners, and then on his own after he bought their shares of the business over the next few decades, Callanan made "a fortune" in the wholesale grocery business, according to one trade magazine, in particular through importing Irish bacon and other "articles of food dear to the native born Irishman." His other most profitable offerings were French olive oil, Spanish altar wine, and his own "house blends" of coffee and tea, which were processed and repackaged at a plant he operated in New Jersey. Callanan succeeded in part because he was a cutthroat, litigious businessman who had no qualms backing out of handshake deals if he sensed that he could squeeze more profit out of a supplier or customer. Callanan invested those profits in rental properties—both residential and commercial—near Washington Square and in what are now the SoHo and Times Square neighborhoods. He was an avid sailor too, joining three yacht clubs and buying an expensive racing sloop.

Callanan successfully used his wealth to shape municipal policy, becoming, as the *New York Tribune* observed, "one of the most prominent and influential Irish-American Catholics in this city." Part of Callanan's renown resulted from his work as a political

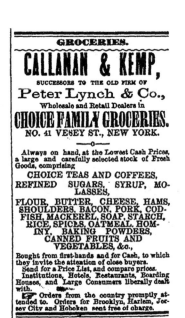

LAURENCE J. CALLANAN

An early ad for Callanan & Kemp, which ran soon after Laurence Callanan purchased the ownership stake of his mentor, Peter Lynch, alongside a photo of Callanan himself, taken circa 1902, when he was about sixty-six.

"reformer" leading the effort to create an alternative Democratic organization to Tammany Hall. But his most important public legacy may have been his role fomenting opposition to the city's plan, announced in 1891, to turn Battery Park into a train yard. "Mr. Callanan helped to work up such a sentiment against the plan," noted the *Times* years later, "that the park was saved."

Despite Callanan's wealth and prominence, his personal life was far from carefree. He and Ellen had eight children, but only one lived to adulthood. Three perished in 1873 in a twenty-three-day span from diphtheria, a bacterial infection that suffocates its victims by destroying their lung tissue and swelling their throats so much that the passage of air is nearly impossible. It must have been especially traumatic to watch helplessly as their children suffered such horrible deaths.

At the dawn of the twentieth century, as the center of the New York business world moved farther and farther uptown, Callanan stuck stubbornly to his lower Manhattan location, doubling down on his investment by purchasing the building next door and combining 41 and 43 Vesey into a huge, five-story wholesale showplace. That investment did not pay off, and by the early 1910s the business was losing the modern equivalent of a million dollars a year. Still, Callanan had plenty of money and real estate to pass on to his heirs when he died in 1913 at age seventy-seven.

Most others who climbed from the unskilled ranks to business ownership had much more modest success. William Cruise and his wife, Julia, both from King's County, left Ireland in about 1846 and settled in Liverpool, where William worked as a laborer and their first two children were born. In 1852, however, they immigrated to New York. William started out there as a day laborer, but by 1855 he was employed as a sugar baker, an employee of a sugar refinery who heated the juice extracted from sugarcane to create the refined sugar crystals that consumers preferred. In 1858, however, Cruise became a grocer, first in Ward Five and then in Ward Nine on Christopher Street near the Hudson River.

But this modest success apparently did not make Cruise a happy man. He was especially angry that the Civil War seemed likely to grant equal rights to African Americans and potentially legitimize interracial marriage, things that many New Yorkers — both native-born and immigrant — adamantly opposed. At the commencement in 1863 of the Draft Riots — the great uprising of New Yorkers against the Civil War draft, which lasted four days and resulted in more than one hundred deaths and many more injuries — Cruise led a gang to the Worth Street home of an interracial couple, William and Ann Derrickson. "He's the big n****r we want," cried Cruise. "We'll hang him to the lamp-post." When Cruise and his gang burst into the Derricksons' apartment, William had already escaped out the back window, thinking the rioters would spare his white wife and their eight-year-old son, Alfred. But Cruise and his accomplices viciously set upon the dark-skinned boy, beating him with clubs and cart rungs; Cruise himself hit Alfred with an axe. "For God's sake," screamed his mother, "kill me and save my boy." That's exactly what the rioters did. Since the jury did not know for sure who struck the fatal blow, Cruise was convicted only of assault with the intent to kill. For Derrickson's brutal murder, he was sentenced to just two years and four months at Sing Sing, the state prison forty miles north of New York City on the Hudson River.

Julia Cruise apparently could not keep the grocery afloat in her husband's absence and used up their savings supporting her family. When William was released from prison, the Cruises moved to Brooklyn and William became a day laborer once again. By 1874, however, he had rejoined the grocery trade, opening a shop facing the Brooklyn docks just west of the Navy Yard (in a neighborhood that was nameless back then, but is now known as Vinegar Hill). But there is no indication that it was a thriving enterprise, and the Cruises may have drunk away most of the profits. Julia and William both died of liver disease — the coroner specified cirrhosis in William's case — in 1878 and 1880, respectively.

Like onetime day laborers, tradesmen and peddlers also frequently became business owners. Artisans, of course, often started the kinds of businesses for which they had once worked as journeymen. Patrick Fitzpatrick from Mountmellick in Queen's County, for example, worked as a baker at the huge State Emigrant Refuge on Wards Island in his early years in New York but by 1880 ran a bakeshop. Blacksmith Patrick McCusker eventually owned a livery stable. Lamp maker Andrew Maloney ultimately operated a lamp shop, while carriage painter William Doherty became the owner of a carriage-making business.

It took Doherty decades to progress from journeyman carriage painter to business owner. Born in Coleraine at the northern tip of Ireland, as a young teen Doherty served an apprenticeship as a coach painter with his older sister's husband and then worked as a journeyman coach painter in England before immigrating to New York at age twenty-one in 1848. After his arrival, Doherty toiled for another two decades as a coach painter in New York before he bought a carriage-making business in Westchester Village, now the Throgs Neck neighborhood of the Bronx. He and his wife, Margaret,

WILLIAM DOHERTY,
Successor to J. Frost,
CARRIAGE MAKER,
Westchester. N. Y.

Carriages, Light Wagons, &c., Made, Repaired, and Painted in the Best Manner.
ALL ORDERS PROMPTLY ATTENDED TO.

An advertisement for William Doherty's carriage business from 1871, shortly after he purchased it.

became active members of the Episcopal Church there, and Doherty continued to operate the business until his death at age seventy-two in 1900.

For most artisans, however, there was no particular link between their original occupational training and their eventual business pursuit. Baker James Slattery became a contractor. Carriage trimmer Henry Hewson opened a fancy goods shop. Carpenter John Connelly became a grocer, as did type founder John Crimmins. Printer James Cleary became a boardinghouse operator and later an "innkeeper" in Queens. Tailor James McGreevy opened a photography studio.

The bulk of those who climbed the socioeconomic ladder to become business owners started out, like these folks, as blue-collar workers, but many immigrants who initially worked in New York as peddlers also made the transition to brick-and-mortar businesses. In fact, 30 percent of the peddlers tracked for ten years or more eventually operated storefront enterprises. Although it might seem intuitive for these business owners to concentrate on whichever wares they had sold during their peddling days, in fact they seem to have been guided by the market and by opportunity more than by their previous experience. Peddler Michael Murray from County Mayo went into the stone supply business. Fruit peddler Robert Thomas from Dingle opened a fancy goods shop. Book vendor Hugh Corcoran from Granard in County Longford became a tea merchant.

Peddlers were especially attracted to the grocery trade. Michael Doyne, for example, a native of Dublin, arrived in New York in November 1848 and by the summer of 1850 was peddling books as the agent of a publishing house. Four years later, he had opened a grocery in Brooklyn. By 1860, however, he had relocated his store to Morrisania, in the southwest corner of what is now the Bronx. Land was cheap there, and Doyne could afford to buy a $2,000 house in Morrisania while keeping more than $600 in the Emigrant

Savings Bank as an emergency fund. Morrisania real estate was a shrewd investment. A decade later, Doyne's two properties there were worth $12,000. Michael and his wives (first Ellen, later Mary) ran a food shop there until 1873, when Michael died at age fifty-nine.

Lower-status white-collar workers — clerks, agents, salesmen, and the like — also frequently rose to business ownership. About half the Famine immigrants who started out as clerks and could be tracked for at least ten years ended their careers as business proprietors. Some of these transitions were predictable. Drug clerk John Sidley from Waterford eventually opened his own drugstore. Grocer's clerks Peter Warren from County Roscommon and Peter Farrell from County Longford became grocers, while liquor store clerk Michael McAnnena from Tyrone managed by 1870 to start his own liquor shop. In most cases, however, clerks did not initially work in the same retail field that they eventually entered themselves.

Farrell is the rare Famine immigrant whose work history in America can be documented nearly from the day he landed in New York. He arrived in America on July 1, 1850, at about age twenty with his mother, Mary, and younger sister Rosanna. The Farrells clearly had more money than typical Irish immigrants, as they made the transatlantic journey in a second-class cabin rather than in steerage. Twenty-six days after Peter first set foot in America, a census taker found him living in the Irish neighborhood in Brooklyn just west of the Navy Yard and working there as a grocer's clerk. By 1853, when he opened an Emigrant Savings Bank account with an initial deposit of $74, Farrell was operating his own grocery in the same locale. It was around then that Farrell married Lucy Kiernan, who had emigrated from Longford as a child in about 1840.

Peter had a knack for business and soon decided to diversify his retail operations. In early 1864, as the Civil War convulsed the nation, he moved to a less crowded part of Brooklyn and, while continuing to operate the grocery, opened both a mortuary and a livery stable. The mortuary was the first in the neighborhood, now known as Boerum Hill, where Farrell soon became "widely and popularly known and highly respected." The funeral parlor thrived in part because Farrell had an "unfailing good nature and cheery disposition," reported the *Brooklyn Citizen* at the time of his death in 1894, by which point sons John, James, and Peter Jr. were running the family businesses due to their father's severe rheumatism. Six members of the Kings County Undertakers Association acted as pallbearers at Peter's funeral, "one of the largest seen in this city in years."

Like Peter Farrell, the Muldoon brothers came from a family with resources but apprenticed as clerks before risking their savings on a business of their own. Thomas, Peter, and Patrick Muldoon were teenagers when they arrived in New York in November 1852 with their widowed mother, Alice, and three other siblings. The family had been comfortable farmers in County Louth, but perhaps the death of Alice's husband prompted her to take her children to New York, where Alice's older brother Peter McLoughlin had settled a quarter century earlier. Peter loved New York. "This is the best country in the World," he had written to his brother in Ireland in 1829. "There is no want[;] there is room and a living for all but you may depend they must Work for it." Peter McLoughlin definitely worked for it. By 1834 he had become a liquor dealer in Five Points at 472 Pearl Street. His business thrived, and he shrewdly invested his profits in real estate in the growing Irish enclaves in Wards Four, where he lived, and Six, where he did business.

It is not clear to what extent Peter McLoughlin helped his sister and her children when they decided to move to New York in 1852. Alice Muldoon, along with four of her sons and two of her daughters, made the voyage in steerage, even though Peter could have easily afforded to send them cabin tickets. And he did not immediately set them up in business, though perhaps that was because Alice's boys were so young. In 1855, seventeen-year-old Patrick was working as a clerk and boarding with his employer in affluent Ward Nine. Nineteen-year-old Peter toiled there as a waiter and he too boarded where he worked. Thomas was a clerk in Ward Nine as well, where Alice and her daughters also lived. By then Peter McLoughlin had passed away, but the Muldoon brothers probably got additional advice from their cousin John McLoughlin (son of another of Alice's brothers), who had come to America in 1849 at age nineteen and was running a New York grocery by 1855. A year later, the three Muldoon brothers founded their own grocery business on Pearl Street, just four doors down from where their uncle had once operated his saloon. In 1858, they opened a second location (that also sold wholesale) at 409 Grand Street in Ward Thirteen.

The Muldoons appeared to be shrewd entrepreneurs. Dun & Company called Thomas "an honest industrious business man of good character and habits" and reported that he had "a good bank A/C." Indeed, the three brothers accumulated $4,000 in the Emigrant Bank by 1860.

But prosperity did not guarantee longevity, for either New York's Famine immigrants or the businesses they started. Peter Muldoon died in 1868 at age thirty-two. Thomas passed away five years later at age thirty-nine, a few years after he and Patrick had dissolved their partnership and decided to operate independently. Patrick, however, didn't fare well on his own. His "habits are not the best," Dun & Company reported in 1869, "and we learn that he is now in some difficulty—having been sued & levied upon by the sheriff." He remained in the grocery business until about 1874, but then left it to run a cigar shop on Chatham Street around the corner from Pearl. But according to the Dun investigators, that store "failed" in 1878 and Patrick left town, "debts unpaid. There are several judgments vs. him." It's not clear what became of Patrick. His cousin John McLoughlin, meanwhile, moved to the Park Slope neighborhood of Brooklyn and ran a grocery there at 556

Sixth Avenue until his retirement. That small frame building is still standing, and as of 2023 a grocery was still operating in the same space.

While most Famine immigrants who ended their lives as business owners began their American careers on a lower rung of the socioeconomic ladder, some were able to immediately start businesses upon arrival in New York. Most of these immigrants had operated successful retail establishments in Ireland and were reentering those same lines of work in Manhattan. Constantine Duffy, for example, arrived in New York in 1849 from the small town of Ballybay in County Monaghan, where he ran a shop (probably a grocery) with his eldest son, Patrick, who had made the trip to America a year before his parents and six siblings. They quickly opened a grocery together on Ninth Avenue. Patrick soon branched out on his own and started a liquor store on East Thirty-Fifth Street, while Constantine remained a grocer on the West Side and obsessively plowed his profits into East Harlem real estate. His holdings became so vast that he eventually quit the grocery business in order to devote his full attention to the construction of tenements and brownstones on his dozens of lots, which were eventually worth hundreds of thousands of dollars. Patrick died before his father, but after Constantine passed away intestate in 1882, his surviving children fought bitterly for many years over his huge estate.

Eugene McSwyny, born in 1799 thirty miles northwest of Cork city in the market town of Millstreet, also came to America with money and business experience but, unlike the Duffys, he struggled. A "master draper" by trade, Eugene and his wife, Julia, could afford second-class fares on the "poop deck" when they emigrated in the summer of 1850, which kept them out of steerage and also guaranteed they would not have to share a bed with strangers. And because the McSwynys were traveling with their six children, aged four to twenty, they probably had an entire second-class cabin to themselves.

According to Dun & Company, McSwyny brought several hundred pounds sterling with him when he emigrated and used that cash to quickly set up "McSwyny & Co., Drygoods," in a choice corner storefront on Sixth Avenue and Fourteenth Street, selling fabric, thread, linens, and draperies. But McSwyny, wrote a Dun agent, "not much acquainted with the manner of doing business in this country," did not find that location satisfactory. He moved his operation to Third Avenue and Twenty-First Street, but still unhappy, he relocated to a much cheaper storefront in Williamsburg, Brooklyn. There, Dun & Company reported, he appeared "to be getting on very well," paying just $50 a month for rent while making $50 per day in sales.

Nonetheless, McSwyny did not thrive. He was perennially dissatisfied and continued to move the business constantly—sometimes more than once a year—eventually transferring it back to Manhattan. This lack of stability indicated to Dun & Company that McSwyny was "neither responsible nor reliable." Yet he did not go out of business either. In 1870, a year before McSwyny retired, he reported a net worth of $1,000, well above average for a Famine immigrant, but no more than he had brought with him from Cork twenty years earlier. Nor did he get much time to enjoy his retirement. On December 26, 1872, after what the *Tribune* called "the severest snow-storm in years," McSwyny went outside, slipped and fell on some ice, and dislocated his hip. He was brought to St. Vincent's Hospital, but complications set in, and he died there, at age seventy-three, two weeks later.

———

Many aspiring entrepreneurs could not afford the start-up costs for a saloon, grocery, or dry goods business, and this explains why the junk trade was the third most-popular business among Famine immigrants. Aspiring junk dealers did need some capital to buy their initial stock of goods, but they could also gather their wares themselves by scavenging around town on foot or by boat along the shoreline. In fact, boatmen were a prime source of a junk dealer's stock, finding scrap metal, old rope, bottles, and other refuse along the waterfront that might make both the waterman and the junk dealer some money. Children could also scavenge around town for items for their parents' junk shops. To discourage theft, the law forbid junk dealers from buying or selling precious metals. They could not even legally sell tools or furniture "in a sound, unbroken or undamaged condition." Immigrants also needed money to rent a retail space in which to open a junk shop, but in a pinch the novice junk trader might display his merchandise in his tenement yard.

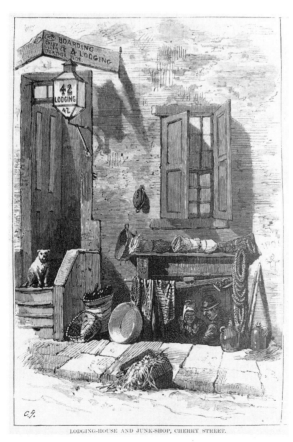

LODGING-HOUSE AND JUNK-SHOP, CHERRY STREET.

Michael Carroll's basement junk shop in Ward Four on Cherry Street displayed typical merchandise: old rope, used bottles, and discarded baskets. Valuable or pilfered goods would have been kept inside.

Some junk dealers thrived. Twenty-four-year-old Bernard Sheridan from County Fermanagh, for example, arrived in New York in 1852, settled in the northwest corner of the Five Points neighborhood, and took work as a day laborer. But around 1855, when he placed $60 into his new Emigrant Savings Bank account, he transitioned into junk dealing. Sheridan was apparently an adept businessman — by 1859 his bank balance had risen to $600. Soon thereafter he opened a Canal Street furniture store, which he ran until at least 1875.

Another junk dealer who eventually transitioned to a more profitable enterprise was Lawrence "Lanty" Ryan, who immigrated to New York as a teenager in 1854. Ryan tried to open a saloon on Baxter Street in Five Points around 1858, but when that business failed, he entered the junk trade, in which his father and brother were already engaged. By 1866 he had moved to Ward Seven and continued operations there as a junk dealer, but soon thereafter he became a "dealer in paper," buying used paper and rags from garbage scavengers that he then resold to paper manufacturers. Lanty prospered in this business until he retired around 1900 and lived, as he put it, on his "own income," probably the rents from the tenements in Ward Seven, Ward Nineteen, and the Bronx that he had purchased with his paper-business profits. He was living in the Bronx on the Grand Concourse with two spinster daughters when he died at age ninety-three in 1933.

Ryan and Sheridan were not exceptional in using the junk trade as a springboard to more lucrative businesses. Daniel and Susan Bradley from Letterkenny in County Donegal arrived in New York in 1849 with their two children, settled on the bend of Mulberry Street in Five Points, and by 1853 had opened a junk shop there. In 1858, Daniel attempted to move into the liquor business on Spring Street in Ward Fourteen, but quickly left that trade and attempted to sell stoves instead. That didn't pan out either, and soon he was back in the junk trade. Yet he did not give up his dreams of running a more lucrative establishment. In 1868, Bradley opened a livery stable in Five Points, and the next year moved it to Monroe Street in Ward Seven.

Bradley grew from a small-time livery operator to a horse-and-carriage mogul when he devised a way to guarantee steady and lucrative business for his coaches and drivers. In the 1880s, he began paying the managers of the Astor House, a posh Broadway hotel that was the haunt of rich tourists and Tammany Hall politicos, for the exclusive rights to supply the livery cabs that took the hotel's customers to their destinations around town. Bradley held that contract for a quarter century and eventually arranged similar deals with other hotels. He often dispatched the carriages himself from the front door of the Astor House, using his charm to ingratiate himself

The front of the Astor House on the west side of Broadway facing City Hall Park in 1867, a decade or so before Daniel Bradley secured the exclusive rights to supply livery cabs to its patrons.

with hotel regulars like Tammany chieftains William Tweed, John Kelly, and Richard Croker. In fact, Croker came to rely on Bradley for advice about Lower East Side politics. When Bradley died at age eighty-seven in 1912, the press called him "one of the oldest and best loved residents of the famous Seventh ward."

While many junk dealers succeeded handsomely, others found the trade difficult. Francis McMahon emigrated from County Monaghan in 1848 at about age twenty and by 1851 was working as a junk dealer in Five Points. Over the course of the next decade he moved his business constantly — to Ward Thirteen, Ward Seventeen, Ward Eighteen, and finally back to Ward Seventeen. Yet he was always just scraping by. After a decade in the junk trade, his net worth was only $100. Tim Slattery, who arrived in America from County Kerry in 1851, probably worked initially in New York as a day laborer but did business as a junk dealer in Brooklyn from at least 1857 to 1860. By the 1870s, however, he had given up the junk trade and was back at day labor. But failure as a junk dealer did not necessarily mean an immigrant was living hand to mouth. John Dennison tried and failed several times to establish himself as a junk dealer in Brooklyn, but nonetheless maintained a balance of $500 in his savings account throughout those unsuccessful efforts.

While some junk dealers struggled to remain in business, others had to fight to stay out of jail. Neighborhoods like Five Points and Corlears Hook were known for both their thieves and the fences who bought stolen merchandise, and junk dealers were infamous for trafficking in stolen property. Children, in particular, found that they could sell metal ripped from buildings, merchandise pilfered from wagons, or retail goods stolen from store displays to their neighborhood junk dealers. To try to prevent junk shops from fencing stolen goods, New York required junk dealers to post a $250 bond, which they would forfeit if they were convicted of buying purloined property. Nonetheless, many junk dealers trafficked in such items.

One was Five Points junk dealer James Boyce from County Donegal, who arrived in New York in 1852 at age twenty-three and by 1857 was a junk dealer with over $850 in savings, a windfall built in part on fencing stolen property. In 1865, a thirteen-year-old boy pilfered hundreds of spools of silk thread worth $1.25 each and sold them to Boyce for five to ten cents apiece, allowing the junkman to make a hefty profit when he resold them to unscrupulous retailers. Despite being arrested for this crime, Boyce avoided jail and stayed in the junk business until his death at age fifty-two in 1881.

Like junk shops, boardinghouses were another business with low start-up costs that appealed to many Famine immigrants. In Irish enclaves, a boarding "house" might be no more than a tenement apartment that the proprietors rented in the very same building in which they lived. Yet other boardinghouse keepers leased or purchased whole buildings in which to house their operations. In either case, the proprietors would need to outfit the rooms with beds, sheets and blankets, and perhaps a table and chairs. Then they sought customers, charging by the month, week, or even day. Those who also wanted to be fed (boarders) paid more than those who merely wanted a place to sleep (lodgers). Many boarders would leave their workplace at "dinner" time (what is now called lunchtime) to eat their midday meal in their boardinghouses before returning to work for the rest of the day.

Some boardinghouse keepers made huge profits. Jeremiah and Honora Perry from northwest County Kerry arrived in New York in 1849 and 1851, respectively, and settled in the Kerry enclave along the Hudson River in Ward One. In 1852, they were running a boardinghouse at 139 Cedar Street, a block south of where the World Trade Center would later sit. Business must have been brisk and lucrative. Their bank balance grew from $139 in May 1852 to more than $1,000 twenty-six months later. The Perrys decided to take their hard-earned savings and leave the city. In the spring of 1855, they bought farmland 250 miles northwest of Manhattan in Allegany County, New York, and left their son Edward in Manhattan to continue operating the profitable lodging business.

An advantage of running a boardinghouse was that a husband could leave much or all of the work to his wife and seek a second job to supplement the family income. Widower Philip McQuade, for example, was about fifty years old when he arrived in New York in January 1848 with some brothers, nieces, nephews, and a fourteen-year-old son, Philip Jr. The elder Philip initially worked as a laborer, but around 1852, having recently married Mary Kelly, he opened a boardinghouse in Five Points. To save as much as possible, McQuade continued to work as a laborer while leaving most of the boardinghouse responsibilities to Mary. By 1855, they and Philip Jr. (now also working as a laborer) had saved over $500. During the Civil War, the McQuades moved their boardinghouse to Ward Four and soon thereafter Philip Sr. began working as a deliveryman while Mary continued to run the lodging business. When he died in 1868, she became its sole proprietor.

While most women feared the financial consequences should a spouse pass away, some became *more* prosperous once they became widows and could operate their businesses without their husband's interference. Ann Giltenan Delany and her husband, laborer Jeremiah Delany, for example, never managed to save more than $50 while he was alive, even though they had no children to support. But after Jeremiah died in the late 1850s, Ann opened a small boardinghouse (it had six occupants in 1860) and also took in washing. Ann never remarried, but in the first decade after Jeremiah's death, she managed to save nearly $700.

Uptown boardinghouses in new tenements, like Ann Delany's, could be clean and comfortable, but those in impoverished locales, such as the one in Five Points run by Alexander and Kate Sullivan, were often quite inhospitable. "Sandy," Kate, and their daughter

Mary were born in the shadow of Mount Knockatee in the County Kerry parish of Tuosist, just down the road from the birthplace of laborer turned cork peddler Cornelius Sullivan (though if the two families were related, they were not close kin). Arriving in New York far more impoverished than the typical Famine immigrants, Sandy and Kate found getting by in the city to be quite difficult, even more so when forty-year-old Kate and eighteen-year-old Mary gave birth a few months apart in early 1855. It was Kate's second child in eighteen months. The situation was made even more challenging because Mary and her baby, John, were forced to live with Sandy and Kate and Mary's three surviving younger siblings because Mary's husband, Patrick Shea, had abandoned her and moved to Chicago. With so many mouths to feed on Sandy's day-laborer wages, Mary left little John at home with Kate and took a day job as a domestic. In addition to caring for all those kids, Kate helped bring in more income by opening a basement lodging house in the dilapidated wooden tenement at 35 Baxter Street in the Lansdowne enclave.

BACKGROUNDS OF CIVILIZATION.—MRS. SANDY SULLIVAN'S GENTEEL LODGING-HOUSE IN BAXTER STREET.—See page 209.

Sandy and Kate Sullivan's lodging house at 35 Baxter Street in Five Points. Lodgers paid just six cents per night to stay there, though for that price they were not guaranteed their own bed.

Several newspaper reporters visited the Sullivans' boarding-house in the summer of 1859 on a tour of the "abodes of the poor." The establishment consisted of three ten-by-ten-foot rooms. In each, stated one of the reporters, "there were bunks arranged along the wall, two or three deep," just as in the steerage compartment of a ship, so that lodgers might have to climb over other guests to reach their assigned places. Sandy promised the incredulous visitors that the bedsheets were " 'clane and dacent sure,' that they were washed 'onst a week,' every Thursday, and that the place was quite sweet." But according to the journalists, the rooms reeked of "fetid odors..., and the floor[s] and the walls were damp with pestiferous exhalations....Not the slightest breath of air reached these infernal holes, which were absolutely stifling with heat." What the Sullivans' lodging house lacked in cleanliness, however, it compensated for in value. They charged just six cents a night, enabling recently arrived immigrants to scrimp and save so they could quickly pay for the emigration of siblings, send money to parents in Ireland, or accumulate enough to start businesses. Sandy died in the summer of 1862, and Kate probably supported herself and her children taking in lodgers in Five Points for at least another decade, until her children were able to help support her.

In some cases, how poorly a boardinghouse keeper fared can be documented. Jeremiah Tannian from County Galway, for example, immigrated in 1848 to New York, where he eventually went by Tannahan. He had trained as a blacksmith, but in New York he married boardinghouse keeper Mary Burke (probably after patronizing her establishment) and made running the boardinghouse his occupation also. At first they did well — their bank balance rose from $80 in 1852 to $247 by the end of the following year. But the business did not thrive over the long term. Mary died sometime before 1870 and though Tannahan remarried, he had to spend his later years in New York as a day laborer. With seven mouths to feed, Tannahan sometimes needed to take charitable donations of coal to keep his family warm. And in April 1883, at about age sixty, with "health failing, no work, and destitution" staring him in the face, according to municipal records, he asked to be admitted to the city alms-house, probably so that his children (now adults) would not have to pay his medical bills or feed him. He passed away eight months later. His story reminds us that not every Famine immigrant who managed to become a business owner was successful and that some ended their lives no better off than when they arrived in America.

Other Famine immigrants started businesses designed to profit from such misfortunes. To stave off admission to the almshouse, someone like Tannahan might have tried to secure a loan from a pawnbroker, and one Famine immigrant who entered this business, Henry McAleenan, fared extraordinarily well. Born in rural County Down around 1829, McAleenan arrived in New York eighteen years later. He settled in Five Points, became a peddler, and by the spring of 1855 had saved $450 in his Emigrant Bank account. McAleenan took that money and, in partnership with his brother Hugh, opened a pawnshop at 62 Mulberry Street in the heart of Five Points. The busi-ness thrived, reported R. G. Dun & Company, because Henry "is shrewd and keen at a bargain." Soon the brothers opened a second location on Eighth Avenue and West Twentieth Street. By the 1870s, the McAleenans had left Five Points behind, with Henry taking over the Eighth Avenue location while Hugh set up a new pawnshop on the East Side. Henry continued to prosper, and like so many of his successful Famine compatriots, he invested his profits in real estate. Henry bought up prime lots along Herald Square on the corner of Sixth Avenue and West Thirty-Fourth Street when it was "practically a wilderness," wrote one admiring journalist, and opened a second pawn location there in the 1890s as well as a third in Brooklyn. Real estate developers offered him increasingly astounding sums for his Herald Square lots in the first decade of the twentieth century so they could build huge retail palaces in the increasingly fashionable locale, but McAleenan refused to sell at any price. In 1910 he gave virtually all his property to his six children to avoid inheritance taxes, and he passed away in his spacious apartment on Broadway and West Eighty-Sixth Street at age eighty-four in 1913.

While half the Famine immigrant business owners ran saloons, groceries, junk shops, and boardinghouses, the other half were engaged in an astounding variety of other enterprises. Some of these entrepreneurs, like Eugene McSwyny, clearly utilized funds brought from Ireland to enter the ranks of New York's merchant class, but most — such as brothers Francis, Patrick, and John Morgan — brought little if any money with them from Ireland to finance businesses and instead accumulated most of their start-up capital in America.

Like many families, the Morgans used chain migration to come to the United States from County Cavan, arriving as teens (or, in Francis's case, as a preteen) in 1844, 1847, and 1848. They entered their first business — the soda water trade — by sheer happenstance. Patrick Morgan is listed in the 1850 census as a stable hand, a common job for a teenaged Irish immigrant recently arrived in New York. The owner of that stable also operated a business brewing carbonated beverages and Patrick boarded with some of those workers. This was apparently how he and Francis got the notion to become soda makers. The 1854 city directory identified Patrick as a "rootbrewer," while that same year Francis identified himself as a maker of "gingerpop." They eventually decided to locate their business in Ward Twenty on the West Side.

John, meanwhile, the youngest of the Morgan brothers, was working as a printer, but seeing his brothers' success, he started his own root beer business in 1858, five blocks north of where Patrick and Francis made their "sarsaparilla" and other "waters." Rather than compete with them, John soon switched his focus to cider and after a decade in that trade owned $5,000 in Manhattan real estate.

But his brothers had done even better. They had shrewdly invested their profits in empty lots between Madison and Fifth Avenues in what would eventually become Midtown. In 1872, they estimated the value of those real estate holdings at $100,000 (of which $30,000 was owed to lenders). But their soda company, which Dun & Company appraised at $25,000, was entirely debt free. "They do a strictly cash business, both ways," noted the credit rating firm approvingly, "taking no risks and asking no favor."

Despite already being "wealthy" from soda making, according to the Dun investigators, Patrick and Francis craved still more. In the mid-1870s, they decided to open a second business focused on moving and storage. Patrick ran the new enterprise at first, leaving Francis to look after the soda water operation, but eventually the two devoted their full attention to Morgan & Brother Storage and transferred their soda water business to their kid brother.

All three Morgans became prominent members of the West Side Irish American community, which grew substantially in the post-war years as more and more Famine immigrants could afford to move away from the dilapidated tenements of Five Points and Ward Four. Patrick took a leading role in Democratic politics in Ward Twenty, while Francis married the niece of a powerful Democratic politico, John "the Big Judge" Connolly. Their moving and storage business, eventually renamed Morgan Manhattan, operates to this day. John, less wealthy than his brothers, actually became the best-known of the three. He personally drove a horse-drawn cart around the Upper West Side to persuade saloonkeepers and restaurateurs to stock his soft drinks and hard cider. John also served as a trustee of the New York City schools, akin to a seat on the modern-day board of education, for more than a decade. "A man of great kindness of heart and charitable impulses," noted a biographer, "he was universally liked and respected." In the 1950s, John's grandson expanded the reach of the family soda business by merging it with White Rock Beverages, a midwestern mineral water company, and began selling Morgan products under that name. They still produce soda water in a plant in Queens and remain a favorite New York brand.

The horse-drawn wagon that John Morgan drove about the Upper West Side to sell his root and ginger beers probably looked something like this image of a New York "mead, ginger and root beer cart" from about 1840.

While some businessmen, like the Morgan brothers, succeeded in their very first enterprises, it was common for Famine immigrants to make two or three attempts before they finally established a firm foothold in the business community. John and Maria Regan, for example, opened many businesses seeking just the right combination of location and product. They apparently met in New York, and by 1854 John was working as a clerk in a Five Points liquor shop. The following year, with an impressive $700 in savings, the ambitious couple crossed the Hudson and opened a grocery in Hoboken. It apparently flourished at first. By 1860, the Regans owned $5,000 in real estate and $600 in personal property. Soon they converted their establishment, five blocks from the Hudson River waterfront, into a saloon, but that business floundered, so they closed it and moved back to New York. We don't know what they did there initially, but by the end of the Civil War, they had opened an "eating-house" in lower Manhattan, on West Street. Oysters were clearly one of their most popular dishes. In 1867, the Regans placed an ad in the *Herald* seeking "a boy to open oysters and make himself generally useful." The establishment must have been moderately successful, because in 1870 the Regans reported a net worth of $1,500, significantly lower than in 1860 but still fairly impressive. Seeking a better situation, however, the Regans moved back to Hoboken in the early 1870s, opening Regan's Oyster Saloon at 6 Newark Street just steps from the bustling waterfront. Regan's must have been a busy place. Even with sons William (age twenty-one) and John Jr. (age seventeen) working full-time at the restaurant in 1879, the Regans still needed more help. They advertised in New York that summer for "a smart boy, to open oysters and wait on table." Perhaps John and Maria needed the help because their health was failing. John died in 1880. Maria took charge of the saloon after his death, but she passed away, at age fifty, later that same year.

Women tended not to experiment with as many different business ventures as men, in part because the number of enterprises they could operate within the bounds of nineteenth-century propriety was limited. Washing clothes, peddling fruit, and operating a boardinghouse were really the only businesses women could run without prompting raised eyebrows from some segment of New York's population. Selling ladies' hats or undergarments was also acceptable, but these were usually done, at least initially, in conjunction with a husband.

As we've seen, husbands tolerated, and may have even encouraged, their wives to operate businesses while they earned a wage. Yet even if a woman ran a shop or boardinghouse entirely on her own, the discriminatory laws of this era stipulated that every penny a woman earned belonged to her husband. Husbands might drink or gamble away a female entrepreneur's hard-earned profits or with-hold it from stepchildren out of spite, and their wives had no legal recourse. Even opening a bank account in her name alone offered no protection from a husband's profligacy or ill will.

This fact was made painfully clear in the legal battle that took place over the profits from the hat shop that Joanna Condon Boyle started with the help of her husband, Terence Boyle. He came to America from County Armagh in 1849 and in February 1855, at age thirty-eight, married Joanna, sixteen years his junior and the American-born child of Irish immigrants. She had worked as a hatmaker before their marriage, and a month after their wedding Terence rented a storefront on Eighth Avenue just north of Fifteenth Street so Joanna could open a millinery shop. Joanna spent $300 on raw materials to make her initial stock of hats and bonnets, using $100 she brought to the marriage plus $200 in credit secured in her own name. She proudly hung a sign outside the shop that read "Mrs. Boyle's Millinery."

Joanna must have had a great sense of style and a knack for business too because the shop flourished right from the start, and after a few months Terence decided to make it his full-time voca-tion as well. He traveled around town buying the necessary raw materials from dry goods dealers and handled the finances, while Joanna made the hats, supervised the milliners they eventually hired to keep up with demand, and waited on customers. The prof-its were substantial. Every time the balance in their Emigrant Sav-ings Bank account hit $500, they opened another one.* By January 1862, they had eight Emigrant accounts.

Terence was not foolish enough to keep all the Boyles' financial eggs in one basket, even a basket like the Emigrant Bank, which

---

* To encourage the poor to open savings accounts, New York law stipulated that accounts holding $500 or less would earn more interest than those with higher bal-ances. To circumvent this rule and earn the maximum interest on all their savings, the Boyles, like most Emigrant Savings Bank depositors, opened a new account each time one of their old ones reached $500. They repeated the process as many times as neces-sary to ensure that all their savings earned the highest possible interest rate.

promised to invest depositors' funds conservatively so they would not have to worry, in the days before deposit insurance, about losing their nest eggs in case of a bank run. Despite the inconvenience, the Boyles prudently spread their savings around town. By May 1862 Terence had deposited in his name, in addition to $5,550 at the Emigrant Savings Bank, another $522 at the Bank for Savings, $500 at the Bowery Savings Bank, $500 at the German Savings Bank, $450 at the Greenwich Savings Bank, $500 at the Irving Savings Institution, $500 at the Manhattan Savings Bank, $530 at the Mariners' Savings Bank, $400 at the Seamen's Savings Bank, and $400 at the Sixpenny Savings Bank—for a total of almost $10,000 in bank deposits. In addition, there was $1,499 in Joanna's name at three different banks. And just in case of a true financial catastrophe, they had $1,000 in gold coins they kept at home. Their savings was the equivalent of more than $380,000 today.

Joanna's second-class legal status as co-owner of this small fortune became evident when Terence died later that spring. In his will, he left $3,500 of that $10,000 to Joanna and $250 each to his brother Richard (who ran a crockery shop on Third Avenue) and his sister Sarah (who lived in Ireland), directing that the remainder be put in trust for Terence and Joanna's one surviving child, two-year-old Annie. According to the terms of Terence's will, the money would not become Annie's until she married. If she died before marrying, the trust fund would be split between Richard and Sarah.

Richard Boyle, however, was not pleased with his paltry share of his brother's fortune. He knew about the gold coins, which Joanna claimed were hers and therefore not covered by the will, and he sued to get them put into the trust so that he might eventually get his hands on them.

The facts of the case that went before a probate judge in 1864 were not in dispute. While Terence and Joanna had eventually changed the sign outside the shop to read "Boyle's Millinery," Joanna had remained the primary operator of the business. Her name was the only one on the shop's business cards. She designed and sold the hats. And no one disputed that the gold coins had been bought with proceeds from the business.

Yet none of that mattered. The judge ruled that according to the laws in place at the time the shop opened, anything of value acquired by a married woman automatically become the sole property of her husband. Even the bank accounts that were in Joanna's name alone were legally Terence's. His will directed that they become Joanna's property after his death (that was part of the $3,500 she got), but he could have bequeathed them to anyone he chose. All Joanna was legally entitled to was the $100 she brought to the marriage, plus accrued interest on that tiny sum. New York had changed the law pertaining to businesses owned by married couples in 1860, stipulating that henceforth such enterprises were equally the property of husband and wife. But because the Boyles had opened their shop in 1855, the judge ruled, the 1860 law did not apply. Richard, as Terence's executor, was given control of the gold coins.

At first, it looked as if Richard's legal maneuver might pay off. Joanna remained in the millinery business on Eighth Avenue into the early 1870s, at which point she apparently passed away, having burned through most of her savings. Orphan Annie, who had lived the first ten years of her life in relative wealth and comfort, was in 1880, at age twenty, toiling as a domestic in a boardinghouse on West Twenty-Third Street. She clearly wasn't receiving much if any trust-fund income from her miserly uncle. Years went by, and still Annie could not find a mate. Only in her mid-thirties (making her quite the old maid by the standards of the day) did Annie finally find a husband and receive her father's bequest. Her new spouse, Augustine Healy, was himself an American-born trust-fund baby of Irish immigrants who had done extraordinarily well — in their case, in the dry goods trade. His family had spent summers at a country house in Far Rockaway in Queens, and after the wedding Augustine took Annie there to live full-time while supporting them off the proceeds of real estate investments and his share of the profits from a haberdashery he owned on Broadway in Manhattan. When Augustine died in 1903, however, Annie moved with their two children back to Manhattan, to a town house on the Upper East Side and eventually to another in Prospect Heights, Brooklyn, where she lived comfortably until she died of complications from pneumonia in 1919.

Had Annie Boyle Healy started her own business, she would have had more rights to the proceeds of the enterprise than her mother. But not a whole lot more. The notion that women could, or even should, have an equal say with men over the disposal of family assets would not be codified in American law until well into the second half of the twentieth century.

———

Joanna Boyle probably took some pride in knowing that she had succeeded spectacularly in business while many Irish American men had failed at running their own commercial enterprises. Of those who operated businesses when they opened Emigrant Savings Bank accounts in the 1850s, only three-quarters finished their careers in that occupational category. The rest typically went back to the vocation they had followed before opening their businesses. Boardinghouses were the most likely business to fail. Nearly a third of the male boardinghouse keepers with accounts at the Emigrant Bank in the 1850s were no longer in business by the end of their working lives. The second-most-likely businesses to fail were saloons (more on that in the next chapter). Many of these unsuccessful entrepreneurs fell all the way back down the socioeconomic ladder to the ranks of the unskilled, often working as day laborers but also frequently as porters and cartmen, unskilled positions that had an entrepreneurial component. Still others who failed at business became clerks, assisting with the operation of businesses very similar to those they had recently run themselves.

Occupational Mobility of Male Famine Immigrant Business Owners

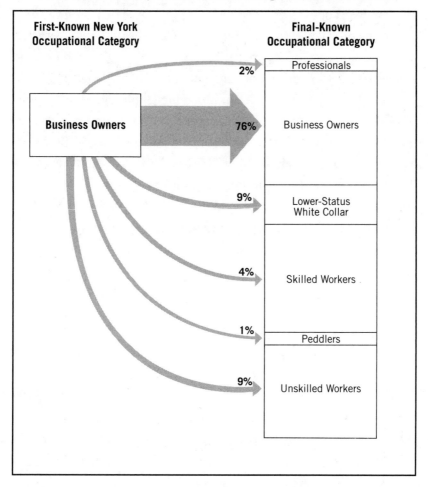

Nonetheless, the bank accounts of even the unsuccessful business owners epitomize the old adage that it is better to have tried and failed than never to have tried at all. The Famine Irish who had once owned businesses but ended their lives in unskilled occupations had 60 percent more money in their bank accounts when they ultimately closed them than did unskilled workers who never attempted to start a business. It is not clear why this was the case. But it appears that more often than not, ambition and a willingness to take risks paid dividends in Civil War–era New York no matter what rung of the socioeconomic ladder an Irish immigrant ultimately occupied.

One wonders if Edmund Butler, who left the tiny, impoverished north Cork hamlet of Rathnagard in the spring of 1850 and became a New York waterfront labor magnate, and Thomas Meagher, who grew up fifty miles away in a not much bigger impoverished "townland" in Tipperary and became a successful Manhattan grocer, ever sat together on their adjoining stoops on Willow Place in Brooklyn Heights and mused about how far they had come and how well they had done. A tiny number of Famine immigrants, of course, arrived in New York with both the capital and experience to immediately start businesses, but neither Butler nor Meagher was part of that small group. As with most of the Famine immigrants who eventually became business owners, it took them more than half a decade after emigrating to accrue the experience and capital needed to start their enterprises. Of the Famine immigrants who eventually operated businesses, Butler was part of the minority that succeeded in their very first ventures. Meagher, like most immigrants, required several attempts to find an entrepreneurial formula that worked.

Perhaps the Butlers, in November 1882, invited Kate Meagher, recently widowed, to their home to celebrate their son's election to the New York State Assembly, a position of power and prestige that would have been unimaginable had Edmund remained one of the eighty-nine inhabitants of Rathnagard. As proud as the Butlers must have been on that evening, Kate would have been equally proud when one of *her* sons gained admission to an Ivy League university a few years later. While their paths to success may have differed, Edmund Butler and Thomas Meagher probably thanked their lucky stars that they had survived years of Famine and made it aboard sailing ships bound for the United States. And given how well they had done, they must have agreed with fellow entrepreneur Peter McLoughlin that for aspiring Irish businessmen, the United States was "the best country in the World."

CHAPTER EIGHT

"Few Men Better Known"

Saloonkeepers

JOHN LANE SURVIVED five years of Famine in one of the hardest-hit parts of Ireland, the parish of Kenmare on the Lansdowne estate in County Kerry, before making his way to New York at the end of the summer of 1851. He settled in Five Points and, like most of his Kenmare compatriots, initially sought employment as a day laborer. But by 1855, he had saved enough to try his hand at the liquor trade, opening a saloon at 31 Baxter Street in a huge brick tenement that loomed over the Lansdowne enclave.

Lane's first entrepreneurial venture did not succeed, and the following year he was back at day labor. But John and his wife, Mary Buckley Lane, a native of Tralee who had arrived in New York a few years after John, did not abandon their dream of running their own business. By 1857, the Lanes had opened another saloon, in a run-down wooden tenement up the street at 37 Baxter. Ever searching for a better location or lower rent, over the course of the next seven years the Lanes moved their liquor shop across the street to similarly dilapidated buildings at 30, 36, 40, and 52 Baxter, all on the same block where they had operated their first two saloons. Mary ran the business on her own while John served a short stint in an artillery unit during the Civil War.

All that moving around apparently paid off. By the late 1860s, the Lanes had saved enough money to purchase the tenement at 357 West Sixteenth Street in Ward Sixteen. They reopened their saloon at that location, lived on the premises as well, and rented the remaining six apartments to other immigrants. By 1880, John and Mary no longer operated the saloon, living instead off the tenement's rental income alone. A few years later, they bought a bigger building in a nicer neighborhood on West Thirty-Fifth Street. That tenement was worth thirty to forty thousand dollars by the early 1890s and brought in several thousand dollars a year in rental income, more than enough to support frugal Famine immigrants.

The large brick building in this photo (taken in about 1870) is 31 Baxter Street, the location of John and Mary Lane's first Five Points liquor shop. They continued to operate barrooms on this block into the 1860s.

John and Mary's work ethic, however, did not rub off on the majority of their children. Daughter Johanna did well enough until her husband, carriage driver Patrick T. Feeney, passed away, leaving her with several small kids to support. They eventually moved in with John and Mary, less a reflection on Johanna than on the limited opportunities in that era for unmarried women with children. Johanna's brothers, however, who had far more opportunities, did not take advantage of them. In 1892, thirty-five-year-old Michael was serving three years in Sing Sing prison for assault. Nor was this Michael's first trip "up the river." He had a drinking problem and became violent when intoxicated. While drunk at age twenty-three in 1880, he and a fellow member of the Tenth Avenue Gang indiscriminately attacked pedestrians with a slingshot, a loaded billy club, a butcher's knife, and a pistol. For this rampage, Lane was sentenced to five years at Sing Sing. He was released early, but in 1884 he was again convicted of robbery and assault and sent back to prison for seven years. Yet just a few weeks after returning home in 1891, he got into a fight with a West Side bartender, was convicted of assault, and was shipped up the river a third time.

Yet it was Michael's younger brother Daniel, born in 1862 and a stonecutter by trade, who was the true "scapegrace of the family." In December 1892, Daniel, also an alcoholic, assaulted his own father and stole his seventy-dollar gold watch in order to finance his wastrel ways. When Daniel reappeared six months later and attacked his father again, John pressed charges and demanded that his son be incarcerated, and the incredulous judge assigned to the case complied. By the start of 1894, however, both Lane boys were out of prison and anxiously awaiting the day when their father would pass away (he was a widower by this point) and they could inherit his valuable tenement and divvy the proceeds with Johanna.

The Lane family drama came to a climax in June 1894 as John lay at home on his deathbed, surrounded by his three children, a grandchild, a doctor, a priest, and "a score of neighbors." When

John handed the physician ninety dollars for his services, the doctor declined it and gave the billfold to the widow Johanna. This outraged Daniel—intoxicated as usual—who demanded a share, while Michael scolded his brother for making a scene. As the dying man begged his sons to stop fighting, Daniel grabbed a candlestick and struck Michael a blow that knocked him to the floor. "The two brothers struggled out into the hall," recounted a New York tabloid, and although Michael eventually subdued his younger sibling, "while they were fighting their father breathed his last." The siblings apparently reconciled in time for the funeral but, in the meantime, their bedside brawl had become the talk of the town. As John and Mary Lane discovered, financial success in America did not necessarily bring the better life for their children that the immigrants had anticipated.

Thousands of Famine immigrants aspired to become saloonkeepers like John Lane. In fact, more Famine refugees went into the liquor trade than any other retail business. Most Irish immigrants considered owning a saloon the pinnacle of success. Doctors and lawyers might make more money than liquor dealers and enjoy more prestige, but very few Famine immigrants had the education to qualify for those jobs. Many saloonkeepers, however, made enough money to send their sons to college so that *they* might become attorneys and physicians. For most of the Famine immigrants, therefore, operating a saloon was their highest realistic aspiration, and achieving it was proof that they had "made it" in America. It was, in this sense, the top rung on the Famine immigrants' socioeconomic ladder.

When the Famine immigrants arrived in New York, the city already had a lot of saloons, and Manhattanites opened many more of them to accommodate the newcomers' thirst for whiskey, gin, and beer. In 1856, at the end of the Famine migration, the compilers of the New York City directory counted more than twenty-five hundred liquor dealers, an average of one for every developed block in the city. (That figure does not include the hundreds of groceries that also sold liquor by the glass or growler.) Yet New York's watering holes were not distributed evenly across the city. In predominantly Irish wards like the Fourth and the Sixth, some blocks had as many as two dozen saloons. In Five Points, both retail spaces at the front of a typical brick tenement might be occupied by saloons, and at some addresses there was even a third grogshop in the cellar or a rear building.

Famine immigrants of every vocational background made their way into the liquor trade. Boilermaker Francis Lawler, carpenter John McNulty, coffin maker Benjamin Callan, gardener Thomas Higgiston, gold refiner Edward Dooley, metal burnisher Thomas Cullen, painter William Warner, plasterer James Redding, printer Thomas Heany, stonecutter Christopher Gregory, shoemaker John Kernan, tailor James Dorin, and wood turner John O'Flaherty all left their artisanal trades to become saloonkeepers.

Even menial workers could realistically dream of one day running the corner saloon. Longshoreman John Green, night watchman Thomas Owens, poorhouse orderly James Woods, and porter John Gilvary all became liquor dealers. But the most common first job in America for Irishmen who became saloonkeepers was the most menial of all—day laborer. Bernard Galligan from Cavan, Peter McCarty from Cork, Peter McGoldrick from Donegal, Daniel O'Connor from Kerry, Patrick Scanlon from Sligo, and Andrew Watson from Westmeath were just a few of the many day laborers who eventually ran their own bars.

Some Famine immigrants did not need to work initially in a blue-collar vocation in New York before becoming saloonkeepers. Michael Murphy, a native of Castletownroche in Cork, immigrated in September 1855 at about age fifty with his wife, Mary, and all six of their children, ranging in age from five to twenty. A few months later, he was operating a saloon in Ward Four. In his first nineteen months in business, Murphy managed to increase his Emigrant Savings Bank balance from $40 to $500. He eventually moved his bar to the waterfront in Ward Seven, where he became a major player in ward politics — especially impressive given that he came to America at a relatively advanced age and was not educated enough to write his own name.

Patrick Reynolds also entered the saloon trade quickly. Not long after arriving in New York in 1849 with his wife, Kate, and their ten-month-old daughter, Reynolds had a bar in Five Points. That his brother was a priest in Ireland suggests that the family had been one of means in County Leitrim. After a couple of years in New York, Patrick had accumulated enough capital to rent the entire tenement at 510 Pearl Street, the location where he operated that first saloon. But his success also exposed him to the violent side of Five Points life. One day in November 1852, one of his tenants, Charlotte Connery, who ran a boardinghouse in her apartment, staggered into Reynolds's bar with her hands around her neck and blood streaming out between her fingers. A boarder, jealous that Connery was becoming romantically involved with another man, had slit her throat with his straight razor. Reynolds helped take Connery to the hospital, but she died a few hours later. Dangerous though it might have been, business on Pearl Street was good. Reynolds's bank balance grew from $100 in March 1852 to $971 just twenty-two months later.

Given the substantial profits that barkeepers like Murphy and Reynolds were making, it's no wonder that so many immigrants strove to become liquor dealers. But it was not necessary to have arrived in New York with significant savings, as those saloonkeepers probably had, to reap the rewards of the liquor trade. Michael J. Higgins came to America from Maynooth in County Kildare in

1849 at age twenty and a few months later had landed a job as a waiter on Chatham Street, a busy commercial thoroughfare on the southeast edge of Five Points. By 1852, he had opened a bar there, although he soon moved his watering hole to an even busier location on Broadway at the corner of Canal Street. There, business really took off, so much so that Higgins had trouble keeping up with the demands of his customers for food and drink. A help-wanted ad run by Higgins in the *Sun* sought "one first-rate oyster-man and two good waiters, and one girl to do general work." From 1852 to 1855 his bank balance rose from $100 to more than $1,000. He managed this feat in part by continuing to live with his mother and five adult siblings even though he could have easily afforded a place of his own. Still, wealth was no guarantee of health in ante-bellum New York. Higgins died of tuberculosis at age thirty-two in January 1861.

The profits that James and Margaret Meehan generated in their Five Points porterhouse on Orange (now Baxter) Street were also spectacular. From August 1853 to June 1854, they saved $1,100, despite competing with two dozen other watering holes on the very same block. Only in February, when many of his customers were presumably unemployed due to seasonal slowdowns in the labor market, did the Meehans fail to save at least $100. Yet again, prodigious profits could not protect the publican's health. James died from an unknown ailment, at age thirty-three, in 1857.

The funds that immigrant business owners had on deposit at the Emigrant Savings Bank were often just a small portion of their profits, because it made sense in the days before deposit insurance to distribute one's money among several banks, just as Terence and Joanna Boyle had done. We can document the full savings of the Famine immigrants with certainty only in the rare instances when legal proceedings caused courts to order an inventory of their assets. Such was the case for Thomas Fenton, who arrived in New York in 1849 at age thirty-two from a rural part of County

Waterford along the Blackwater River. Fenton worked as a gardener at the Catholic Orphan Asylum on Fifth Avenue between Fifty-First and Fifty-Second Street during most of his first ten years in New York, saving nearly $800 in that decade. But in 1860, soon after marrying Mary Delany, Fenton laid down his spade and shovel, closed his Emigrant Bank accounts, bought a house on a large lot at the corner of Tenth Avenue (now Amsterdam) and West 161st Street, and opened a saloon there. Thomas operated a pub with Mary in that narrow stretch of northern Manhattan between Harlem and Washington Heights for nearly forty years. They never had children and lived unpretentiously, and when Thomas passed away in 1899, a few years after Mary's death, the courts appraised the value of his tangible possessions at just $60.

Psychologically scarred by their experiences, Famine immigrants like Fenton often remained obsessively thrifty in New York even when they could easily have afforded to splurge now and then. Fenton, it turned out, was one of these misers. This fact became evident after his death when, following the appraisal of Thomas's meager possessions, the court allowed his heirs to open a tiny safe found in his home. Inside, they discovered passbooks for thirty different bank accounts, with balances totaling $90,000, and another $24,000 in cash and securities (the total was equal to about $4.25 million today). Furthermore, Thomas had a real estate portfolio that was worth about the same amount; it included an entire block in his neighborhood on the west side of Amsterdam Avenue. Fenton's siblings, their children, Mary's family, and Thomas's young second wife, whom Thomas had married a year before his death, fought for years over this huge estate.

Fenton, Murphy, Reynolds, and Lane all appear to have succeeded in their very first ventures as barkeepers. For many Famine immigrants, however, it took two or three attempts before they could establish a profitable liquor business. Thomas Murphy, for example, arrived in New York from County Kildare in 1850 and by

1852 was operating a bar on Pearl Street in Five Points. He had to give up the saloon and become a porter for a while and then a clerk, but by 1860 he was back in the liquor business. Likewise, brothers James and Patrick Simmons came to America from County Limerick when they were both about twenty in 1851. Patrick decided to become a coal miner in central Pennsylvania, but James stayed in Manhattan, where he managed to open a saloon by 1857. That first effort failed, and in 1860 Simmons was tending bar in someone else's pub. Simmons again had his own saloon by the end of the Civil War, however, this time in Brooklyn, but lost that one as well. He returned to barkeeping for good in 1869, by which point he had $800 in his Emigrant Savings Bank account and was the proud owner of a $75 gold watch. He ran this bar, at 25 York Street in Brooklyn, until his death in 1885 at age fifty-four.

———

Whether Famine immigrants succeeded in the liquor trade on their first try or their third, politics would quickly become nearly as important a part of the business as whiskey and gin. Some saloonkeepers got involved in politics because it helped business. In the Famine era, all municipal and federal jobs, even the most menial like letter carrier and street sweeper, were obtained through the blessings of some political leader. In the case of employment from the city, the mayor would delegate the appointments to his commissioners, who would dole out the positions to the aldermen who represented each of the city's twenty-two wards. If a ward was represented by an alderman of a different party than the mayor's, however, the commissioners would allow the ranking party member from that ward to distribute the jobs. The aldermen would split the patronage positions among their district leaders, and the district leaders would divide the spoils among their block captains, who in nineteen cases out of twenty were saloonkeepers. The immigrants quickly learned that this was how city jobs were doled out, and that if they hoped to obtain one, they should patronize the pub of a politically powerful saloonkeeper and make it known that they would like to be considered for one of the patronage plums. Thus, a saloonkeeper's political clout brought additional customers into his bar.

But it took more than buying a few glasses of beer to qualify for a patronage position in the city government. To get the saloonkeeper's support, an Irish immigrant might need to show up at the ward's Democratic primary meeting (invariably held in the back room of a saloon) and help the barkeeper's handpicked candidates win the nominations. Sometimes this meant merely voting for the saloonkeeper's preferred ticket, but in other cases it meant fighting—literally—on his behalf. In the late 1840s and early 1850s, supporters of the rival Democratic tickets often engaged in hand-to-hand combat (Michael Quigley's specialty) to secure control of the primary meeting. Once the nominations were set, the aspiring street sweeper or road paver might be asked by the saloonkeeper to post handbills advertising the party's nominees and any parades or political meetings being held to promote their candidacies. Then, on election day, an immigrant currying favor with his neighborhood liquor dealer would promise to deliver the voters from his tenement, or from his particular parish in Ireland, to the polls to vote for the saloonkeeper's patrons in City Hall. Only after the immigrant had made good on such promises would he qualify for consideration for one of the jobs the saloonkeeper might offer.

Immigrants could count on their saloonkeepers for more than just jobs. If they needed a loan, the local liquor dealer was often the first person to whom they would turn. If the immigrant or one of his family members got arrested, the saloonkeeper could pull strings to get the charges dropped or reduced. If someone in the immigrant's family was sick and they could not afford a doctor, the saloonkeeper might send one, at his own expense, before even being asked. And if the immigrant lost his job and the saloonkeeper could not find him one, food, fuel, and even clothing might arrive on the unemployed man's doorstep, courtesy of the liquor dealer or the ward heeler to whom he answered. In an era before government-run social safety nets, saloonkeeper-politicians in cities like New York operated their own extensive private welfare system.

Just as ordinary Famine immigrants might woo their local saloonkeepers in the hopes of landing a city job, liquor dealers had to court politicos higher up the party hierarchy to ensure that they continued having the opportunity to dispense patronage. One who succeeded at this important task was James McGillin from Bodoney Lower parish in County Tyrone, who immigrated to New York at age nineteen in 1854. Like so many immigrants from that parish, McGillin initially worked in New York as a charcoal peddler, but by the close of the Civil War he had become a saloonkeeper in Brooklyn. For decades, reported the *Brooklyn Daily Eagle* in 1889, McGillin's "resort" at the southeast corner of Grand and Roebling Streets in Williamsburg was the favorite haunt of Irish-born politicos "who formed a coterie known as the Knights of the Round Table." This jolly band included "ex-Commissioner John W. Flaherty, ex-Commissioner Gallagher, James Langan, George B. McGrath and the late James J. McCormick, George McKay, . . . Cas Sparks and others." By the time McGillin passed away at age fifty-four in 1889, "there were few men better known" in that part of Brooklyn. The two-story brick building where McGillin and his wife, Bridget, operated their saloon (and lived as well) still stands at that Williamsburg intersection.

A saloonkeeper's political influence might win him customers, but there were other forms of political activism that could attract patrons to a liquor dealer's place of business. Mortimer "Murty" O'Sullivan, for example, who usually went by "Sullivan" in New York, left Kenmare in County Kerry as a sixteen-year-old in 1851, settled in the Lansdowne enclave in Five Points, and later in the decade helped organize a Five Points militia company, the Kenmare

Guards. Politicians curried favor with militia company leaders because those officers might, with the right inducements, muster their men on behalf of an aspiring officeholder on election day.

THE VOTING-PLACE, NO. 488 PEARL STREET, IN THE SIXTH WARD, NEW YORK CITY.

The circular objects hanging on the wall of Alderman John Barry's saloon on Pearl Street in Five Points are targets used by a militia company that probably held its meetings in the back room of the saloon. Murty Sullivan probably hung the targets of the Kenmare Guards on the walls of his Baxter Street watering hole.

But Sullivan did not obsess about politics to the exclusion of all else. He also organized the Kenmare Hurlers, a Five Points athletic club that competed in that popular Irish sport, in which players on a large field used a wooden stick with a flat end (called a hurley) to knock a ball into a goal or through the uprights above it. The Lansdowne emigrants may have arrived in New York dirt poor, but they spared no expense when it came to their beloved pastime. On a March weekend in 1859, the club set out from Five Points for the Elysian Fields in Hoboken, reported the *Irish-American*, with its equipment and picnic supplies "in a large four horse wagon,...covered and sorrounded [sic] with white canvass, on which was painted in large letters the words 'Kenmare Hurlers.'" An Irish flag flew atop the wagon as it made its way to the Hudson River ferry landing on Barclay Street. Club members had spread word throughout the city that they would take on any other hurling club that might appear at the fields and promised to back up their boasts of invincibility with appropriate wagers. No other teams appeared, however, so after Sullivan and another club leader called the men to order, the Kerrymen "had a few sharp 'brushes' among themselves. The men were in fine condition and played with much spirit....The fleetness of some of the players in whipping along the ball front-wise and crosswise, and in every direction, showed that they were in excellent practice." Sullivan's leadership role in both a Five Points militia unit and a hurling club must have helped boost business in his saloon. He undoubtedly contributed conspicuously to the treasuries of both organizations in order to impress his customers and win their respect.

Still, such largesse did not guarantee success as a saloon operator. Sullivan's first grogshop, opened at 149 Worth Street in about 1858, was a failure. The collapse of that business may have resulted in part from the fact that Sullivan had boasted in New York that his brother Daniel was the Irish freedom fighter Daniel O'Sullivan, who made international headlines when he was convicted of treason in the spring of 1859 in Tralee. The revolutionary eventually heard that there was a New Yorker claiming to be his sibling and sent a letter to the *Irish-American*, published on December 31, 1859, stating that his only brother in America was named Jeremiah and lived in Massachusetts. Perhaps this explains why Murty's business dried up and he was forced to take work in 1860 as a painter to support himself, his wife, Ellen McNamara Sullivan, and their two small children. But Murty's second foray into the liquor business, a porterhouse he opened on Baxter Street in 1862, was a resounding success, and he accumulated $1,175 at the Emigrant Savings Bank by 1864. Yet Murty could not enjoy his success for long. He died that year, at age twenty-nine, of heart disease, after which Ellen took over the business.

The Famine Irish saloonkeepers who dabbled in politics but did not seek elective office typically avoided citywide publicity, lest their patronage plums and other sweetheart deals attract too much scrutiny. But every once in a while, an incident brought them into the public spotlight. That was the case in 1876 for the O'Connor brothers from Castleisland, Kerry. The O'Connors, like many families, had used chain migration to get to America. In the spring of 1849, Daniel and David landed in New Orleans with the intention of settling in Cincinnati. Six months later, their parents and brothers John and William moved to New York and settled in the Kerry enclave near the Hudson River waterfront in Ward One. David and Daniel eventually joined them there, as did a sister and the fifth brother, Bryan, who emigrated in 1851. Two years later, the five O'Connor brothers (all in their early twenties at that point) were working as day laborers. By 1855, however, Daniel had become a grocer and John had opened a porterhouse, both located on the southernmost stretch of Washington Street, near the Battery. David opened a saloon there a few years later, and Dan converted his grocery to a saloon soon thereafter.

The part of Washington Street that the O'Connors inhabited became known as the "Kerry Block" due to the concentration there of immigrants from that county, and David and Daniel (known universally in the neighborhood as "Dan D.") became two of the enclave's most prosperous and prominent business owners. Yet their life was far from easy. Dan's wife, Elizabeth, and his brother Bryan both died in the mid-1850s. Dan got remarried in about 1858 to Margaret O'Connor, but their first child, Julia, died in 1861 before reaching her second birthday. Margaret herself succumbed to cholera in August 1867. Dan got married for a third time, in 1871, to a native of Castleisland twenty years his junior named Elizabeth, who had come to America three years earlier. But a few days after giving birth to their first child in January 1873, Elizabeth died at age twenty-three of puerperal fever, an infection of the uterus common after childbirth in those days.

While Dan's personal life was painful, his saloon business was profitable. In the mid-1870s, Dun & Company estimated his net worth at $18,000 to $20,000, the equivalent of about $500,000 today. In addition to being the Kerry Block's wealthiest residents, Dan and his brother David were also the enclave's political power brokers. "For years, the O'Connors have held full sway," reported the *Herald* in 1876, with Dan D. (the youngest but apparently most charismatic of the brothers) acting as head of the clan. He could do so, explained the *Herald*, in part because his "liquor store" was "the resort of all the wild youths in the neighborhood," and the O'Connors could count on these toughs to deliver the vote of the southwest portion of Ward One for the O'Connors' anointed candidates.

That year, however, a rival faction known as the Stable Gang, headquartered a block to the east on Greenwich Street and led by "Buck" Shanahan, attempted to challenge the O'Connors for supremacy. Tempers rose steadily until June, when Buck and David exchanged blows outside Dan's saloon. Buck eventually threw David to the ground, "and an old fashioned hand-to-hand fight soon began" between the two men's supporters, the *Herald* reported. Because they were battling on Washington Street, the Kerrymen could gather a larger force than Shanahan and gained the upper hand. "In the mêlée, however, Shanahan drew a revolver and fired at O'Connor, wounding him in the left forearm." Shanahan then retreated east to Stable Gang territory, where he barricaded himself behind the bar in a saloon and managed to shoot another leader of the Kerry faction, Michael Callahan. With the police of the district controlled by the O'Connors, the members of the Stable Gang were the ones arrested at the end of the riot. It is not clear how long the O'Connors retained control of that portion of Ward One, but Dan D. continued to live and do business on the same block of Washington Street until his death, at age sixty-three, in 1891.

Like most saloonkeeper politicos, the O'Connors were not well-known outside their ward. But Walter Roche, a Five Points liquor dealer who became a neighborhood ward heeler, eventually rose to citywide fame, or to be exact, infamy. Roche arrived in New York at age twenty-one in May 1848 with eleven other family members. That Walter's parents, Patrick and Catherine, could afford so many ship tickets at once suggests that the family was fairly well off. The manifest of the ship that carried them to America lists Patrick as a farmer, and it is likely that the family had owned some land in their native County Carlow. Walter's brother, Thomas, had been a grocer in Ireland, further indicating that the family was one of at least moderate means. Walter himself had trained as a draper.

Perhaps assisted by his large network of kinsmen, Walter by 1853 had opened a porterhouse at 19 Mulberry. Like many saloonkeepers, he was ambitious. In 1854, Walter was running a second Five Points grogshop, Monroe Hall, at 514 Pearl Street in the southwest corner of the neighborhood. Two years later, still in his twenties, he had a third saloon, at 57 Centre Street.

Roche also had political aspirations. This may explain why he chose to live in the Five Points boardinghouse of Irish immigrant Hannah Brennan, whose American-born son Matthew was one of the most powerful politicos in Ward Six. In fact, Monroe Hall was originally Brennan's establishment, which Roche took over when voters elected Brennan the district's police justice in 1854. Roche increased Monroe Hall's business by converting the conventional males-only watering hole into a "concert-saloon" whose "pretty-waiter-girl[s]" were as much an attraction as the musicians who performed there. With the assistance of the Brennan clan, Roche quickly amassed political influence on lower Mulberry Street. Young workingmen from that part of the ward organized a combination militia company and political club known as the Walter Roche Guard in honor of their favorite saloonkeeper. The minor patronage appointments Roche began receiving at this point also reflected his growing power in the ward.

At the beginning of 1857, Roche was a rising Ward Six politician who, if he played his cards right, might one day win a spot on the board of aldermen. But events at the state capital in Albany that winter ended up making Roche one of the best-known, and wealthiest, politicians in all of New York City. The Republicans who controlled the legislature decided in that year to revise the city's charter in what they characterized as an effort to "reform" New York's corrupt politics. Two of these reforms affected Walter Roche. In the first, the legislators disbanded the city's police department (headed by the mayor) and replaced it with a new one run by a board chosen by the legislature. Believing that Irish-born officers did not enforce the city's liquor laws (and in particular the ban on selling alcohol on Sundays), the new board fired almost all the Irish patrolmen and replaced them with native-born officers, many of them supporters of the anti-Catholic, anti-immigrant Know Nothing Party, a fact that infuriated New York's Irish-born inhabitants. The new charter also reorganized the city's Board of Supervisors, which approved every single payment made by the municipal government. The legislature mandated that the revamped board's twelve members be split evenly between the city's two most popular political parties, thereby forcing Democrats (who usually controlled city government) to give Republicans the opportunity to block corrupt expenditures.

The new legislation brought Roche to the attention of all New Yorkers. After a slugfest on the steps of City Hall in which members of the old police force (which refused to disband) and the new Republican-led force fought for supremacy, and a ruling by the state's highest court in favor of the Republicans, the new patrolmen finally took over on the first of July. When the new officers appeared in Five Points, however, members of the Roche Guard showed their disdain by chasing the new policemen out of the neighborhood. The Irishmen pursued the patrolmen all the way to the Bowery, where the adherents of the Irish American politicos who controlled that area took offense at this incursion by the Roche Guard onto their turf. A full-scale riot ensued, in which nearly a dozen New Yorkers (many of them members of the Roche Guard) were killed.

The involvement of his political club in one of the deadliest riots (still to this day) in all New York City history did not stifle Roche's climb up the political ladder. A few months later, Brennan helped Roche secure one of the six Democratic nominations for the new Board of Supervisors. The general election was a mere formality, and in January Roche was sworn in for a five-year term, immediately vaulting him from a ward-level politico of middling importance to one of the most powerful officeholders in the city. Roche was the first Famine immigrant elected to citywide office.

Walter scaled back to a single saloon (Monroe Hall) after being sworn in, but he nonetheless became a rich man over the ensuing years, and not as a result of his salary or the profits generated by his bar. Even though the Board of Supervisors was split evenly between Republicans and Democrats, those doing business with the city still showered the board's members with business and bribes to curry their favor and ensure that the supervisors approved their inflated invoices. One of Roche's colleagues on the revamped Board of Supervisors was William M. Tweed, and as Tweed rose to become "Boss" of the city's Democratic Party by 1865, Roche rode his coattails to additional illicit riches.

To hide the Tweed Ring's ill-gotten gains, the Boss and his henchmen eventually founded savings banks and made themselves directors of these financial institutions to help camouflage the flow of money into their pockets. Roche was not a part of Tweed's innermost circle, but the fact that Roche became a vice president of both the Guardian and Bowling Green Savings Banks, two of the Ring's money-laundering conduits, indicates that he was involved in (and profited from) the political machine's plunder. Roche served as president of the Board of Supervisors in 1868 and 1869 and in those years oversaw the approval of the Ring's most corrupt city contracts. Roche owed that position to the fact that, as one

Republican newspaper put it, "he understands every nod and wink of the mighty Tweed."

Roche stepped down from the Board of Supervisors in June 1870, after thirteen years in office. All that time he had continued to oversee Monroe Hall and he had taken over a kinsman's saloon at 29 Mulberry Street at the start of the Civil War as well. As soon as he left office, the forty-three-year-old Roche married twenty-six-year-old Mary Amelia Doherty, the American-born daughter of an Irish immigrant cartman turned contractor who had made a

Walter Roche along with five of his children in an undated photo. The woman seated to Walter's right is apparently not his wife, Mary Amelia, but another relative.

fortune buying dozens of lots in the 1840s in and around what would eventually become Times Square. (Mary Amelia and her siblings wisely held on to most of this real estate portfolio into the early twentieth century, pocketing the ever higher rents and exponentially increasing the family fortune in the process.) After their wedding, which was held at St. Patrick's Cathedral on Mott Street (predecessor to today's building of the same name in Midtown Manhattan) and attended by dozens of the city's most important politicians, Walter and Mary Amelia left by steamship for a three-month European honeymoon, "chiefly at the Lakes of Killarney." A year after the wedding, Mary Amelia gave birth to the first of their six children.

By that point, Roche's connection to Tweed was coming back to haunt him. In the summer of 1871, the *New York Times* began publishing an exposé of the Tweed Ring's corruption. Investigators eventually examined the finances of the Ring banks and discovered that some of the Ring's leaders had used money deposited by the banks' customers to finance their opulent lifestyles. The first Tweed ally found to have done so was none other than Walter Roche, who, although he had no account there, suspiciously took tens of thousands of dollars from the Bowling Green Savings Bank just a few days before he and Mary Amelia departed for their lavish honeymoon. Fearing that their savings had been stolen, the bank's customers rushed in such large numbers to withdraw their money that the bank became insolvent and had to close. The Guardian, the other bank Roche helped operate, defaulted the same week.

Roche returned the tens of thousands of dollars to the Bowling Green Bank and conveyed hundreds of thousands worth of real estate to the Guardian in an unsuccessful attempt to save them, but their depositors filed civil suits against him anyway. The targets of large civil actions in that era were arrested, and Roche's warrant was served by none other than his mentor, Sheriff Matthew Brennan (Brennan and his brothers were also directors of some Ring banks). Trials led to several large judgments against Roche, but the city officials assigned to track down his assets reported that he had none to be seized. Roche may have successfully hidden his Tweed Ring loot, or he may have frittered it away — Roche supposedly lost some of the "borrowed" funds on stock market speculations.

Thanks to his wealthy wife (whose assets the banks' creditors could not touch due to the passage of "married women's property laws" that were enacted too late to help milliner Joanna Boyle), the Roches could continue to enjoy a life of luxury even after the collapse of the two banks in which Walter had supposedly invested all his assets. With his political career in shambles, Walter moved his family to a property owned by Mary Amelia in the Bronx. But in the 1890s, they returned to Manhattan and lived there with their children and a staff of servants in a town house at 350 West Fifty-Seventh Street. Roche even managed to secure a minor patronage appointment. He died at home, at age seventy-seven, in 1904.

———

For their roles in dispensing jobs, loans, and a helping hand to those in need, Irish saloonkeepers were viewed by their fellow immigrants as pillars of their communities. But some liquor dealers — those who enhanced their profits by selling sex in addition to alcohol — were not so highly esteemed. Some barkeeps might lease a single bedroom behind or above the bar to a lone sex worker, but others offered the services of several or even a dozen. Few of the Famine immigrants seem to have run brothels in their first decade in New York, though many would have worked in them. Yet the stories of the Irish-born brothel keepers who had immigrated just before the Famine and opened accounts at the Emigrant Savings Bank in the 1850s provide insight into this variant of the liquor business in which some Famine immigrants eventually participated.

Prostitution was illegal in Civil War–era New York, but the police rarely raided brothels unless neighbors complained that they were "disorderly." Five Points and Corlears Hook were both notorious for their bordellos, yet sex workers operated most brazenly in the portion of Ward Four along Water and Cherry Streets between James and Dover. On Cherry Street, exclaimed one shocked visitor, women exposed "their naked persons before the windows" of their brothels "to attract the notices of persons passing by." When clothed, according to another writer, the sex workers in this neighborhood wore dresses that were "flashy, untidy, covered with tinsel, while they are loaded down with brass jewelry." Even dressed, these women were easy to identify because they wore their dresses unfashionably short with "arms and necks bare."

One Ward Four brothel, at 277½ Water Street, was run by Mark and Mary Ann Driscoll. Mark was the American-born son of an Irish immigrant father and a New York–born mother, while Mary Ann was a Famine immigrant who had left County Roscommon in 1846 at age sixteen. When they opened their Emigrant Savings Bank account in 1853, Mark told the bank secretary that he was a sailor, but a year later he reported that he had become a boarding-house keeper on the north side of Canal Street, at the corner of Baxter, in Ward Fourteen. Yet their nine "boarders" were sex workers employed by the Driscolls. Soon Mark and Mary Ann moved their bordello to the heart of the Water Street red-light district.

It took a tough man to run a Water Street brothel because the sailors who frequented these establishments had a penchant for violence. The brown-haired, blue-eyed Driscoll had a wiry physique but had survived his share of knife fights. He had one scar on the bridge of his nose and another that ran from his left eyebrow, across his forehead, and nearly to his hairline. The tattoo on his left forearm, depicting a voluptuous woman astride an anchor, signaled to his sailor patrons that he had once been a member of their fraternity. The Driscolls were skillful entrepreneurs, and a couple of years after relocating to Water Street they had amassed $1,000 in their Emigrant Bank accounts.

Brothels were renowned for thievery as well as violence. Bordello operators like the Driscolls trained their female employees to sneak money out of their customers' wallets while the men had their attention focused elsewhere, knowing that a client was unlikely to press charges with the police. When a customer complained to the Driscolls in November 1857 that a sex worker in their establishment had stolen his money, Mark took offense and a fight broke out. One sailor and one sex worker were killed, and Mary Ann's brother (who tended bar for the couple) was stabbed as well but survived.

Mark, twenty-five years old by that point, escaped this incident unscathed, but he and Mary Ann could not stay out of trouble for long. The couple, who had moved across the street to 274 Water and had four children by 1860, apparently found themselves in financial difficulty once the Civil War started. Mark enlisted in the navy but in the summer of 1863, he snuck off his ship (which was docked

The scene inside a saloon and brothel on Water Street in the summer of 1868. The clientele, according to the article accompanying this woodcut, were mostly foreign-born sailors, and about half the sex workers were Irish immigrants.

in New York) to drink. He was caught, and a military tribunal sentenced him to six months at Sing Sing. Mary Ann was no innocent herself. When the Draft Riots broke out in July 1863, just before Mark's arrest, she took advantage of the chaos to loot furniture and bedding from a hotel around the corner from their place of business. She was caught red-handed and arrested but, like most of the Draft Riot looters, she was never prosecuted.

These brushes with the law did not prompt the Driscolls to reform their ways. In 1867, one of their sex workers made the mistake of stealing too much money—$150—from a customer. Instead of complaining to the Driscolls, he pressed charges, as did another man who claimed that Mark had taken $10 from him that same night. Driscoll and his employee, Mary Maloney, were convicted of grand larceny, and the judge sentenced Driscoll to two more years at Sing Sing. Mark apparently fell ill in prison; he appears to have died in Manhattan in February 1868. Mary Ann may have died soon thereafter. Or she may be the "Mary Driscoll" of Water Street who, drunk and despondent, unsuccessfully attempted to drown herself in the East River in 1880.

The Driscolls' bordello, despite its notoriety, was not the most infamous on their block. That honor belonged to Christopher "Kit" Burns, who ran Sportsman's Hall at 273 Water beginning in 1858. Burns had emigrated from Ireland as a child in the early 1840s. In 1860, he lived in his bordello with his wife, Mariah, their daughters Annie (age thirteen) and May (age eight), and seven sex workers. Yet Sportsman's Hall was known less for the sex that was sold upstairs, and more for the rat baiting that took place in a crude amphitheater in the basement. There was no shortage of rats in this waterfront neighborhood, and Burns's raucous customers, sitting on rude wooden benches, placed wagers on how many rats each specially trained dog could kill in a specified period of time. Facing increasing pressure from the police and religious leaders to close his notorious haunt, Burns agreed in 1870 to lease Sportsman's

Hall to a charitable organization, which converted it into a "home for fallen women." That charity continued operating there among the brothels and sailor bars until almost the end of the century.

The reason reformers sought to establish such homes for "fallen women" right in the middle of the city's red-light districts becomes evident in the story of another Water Street brothel keeper, Pete Dawson. Dawson was a native of County Carlow who, like Burns, had arrived in New York as a child. In November 1851, when the twenty-five-year-old Dawson opened an Emigrant Savings Bank account, he was running a grocery on Cross Street in the heart of Five Points on a block full of boardinghouses catering to sailors. Perhaps familiarity with these customers provided Dawson his entrée to the brothel business. He soon established a bordello at 310 Water Street along with his wife, Rebecca Kohler Dawson, a German immigrant, though by 1855 they had moved it a block away to Cherry Street. Theirs was a larger operation than that of the Driscolls, with more than a dozen women entertaining customers in thirteen bedrooms situated behind two bars at 58 Cherry. The Dawsons' bank account reflected the huge profits that brothel keepers could make. Their balance rose from just $100 in November 1851 to nearly $2,500 just twenty-one months later. Their Emigrant Bank holdings never grew much higher because the Dawsons began hedging their financial bets by making deposits (often in Rebecca's name) at other banks and plowing still more of their profits into Manhattan real estate.

According to the *Times*, Dawson was "an Irishman...of gentlemanly and winning address," but that amiable exterior was reserved for well-behaved customers and the press. It took ostentatious displays of brutality to keep both the sex workers and their clients in line. When his "girls" attempted to quit, he would beat them violently, kicking them in the face with his hard-heeled boots and dragging them back to their rooms. Dawson's wife threatened the women with violence as well. If they tried to run away, the

Dawsons could call on the Ward Four police (whom the Dawsons bribed extravagantly) to track the girls down on trumped-up charges of theft and return them to the brothel. These were the circumstances that inspired reformers to set up houses of refuge amid the brothels, so women seeking to "repent" could find shelter and assistance before the brothel keepers and their police abettors could track them down.

The Dawsons' luck ran out, however, long before the reformers descended upon Water Street after the Civil War. In 1858, a reform-minded mayor, Daniel F. Tiemann, took office promising to root out vice and corruption. When he demanded that the police arrest a brazen brothel keeper in the city's most notorious red-light district, Dawson was the unfortunate whose house was raided. At 11:00 p.m. on Tuesday, July 13, 1858, more than two dozen policemen stormed the Dawsons' place and arrested all forty-eight people in it — Dawson and his wife, the one barkeeper on duty, the musicians, about thirty patrons (mostly foreign-born sailors), and more than a dozen sex workers. They all spent the night in jail.

The following morning, the mayor himself presided over the court proceedings. This was when the sex workers' claims of virtual imprisonment first surfaced. The courtesans also complained that Dawson required them to have sex with Black men as well as white. (Many brothels at the time would only pair Black customers with sex workers of color.) "Any man is good enough so long as you get the money," Dawson purportedly told them. Newspapers across the nation covered the story.

Dawson pled guilty to keeping a disorderly house, and the judge in the mayor's court dismissed the charge that Dawson had imprisoned his female employees against their will. The magistrate also dropped all charges against Rebecca. At that point, Pete undoubtedly expected nothing more than a fine, the typical punishment for keeping a disorderly house. He was shocked when the judge, in keeping with the mayor's campaign promises, decided to make an example of him and sentenced him to two months in jail. That punishment seemed comparatively light, however, given that the same court gave four of the sex workers *six-month* sentences for disorderly conduct and vagrancy.

Newspaper editors railed at the injustice of the Dawsons' employees receiving longer sentences than Pete. But he did finally get his comeuppance. Pete, it turned out, had been arrested in September 1857 for stabbing a prominent resident of Brooklyn on the street there when the Brooklynite made a remark about one of Dawson's sex workers to which the brothel keeper took offense. The man nearly died, and when a jury convicted Dawson of assault with the intent to kill in December 1858, the judge sentenced Pete to nine and a half years at Sing Sing. "The prisoner was completely overcome by the sentence," reported the *Times*, "and wept like a child." To make matters even worse for Dawson, it turned out that while he had been in jail for his previous offense, Rebecca had taken "nearly $5,000 of Pete's money," according to a press account, and fled back to her German homeland accompanied by "a big Irishman."

Dawson clearly had more money socked away somewhere, because he could pay his attorney, a former judge, to appeal his conviction all the way to the state's highest court. That effort was unsuccessful, but the governor eventually commuted his sentence, and Dawson was released in April 1864. What became of him after that is unknown.

———

While most Irishmen and -women involved in New York's liquor trade were retailers, the industry relied upon an extensive network of suppliers and importers, and a significant number of the Famine immigrants ran these businesses as well. Callaghan McSwiney, for example, was born in the city of Cork, where his large family ran several successful businesses, including a gristmill, a distillery, and liquor retailing as well. Two of McSwiney's older brothers were Roman Catholic priests — one, Patrick (eighteen years older than Callaghan), became dean and then president of the Irish seminary in Paris.

By the time Callaghan emigrated, at age forty, he and his wife, Honoria, had a large family of their own. Callaghan and his eldest son, Patrick, made the voyage first, in 1849, to Philadelphia. McSwiney deposited his son at the College of St. Thomas of Villanova outside Philadelphia and then moved on to New York in time to greet Honoria, seven more of their ten surviving children, and Honoria's younger brother Maurice, all of whom arrived in New York in October 1850. That they could afford the more expensive direct passage from Cork to New York demonstrates that they were not a family that had been impoverished by the Famine, as did the fact that they had booked berths in cabins rather than in steerage.

Once he got settled in Manhattan, Callaghan became a distiller there. He initially set up his operation in Corlears Hook, but eventually moved it to 342 Water Street (just a block northeast of the aforementioned brothels) and there branched out into selling wine and liquor "coloring" to other alcohol producers. He also changed the spelling of his surname to McSweeny, perhaps in the belief that it made the name more American. Honoria, meanwhile, gave birth to a son named Francis, her fourteenth child, in 1857, but she passed away in her late forties a few years later. Yet "O'Callahan McSweeny," as he was now known, continued to prosper. In 1864, the tax authorities assessed the value of his businesses at $50,000; at that point he had more than $3,500 on deposit at the Emigrant Bank. Meanwhile, one of his sons became a doctor and two trained, like their uncles, for the priesthood in Rome after completing degrees at New York's College of St. Francis Xavier. When McSweeny died suddenly in 1865 at age fifty-six, an obituary called him "remarkable for his strength of mind, loftiness of aim, and nobility of spirit. He was a perfect gentleman, and what is of still greater value, an earnest Catholic, faithful to all his duties.... [H]e leaves many to regret his sudden departure from amongst them."

O'Callaghan and Honoria McSweeny.

William Rudkin was another Famine immigrant who prospered supplying the liquor trade. Trained as a druggist, Rudkin left the town of Carlow, his birthplace, and opened an apothecary on Merrion Row in an affluent part of central Dublin just off St. Stephen's Green. But the Famine and the resulting economic doldrums apparently affected business even in that prosperous locale. In the spring of 1851, forty-four-year-old William and his eighteen-year-old son of the same name took a steam-powered ferry from Dublin to Liverpool and there boarded the S.S. *Hemisphere* for New York. His wife, Catherine, and their four other children made the trip three months later.

Like the McSwineys, the Rudkins brought significant savings with them from Ireland. William may have entrusted their nest egg to Catherine, because he opened his Emigrant Savings Bank account with an initial deposit of $400 just three days after her arrival. By that point, Rudkin had already resumed work as a druggist, though not running his own shop. In 1860, when he finally started an American business of his own, it was not in the drug trade and not as a retailer. Instead, he used his chemistry background to manufacture "flavoring extracts" that distillers could use to disguise their cheap booze as fine spirits. For twelve dollars, boasted one of his advertising flyers, distillers could buy a pound of Rudkin's Holland Gin Oil, enough to make sixteen barrels of American alcohol taste like Dutch gin in a fraction of the time and at a fraction of the cost. Rudkin sold oils that could flavor alcohol to taste like bourbon, brandy, cognac, port, rum, scotch, sherry, whiskey, and even Bordeaux wine. This trade was lucrative. In 1860, when he entered the liquor-flavoring business, Rudkin told the census taker that his net worth was $800. Twelve years later, that figure had mushroomed to more than $30,000, about half of which he invested in government bonds; he used the other half to purchase the four-story brownstone (still standing) that he and his family owned at 594 Henry Street in what is now Carroll Gardens, Brooklyn. Some

Paintings of William Rudkin and his wife, Catherine Connolly Rudkin.

New Yorkers wondered if Rudkin could have made his small fortune so rapidly in legitimate enterprises alone. "Some say that old Rudkin manufactures female [abortion] pills, on which he makes money rapidly," reported one of Dun & Company's informants in 1868, but "others deny it." Whatever the case, the Rudkin business, eventually taken over by his sons, continued to operate into the twentieth century.

———————

Most of the immigrants who became saloonkeepers remained in that business for the rest of their lives if they could. But some decided to diversify their business pursuits, knowing that it was wise to have another source of income should their liquor shop suddenly fall on hard times. Peter McGoldrick, for example, arrived in New York in April 1851 (apparently having left his wife, Ann, and their baby in Ireland) and, after toiling as a day laborer for a little over a year, withdrew his $140 bank balance and left for California, presumably hoping to strike it rich in the Gold Rush. He returned to New York two years later with $550, a sizable profit for his California adventure, but certainly not a fortune. McGoldrick then sailed for Ireland, and several years later when he re-emigrated with his wife and children, they settled in Brooklyn, where Peter became a saloonkeeper directly across the street from the Navy Yard in partnership with a kinsman, Neal McGoldrick, who had spent most of his first ten years in New York working as a morocco dresser.

The Navy Yard district was a propitious location for a saloon, and Peter and Ann flourished. Soon Peter and Neal were operating four saloons, all in the same vicinity. Besides their retail businesses, they were partners in several local distilleries as well. Irish immigrants in this part of Brooklyn were famous for producing Irish poteen (a fiery spirit distilled from malted barley) without paying excise taxes—in 1867, in fact, authorities confiscated a keg of the illicit brew from Peter. He and Neal had a falling-out in 1870, causing Peter to sell his stake in their businesses and leaving him with just one saloon but $10,000 in real estate. Peter used the proceeds from the dissolution of that partnership to try his hand as a real estate speculator. "Peter McGoldrick, Esq., is putting up four elegant mansions on the corner of Washington and Park avenues, at a cost of $150,000," reported the *Brooklyn Daily Eagle* in 1871. This was just the kind of puffery a novice real estate developer like McGoldrick loved—he had actually paid only $3,250 for the lots, and the buildings would not cost much more than that sum. His speculation appears to have paid off. The McGoldricks continued to operate their liquor shop and now collected rents from their Washington Avenue properties as well. They also became major donors for the construction of a Roman Catholic church in their neighborhood, and in 1882 Peter could afford to travel to Rome to see one of his sons ordained as a priest. Another became an attorney. Peter and Ann lived in one of the four "mansions" (really apartment buildings) and operated a saloon on the ground floor of another until his death in 1892.

Bernard Woods was another saloonkeeper who successfully branched out into other pursuits. Woods had farmed the rolling green hills of Monmurry in northeast County Monaghan with his father, Felix, until "Barney" emigrated in 1851, at age nineteen, with his fifteen-year-old sister, Bridget. She probably got a job in Manhattan as a domestic servant, while Barney moved to a sparsely populated part of north Williamsburg in Brooklyn, began work as a day laborer, and married Ann Flanagan. In 1856, he took the ferry to Manhattan and put $300 into an account at the Emigrant Savings Bank. It must have been an emergency fund—he did not visit the bank again until 1861, the year he opened a liquor shop in the small brick tenement that he, Ann, and their sons Henry and George inhabited. George died young, as did another son, but Ann and Barney eventually had one more son and three daughters who lived to adulthood.

The Woodses' saloon sat two blocks from the East River on the very northern edge of residential Williamsburg. To the east lay iron and brass foundries, varnish factories, a quinine works with its acid sheds, and hundreds of empty lots. To the north and west toward the river sat noxious oil refineries, an equally noxious gasworks, and two giant coal sheds sitting beside three enormous "coal bins," each longer than a football field, connected to the Philadelphia and Reading Coal and Iron Company's three docks via an elevated, steam-powered tramway. This machinery enabled the filthy, coal-dust-covered laborers employed there to unload dozens of tons of coal daily, and these hungry and thirsty workers poured into the Woods saloon before and after work. Becoming so familiar with so many north Brooklyn voters, Barney became "a power in politics," according to the press, and though he never held elective office, leading politicians sought his advice, curried his favor, and passed along valuable patronage opportunities. Meanwhile, Ann and Barney invested their saloon profits in neighborhood real estate, including the tenement where they lived and worked. By 1870, they owned $20,000 worth of buildings and lots.

One of those real estate investments became Barney's claim to fame. Next door to the tenement where the Woods family resided, at the southeast corner of Wythe Avenue and North Ninth Street, was a hundred-foot-square "athletic hall." Barney purchased it and rebranded it as Woods' Athletic Grounds. He did so in the late 1870s just as pedestrianism, the competitive marathon race-walking craze, was sweeping America and briefly making Bartholomew O'Donnell, Brooklyn's faux octogenarian, famous. Sometimes Woods would organize these race-walking events himself, offering prize money and charging a race entry fee in the hopes that those receipts plus the money he charged spectators would surpass the sum laid out for awards. In other instances, Woods rented the hall, which a reporter described as "a miniature of the Madison Square Garden," to race organizers and added to his profits by selling drinks to the spectators. Woods' Athletic Grounds was also a popular venue for amateur boxing matches, union gatherings, political meetings, and rallies held in support of the Irish independence movement. Woods operated the hall until he was in his mid-sixties, at which point he and Ann retired to Flatbush to live with their son John, a priest. Henry, their eldest son, became an attorney. Barney passed away at about age seventy-five in 1906 from influenza. And while Woods's sporting hall was demolished decades ago, many of the three- and four-story brick buildings on that stretch of Wythe Avenue today are the very ones that sat there in the heyday of Woods' Athletic Grounds.

An undated photo of Bernard "Barney" Woods, saloonkeeper and proprietor of Woods' Athletic Grounds.

To most Famine immigrants, it must have seemed as if saloonkeepers could not fail. New Yorkers' demand for booze appeared insatiable, and Irish immigrants, unaccustomed in the old country to having much cash, took pride in buying rounds for each other at their neighborhood watering holes, enriching the saloonkeeper in the process. The average immigrant liquor dealer had two and a half times more money in his Emigrant Savings Bank account than the typical Irish-born New Yorker. Furthermore, saloonkeepers were much more likely than others to have accounts at more than one bank, meaning that the wealth gap between them and the average immigrant was probably greater still.

Yet not every Irish saloonkeeper succeeded. About a quarter of the Famine Irish liquor dealers ended their work lives as employees of someone else, sometimes as clerks or agents, but in other cases as cartmen or — occasionally — as menial day laborers. In fact, saloonkeepers failed in business at about the same rate as New York's other Irish entrepreneurs.

It is usually impossible to determine why some immigrants did not succeed as liquor dealers. In several cases, however, the causes of saloonkeepers' business troubles can be identified. Some expanded their operations too aggressively, and a spectacular case of such overexpansion was that of Michael Halpin. He and his older brother, Peter, worked as gardeners in County Meath before they immigrated to New York in 1848 with their sister and her infant child. Upon arrival, they settled in Ward Sixteen on the West Side just above Fourteenth Street. In 1850, Peter became a saloonkeeper there on Seventh Avenue. Michael made an abortive attempt to enter the liquor business on Ninth Avenue at the same time but soon had to take a job as a clerk instead. He reentered the saloon trade in 1853, however, and this time he succeeded, at least initially. For most of the 1850s, he operated a watering hole at 82 Ninth

Avenue, but toward the end of the decade he began expanding his operations, growing to three saloons in 1856, four in 1858, seven in 1860, and nine in 1861. For a while, he even had his own alcohol-rectifying operation where, using flavorings such as those sold by William Rudkin, he produced specialty liquors for his saloon empire.

To all appearances, Halpin was a wealthy man by this point, boasting to the census taker in 1860 that he owned real estate worth $20,000 and an additional $15,000 in personal property—a total equivalent to about $1.25 million today. He had also become a leading figure in neighborhood politics, representing the ward on citywide Democratic committees, helping to choose the nominees for important offices like alderman, and hosting the ward's Democratic primary meetings (where liquor flowed like water) at his flagship location at the southeast corner of Ninth Avenue and West Seventeenth Street.

Halpin clearly believed that coveted corner retail locations were worth their high rents due to the heavy foot traffic that passed them each day. At the peak of his expansive enterprise, in 1861, he was operating saloons on Tenth Avenue at the corner of West Twenty-Fifth Street, First Avenue at the corner of East Twenty-Fourth Street, and at seven corner locations on Ninth Avenue stretching from West Thirteenth all the way to West Forty-Second Street. "He is well calculated for this line of business," gushed the examiner from R. G. Dun & Company sent to evaluate his creditworthiness. He "keeps a fast house and makes a good appearance."

But Halpin had expanded his business too aggressively, and over the course of the Civil War his saloon empire collapsed. Tens of thousands of young men—the city's heaviest drinkers—left New York to fight in the war. During the conflict, his saloons apparently could not unload enough beer and whiskey to cover those hefty corner-lot rents. He may have had to sell some of those properties (or their leases if they were rented) to pay the debts he had incurred during his flurry of expansion. Whatever the case, Halpin's business shrank from nine saloons in 1861 to eight in 1862, six in

1864, and just two in 1866, the year he passed away at age fifty-three. At the time of his death, Halpin still lived in luxurious sur-roundings. The items sold off at his estate sale included a "fine rosewood Piano," a "rich Velvet Tapestry," "Hall Oilcloths,...heavy Curtains," "fine Carpets," and "also all the fine Wines and Liquors removed from Tammany Hall [where it had been shipped on con-signment], they being a fair assortment and belonging to the estate of the late Michael Halpin, Esq." In the end, however, proceeds from the sale of his real estate holdings and personal property did not quite match his outstanding debts, forcing his widow, Margaret, to live in much more modest circumstances until her death three years later, at age forty-two.

Some immigrants who failed in the liquor trade did so primarily as a result of personal shortcomings. Thomas "Hugh" Keane, for example, emigrated from Castlebar, County Mayo, in 1850 at age nineteen and by 1855 had established himself as a liquor store pro-prietor at 104 Mott Street, just north of Canal in Ward Fourteen. He later moved his retail operation to Baxter Street in Five Points and then Cherry Street in Ward Four, before finally settling on a location facing the East River waterfront at 173 South Street in the same ward. Keane was a shrewd businessman and sales must have been good at that dockside location. He plowed his profits into a wholesale liquor business and Manhattan real estate and also became a Democratic leader in the ward. Like a significant number of successful saloon-keepers, Hugh Keane aspired to greater things, so in the early 1880s he handed the day-to-day operation of his liquor shop to Hugh Jr. and began to dabble in real estate full-time.

When Mary Ann Geraghty Keane, Hugh's wife of more than thirty years, died in 1884 and left him with nine children to care for on his own, Hugh quickly married Mary Connell, a wealthy American-born widow ten years his senior. They lived, along with most of his children, in Stamford, Connecticut, in a twelve-room mansion nestled on eighteen wooded acres. Yet in 1887, just two years after she married Hugh, Mary also passed away. The apparently wealthy Keane, now fifty-six, did not lack for new marriage prospects, however. In April 1889, he wed American-born Helen Agnes McMullen, thirty years his junior and described by the *World* as an "imposing looking blonde." She wanted to live in New York, and Hugh apparently promised her a "handsome house" on Fifth Avenue. So right after the wedding, Hugh put the Stamford estate up for sale, and he and Helen moved back to Manhattan.

Helen evidently imagined that she and Hugh would soon be gracing the New York society pages, but they ended up on the police blotter instead. Hugh, at this point fifty-eight, was described by a reporter as "a bright-eyed, white haired and garrulous old gentleman, scrupulously neat and polite." But he was also a jealous man. Enraged at what he perceived to be Helen's ceaseless flirting with younger men, Hugh took to locking her in a room when he went out in order to keep her away from his perceived romantic rivals. Keane continued to be convinced that, even locked away, Helen harbored affections for other men, so in the summer of 1892 he brought her to a "cheap flat" he rented on Fifth Avenue at West 113th Street in Harlem (thereby fulfilling his promise that he would provide her a home on that famous thoroughfare) and then disappeared. A month later, Helen sued Hugh for abandonment and lack of support, and the police eventually tracked him down to a run-down, five-dollar-a-week boardinghouse sixty miles north of Manhattan in the Hudson River Valley.

It turned out that in addition to having trust issues, Hugh had a gambling problem. He "had not a cent," he told the magistrate assigned to his case, because he had lost $60,000 (equal to about $2 million today) in risky speculations on Wall Street, frittered away about $6,000 more in losing wagers at a horse-racing track in New Jersey, and squandered large sums in other ventures in hopes of quickly recouping those losses.

Helen, however, disputed her husband's cries of poverty. Her attorneys insisted that Keane had been a successful investor and that he was hiding his wealth from a wife he now regretted having married. Helen sued Hugh again in 1894, claiming that after the previous estrangement, he had induced her, under false pretenses of reconciliation, to sign away her stake in real estate he had bought in her name. Once she did so, she claimed, Hugh abandoned her again and refused to support her.

In 1895, the couple reached an out-of-court settlement, and Hugh passed away five years later. Helen never got her fine home on Fifth Avenue. After Hugh's death, she married a French-born carpenter. The couple never had any children, and Helen had to work as a dressmaker, advertising custom-made "gowns" for "$7 and up" in small newspaper ads. She passed away at age forty-eight in 1911.

Although Hugh Keane may have self-destructed in spectacular fashion, his story would not have deterred other Irish immigrants from venturing into the saloon trade. After all, Keane had not actually failed as a liquor dealer. His mistake was to gamble away all his profits. Famine immigrants recognized that saloonkeeping was the most lucrative trade they could reasonably hope to enter, that the business brought not only profits but also prestige and potential political prominence, and that saloonkeepers' sons were especially likely to attend college and become priests and attorneys. There was no guarantee of such an outcome, of course, as John Lane learned too well. Still, just the possibility of saloon riches enticed thousands of Famine immigrants to enter the business. Most, to be sure, did not do as well as miserly Thomas Fenton. But saloonkeepers' impressive bank balances—higher than those of any immigrants other than doctors and lawyers—reflect why the Famine generation would always see running a saloon as the pinnacle of success.

PART III

CHAPTER NINE

"Well-Cultivated Fields and a Good Bank Account"

The New York Irish Beyond New York

SEVERAL HUNDRED THOUSAND Famine refugees focused their energies on climbing the socioeconomic ladder in New York City itself. They laid down roots in the city's Irish neighborhoods, used their networking skills to snag the most advantageous employment opportunities, and saved their money. That way, when the time was right, they could move to a nicer part of town, switch to a less strenuous occupation, open a business, or buy a home. New York (or perhaps Brooklyn or Jersey City) became their permanent American home.

Yet for several hundred thousand more Famine immigrants, the city was merely a way station en route to their ultimate destination. Sometimes the immigrants paused in New York for only a few days or weeks before moving on to their eventual place of residence. In other cases, the death of a loved one or meeting the man or woman of their dreams meant that an intended short layover in Manhattan became an extended residence there. Even in such cases, many of the Famine Irish eventually fulfilled their original resolution to settle elsewhere in the United States.

Take the family of Peter Lynch, from the tiny rural townland of Rahood (pop. 148 on the eve of the Famine) in County Meath, whom we met in the Introduction. This farm family—widowed matriarch Catherine, her eldest child, Peter, his new wife Mary McFadden Lynch, and four of Peter's younger siblings (Jane, Mary, James, and Ellen)—left Ireland in the fall of 1846, one year after the initial appearance of the potato blight. When the first mate of the sailing ship carrying them to New York asked where in North America the family intended to settle, Peter said, "Illinois," where the Lynches apparently planned to resume the farming life they had known in Ireland.

But when they arrived in New York on the eighth of December, the Lynches decided to remain in Manhattan, perhaps because they learned that jobs were scarce in Illinois in the winter months. They may have also needed to earn some money to finance their trip to the midwest and make a down payment on a good farmstead. Besides, staying in New York would enable the Lynches to

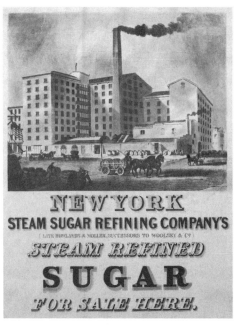

The New York Steam Sugar Refining Company's plant on the Hudson River, where Peter Lynch worked as a laborer during his first decade in the United States.

reconnect with Peter's eldest sibling, Ann, who had come to New York a year earlier and taken work there as a domestic. Peter, thirty-one years old when he landed in Manhattan, found employment as a laborer at the massive nine-story New York Steam Sugar Refining Company plant near the Hudson River in Ward Eight. He and Mary took an apartment on Charlton Street one block away from the facility. Jane, like Ann, became a domestic servant. James, still a teenager, became a grocery clerk.

For some reason, the Lynches did not move on to Illinois when spring arrived. Perhaps the drudgery of farm labor seemed less appealing once they had tried something different. Or they may have found it harder than anticipated to save the money needed to buy a midwestern farm. Even after six years in New York, the Lynches had accumulated only $150, which Catherine, Peter, and James deposited in two accounts at the Emigrant Savings Bank. Soon, however, they figured out how to squirrel away more of their meager pay. Ellen, only eleven when she arrived in New York, was now old enough to add to the family's income by taking a job as a domestic. Perhaps Peter (who in 1852 still worked at the sugar refinery) and James got raises. In any case, by 1853 they had doubled their savings, and by the end of 1854 they had doubled it again. In the middle of 1856, their nest egg peaked at $1,671, equal to $63,000 today. It was then that Peter and Mary finally moved west.

Yet they did not settle in Illinois. In the decade since the Lynches had landed in New York, the price of land in Illinois had skyrocketed. Most frugal Famine immigrants would not pay $50 or $75 per acre for a farm in that populous state when land could be had for $1.25 an acre five hundred miles farther west. So in the summer of 1856, Peter took a ferry across the Hudson, boarded a train, and traveled the twelve hundred miles to St. Paul, Minnesota. From there, he ventured forty miles farther to the tiny new settlement of Faxon, along the Minnesota River in Sibley County, where he laid claim to eighty acres of land for only $100.

If Peter was looking to get away from the crowds in New York, he had succeeded. At that point, Faxon had no more inhabitants than Rahood, but Faxon's residents were spread out over twenty times the space. Peter probably built a crude lean-to on the property to mark it as occupied and satisfy the requirement that he "improve" it in order to keep the homestead. Then he returned to New York.

A year later, in 1857, Peter brought his wife, Mary, brother James, and perhaps sister Ellen as well to Minnesota. Peter and James probably did not have time to finish building a more substantial log cabin on the farm before winter set in; when the Minnesota census taker made his rounds in St. Paul that November, he found Peter, Mary, and James living there together. James, who suffered from asthma, was working as a store clerk, just as in New York. Peter reported, despite having toiled for the previous decade in the sugar plant, that his occupation was farming.

The following spring, he and Mary settled on the Faxon farm for good. James remained in St. Paul working as a store clerk, and by 1860 Ellen had moved into the log cabin with Peter and Mary. There was no shortage of logs for the construction of such housing, as most of the Lynches' "farm" (like all the others in the vicinity) was covered in trees. As a result, Peter reported in 1860 that his eighty acres were worth only $150, giving a sense of how little demand there was for tree-covered acreage in this far-flung locale. It was inhospitable too. Nothing they had experienced in Ireland could have prepared them for the frigid temperatures or blizzards that were common in Minnesota each winter. Peter's sisters Ann and Jane, meanwhile, continued to work as domestics in New York. Ellen eventually returned there to earn money as a domestic as well.

Despite the hardships involved in building a farm from scratch in an isolated valley in rural Minnesota, Peter and Mary eventually prospered there. Before long they could afford to replace their log cabin with what a contemporary described as a "commodious frame dwelling." By 1870, they had doubled their acreage and Peter estimated its value then at $1,500, more than most of the neighboring farms. At that point, Peter had cleared the trees from only 20 of his 160 acres. Yet he must have been proud that he now owned a plot of land bigger than all of Rahood. In addition, he and Mary had two oxen, four milk cows, six steers, and six pigs. On occasion, however, bears came out of the woods at night and made off with a pig. Like most of his neighbors, Peter grew a mix of wheat, corn, and oats — he harvested 450 bushels in 1869. He also brought in 35 bushels of potatoes and the cows produced enough milk to make 300 pounds of butter annually. The Lynches had no children, so a teenage Irish-born kinsman named John Lynch helped Peter work the farm.

Although separated by hundreds of miles, the Lynch siblings must have felt the pull of family ties grow stronger as they aged. After Peter's wife, Mary, died in 1877, Ellen moved to Minnesota to

Settlers in Faxon, Minnesota, built this structure in 1859 and christened it the Church of St. John. The crude nature of the structure reflects the hardships these Irish immigrants had to endure to build communities in such remote locations.

keep house for her brother. By 1880, James had joined them too. And by 1885, all six siblings — Peter, Ann, Jane, Mary, James, and Ellen — had reunited in the farmhouse in Faxon, four thousand miles from the cabin in Rahood where they had grown up. They lived together until Peter and James both died in the first week of April 1891, of complications from influenza.

Peter's probate records confirm that he had been a successful farmer — he passed away with plenty of assets and not a single outstanding debt. Peter did not have a bank account at that point, but he did have $500 in cash stashed inside the farmhouse. The rest of Peter's liquid assets, a little over $2,000, had been loaned out to his neighbors at 7 percent interest. Peter's will ordered that these loans be called in and the proceeds split among the four sisters. Peter also bequeathed the farm to them. They sold it and used some of the profits to buy themselves a house in the nearest significant town, Belle Plaine, while using the rest of the bequest to support themselves in their old age. Ann, the eldest of the four, passed away in her seventies in the late 1890s. Mary and Jane died of pneumonia on the same day in January 1907, when they too were in their mid-seventies. The baby of the family, Ellen, died in Belle Plaine in 1926 at age ninety. The names carved on the tombstones surrounding the Lynch family plot in Faxon — Carney and Cavanaugh, Donovan and Duffy, Fahey and Fitzgerald, McCarthy and McCormick, O'Connell and O'Keefe, Shaughnessy and Sheehan — reflect that the Lynches were just one family among tens of thousands who, after initially fleeing the Famine to New York, decided to go west, where they believed that they had a better chance to achieve the financial security that had been so elusive in Ireland. For these people, as for so many immigrants, New York was a springboard — one whose characteristics were constantly changing due to the impact of the multitudes who inhabited it. But as these onetime Irish New Yorkers landed elsewhere, they transformed the rest of the United States just as profoundly as they had changed New York.

It's impossible to determine precisely how many Famine refugees resided in New York before eventually relocating elsewhere. We know that 1.3 million Irish immigrants came to the United States in the decade beginning when Famine first struck in 1846, and that 960,000 of those immigrants landed in New York. Many of them, like Peter Lynch, were asked where they planned to settle, and about half indicated New York City as their intended home. Yet in 1855, there were only about 150,000 Famine immigrants living in Manhattan. Of the remainder, a few (no more than 5 percent) had returned to Ireland. A much larger proportion (perhaps 20 or 25 percent) died before 1855. The rest, after living in New York for a while, eventually moved elsewhere. So apart from the dead and the return migrants, it seems that for every immigrant who stayed in Manhattan, there was another who decided they could do better outside New York City.

Some Famine immigrants stopped in New York merely to regain their health after the taxing ocean voyage, earn some money, and gather intelligence about where to build new lives. They never considered themselves New Yorkers. But others, like the Lynches, spent years in New York City. It is where they fell in love, started families, learned vocational skills, opened businesses, and became part of the social fabric. New York reshaped them. Their Irish *and* New York experiences helped transform communities across the United States.

Which Irish New Yorkers chose to leave the city? In terms of occupations, it was roughly a cross section of the Irish community. Among the Emigrant Savings Bank's customers, three-quarters of the "leavers" were those who started out in America as unskilled or skilled manual workers, roughly equal to their proportion of the bank's overall customer base. Unskilled workers outnumbered skilled craftsmen by an eight-to-seven ratio among the bank's clients, but among those who left New York, skilled workers outnumbered the unskilled by the same ratio. The one group who migrated out of New York in highly disproportionate numbers were clerks, who probably hoped to use their Manhattan retail experience to open businesses in their new locales. Conversely, Irish-born business owners were much *less* likely than others to relocate, probably because they were doing well enough financially that they were reluctant to risk starting over someplace else.

While it is difficult to differentiate leavers from stayers demographically, where the movers settled can be ascertained. Most did not go very far. About a quarter of those who left New York City ventured no farther than Brooklyn, then a separate municipality and accessible only by ferry from Manhattan and the mainland. A wide variety of Famine immigrants relocated to Brooklyn. Some were struggling day laborers like Bartholomew O'Donnell, who organized race-walking marathons to support himself in his old age. More often, the Brooklyn transplants were flourishing artisans or business owners, such as waterfront labor contractor Edmund Butler and his next-door neighbor, grocer Thomas Meagher. These Famine refugees were successful enough to want to buy their own homes but could comfortably afford to do so only across the East River in Brooklyn. Thirty-four percent of the Emigrant Bank's Famine-immigrant customers who relocated to Brooklyn eventually purchased a home, versus only 10 percent of those who remained in Manhattan.

The second most popular place to relocate for those leaving Manhattan—constituting nearly a quarter of the total—was the rest of New York State other than Brooklyn. Again, many of these movers remained close to New York City. The most common destination for this group was Westchester County, especially its very southern tip, which is now the part of New York City called the Bronx. Some of these transplants were struggling immigrants such as the Civil War veteran Thomas Norris, whose life improbably

318

turned around when he got arrested for buying untaxed cigars. Others were successful tradesmen such as the carriage painter William Doherty, who bought a Westchester carriage-making business. For those who left Manhattan but still stayed in the state of New York, the next most common places to settle were the other locales that would eventually become part of New York City—Queens County and Staten Island. Overall, three-quarters of the Famine immigrants who left New York City but stayed in the state settled in what would eventually become the city's four "outer boroughs." The remainder spread out across the rest of the state, though a particularly large number ended up in or near the state capital in cities like Albany, Troy, and Schenectady.

Among the Irishmen and -women who settled in upstate New York are the only Famine immigrants who can be definitively identified on my own family tree. These are my aunt Vivian O'Connor Molloy's great-great-grandparents John and Honora Killeen. John was born in 1827 in Kilmaley parish in central County Clare. At the beginning of the Famine, he immigrated to Dundee, Scotland, perhaps lacking the funds to buy a ticket to America. A few years later, though, he managed to pay his way to New York. It is not known whether John ever lived in New York City, but by 1854 he had settled on the shores of Lake Ontario in Porter, New York, just north of Buffalo, and was working for the New York Central Railroad as a day laborer. Killeen was one of hundreds of Irish immigrants hired to build and maintain the spur lines that connected Buffalo and Niagara Falls to Lake Ontario and Rochester.

In the early 1850s, Killeen married Honora Greene, whom he had known back in Clare. She had arrived in the United States several years after John. Honora gave birth to their first child, Michael, in 1854 when she was twenty. They had their fourteenth, Lizzie, in 1875.

John supported that huge family working for the New York Central for half a century, first in Porter, then in Niagara Falls, and finally in Buffalo. He toiled as a day laborer into the 1860s, and then as a clerk of some sort for the railroad during the latter half of the Civil War, before returning to day labor in the 1870s. In the 1880s, John managed to secure less grueling work by helping to direct traffic in Buffalo's railyards as a flagman and signal operator until he finally retired, at age eighty, in 1907. When John passed away in 1911, a Buffalo newspaper called him "one of the city's best-known residents."

———

The next most popular place for Irish-born New Yorkers to resettle, accounting for about 15 percent of the total, was New Jersey. Most of these transplants went no farther than Jersey City, which lay immediately across the Hudson from lower Manhattan. Jersey City was where charcoal peddler James Devlin from Bodoney in County Tyrone eventually set up his charcoal manufacturing operation. The next most common New Jersey destinations for ex–New Yorkers were Hoboken (just north of Jersey City), where John and Maria Regan opened their oyster saloon, and Newark, a few miles west of Jersey City. As was the case with Brooklyn, cheaper real estate prices drew many of these Irishmen to New Jersey. Fifty-seven percent of the Emigrant Bank customers who moved to New Jersey managed to buy their own homes by 1870, five and a half times the rate for depositors who remained in New York City.

There were plenty of Irish immigrants in New England, but relatively few settled there after living in New York. Moving to the South was even less popular. Irish immigrants did not want to compete with lowly paid free Black Southerners or unpaid enslaved people for the manual labor and domestic service jobs for which they were most often qualified. The immigrants found such competition degrading, because they knew that in the South, many dangerous jobs — such as moving five-hundred-pound bales of cotton on and off riverboats and ocean vessels — were given to the Irish because the work was considered too hazardous for the enslaved, who by the 1850s might be valued at as much as a thousand dollars each. If an Irish immigrant was crushed by a falling bale of cotton, in contrast, it cost his employer nothing at all. As we have seen with the case of the collapsed warehouse in chapter 3, businesses in those days were not required to pay the medical bills of injured workers or even death benefits to the families of those killed at work. As a result, the Irish usually avoided relocating to states that allowed slavery.

Still, a few Irish immigrants did move to the South. Christopher Burke, from Westmeath, for example, had already been employed as a painter in Ireland before he emigrated at age thirty-one in 1847. He plied his trade as a journeyman in New York for eleven years, but at the end of 1858 he withdrew his $435 in savings from the Emigrant Savings Bank and moved with his wife, Catherine, and their three children to Macon, Georgia.

There Burke became partners with Scotsman Henry Lovi, an already established Macon painter. At first it appeared that Burke had erred badly, as the Civil War severely disrupted business in the South. Lovi, believing that the devastation wrought by the war would make it impossible to turn a profit, moved to Chicago. But Burke, who somehow avoided military service, decided to stay in Macon and after the war he announced in the press that he was resuming house and sign painting on his own and that he sold paints as well "at moderate prices."

Despite the postwar recession in the South, Burke's business was a success. He became well-known for the artistry of his sign painting and the press called him "one of Macon's most popular Irishmen." By 1870, Burke owned a house worth $3,000 and in the ensuing years he won a seat on the Bibb County Commission, the county's governing body. When Burke passed away in the summer of 1884, his funeral was the largest Catholic memorial service ever held in Macon.

In Southern seaboard cities such as Baltimore, Savannah, and New Orleans, there were significant numbers of Irish day laborers. But the Famine immigrants who moved to the slave states from New York relocated there primarily to become peddlers, tradesmen, business owners, and farmers. Still, that number was relatively tiny. In 1860 more Irish immigrants resided in the ten square miles of Manhattan below Forty-Second Street than lived in the entire 770,400 square miles of territory that would become the Confederate States of America, reflecting the intense determination of the Famine Irish to avoid settling there.

———

The midwest and upper midwest were far more popular destinations for Famine immigrants who decided to leave New York. Many of these midwestern transplants moved there to resume the farming lives they had known in Ireland. New York's most widely read Irish newspaper of the antebellum period, the *Irish-American*, often urged its readers to venture westward and become farmers. Going west gave one "that independence which industry and energy combined with thrift and prudent foresight, never fail to secure in these new realms of teeming fertility." Already existing farms could be purchased for as little as three dollars an acre, "depending on the nature of the soil and its proximity to a city or town, or a railroad station," one of the paper's correspondents reported in 1859, while forty acres of virgin land on the frontier of white settlement could be bought from the government for just fifty dollars. Another advantage of farm life out west was that there, "the natives" had "none of the narrow-minded, intolerant bigotry of some of our Eastern neighbors." (The writer was describing native-born white Americans, not Native Americans.) Instead, "a good, generous, hearty, benevolent feeling pervades the whole of the Western country."

It was not safe for Famine immigrants like Peter Lynch to farm what was then the far western frontier until the Native Americans who had called those lands home for centuries had been forcibly moved farther west, and a few of the Famine immigrants played a leading role in that process. One who did so after first becoming a New Yorker was Edmond Butler. Well educated in his native Clonmel, Butler was the first in his family to immigrate to America, leaving behind a widowed mother and four siblings when he sailed for New York in 1848 at age twenty-one. Butler initially found work in Manhattan as a schoolteacher, but by 1854 had secured employment as a proofreader at the *New York Mercantile Journal*. Four years later, he had been promoted to a writing position, and two years after that he became a junior editor at the *New York Tribune*.

Political connections forged at the *Tribune* helped Butler land an appointment as an army lieutenant in October 1861, six months after the start of the Civil War. But because he had no military experience, the army sent Butler to Leavenworth, Kansas, where he supervised Confederate prisoners and Union military recruitment. Butler apparently liked army life, because when the war ended and most soldiers returned home, he remained in the army in Kansas, accompanied by his wife, Kate, and their son. After the war, Butler's regiment was ordered to keep the Indian tribes of the Great Plains away from the railroads and on their reservations. Over the course of the next thirteen years, as Edmond's unit attempted to accomplish that goal, he and Kate had seven more children.

Toward the end of that period, after the death of General George A. Custer and his troops along the Little Bighorn River in southern Montana in the summer of 1876, the army sent Butler's regiment there to help subdue the Sioux and Cheyenne Indians led by Crazy Horse, who had defeated Custer. The regiment, numbering about four hundred men, trudged through blizzard conditions and temperatures that dipped as low as -28°F in early January 1877 before Butler and his men found Crazy Horse and about six hundred of his warriors waiting for the Americans atop a series of high ridges known as Wolf Mountain.

The general in charge of the operation ordered a company of about 125 men to attack the Indians up the gentlest slope, to the Americans' right, but the Indians expected that move and easily repulsed it. Butler, now a captain in command of a third of the regiment, was then ordered to lead his unit in a second attack, this time on the left, via the steepest route up the mountain. At first things also went poorly for Butler's unit. "It seemed to those who watched the movement that nothing could save this company from decimation," especially after Butler's horse was shot out from under him, he wrote soon after the battle. But the Irishman, now on foot like the rest of his troops, led the force charging up the steep ridge "and the impetuous rush of the men...demoralized their opponents" and caused them to flee.

The victory at Wolf Mountain precipitated Crazy Horse's surrender a few months later, and for his bravery Butler received the Congressional Medal of Honor, the nation's highest military award.

This image of the Battle of Wolf Mountain shows the Native Americans' positions on top of the hills and Edmond Butler leading his men up the steep incline on the left to attack Crazy Horse's warriors.

LIEUTENANT-COLONEL EDMOND BUTLER, U. S. A.

Edmond Butler toward the end of his military career.

He was stationed in Montana for most of the remainder of his career, and upon his retirement from the army in 1891 at age sixty-four, he became a lawyer there. He passed away three years later from acute appendicitis while vacationing in France — leaving behind a legacy that included both gallant military service and a prominent role in the removal of Native Americans from the land promised to them by previous generations of Americans.

The Famine immigrants who left New York to become farmers could choose from thousands of communities in the vast swath of farmland stretching from Ohio to Iowa and Michigan and Minnesota. In making decisions regarding where to buy or claim a farmstead, Irish Americans relied on advice from members of their social networks. If they didn't know someone who had already moved west to farm, then someone in their kinship, church, or Irish county social circles certainly did. When all else failed, the press was full of recommendations. That same correspondent of the

Irish-American who touted "the Western country" specifically advised his readers to consider the region immediately southwest of St. Paul, Minnesota, where "many tempting inducements are offered to build up a colony of old friends and acquaintances" from the old country. The area, the author noted, had "a settlement of some 3,000 Irish population within an area of forty miles, which did not contain a single white person some five years ago. Every one around there now is very comfortable, and all are in high expectation of being wealthy."

Two of those early Irish settlers were Michael and Ellen Egan. We know very little about Ellen's origins, but Michael was born in a rural part of southwest County Clare in about 1828 and emigrated in 1850, three years after his father. Michael spent his first year in America doing day labor in western New York but then moved to Massachusetts, where he "worked on a railroad." Six months later, he joined his father in New York City and found a job there as a laborer at a train depot. Egan remained in New York City for six years until, in 1857, he and Ellen withdrew the $85.75 in their bank account, departed the city with their newborn, Michael Jr., and bought eighty acres of land in southeast Minnesota for $100.

Of the hundreds of townships in which the Egans could have purchased a farmstead in that part of the state, the Egans chose — of all places — Faxon, the very settlement where Peter and Mary Lynch had become farmers. There is no indication that the two families knew each other before migrating to the upper midwest. The Egans came from southwest Ireland while the Lynches were born in the east midlands. Peter was employed in a sugar refinery in New York while Michael worked at a rail depot. They also resided in different New York wards. Yet somehow, they ended up living about a mile apart in adjoining sections of Faxon, twelve hundred miles from the west side of Manhattan. Word had clearly spread throughout New York's Irish communities that Faxon was a place where the Irish were setting up a "colony." Irish immigrants constituted only 7 percent of Minnesota's population in 1860, and Sibley County was predominantly German, but 70 percent of the ninety-five households in Faxon that year were headed by Irish-born men like Egan and Lynch.

The Egans' early years in Minnesota were rough. Their "first house, like that of many pioneers, was made of logs, without [a] floor," recounted someone who interviewed the Egans, and had "split oaks for a roof." The whole thing measured just fourteen by fifteen feet, making it no bigger than the tiniest Five Points tenement apartments. Like the Lynches, the Egans eventually built a finer, bigger home, giving them ample space for the six additional children Ellen had after arriving in Minnesota. Even in their new house, however, life was far from easy. The Egans survived both an "Indian massacre" in their vicinity in 1862 and the "grasshopper plague" of 1876 which, luckily for the family, was less severe in heavily wooded parts of the county like Faxon. The Egans weathered these storms, doing well enough that they could afford to buy more land and increase the size of their farm to three hundred acres. Unlike Peter Lynch, Michael Egan took an active role in township governance. He served as justice of the peace when the town first established a government in 1858, and his neighbors held him in high enough esteem that they later elected him chairman of the town board.

Egan retired from farming sometime in the decade after 1885, retaining 185 acres of his farmland and renting it out to others because his surviving children chose to live in Minneapolis, St. Paul, and Butte rather than take over the family farm. Michael and Ellen moved in with their daughter Mary, whose husband, also a Minnesota-born child of Irish immigrants, was a policeman in Minneapolis. When Ellen died in 1898, Michael had her buried not in Minneapolis, but back in Sibley County in a Catholic graveyard high on a hill overlooking the Minnesota River. After Michael passed away in Minneapolis in 1902, he was laid to rest in the same cemetery. Egan had done well—the land he had bought for $1.25 an acre in 1857 was, at his death forty-five years later, worth forty-three times what he paid for it. He left his four children an estate worth $9,700, the equivalent of about $350,000 today.

Minnesota was by no means the only place where New York's Famine Irish relocated to farm. Wisconsin was a more popular destination. Patrick Dolan from County Kilkenny, for example, lived

The Region of the Midwest Favored by Famine Immigrants Who Became Farmers

in Corlears Hook and worked as a day laborer from his arrival in 1849 through at least 1855. The Emigrant Bank secretary recorded his surname as "Doolin," indicating how Patrick pronounced it. Never able to save more than $20 in his bank account, Patrick and his wife, Mary, took their two young sons and left New York in about 1856 for Walworth County in southeast Wisconsin, where they rented land and became farmers. They were the rare Famine immigrants who left New York for a life in agriculture but never apparently purchased their own farm.

Whether one bought a farm right away or waited a few years to do so, success in agriculture required the same skills as operating virtually any other business — hard work, entrepreneurial instincts, knowledge of your products and market, and an appetite for risk-taking.* Adam Strain from rural County Down clearly mastered all those skills. Arriving in New York at age twenty-seven in the summer of 1850, Strain saved $843 in eight years working as a porter in a Manhattan drugstore. At that point, he, his wife, Sarah Sloane Strain, and their two children moved to Marquette County in central Wisconsin, where they spent about $800 on a farm. As his family grew, Strain used the profits from his initial harvests to buy a larger, more expensive property in a different part of the county. Known as "a good neighbor" and a "most indulgent father" to his five surviving children, Strain was also a devout Presbyterian and an active Mason. When he passed away suddenly, apparently of a heart attack, while getting into the bath at age fifty-nine in 1882, the local press called Strain a "wealthy" man and a model of both "thrift and enterprise." He had "handsome farm buildings, the best of stock, broad, well-cultivated fields, and a good bank account."

---

* Because of the high status of farmers within their communities, as well as the fact that farming — like owning a business in New York City — required the investment of capital and the risk of its loss, farmers who owned their own land occupied the same elevated position on the Irish socioeconomic ladder in rural America as their countrymen who owned businesses in urban settings.

Harvesting hay in the upper midwest in the late nineteenth century. Note on the right a steam engine on wheels, used to power threshers; these were man-ufactured in Oswego, New York, under the supervision of Irish-born machin-ist turned factory superintendent John Sinnamon.

Despite the substantial profits made outside New York by Fam-ine immigrants such as Strain, some of the Irish who left the city to farm ultimately decided that they had made a mistake. Felix Quinn arrived in New York in 1853 at age twenty and may have worked in a stable when he first settled there. By 1858, Quinn had moved to Brooklyn with his wife, Rose Ellen McArdle Quinn, and become a hay retailer. In 1860, however, the Quinns were living 150 miles northwest of New York City in Delaware County on a farm they had purchased there. But Felix didn't last long as a farmer. A few years later, he was once again selling hay and other feed for horses, first near Prospect Park in Brooklyn and after the Civil War from a storefront in Cooper Square in Manhattan. In the meantime, Rose Ellen gave birth to ten children in fifteen years. Perhaps that was why she and Felix bought the four-story brownstone at 409 Putnam Avenue (still standing) in what is now the Bedford-Stuyvesant neighborhood of Brooklyn. Felix and Rose Ellen lived there with their eight surviving children, all daughters. Felix died at age forty-four in 1876; Rose Ellen quickly married a Brooklyn streetcar conductor (himself a McArdle) and had three more children, all sons. Felix may have died young, but most of his offspring lived long lives. His youngest child, Frances, resided in Brooklyn until she passed away there in 1963. Hard as it is to believe, there were children of Famine immigrants still living in New York more than 115 years after Black '47.

———

While thousands of Famine immigrants moved to the midwest to become farmers, many more relocated to that region who had no interest in agricultural work. As was the case with those who left New York to pursue farming, networking often determined where in the midwest these immigrants settled and what occupations they chose. At least three of the New York City gasmen from the Dingle Peninsula with accounts at the Emigrant Bank moved in the 1860s to the same small Indiana town, Greencastle, situated on the rail line that connected Indianapolis to St. Louis. Two of these men, James Moriarty and John Forhan (former brothers-in-law from Castlegregory), became railroad track workers, while Bartholomew "Batt" Finn, from the town of Dingle, worked in a nail mill. Despite holding these menial jobs, all three were able to purchase modest homes — worth $300 to $600 — by 1870. Even so, their lives in Indiana were far from secure. Moriarty died on the job in 1877 at age forty-seven. He stepped off a siding onto the main tracks to allow a slow-moving freight train to go by on the siding, not realizing that an express was hurtling toward him from the opposite direction. According to a press account, the impact with the express "tossed" Moriarty "upon [the] passing freight" train, from which he was "retossed under the wheels of the express, and ground to pieces."

Moriarty perished tragically young, but Finn, "who was a

perfect specimen of manhood," according to the press, worked at the nail mill alongside several of his sons until he was nearly eighty. Even at that age, the father of eleven "was as strong, apparently, as the average man of sixty." The same newspaper claimed that Finn was 106 years of age, "possibly the oldest man in Indiana," when he passed away in 1915. But this Bartholomew, like marathon race walker Bartholomew O'Donnell in Brooklyn, had taken to exaggerating his age late in life. Finn was probably eighty-eight when he succumbed to an enlarged heart and "senility."

Artisans were more likely to move west than the unskilled, and did so because the shortage of tradesmen in the midwest attracted many dissatisfied New York craftsmen. Carpenter Daniel Curtin from County Limerick relocated to Hudson, Ohio, just south of Cleveland. Brass finisher Robert Baxter from Belfast ventured farther west, to Detroit, while painter Robert Armstrong and his wife, Hannah, from Cavan, went farther still, to Milwaukee, where he spent the rest of his life as a house painter, eventually owning his own painting business. That life ended suddenly on November 25, 1890, when Armstrong, then seventy years old, was using the outhouse behind his paint shop and somehow fell through the seat and into the "vault" below, where months of urine and feces had collected. By the time he was found two days later, he had suffocated on the noxious privy contents.

Among the artisans who moved west after years in New York were the very first customers of the Emigrant Savings Bank, tailor and "tailoress" William White and Bridget Flanagan White, assigned account number 1 on the day the bank opened, September 30, 1850. Bridget and William had emigrated as teenagers a few years before the Famine and married in New York soon thereafter. Perhaps due to the low wages tailors could command, they had saved only $100 by 1850, but this was not due to any lack of effort by Bridget, who continued taking in needlework even after the couple began having children in 1845. Bridget was a determined saver, something not surprising, given that she was first in line at the bank on its very first day of business. She and William did not make a single withdrawal from their account until January 1856, by which point they had accumulated more than $700. To help with saving, the Whites took in boarders in addition to their needlework.

But on September 30, 1856, six years to the day after Bridget had opened their account, the Whites turned in passbook number 1, withdrew all their savings, and used their nest egg to purchase a brick home on four acres of land on the northern edge of Bloomington, Illinois. Bridget, a devout Catholic, must have liked that their house was across the street from the Church of the Holy Trinity, where she became a "very active" parishioner. While life in Bloomington was slower than New York, it wasn't easier for the Whites. An attempt by William to open his own tailoring business may have saddled the Whites with debt. In the winter of 1864, William advertised that he needed to sell their home. "This property will be sold cheap, for cash," said the notice. The Whites apparently remained in their house, renting it from whoever bought it.

In 1870, the Whites became homeowners once again—or, to be more precise, Bridget did. This was made possible by Bridget's younger brother Patrick Flanagan, who had come to America at the height of the Famine in 1851, perhaps with some financial assistance from his sister. After spending two years in Cleveland, Patrick had ventured to California, where he "engaged in mining some six years, and was quite successful." Patrick tired of life in mining country, however, so in 1859 he joined his sister in Bloomington and spent about $5,000 on a farm just north of town. The bachelor boarded with the Whites in his first years in Illinois before marrying another Irish immigrant. Patrick soon became, in the words of a Bloomington newspaper, "one of the most well-to-do and respected Irish citizens of the county," with a flourishing farm specializing in dairy products and Irish potatoes.

Flanagan apparently bought the Whites' house from his sister and brother-in-law when they faced their liquidity crisis in 1864, or else he acquired it soon thereafter. In any event, in 1870 he transferred the deed to Bridget. Leaving William out of the transaction turned out to be a wise decision. A few years later, William again failed at running his own tailoring business and had to return to wage work as a journeyman. He was employed by a Bloomington clothing shop when, like so many tailors, he died from tuberculosis at age sixty-two in January 1880. (Working for years in rooms suffused with dust and tiny fabric particles expelled from sewing machines damaged tailors' lungs and made respiratory ailments like tuberculosis particularly deadly for them.) Patrick passed away a few months later at age fifty. But Bridget, with the security of owning her home free and clear, stayed in it for nearly thirty more years after William's death, living with her widowed daughter (also named Bridget) and that daughter's little girl.

Having become "one of the oldest of Bloomington's residents," Bridget Flanagan White passed away "from the debilities of old age" at eighty-seven in the summer of 1909. After spending more than half a century in Illinois, Bridget probably did not think much about the fifteen years she had spent in New York City, or about the burst of pride she must have felt when she was told in 1850 that she was the very first customer of the new Emigrant Savings Bank. Despite how diligently she had worked to save, Bridget would not have had such a comfortable retirement had she not had a well-to-do brother to bail her and William out of their financial predicament in 1864. Even so, moving west enabled many Irish immigrants to have the economic security that came from owning a home, something only a handful of them could achieve in New York.

———

Like William and Bridget White, many Famine immigrants who left New York hoped to start businesses. John L. Vaughan, for example, was born and raised in the market town of Kanturk in County Cork but "served an apprenticeship in the dry goods business" in Belfast before emigrating in 1850 with his sister Anne. In New York, John resumed work as a dry goods clerk and Anne married another immigrant in the same vocation, Kerry native James Hoare. In 1857, believing that they had acquired enough expertise to run their own dry goods enterprise, the three of them took their $900 in savings and moved to Dubuque, Iowa, where John and James opened their own dry goods emporium.

The partnership thrived at first, in part because they had little competition in the frontier town when they arrived. It was clear to Dubuque's residents, reported an investigator from the R. G. Dun & Company credit rating agency, that Anne's husband, Hoare, was the brains of the operation and that he took on her brother, Vaughan, as a partner only to appease his wife. But "both are habitual drunkards," claimed the investigator, and to make matters worse they "frequently invite their clerks to drink with them." One of the two partners, it was said, probably Vaughan, "spends his Sundays in dives" and is "addicted to gambling." Yet the credit investigators admitted that the duo made money—lots of it—though apparently thanks mostly to Hoare. He and Vaughan each reported $8,000 in assets in 1860, just three years after relocating to Iowa, and they had accumulated double that by 1866.

At that point, the duo had a falling-out, dissolved their partnership, and began competing with each other, which must have been awkward for Anne. The rivalry quickly came to an end, however, when Anne's husband passed away in 1868 at age forty. The death of his competitor, however, did not improve Vaughan's situation. Lacking his brother-in-law's business savvy, Vaughan took on more debt than was prudent and in 1873 had to declare bankruptcy and close his shop.

Most failed Famine entrepreneurs quickly got back to work on a new venture, but the forty-five-year-old Vaughan took a different path. He moved in with his sister (to whom he owed thousands, according to Dun & Company) and her son and mooched off them for the rest of the decade. That gave Vaughan plenty of time to ingratiate himself with Dubuque's Democratic power brokers. At the end of 1879, after years of unemployment, Vaughan was elected to a four-year term as Dubuque County coroner—a job that, in Dubuque, did not require any medical expertise, only political connections. (Underlings performed the actual autopsies.) After his term expired, Vaughan again relied upon Anne for support, and other than two short stints in patronage positions, he remained dependent upon his sister and her son (who by this point was working for the post office as a letter carrier) until he passed away at age sixty-five in 1893.

A more typical (and less lazy) immigrant entrepreneur was Michael R. Curran from Monaghan, trained like Vaughan as a dry goods clerk. After spending seven years working in that capacity for three different retailers in New York, Curran opened his own dry goods establishment there in 1859. The business failed in 1869 and after a brief stint as a policeman, Curran moved with his wife, Margaret, and their five surviving children to Kansas City, Missouri, and reentered the dry goods trade, operating initially under the name of his fifteen-year-old son, James, to evade his New York creditors. That business quickly folded as well, but unlike Vaughan, Curran was determined to succeed as a retailer. In 1872, he opened a fruit shop while simultaneously seeking the Democratic nomination for county coroner. (What was it that drew failed dry goods dealers to that work?) When both the produce and political efforts floundered, Curran tried retailing soda water. A year after that, in 1875, he closed the beverage business and opened a bakery in the same storefront. That flopped as well, forcing Curran to find work as a dry goods clerk once again. Determined to be his own boss, however, Curran became a dry goods peddler in 1880. He returned to clerking two years later before making one last entrepreneurial effort by opening a restaurant. A few months after it opened, though, Curran passed away at age fifty-nine. Despite Curran's inability to prosper in any of his western ventures, his wife, Margaret, and their children still felt that the frontier held the most promise for enterprising Americans. They moved to Colorado, where son James invented the billboard (or so he claimed) en route to becoming a wealthy advertising executive.

Many other Famine immigrants ventured west to improve their entrepreneurial opportunities. One of these, Patrick Drew, was born near the town of Limerick in 1829 and arrived in New York in the spring of 1850 with his father and two younger siblings. He must have had some training as a mason before leaving Ireland, because he immediately found work in that trade in Manhattan. Yet the ambitious young man apparently heard that even greater opportunities awaited outside New York. Late in the summer of 1854, he withdrew the $77 he had accumulated at the Emigrant Bank, closed his account, and headed west with his wife, Ellen, and their newborn daughter, Mary.

The Drew family settled in Milwaukee, then a frontier town, where Patrick found plenty of demand for his building-trade skills. Speculators, in fact, were desperate to find contractors willing to take charge of their building projects. Knowing he could make far more money as a contractor than a mason, Drew leaped at that opportunity. "Under the direction of Mr. Drew many of Milwaukee's largest buildings were erected," noted a local newspaper years later, and the Drews became wealthy as a result. Patrick also served as one of his neighborhood's civic leaders, representing Milwaukee's First Ward in the state legislature on four different occasions and leaving his family an estate worth more than $37,000 (equal to about $1.3 million today) when he died, at age seventy-four, in 1903.

A photo from 1903 of Patrick Drew, the New York mason turned Milwaukee builder and Wisconsin legislator.

Some Irish immigrants who were already running very profitable business ventures in New York nonetheless left the city seeking even greater success, but sometimes such acquisitiveness backfired. Dr. John D. Durkin and Mary Burke, both born in County Mayo, arrived in America in 1851, met in New York a few years later and, by 1855, were married and living in Ward Ten on the Bowery, where John set up a medical practice. He was a "consumption doctor," one who specialized in the lung ailments so common in this era, when diseases like tuberculosis were omnipresent and easily spread in the confines of crowded tenements. Business on the Bowery was brisk and lucrative. Starting with $450 in the Emigrant Bank in April 1856, the Durkins increased their savings to $2,925 in just two years.

Yet Dr. Durkin craved more. In 1859, the Durkins moved 250 miles northwest to Syracuse, where some family members already resided. John bought a lot in the downtown business district and took out a loan to finance the construction of a four-story brick building. Durkin would house his family there, operate his practice in the building as well, and lease the rest of it to other businesses. But the investment didn't pay off. On Wednesday night, April 24, 1861, Durkin's heavily mortgaged building was consumed by fire. Police suspected Durkin of arson but could not prove his involvement to the satisfaction of a grand jury, so the doctor proceeded to collect on his insurance policy for both damage to the structure and the destruction of his "personal property of the most costly character." The following year, however, dogged detectives found the prized possessions that Durkin claimed had been incinerated in the blaze. The doctor fled to Detroit to avoid arrest, but he was apprehended, extradited, convicted of arson, and sentenced to seven years in prison. In January 1867, after serving four years, Durkin was set free, but in the meantime Mary had left him.

Durkin tried for a fresh start by moving to Scranton, Pennsylvania. By treating patients both in town and in nearby coal country, he was soon raking in cash again. Only a few months after Durkin's arrival in town, his landlord noticed that the physician had "quite a big pile of money" in his examining room. One of Durkin's patients apparently noticed as well. Before dawn on May 29, an intruder entered the office and grabbed the money. When Durkin, who was living where he worked, tried to stop the thief, the forty-eight-year-old physician was beaten to death. His murderer was never found.

The most popular relocation destination for New York City's Famine immigrants—other than the rest of New York State and New Jersey—was, of all places, California. To the Irish, America was a land of opportunity and wealth, and by the early 1850s, California struck many as the location that best exemplified those ideals. Most of the Famine immigrants arrived in America too late to participate in the Gold Rush of 1849 because even if they immigrated in time, they had rarely accumulated the capital needed to finance the long journey to the West Coast. By the mid-1850s, when many Famine immigrants could afford the trip to California, the Gold Rush was waning. Nonetheless, many Americans — immigrants as well as the native-born — continued to move to California anyway, attracted by its reputation as the location where wealth and upward mobility were most easily attained.

In this era, the voyage from New York to San Francisco (the gateway to mining country) was nearly twice as long as that from Liverpool to New York. The journey required taking a sailing ship southward along the Eastern Seaboard 1,200 miles to the southern tip of Florida, then continuing another 1,200 miles through the Gulf of Mexico and around the western tip of Cuba to Panama. After disembarking there and crossing the isthmus by foot, horse, or carriage, the adventurer took another sailing vessel 3,300 miles to San Francisco Bay. (In this era, twenty years before the completion of the transcontinental railroad, hardly anyone took the overland route to the West Coast.) And as on the transatlantic journey, most passengers had to feed themselves during those months of travel. As a result, only the most adventurous immigrants made the trip to California.

A few Famine immigrants who lived initially in New York did manage to arrive in California quickly enough to make money mining. Members of the Canty family had a head start in the race up California's socioeconomic ladder because some of them had come to America before the Famine. Hailing from a tiny rural townland in west Cork just north of Skibbereen, Ellen landed in New York in 1840 along with her husband, Jeremiah Regan. Ellen's brother Michael left Ireland five years later, while their siblings Timothy and Julia, along with their mother, Johanna, emigrated in 1847. This last group brought with them Ellen and Jeremiah's eleven-year-old daughter, Margaret, who had not seen her parents since she was four. Two more Canty siblings, Thomas and Daniel, arrived around the same time.

In the summer of 1850 most of the Cantys, along with their sister Ellen Canty Regan and her husband and children, were living just west of Five Points, and the men were all working as candy makers, a trade Ellen's husband apparently learned in New York and taught to his brothers-in-law. The family was not doing badly — Michael had saved $283 by 1851. Still, he had to squeeze himself, his wife, Ann, his baby, Thomas, his mother, Johanna, his uncle John, his brother Daniel, and two boarders into their tiny apartment (350 square feet at most) to enable them to build that nest egg. Ellen and Jeremiah's flat around the corner was just as crowded.

Seeking a way out of that life, Jeremiah Regan left with Daniel Canty for California in the summer of 1850, hoping to strike it rich as miners. They were joined by another Canty brother, Thomas. By early 1851, the threesome were sending their kin in New York money — lots of money. Eight hundred dollars arrived in April 1851; Ellen got $500 from Jeremiah in June; and Johanna received $600 from sons Thomas and Daniel in July. These were life-altering sums for recently poverty-stricken tenant farmers in west Cork. Over the next several years, Johanna and all the remaining Canty siblings and their spouses and children joined the fortunate trio in California.

Members of the Ruddock family, born fifty miles from the Cantys in northeast Cork, also departed New York hoping to strike it rich as gold prospectors. Brothers James and John, who had emigrated in 1849 and 1851, respectively, and worked as wood sawyers in New York, left for California in 1852 to join three other brothers — Andrew, George, and Benjamin — who were already panning for gold in the foothills of the Sierra Nevada. A year later, James Ruddock sent for his wife, Mary, and their three children. John soon married an Irish immigrant from County Clare whom he met in California. Initially, they did well. James "owned and mined in several rich placer claims on Wood's Creek" near Jamestown, 125 miles east of San Francisco, while Mary ran a boardinghouse there that catered to other miners. John worked as a miner too.

Yet most of these Famine immigrants who started out in California as gold prospectors did not last long in that vocation. Jeremiah Regan had moved to San Francisco by 1852 and returned to confectionary work. Soon thereafter he opened his own candy shop at 33 Montgomery Street; his brother-in-law Daniel Canty became his clerk and bookkeeper. Timothy Canty opened a tailor shop five blocks up Montgomery from the sweet shop, while Thomas Canty ran a "liquor saloon" a half mile to the south. Michael was the only Canty brother without a brick-and-mortar business by 1860. He ran a fruit stand and occasionally did day labor as well.

Jeremiah Regan ran this half-page ad in the San Francisco city directory in 1858, just as his business was starting to take off.

The Ruddocks remained in mining country far longer than the Regans and Cantys. Yet in hindsight, it would have been smarter had they taken their initial prospecting profits and quickly invested them in San Francisco as Regan did. Instead, the Ruddocks plowed much of their revenue into additional mining properties that did not pan out (in the truly original sense of that term). John, James, and the other brothers who had joined them continued to live and work in the Jamestown vicinity past 1860 and identified themselves as "miners" to census takers, but to make ends meet they divided their time, recalled one of their sons, between "mining, merchandising, stock-raising and lumbering." With moneymaking prospects drying up there during the Civil War, the Ruddocks eventually relocated to San Francisco too, though they often couldn't bear to part with their mining properties. John spent most of his time as a San Francisco day laborer, occasionally returning to Tuolumne County to work his claims, until his death at age fifty-eight in 1879. His brother James toiled into his fifties as a sawyer and into his early seventies as a day laborer.

But these apparently precarious occupations concealed a good bit of financial success and stability. James and Mary Ruddock owned their San Francisco home on Ivy Avenue free and clear (it sat on the site now occupied by the San Francisco Symphony) and retained some mining property as well until they passed away in 1903 and 1905, respectively. John Ruddock and his wife, Ellen, meanwhile, purchased their house on Bartol Street three blocks from the waterfront. In 1875, John purchased an empty lot around the corner at 322 Vallejo Street for $1,000, took out a $2,600 loan for four years at 9 percent interest, built two residential buildings on the lot, and began renting out six of the units, while he and Ellen moved into a seventh. The loan came from the Hibernia Bank, San Francisco's answer to New York's Emigrant Savings Bank. John gifted the property to Ellen at his death, and she supported herself as a landlord for the next thirty-one years. In 1900, by which point Ellen had paid off the property's mortgage, the apartments were full of Italian immigrant dockworkers and their families. Ellen survived the 1906 San Francisco earthquake and resulting fire and luckily had insurance on her property, allowing her to rebuild. She passed away at age eighty-six in 1910.

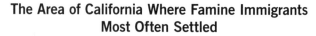

The Area of California Where Famine Immigrants Most Often Settled

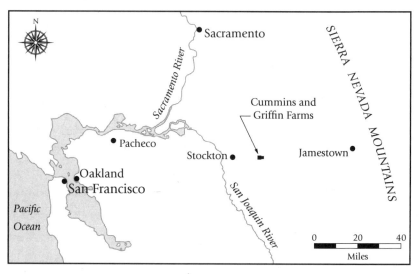

Unlike the Cantys and Ruddocks, most of the Famine immigrants who moved to California did not even try mining. Many had much less dramatic lives with relatively little occupational change. William Fivey tended steam engines in New York and did the same for decades in San Francisco, mostly on steamships that plied the northern California coast. Michael Arthur, who came to America in 1851, was a blacksmith in New York and remained one in Eureka. Laurence Burd from Meath was a bricklayer in Manhattan as well as in San Francisco until his death in 1877.

Others moved up the California socioeconomic ladder only to fall back down. Michael F. Cummings from Castlegregory, a book-binder in New York, ended his life in that trade at the state print-ing office in Sacramento, though in the intervening years he had tried his hand as a painter, a gilder, as undersheriff of San Fran-cisco County, and as editor of a short-lived West Coast news-paper called *The Irish Nationalist*. John M. Foy from County Cavan worked in New York as a clerk before becoming a liquor rectifier (a distiller of highly alcoholic beverages) and then briefly a liquor retailer. Apparently unsatisfied, Foy, his wife, Mary Butler Foy, and their three sons and two daughters headed for San Francisco. There, John put the science behind his alcohol-production experience to good use as a chemistry teacher at St. Ignatius College. When Foy joined the Jesuit institution's faculty, it boasted in advertisements that "a complete philosophical apparatus has been received from Paris," and its "laboratory contains over two hundred and fifty pure chemicals, and all that is necessary for the most complicated manipulations and analysis." But if Foy's work as a chemistry teacher was a step up from his first American job as a clerk, he could not manage to maintain that foothold. By the mid-1880s, he was working as a bookkeeper, and in 1890, at age sixty, he became a salesman at Morganstern's trunk and valise shop. Foy soon returned to bookkeeping, however, and passed away in San Fran-cisco in 1904.

Yet the majority of Emigrant Bank customers who moved to California enjoyed upward socioeconomic mobility. David G. Bart-nett emigrated in 1848 from the Cork town of Fermoy. He toiled as a porter in an "India Rubber Factory" with his brothers and half brothers during his first half decade in New York, but then learned the blacksmith's trade before going to California in the early 1860s. Bartnett settled in the hinterlands of the East Bay, twenty-five miles northeast of Oakland, and set up the first blacksmith shop in the village of Pacheco. The only shopkeeper in town, Bartnett soon began selling whatever the local farmers might need. His "general store and blacksmith shop" served as "the community hub of Pacheco" for more than a half century, until his death in 1918. At that point his assets, willed to his four children, were appraised at $13,500, equal to more than a quarter million dollars today.

The three siblings of Michael Cummings, the New York bookbinder whose ascent up the California socioeconomic ladder proved so fleeting, also did far better in California than they probably would have had they remained in New York City. John, a book peddler back east, moved to the fertile San Joaquin Valley (where he went by "Cummins") and acquired farmland near Stockton that eventually totaled 980 acres. No wonder it was worth $60,000 in 1880 — it yielded 10,000 bushels of wheat per year. John's sister Ellen and her husband, John Griffin, also from Castlegregory and a day laborer in New York, owned the 2,000-acre farm next door. They brought in 40,000 bushels of wheat annually, a mind-bogglingly bountiful harvest for Irish-born farmers in other parts of the United States. After John died of cancer in 1881, Ellen managed the large "ranch" and its many employees "with admirable executive ability and sagacity" (and with some help from her two unmarried adult daughters) until her own death in 1909. The youngest sibling, Patrick Cummings, a gashouse employee in New York, preferred city life in the west. He settled in San Francisco and became a policeman and then a lawyer. Cummings, however, was the rowdy, brawling kind of lawyer. Despite being a widower with a teenaged daughter to care for, Patrick persisted in his hard-drinking ways and drowned in San Francisco Harbor in 1884, having apparently fallen off a wharf while drunk.

The onetime Five Points confectioners from the Canty family also exemplified the promise of Civil War–era California to the

Famine immigrants. Ellen Canty Regan's brothers were all some-what successful, though not nearly as much as one might have expected given those huge remittances they initially sent from California. Thomas Canty, with some fits and starts, remained in the liquor and grocery business for the rest of his life. Timothy Canty, who apparently never married, ran a small tailor shop—rarely in the same location for very long—until he died in 1882. Daniel Canty and a German immigrant partner bought brother-in-law Jeremiah Regan's candy business in about 1867 (with Daniel's financing provided by Regan), and Daniel remained in that trade until he passed away in 1889.

Michael Canty seemed to have the most precarious life of the Canty siblings. He subsisted for years as a fruit peddler and occasionally had to rely on day labor to support himself, his wife, Ann, and their six children. Perhaps sensing that precarity, Michael—unlike his brothers—made it a priority to buy his own home, purchasing one by 1865 on a half lot at what was then the southern end of town, about ten blocks south of Market Street. He remained in it, living with sons Michael Jr. and William (both harness makers) until his death, at age eighty-three, in 1894.

The family of the final Canty sibling, Ellen, did truly strike it rich. Californians, it turned out, were voracious candy eaters, and her husband, Jeremiah Regan, apparently had a keen understanding of the tastes of his retail and wholesale customers. Regan became one of the biggest purveyors of confections on the entire West Coast. As mentioned above, he sold the business to brother-in-law Daniel Canty in 1867 because he was so wealthy that he no longer needed to work. That was because Regan had poured his candy profits into San Francisco real estate and could support his family on the rental income alone, which, by the time of his death, in 1881, amounted to $25,000 *per year* (the equivalent of about

$750,000 annually today). He left his children an estate appraised at $325,000.

Yet Ellen did not live to enjoy that fortune. On the first day of summer, 1858, the forty-seven-year-old was hanging laundry out to dry on the roof of 33 Montgomery Street, which was both the Regan home and the location of their candy business. In stepping down a small ladder from one level of the roof to another, Ellen slipped, and her leg crashed through a skylight, "severing the muscles, arteries and tendons...clear to the bone," according to a news account. She lost so much blood, so quickly, that she bled to death. Jeremiah never remarried.

———

It would appear, based on stories such as those of the Cantys and Regans, that the Famine immigrants who moved west fared better than those who remained in New York City—and the data support that impression. Unskilled workers were nearly 50 percent more likely to ascend beyond that rung of the socioeconomic ladder if they left the New York area: 38 percent of the unskilled who remained in New York ended up climbing higher than their original station, but 55 percent of those who relocated made that leap. Moving also significantly improved one's chances of becoming a business owner: 28 percent of the Irishmen who stayed in New York ended their careers as business owners, but 39 percent of those who left the region achieved that status. For those hoping to reach the very top rung of the Irish American socioeconomic ladder, bidding farewell to New York also enhanced one's odds. Famine immigrants who left the New York area were four and a half times more likely to become doctors and lawyers (mostly the latter) than those who remained in Manhattan. New York City might offer a vibrant Irish American cultural life and a variety of social networks that could help the newcomers find both jobs and spouses, but if one's overriding goal was socioeconomic advancement, then relocating from New York was a smart move.

Comparison of the Initial and Final Occupational Categories of New York's Male Famine Immigrants, Based on Their Final Place of Residence

	FIRST-KNOWN U.S. OCCUPATION OF MALE FAMINE IMMIGRANTS TRACKED TEN OR MORE YEARS	FINAL OCCUPATIONAL CATEGORY OF THOSE WHO REMAINED IN NEW YORK CITY	FINAL OCCUPATIONAL CATEGORY OF THOSE WHO LEFT THE NEW YORK AREA
Professionals	0.9%	1.4%	6%
Business owners	9%	28%	39%
Lower-status white collar	9%	10%	11%
Skilled workers	37%	30%	24%
Peddlers	5%	4%	2%
Unskilled workers	39%	27%	18%

Note: Business owners category includes farmers who own their farmland.

There was more opportunity for advancement outside New York primarily because the barriers to upward mobility were lower the farther one ventured from the East Coast. Shortages of just about every kind of worker in the west meant that opportunities for learning a trade abounded. Yet the upward mobility the Irish experienced outside New York was rarely into the artisanal ranks; instead, it was overwhelmingly into white-collar occupations. This must have reflected a conscious choice by the immigrants. Their goal was not merely to move from one form of manual labor to a higher-status, slightly higher-paying one, but to leave behind blue-collar work altogether. This goal was easier to achieve away from the East Coast, in places where the costs of renting or buying property were so much lower than in Manhattan. Fifty-six percent of the Famine immigrants who left the New York area ended their careers either in a white-collar occupation or operating a business, quite an achievement considering their educational and financial status when they arrived in America.

What was it that separated the immigrants who thrived after leaving New York from those who merely survived? Sometimes it was good luck; sometimes it was good health; sometimes it was having the right training or entrepreneurial instincts; and sometimes it was merely being in the right place at the right time. But in other instances, it came down to a question of character. David Bartnett's half brother Garrett Bartnett, for example, emigrated the same year as David, worked in the same New York rubber factory, also received training as a blacksmith, and also moved to Pacheco. Yet while David was kind and a hard worker, Garrett was greedy and lazy. He became a serial felon, serving four separate sentences (for offenses such as robbery and accessory to murder) in the state prison at San Quentin. He died while incarcerated there in 1907. Surely there were other Famine immigrants who failed to get ahead for similar reasons.

Garrett Bartnett's mug shot for his fourth and final term in San Quentin prison.

The fate of two brothers from west Cork, Daniel and Patrick Donovan, exemplified how health, luck, and hard work could bring drastically different outcomes to immigrants with similar backgrounds who moved west from New York. Daniel and Patrick were born in the rural hamlet of Driminidy, five miles north of Skibbereen. The tiny townland of 375 inhabitants lost more than half its population during the Famine. Many, like their mother, Ellen, had perished. But some emigrated. Among them was Daniel who, with his wife, Mary Brickley Donovan, sailed via Liverpool to New York late in 1850, when he was twenty-five and she was twenty-four. Mary left behind a widowed mother and two siblings who were expecting Mary to send money to support them or finance their emigration to America. Daniel had left his widowed father plus eight siblings—John, Patrick, Cornelius, Timothy, Jeremiah, Richard, Dennis, and Honora—who counted on the same from Daniel. To ensure that they could focus on work and saving, Daniel and Mary left their two-year-old son Cornelius in Ireland with his grandparents, aunts, and uncles.

Daniel and Mary did not disappoint. He had trained as a carpenter in Ireland and found ready employment in Manhattan's booming construction industry. Mary probably worked until her second child, John, was born in 1852. That March, eighteen months after their arrival in New York, the Donovans had saved $120. They probably used some of their savings to buy Daniel's brother Patrick a ticket to America. He arrived in March 1853, joined Daniel and Mary in their tenement apartment on East Twenty-First Street, and began working as a carpenter too. Patrick had brought with him Mary's sister Catherine, one of Mary's cousins, and Daniel and Mary's son Cornelius, now five, who had not seen his parents in three years.

While Mary and Daniel must have been delighted to have their son and other kin join them in New York, they apparently found life in the city unappealing. In December 1854, Daniel, Mary, and Patrick withdrew the $600 they had saved between them, closed their bank accounts, and headed west with little Cornelius and John. They did not stop until they had covered a thousand miles, crossed the Mississippi, and reached Iowa City. The name of that settlement was more aspiration than reality when the Donovans arrived there. The town's five thousand inhabitants were spread out far and wide—the entire "city" had only one-eighth the inhabitants of the single ward in New York where the Donovans had lived. Yet the sparse population of Iowa City and its environs was precisely what gave the Donovans more opportunities for upward advancement than they would have had if they remained in Manhattan.

Daniel and Patrick initially split their time in Iowa between carpentry and day labor. After five years in Iowa City, that income, combined with savings brought from New York, was enough to allow Daniel to buy, for just a couple of hundred dollars, a small home at the southern edge of town near the railroad depot. But Daniel did not get much of a chance to enjoy home ownership. He died in June 1862 at just thirty-six years of age. Mary was left with six children—ranging from an infant born after Daniel's death to thirteen-year-old Cornelius—to care for on her own. She never remarried and instead supported the family by operating a saloon in their small, crowded home. The tiny grave marker that Mary bought for Daniel at St. Joseph's Catholic Cemetery on the outskirts of Iowa City reflected how tight the widow's budget would be for the foreseeable future. The matching marker placed on Mary's grave when she died thirty-five years later indicates that the family's fortunes did not improve much in those intervening years.

Daniel's brother, Patrick Donovan, fared far better in Iowa, even though at first things didn't go very well for him either. In the summer of 1856, at age twenty-five, he became a widower, responsible for a one-month-old son. His wife had likely died from the same postdelivery uterine infection that took the life of Elizabeth O'Connor, the wife of the brawling Ward One saloonkeeper Dan D. O'Connor. Not long after, Patrick's son passed away too.

Around 1860, Patrick remarried. His new bride, Ellen Maher, was an Irish immigrant from Tipperary. Rather than stay in town, he and Ellen bought a farm five miles northeast of Iowa City in Cedar Township, yet another Irish farming enclave. All of Patrick and Ellen's immediate neighbors were also Irish immigrants.

352

The Donovans' farm was substantial—280 acres—but only 80 of them were arable. In 1869, their harvest of grain, hay, and dairy products brought in $780, Patrick reported, far more than he could have made as a carpenter. Sometime in the 1870s, however, Patrick and Ellen sold this farm and bought more expensive acreage in the neighboring township of Graham. This farmstead was smaller—only 200 acres—but 150 of them were arable. As a result, it was far more profitable. By 1880, the Donovans were producing a ton of butter per year. Instead of fifteen pigs, they now had a hundred, and their fields yielded 4,500 bushels of corn, three times the yield of their previous farmstead. All this made the Donovans one of the most prosperous farm families in the area, and affable Patrick—who was active in the Democratic Party and the local Catholic church—became "one of the best known men in Johnson County." Patrick and Ellen also raised eight children, born from 1861 through 1877.

Ellen died in 1893 in her early sixties, and a few years later Patrick gifted most of his farmland to two of his daughters. But in return, Patrick required them to execute promissory notes obligating them to pay him an annual annuity until his death. Patrick lived with one of those daughters, Annie, and her husband, farmer Charles Swift, also the Iowa-born offspring of Irish immigrants. Even in his dotage, Patrick continued to lend a hand around the farm. He was out in a barnyard enclosure repairing a fence on a frigid January morning in 1901 when he suddenly collapsed and died at age seventy.

The unusually tall and ornate tombstone that Patrick had erected for Ellen (and onto which his own name was eventually chiseled) at St. Bridget's Catholic Cemetery twelve miles northeast of Iowa City reflected the prosperity that Patrick and Ellen—in contrast to Daniel and Mary—had managed to achieve by leaving New York behind. New York had been the family's gateway to America, as it was for hundreds of thousands of other Famine immigrants. But beyond the teeming metropolis, a land of opportunity had beckoned.

CHAPTER TEN

"A Respectable Life"

The Children of the Famine Immigrants

IMMIGRANTS COME TO America not merely to improve their own circumstances but also to give their children opportunities that would be unavailable in their parents' homelands. Did the offspring of the Famine immigrants fulfill their parents' dreams in this respect? As we've seen, historians have been skeptical. Hasia Diner, author of more than a dozen books on American immigration history, has noted that "in the usual telling of the story of the Irish in America, they are for the most part relegated to the economic bottom until well into the last decade of the nineteenth century." Kerby Miller, one of the foremost historians of the Irish American experience, has likewise contended that the children of the Famine immigrants did not "advance much beyond their parents' status."

Recently, however, economists have generated far more reliable data on the intergenerational mobility of immigrants and their children by using census-linking methods similar to those employed in this book. The economists have written algorithms to automate the process and create huge databases tracking hundreds of thousands of immigrants and their children over many decades. This process does not work very well with Famine immigrants themselves (whose names and ages were recorded very inconsistently by American record keepers), but it has been put to good use tracking their American-born offspring.

The scholars doing this work have found that the male children of the Famine immigrants ended up, on average, significantly higher up the socioeconomic ladder than their fathers. They were a third less likely to work in unskilled occupations than their fathers and nearly three times more likely to hold white-collar jobs. The American-born children of the Famine immigrants did not completely close the gap between themselves and other native-born Americans in what economists call "occupational rank." That would take one more generation. But given how bleak their children's job prospects would have been in rural Ireland, the Famine immigrants had, by coming to America, vastly improved their offspring's opportunities.

———

Looking at what became of the children of the Famine immigrants featured in the previous chapters brings to life the trends borne out by the economists' data. Daughters are harder to trace than sons because most women married and changed their names. And because the immigrants' children were, on average, more prosperous than their parents, fewer of the Famine immigrants' daughters worked outside the home than had their mothers, most of whom had toiled as domestics before marrying and having children.

Nonetheless, many daughters of the Famine immigrants became schoolteachers. Junk dealer Lanty Ryan's unmarried daughter, Gertrude Ryan, was a lifelong public schoolteacher. So, too, was Mary Ann "Minnie" Dean, daughter of a Castlegregory emigrant who moved to Minnesota. She taught school there until age thirty-one, when she died of what a newspaper described as "quick consumption."

Most female teachers left the profession to get married, but those who never wed, or who took up teaching after the death of a spouse, could go on to hold relatively high-status positions. Recall teacher Caroline "Carrie" Sinnamon, who was accompanying her father (machinery shop proprietor John Sinnamon) on a grand tour of the British Isles when he died in a "disreputable house" in Glasgow. She never married and was therefore able to move up the instructional ranks, working as a "model teacher" in both Oswego and New York City (where she did graduate work at Columbia University's Teachers College), as a school principal, and as a faculty member and department chair at the institution eventually known as Oswego State Teachers College. Sinnamon was such a popular principal that her seventh- and eighth-grade students built her, as a gift for use on Lake Oswego, a twenty-five-foot motorboat, which they christened *The Caroline.*

Caroline Sinnamon with one of her students.

Minnie Ledwith followed a similar path. The widowed daughter of Manhattan hay dealer Felix Quinn, she was a beloved teacher in Brooklyn for twenty-four years and then a highly respected principal there for another twenty-six. But her experience teaching for a half century, like that of Carrie Sinnamon, was exceptional.

More women, like Felix Quinn's remaining daughters, ended up in more menial occupations. Catherine Quinn was a bookbindery forewoman until age forty, when she married co-worker Louis Kleid. Ettie and Ida Quinn worked as book sewers (probably in the same shop as Catherine) into their early thirties before they disappear from the census records, presumably married. The youngest, Frances, worked as an office stenographer in 1900 but by about 1904 had married Michael J. Harding, an immigrant from County Cork.

In rural locales, the employment opportunities for women were even more limited. Apparently having trouble supporting his wife, Winifred, and their seven children as a cooper in Brooklyn during the depression following the Panic of 1873, Michael Smee moved his family to the Hudson River Valley town of Claverack, where textile mills were the main source of work for women and children. In 1880, five of the Smee kids were employed at a cotton mill, ranging from Margaret (age twenty) all the way down to thirteen-year-old Ellen and even ten-year-old Mary.

The fate of the Smee girls reflects how life-changing a good marriage could be for women of modest means. In 1900, by which point their father had passed away, the three yet unmarried Smee daughters were still working in the mill as "finishers." A couple of them never married and worked in textile mills for their whole lives. But Ellen's life veered in a different direction when she wed Michael Boyne, a neighbor in Claverack who was also the child of Famine immigrants and who also worked in a mill in his teens and twenties. Michael had both ambition and a knack for business, managing to open a modest mill of his own (apparently in an abandoned Catholic church that he purchased for a hundred dollars), where his employees recycled discarded textile shards and rags into "shoddy" to fill things like mattresses. With the profits from that venture, Michael bought another local mill, and then another. He was able to retire young and send his and Ellen's one child, Edward, to an Ivy League university for college and law school. Edward became a corporate lawyer for the firm known today as Willkie Farr & Gallagher in New York before finishing his career as in-house counsel for U.S. Steel in Pittsburgh. (Edward's cousins, who grew up in much more modest circumstances as the sons of mill workers, also did fairly well. Edward's uncle John Boyne had three sons, for example, and they became an accountant, a cement plant manager, and a lawyer, albeit one with a small-town practice.)

Of course, a bad marriage could be just as life-defining as a good one. Recall that Bartholomew O'Donnell, the financially struggling marathon race walker, had just one child, Margaret. She married cooper William Cowan in 1872 and in the ensuing twenty years gave birth to eleven children. By 1900, she was on her own, struggling to support two of her teenaged children by taking in a pair of boarders and working as a laundress at a hospital while her three youngest were in a home for destitute children, presumably put there by her because she could not afford to support them.

Yet there was much more to Margaret's story than meets the eye. Margaret was not widowed or abandoned. In the mid-1890s, she began seeing another man, a lathe operator named Samuel Roberts who was nineteen years her junior. In 1896, after William complained about the way she flaunted her infidelity, Margaret moved out, taking the older children with her and leaving the younger ones with him. William was the one who had put them in the home for indigent children, as a form of childcare (he was paying for them to stay there) so he could continue working at a Brooklyn flour mill, and he was providing child support for the older children. Roberts was one of the so-called boarders the census taker found living with Margaret and her older children in the summer of 1900.

William, to be sure, had issues of his own. Years earlier, he had been badly injured in an explosion at the flour mill that had left him lame and with some mental impairments as well. In a fit of pique after delivering child support and seeing Roberts still with Margaret and his children, William decided that he would find a new partner too, not stopping to consider that he and Margaret were still legally wed. In 1901, William married a Brooklyn widow, telling her and the minister who married them that Margaret was dead. When he bragged about having a new "wife" to Margaret during another child support delivery, she marched to the local police station and had William arrested for bigamy.

The story made front-page news, although when William pled guilty in court, he was able to publicize his side of the story. The usual punishment for bigamy was years in prison, but given the circumstances, William (whom the press labeled a "fool") was sentenced to just three months in Kings County Jail. Margaret suffered initially as well — the Catholic hospital where she washed laundry fired her once all the sordid details of her long-standing relationship with Roberts were publicized. But William's bigamy conviction did enable Margaret to marry Roberts in 1902. They remained together until she passed away at age sixty-seven in 1921.

It was far easier for the daughters of successful Famine immigrants to marry well. Two of the daughters of Hugh Collender, a window blind maker turned billiard-table-manufacturing magnate (whose story can be found at the beginning of the Conclusion), married Italian noblemen. Or recall Walter Roche, the disgraced Tammany politico who managed to stay out of jail and retain his wealth because most of it belonged to his wife, whose father had wisely invested it in empty lots in what would eventually become Times Square. Walter's son John devoted his life to managing the family real estate portfolio, but his five daughters, who all graduated from local Catholic colleges, could use the family fortune to win the hearts of most any New Yorker they might choose. Marie Roche, the oldest, married a well-known lawyer; Amelia wed a textile manufacturer; Beatrice married a prominent Brooklyn surgeon; and Adele wed a dental supplies manufacturer. Only Corinne, the youngest, never married. She held leadership positions in several Catholic charitable organizations, and even though she never seems to have had a paid position, the press called her a "social welfare worker with Catholic agencies" when she passed away, at age seventy-two, in 1955.

While the Famine immigrants' daughters had narrow employment options, their sons' opportunities were almost unlimited. Nonetheless, some chose precisely the same vocations as their fathers. Bill Quigley, a son of the well-known Battery boatman Michael Quigley, also became a "famous Battery boatman." With a larger-than-life personality just like his dad's, Bill was as beloved in lower Manhattan as his father and was quoted in the New York press even more often. Likewise, all the sons of tailor George P. Fox, that master of self-promotion, worked as merchant tailors. And Andrew J. Kerwin became, "like his father,...a building contractor and real estate operator," reported the *New York Times*. The younger Kerwin's claim to fame was the invention of the "kitchenette," something he first used in hotels that he built to encourage long-term stays. Kitchenettes eventually became ubiquitous in New York's small apartments.

Another son who followed in his father's footsteps was Daniel J. Sullivan, son of Cornelius Sullivan, the laborer turned bottle-cork peddler whose story was recounted in the opening pages of chapters 1 and 2. Daniel also peddled corks, first in Manhattan and then in Brooklyn, though like his father he occasionally turned to day labor to make ends meet. But mental health issues were a bigger impediment to Daniel's prosperity than inconsistent cork sales. According to a Brooklyn newspaper, "Sullivan suffered from religious insanity" and was institutionalized for ten months from 1882 to 1883. He was given a straitjacket when he was released, "and when he felt an attack coming he would go to his wife and have her put him in it that he might do no harm to anyone." But in June 1884, Sullivan got hold of a pistol, walked the couple of blocks from his Red Hook home to the waterfront, and killed himself with a shot to the temple.

It was much more common for a son to enter a different line of work than his father's, but often they remained in the same "occupational rank." That was the case for the son of Thomas D. Norris, the merchant tailor who lost his wife to another man while he was serving in the Union army and had to peddle apples to support his children, until a chance arrest for buying untaxed cigars helped him land a civil service position as a clerk that he held for the last two decades of his life. His son, John D. Norris, also volunteered to fight in a war (in his case, the Spanish-American War) and otherwise worked in a variety of lower-status white-collar jobs, mostly as a salesman. John sold clothes wringers in Denver before the war, insurance in New York after it, and cigars in a San Francisco tobacco shop after that.

The sons of Hubert D. Glynn, for decades the chief clerk at the Castle Garden immigration depot, also chose careers like their father's. Son Henry was a bookkeeper before he died young, at age twenty-six, in 1882. His brother James started out as a paperhanger but became a bookkeeper and clerk until he died from tuberculosis in 1902. And William Glynn was a shipping clerk for more than thirty years before he passed away in 1943.

While some children, like the Glynn sons, followed in their parents' footsteps, more moved modestly up the occupational hierarchy. The son of Joseph Kingsley, a journeyman tailor in New York, became a railroad station agent in Baltimore. Others took civil service jobs that, while not exactly white-collar, were definitely a step up from their fathers' vocations. Jeremiah Griffin, for example, son of the surprisingly successful peddler John Griffin described at the beginning of chapter 4, failed in his attempts to run a butcher shop and a saloon but then had a long career as a policeman. After putting in the twenty years necessary to qualify for a pension, Jeremiah retired from the police department and became a real estate agent.

The children of the lifelong dry goods clerk and lace buyer Robert Lewis also moved up the socioeconomic ladder. Robert Jr. went to medical school at Columbia University and later became a faculty member there, ultimately serving as president of the American Otological Society. Lewis's other son, Thomas, started out in the lace trade but eventually made his living as the owner and operator of an orange and grapefruit plantation in Cuba.

A small proportion of the Famine immigrants' children had lower-status or lower-paying jobs than their fathers, and this was frequently the case with the children of saloonkeepers. The eldest son of Peter Devlin, the Bodoney charcoal peddler who traded in his horse and cart for a saloon on Staten Island, managed to follow his father into the liquor trade, but Peter's five other sons got civil service jobs. The youngest, Eugene Devlin, became a New York City food inspector and was credited by a leading health-food advocate with inventing the modern metal vegetable steamer.

Eugene's brother William initially seemed destined for the role of family ne'er-do-well. William was working as a messenger boy at age sixteen in 1885 when he was dispatched by a Wall Street bank to collect $1,365 from another financial institution. Rather than return with the cash, William and a friend absconded with the money "to see the ice carnival at Montreal." They got as far as Syracuse before they were arrested and returned to New York, where Peter paid his son's bail. Before William had his day in court, however, he fled town and under an alias joined the army, which stationed him in Idaho. Peter tracked William down and brought him home, but the teen soon ran away and enlisted again.

Seven years later, perhaps feeling pangs of guilt, the fugitive came back to New York and turned himself in. Finding that he had been "leading a respectable life" serving his country, the bank and the district attorney agreed to drop the charges. William then landed a job as a New York City fireman. He rose quickly through the ranks, becoming a battalion chief in 1911. Leading his men onto the roof of a burning two-story building on Broome Street in September of that year, the forty-two-year-old widower lost his footing on the pitched roof "and shot over the side," hitting and bouncing off the top of a backyard shed before landing on the pavement in an alleyway "so narrow that a stretcher could not be brought to help the injured man." The prodigal son died four days later from internal injuries sustained in the fall, leaving five orphaned children, all less than thirteen years old, who were taken in by their dead mother's unmarried sister.

Two of William Devlin's brothers were policemen. So, too, was Michael Murphy, son of the Ward Four and Seven saloonkeeper of the same name. Like William Devlin, Michael Jr. rose meteorically through the ranks, perhaps due to his father's political clout, and became one of the force's youngest captains. Murphy's precinct included many of the Bowery's most infamous gambling and drinking resorts, and he demanded huge payoffs to ignore their many violations of the law. In 1886, the press got wind of the fact that Murphy's men had presented a "floral cradle" to the captain's wife as a New Year's present, to which were pinned "three new crisp $1,000 bills" (together worth about $100,000 today), which the patrolmen had extorted from the precinct's shady business owners. As a result of the public uproar, Murphy was transferred uptown, but he retained his rank because a subordinate took the fall for instigating the bribery. Yet in 1894, when the Lexow Committee began a wide-ranging investigation into police corruption, Murphy was indicted for additional bribe taking and suspended. After his arraignment, the fifty-year-old captain increased an already ample drinking habit. He died a year later, before his case could be adjudicated, of "acute disease of the liver."

As was the case with the immigrants themselves, their children who did best were those who started out their adult lives with money or other resources already in hand. Alfred Y. Morgan, for example, prospered running the Morgan family soda company after his father, John, passed away. That wealth, however, could not prevent Alfred from taking his own life in 1926.

The son and daughter of John Cummins, who owned the huge farm near Stockton, California, that yielded ten thousand bushels of wheat per year, also thrived in early adulthood thanks to the advantages of growing up wealthy. Cummins's son, who went by John Commins, used family financing to become "a wealthy real estate man" in the Bay Area. But starting out wealthy in America was no guarantee of ending up that way. In 1902 John Commins, who was then forty, and his wife, Anna Viers Commins, who had married John when he was thirty-two and she was just sixteen, went through a nasty divorce. Anna, who by this point had already given birth to three children (two still living), admitted to some indiscretions. "My peccadilloes must have been of much interest to my husband," she told the San Francisco Examiner upon hearing that John planned to call seventy-eight witnesses against her at the upcoming trial, "as not one seems to have escaped his notice." In her defense, she insisted that "my husband is a jealous old man. If I went out with male friends it was because I was lonesome. He wanted me to stay home like an old woman." The judge ruled Anna an unfit mother and awarded sole custody of their children to John.

But John did not fare well after the breakup. By 1910, he had lost his real estate business and was working as a deliveryman in Oakland and living with his sister, who had not squandered her share of their parents' large bequest. John continued in that vocation and worked as a teamster too before starting a small carpentry business in the 1920s. During the Great Depression, John remarried and moved into a place of his own, but to make ends meet he had to take a job as a cleaner for the East Bay Transit Company. John managed to find work as a bookkeeper by 1940, shortly before he passed away.

Anna ended up no better. Bereft at not being able to see her children, she decided to move to Montana, where two of her siblings lived. A judge granted her just a two-hour visit with her kids in 1902 before she departed. By 1940, Anna was back in California, where her husband worked as a golf caddy while she toiled as a hotel maid. She passed away there in 1958.

Most children of Famine immigrants who started out in comfortable circumstances, however, remained that way. Many sons of successful Famine immigrants, for example, became attorneys. Most had small practices, but Walter J. Bartnett, son of California blacksmith shop proprietor David Bartnett, became nationally prominent. Walter was a whiz kid of corporate finance, brokering deals for New York and San Francisco robber barons and sometimes forcing them to make him a partner in their transactions. In 1908, however, Bartnett was convicted of embezzling funds from customers of a failed bank he had helped run and was sentenced to ten years in San Quentin, where his uncle Garrett had died the year before. Claiming to be "going mad" in prison, Walter persuaded a judge to release him, after serving only about a year, by promising to go to New York to line up financing to fully repay the bank's customers. The deal was inked amid much fanfare, after which Bartnett's conviction was vacated, but the bank's depositors ended up getting very little of their money back. Bartnett, meanwhile, moved to New York and practiced law in relative obscurity, becoming best known as a protégé of Andrew Carnegie in his effort to create international tribunals to adjudicate conflict and eradicate war.

This portrait of Walter J. Bartnett dates from 1908.

WALTER J. BARTNETT

In addition to the law, the Famine immigrants' children were also prominent in journalism. In chapter 2, we met Rosanna and Michael J. J. Kavanagh, the peripatetic shopkeepers who left New York City for Kansas after nine of their ten children passed away. The surviving child, Michael J. Kavanagh, became the editor and publisher of the *Butler City News* in Pottawatomie County, Kansas. The paper did not last long, however, so he became a Sherwin-Williams paint dealer while supplementing his income as postmaster of his small Kansas town. Edward Graves, stepson of machinist Francis Graves, volunteered for the Union army and survived a saber wound at Five Forks and a gunshot injury at Petersburg. Graves went on to become the editor of the *New Haven Union*.

The most well-known newsman among the children of the Famine immigrants was probably Richard V. Oulahan, son of the longtime and underpaid Treasury Department clerk of the same

Newspaper editor and Sherwin-Williams paint dealer Michael J. Kavanagh.

name encountered in chapter 6. Born in the capital in 1867, Dick Oulahan covered national politics for forty-five years, culminating as Washington bureau chief of the *New York Times* from 1912 until his death in 1931. "A man of distinguished appearance" and "unfailing charm," Oulahan was a beloved Washington personality. He was also respected for his reporting prowess and his ability to ingratiate himself with the most powerful national political figures. Oulahan was "especially close to Benjamin Harrison and Grover Cleveland," gushed an obituary, but was an "intimate friend" of their successors as well as their leading cabinet secretaries. Oulahan was so well respected by Washington's leaders that he became, according to one senator, "a confidential and most intelligent adviser" to many of them. Oulahan's chumminess with those he covered, common in those days, came under scrutiny toward the end of his career. Still, when Oulahan passed away suddenly at age sixty-four, he had already won "every honor his colleagues could bestow," and his death was front-page news across the nation.

Richard V. Oulahan, Washington bureau chief of the *New York Times.*

Far more often than becoming journalists or attorneys, the children of the Famine immigrants ran their own businesses. Richard Francis Xavier Smith, son of a St. Louis hardware packer named Philip Smith, owned the National Paper Company there. John A. Donovan, the second eldest son of Iowa farmer Patrick Donovan, operated a hotel in Iowa City and later, for more than a decade, ran the O. K. Restaurant, "the home of good eats, home made pies, and coffee second to none." Daniel C. Stapleton, son of Joliet shoemaker William Stapleton, became a wealthy cattle rancher in Nebraska as president of the Trans Missouri Land Company. Stapleton later moved to Colombia, where he operated an emerald mine, before returning to the United States and settling in Washington, D.C. When Stapleton died there in 1920, he left an estate valued at over $100,000. Stapleton's sister Ellen was also drawn to the Spanish-speaking world, working as a schoolteacher in Mexico and Cuba.

Sometimes the business of the son grew out of the vocation of the father. Patrick McCabe was a brickyard laborer in Rockland County, New York. His sons John and James McCabe became brickyard owners on Staten Island in the 1880s, at one point manufacturing ten million bricks per year. James somehow found time to earn a law degree from Columbia University while presiding over this huge operation. Likewise, John C. Burke, son of a porter named Michael Burke, started out as a cartman but eventually expanded that work into Burke Moving and Storage, which operates in New York to this day (and competes with the moving company started by Alfred Morgan's uncles, Patrick and Francis Morgan).

Many descendants of Famine-era Emigrant Savings Bank customers became prominent politicians. Michael E. Butler, son of waterfront labor contractor Edmund Butler, served two terms in the New York State legislature and was a "political chieftain" in Brooklyn until he died at his daughter's summer home in Quogue in 1926. The Christian Brothers leader known as Brother Justin was not permitted to marry, but his sister's son, attorney John J. Fitzgerald, served ten terms in Congress, the last three as chairman of the House Appropriations Committee. Fitzgerald resigned his seat to return to his legal practice in 1917. (In those days it was the norm for members to voluntarily leave Congress so other party leaders could have a chance to serve.) Fitzgerald spent the last ten years of his career as a judge in Brooklyn before he retired at age seventy in 1942.

Not every congressional career was as distinguished as Fitzgerald's. Thomas J. Bradley, son of a tinsmith named Edward Bradley, was initially a rising star in the Democratic Party. "Bright and popular," recalled the *Times*, Bradley graduated from City College and quickly earned a law degree from New York University. With help from political patron "Big Tim" Sullivan — the child of Lansdowne immigrants from Kenmare — Bradley in 1891 snared a prestigious appointment as an assistant district attorney straight out of law school. Five years later, at age twenty-six, again with Sullivan's help, Bradley won the Democratic nomination for the congressional seat representing the Lower East Side. He triumphed easily in the general election.

Congressman Thomas J.
Bradley.

At that point, however, Bradley's life quickly spiraled downward. "Life's glories were too much for him," observed the *Times*. "He neglected his duties. Drink and high living took possession of him." Alcohol always flowed like water in Tammany Hall, but Bradley imbibed too much even for that hard-drinking crowd. After four years in office, Sullivan refused to support Bradley for a third term. Bradley found this humiliation too much to bear and began imbibing even more prodigiously. On New Year's Day 1901, before his term in Congress had even expired, a policeman found Bradley passed out drunk in the gutter on the Bowery. It wasn't the first time either. Bradley was taken to the "alcoholic ward" at Bellevue Hospital. Although he was released a few weeks later, he was hospitalized again in March and died on April 1, at age thirty-one, of cirrhosis of the liver.

———

For the children of the Famine immigrants, a career as an officer in the military was considered more honorable than one in politics. Arthur Kerwin, another son of builder Andrew Kerwin, graduated from West Point, rose to the rank of colonel while stationed in the Philippines during the Spanish-American War, and afterward served as Manila's police chief for three years. He later became an attorney in Los Angeles. Arthur's sister Gertrude married Paul B. Malone, also a child of Irish immigrants and a West Point graduate. He commanded a regiment in World War I and later rose to the rank of major general. John F. O'Ryan, son of a schoolteacher named Francis O'Ryan, also became a major general and commanded 24,000 men in World War I as head of the army's Twenty-Seventh Division, known as "O'Ryan's Roughnecks." He became a lawyer as well and served as New York City's police commissioner under Mayor Fiorello La Guardia.

Even more prestigious in the Irish American community than having a son in the military was having one in the priesthood. Many of the Famine immigrants' daughters became nuns but, for better or worse, parents were far more likely to boast about their son the priest than their daughter who entered a convent. Saloonkeepers' sons seemed especially likely to become priests, perhaps because they were most easily able to afford the college degree that became a prerequisite for the priesthood in that era. Fordham University (in what was then Westchester County but is now part of New York City) was the most common launching pad for would-be New York priests in that period, although others attended Manhattan College or the College of St. Francis Xavier in New York City itself.

One immigrant's son who became a priest after studying at Fordham was Thomas P. McLoughlin, a son of the Brooklyn grocer John McLoughlin. Father Tom's first assignment to lead a congregation was at the Church of the Transfiguration in Five Points, though by the time he arrived there the neighborhood had become more Italian than Irish. McLoughlin continued his predecessor's policy of segregating the parishioners — requiring the Italians to attend mass in the basement while reserving the main sanctuary for Irish immigrants and the native-born. This infuriated the Italians, who sent their complaints all the way to the Vatican. After years enduring criticism for this policy, Father Tom happily accepted a transfer to a parish in Westchester.

A more popular priest was Monsignor John T. Woods, a son of the Brooklyn barkeeper and "sporting grounds" operator Barney Woods. While Father McLoughlin had both his fans and his detractors, Monsignor Woods was universally "beloved." This "super-priest," reported a Brooklyn newspaper, was so widely admired in part because he ministered not only to his flock in Flatbush, but also to thousands of strangers he met through his role as chaplain at Kings County Hospital. The outpouring of grief from all parts of the Brooklyn populace at his death in 1924 spoke to the generosity "of this valiant leader of Catholicism..., whose true worth as a priest and as a man will ever remain indelibly inscribed on the hearts" of Brooklyn's "men, women and children, regardless of denomination[,] creed or color."

―――――――

The Famine immigrants must have found it hard to bear when their American-born children lost (or even worse, squandered) the financial resources that their elders had so painstakingly accumulated. William V. Collender, the only son of the pool-table magnate Hugh Collender, lasted just a year in the job his father gave him in the family business. When William died at age thirty, a few months before his father passed away, the young man's only claim to fame was as "an enthusiastic yachtsman and a great lover and owner of fast horses." The press did not disclose William's cause of death.

In many instances, however, parents did not live long enough to witness their children's difficulties. Recall mason Patrick Drew, for example, who had moved from New York to Milwaukee and made a small fortune as a builder and state legislator. His eldest son, Frank, went into the family business but died tragically at age twenty-eight of phthisis, a wasting disease that was a common side effect of tuberculosis. Another promising son, James, died at age twenty-two of complications from malaria that he contracted "during a sojourn in the South." The deaths of Frank and James must have broken Patrick's heart, especially because his third son, Thomas David Drew, was an alcoholic ne'er-do-well. Thomas worked off and on as a miner in Alaska and the Yukon, apparently only for as long as it took to buy himself another bottle of booze, until he died of "acute alcoholism."

Patrick therefore had to pin all his hopes on his youngest son, John I. Drew. Initially, John appeared headed for success that could make his father proud. He graduated from Marquette University, became a bookkeeper, and was working in the family building business when his father passed away in 1903. John decided to get out of the cutthroat construction industry soon thereafter and at age forty became deputy treasurer of Milwaukee County. Six years later, John was elected treasurer of the city of Milwaukee, a post he held for sixteen years.

But Drew's career ended in disgrace. He was defeated for reelection in 1932 when, during the Great Depression, questions arose about the favoritism he seemed to show to a local bank that had subsequently gone belly-up. An investigation led to his indictment on charges that he had used the bank as a conduit to embezzle $500,000 from the city. In 1934, before he could be tried for the crime, Drew passed away of a heart ailment at age sixty-seven.

There were plenty of other Famine-immigrant families whose children collectively ran the gamut from exemplars to embarrassments. Recall, for example, shoemaker Richard Sharkey, who, with his wife, Mary Ann, left New York for California, settled in mining country, supplied prospectors with boots and shoes, and raised ten children. One son became a house carpenter; another became a court bailiff; a third worked as a day laborer in a shipyard. A fourth son, Joe, was moderately successful owning and operating small mines, but when that work could no longer support him and his wife, he spent the last twenty or so years of his life employed at an oil refinery.

A fifth son, William, was the family overachiever. He worked his way up in the newspaper business from printer's devil and delivery boy to editor in chief and publisher of the *Contra Costa Gazette*. Gaining notoriety in that position, William was elected as a Republican to the state assembly and soon thereafter to the state senate, where he served for more than a quarter century, including several stints as Republican "floor leader." Sharkey was one of the most prominent progressive Republicans in the state—pushing successfully for limits on the power of oil companies and a major expansion of the state park system. Yet in those days, progressives could also be nativists, and Sharkey was one of California's best-known advocates of immigration restriction. "Senator Sharkey was one of the organizers of the Japanese Exclusion League," noted his own

Senator William R. Sharkey and his brother Charles in a Folsom Prison mug shot.

newspaper proudly. "'Keep California White' was the league's slo-gan," and it aimed to exclude from America not only the Japanese, but also "Chinese, Hindus, and others of the yellow race," and even to strip their American-born children of citizenship and the right to own land in the state.

While the *Gazette* gave prominent coverage to William Shar-key's exploits and covered Joe's death and those of most of his brothers as well, it ignored the notoriety of a sixth brother, Charles. In 1902, after losing a "considerable" sum of money playing cards with a livery stable keeper in a saloon in Sierra City, Charles and an accomplice, both intoxicated, attacked and robbed the winning gambler as he walked home, crushing his skull with a blunt instru-ment. Charles, then twenty-two years old, was convicted of first-degree murder and sentenced to life in prison at San Quentin. In 1920, however, after serving eighteen years, authorities released him, apparently on the condition that he help fill the manpower shortage in the merchant marine. Charles shipped out, but after that he disappears from the historical record without a trace. There isn't any evidence that he ever made it back to the United States.

The children of John Killeen—the Famine immigrant in my own family tree—also ranged from famous to infamous. John worked as a day laborer and in other unskilled positions for nearly fifty years for the New York Central Railroad in and around Buf-falo. The eldest of his six sons, Michael and Thomas, left Buffalo in their twenties for the west. Michael, who had trained as a mason but later worked as a clerk for the New York Central, became a peri-patetic gold prospector. He died of Bright's disease, a kidney ail-ment, at age fifty in 1904. Thomas, who had also worked as a clerk for the New York Central before heading west, settled in central Colorado and became a railroad telegraph operator and then a train dispatcher there. In the same year as his brother Michael, Thomas also succumbed to Bright's disease, at age forty-seven. A third brother, James, ventured west a few years later and opened a plumbing supply business in Salt Lake City, He died there, apparently of a stroke, at forty-eight.

John's three other sons remained in Buffalo. John Jr., a bartender, died at age twenty-three. But Frank Killeen, my aunt's great-grandfather and the second youngest of the six brothers, became very well-known in Buffalo as one of the highest-ranking officers in the city's police department. As a captain, Frank presided over Buffalo's "notorious third precinct." Portrayals of Frank in the press varied widely, depending on the political and ethnic affiliation of the publication. Democrats and Irish Catholics viewed Frank as a brave and loyal public servant tasked with the thankless job of policing the rowdiest part of town. Protestants and Republicans, in contrast, portrayed Frank as the confidant of brothel keepers, "gambling resort" proprietors, and illegal saloon operators, purportedly pocketing lavish bribes in exchange for allowing them to operate with impunity. Reformers like those in the Anti-Saloon League tried to hound Frank out of the department, but he

Captain Frank J. Killeen.

Captain Frank J. Killeen.

managed to serve for twenty years—long enough to earn his pension—before retiring in 1914 at age forty-six. Frank did not get to enjoy much of that pension, however, dying just a year later of heart disease.

Only Henry W. Killeen, the youngest of John and Honora Killeen's sons, lived, like his parents, to a ripe old age. Perhaps this was in part because, as he later recalled proudly, he did only half a day's manual labor in his whole life—toiling as a carpenter's helper before both he and his employer agreed he was not cut out for such work. They were not the only ones who came to that conclusion. Henry won a prized appointment to the U.S. Military Academy but had to return home from West Point after only a few days because he failed the physical.

Yet what Henry lacked in brute strength, he compensated for with what a Buffalo Democratic chieftain called a "big brain." Immediately upon his return from West Point, Henry began studying law and was admitted to the bar on the eve of his twenty-first birthday. He quickly became a prominent Buffalo attorney specializing in representing railroads, streetcar companies, and utilities, particularly in their fights to raise their rates in the face of opposition from political leaders and public service commissions. Henry was hailed as a "brilliant lawyer" with a "quick and piercing mind," and his courtroom victories made millions for his already rich clients and made him a wealthy man as well. He loved his work and retired only reluctantly due to ill health, after fifty years before the bar, a few months before his death, at age seventy-one, in 1943.

———

I didn't know anything about my Famine immigrant ancestors or their children until I started writing this book. I had been led to believe that the family could not find any documents confirming when the Killeens had arrived in America or where in Ireland they had come from. But when pressed, my aunt Vivian was able to track down the Killeen family genealogy buff (there's one in almost every family), who had cobbled the whole story together.

I got in touch with many descendants of the immigrants whose stories I uncovered in the course of my work thanks, in part, to amateur genealogists like the one in my own family who led me to the story of John Killeen. Nowadays, many of these enthusiasts place their family trees, replete with supporting documentation, on Ancestry.com or one of its competitors. The truly avid researchers add photos of their ancestors to these sites as well. Photographs of survivors of the Great Irish Famine are not easy to find, but the generosity of these amateur genealogists in putting their work online led me to virtually all the images of Famine immigrants that grace these pages.

Some of these descendants sought me out. Conor Welch, the great-great-great-grandson of Catherine and William Rudkin (the alcohol flavorings manufacturer), initially wrote to me about his *Italian* ancestors. Six years later, however, he heard about my new book project, told me about Catherine and William (whom I already knew about through the Emigrant Savings Bank records), and offered to share their portraits.

In most cases, however, I had to track down descendants through their online family trees in hopes of finding a photo of their Famine immigrant ancestor. In almost every instance, these family members graciously agreed to let me reproduce their cherished keepsakes. The photo of Timothy Carr, armorer of the Sixty-Ninth Regiment, who posed proudly with his gold watch, was provided by his great-great-grandson of the same name, a retired New York City police officer. Monsignor Robert Gibbons of St. Petersburg, Florida, shared his photos of his great-grandfather, Tammany Hall politico Walter Roche. Pulitzer Prize–winning historian T. J. Stiles directed me to his relatives in Ireland who retain the family's portraits of Jonathan Dillon, who wrote the secret message inside President Abraham Lincoln's pocket watch. Ed and

Connie McSweeny of Monterey, Tennessee, made available the photos of Honoria McSweeny (the mother of fourteen children) and her husband O'Callaghan McSweeny, the liquor distiller. And Kathleen Kavanagh gave me permission to use the photograph of her grandfather Michael J. Kavanagh, whom his parents, Michael and Rosanna, brought to Kansas as a teenager after all nine of his brothers and sisters passed away. Her grandfather thought that "the worst thing he ever did was move to Kansas. He hated the weather and if he could have [he] would have moved back to NYC."

The world of online genealogy also gave me the chance, in June 2023, to do something I had never done before—meet a descendant of one of the Famine immigrants featured in this book. Actually, a descendant of *many* of them. Paul McLoughlin of Boulder, Colorado, is the great-grandson of grocer John McLoughlin, mentioned in chapter 7. John married one of O'Callaghan and Honoria McSweeny's fourteen children, making Paul the great-great-grandchild of O'Callaghan and Honoria. Paul is also a descendant of the Muldoon brothers, who had less success as grocers than their cousin John, and the great-great-great-nephew of Father Tom McLoughlin, pastor of the Church of the Transfiguration in Five Points. Another of Paul's ancestors, Peter McLoughlin, came to America twenty years before the Famine and became rich investing his grocery and saloon profits in tenements in Five Points and Ward Four. His letter calling the United States "the best country in the World," which he wrote in 1829 before he became wealthy, is quoted in chapter 7.

As Paul's pedigree suggests, he is descended from New York's Irish aristocracy. Most of his immigrant ancestors arrived in America with ample savings and prospered almost immediately. Like other successful Famine immigrants, they sent their sons to college, and many of them became priests. (That may be why, Paul told me, his cousin Ed McSweeny is one of the last "McSweeny" descendants of O'Callaghan and Honoria—"too many priests.") Paul's father, Maurice E. McLoughlin, was a senior partner with the prominent

New York corporate law firm White & Case, and Paul himself had been a senior administrator of two New York medical schools and worked for an investment bank on Wall Street. In trying to track down McLoughlin family photos, I learned that Paul is the kind of person who prefers a phone call to an email. But because he was planning to pass through my hometown, Arlington, Virginia, on his way to his fifty-fifth college reunion at Georgetown University, he suggested that we get together immediately after he landed at National Airport so we could chat face-to-face, and I could learn more about his family's rich history. When he told me he would bring Peter McLoughlin's 1829 letter and tell me the story of the "MacSwiney Chalice" as well, I could hardly refuse.

Paul greeted me warmly with a firm handshake and a broad smile when I met him at an outdoor café. To call him an energetic seventy-five-year-old would be an understatement—he had come straight from the airport, but without a suitcase because he had brought his belongings in a very large backpack, which he flung easily over his shoulders when we left the restaurant two hours later. That time flew by as I learned about Paul's career, his family, and its history. The chalice, it turned out, had been made for the celebration of mass in the 1600s for his McSwiney ancestors. What made it unique was that it could be disassembled and therefore more easily hidden at a time when the Protestant invaders of Ireland had made practicing Catholicism a crime. Today, that might seem like ancient past, but to the Famine immigrants, those years in Ireland's history evoked fresh and brutally painful memories.

Seeing the handwritten letter was also a revelation. Another McLoughlin had published excerpts from it a century ago, but examining a copy of the handwritten original led to the discovery that the published transcription contained some mistakes and omissions, providing a good reminder that one should *always* go back to the original source—something I had told my students ad nauseam during my thirty-year teaching career. But just as important as correcting those inaccuracies was seeing Peter McLoughlin's actual handwriting, which conveys the heartfelt emotion behind the words he carefully put to paper with a hand-filled fountain pen 194 years ago. Seeing the actual letter also highlights how frugally Irish immigrants lived. To save money on paper, Peter filled a page with his neat script, but when he got to the bottom of the page, he turned it ninety degrees and wrote twenty lines more. These penny-pinching acts, repeated many times a day, every day of the year, year after year, were undoubtedly those that Peter believed had made him a wealthy man — one respected by both immigrants and natives alike — by the time he passed away, at age sixty, in 1854.

This is a detail from Peter McLoughlin's handwritten letter from 1829, in which he wrote in two different directions so he would not have to use a second sheet of paper. The top line says "this is the best country in the World" and below that he adds that for immigrants to succeed, "they must Work for it and at present very hard."

More than anything else, what I took away from my meeting with Paul was how much his family history, and the history of Irish New York and Irish America, mean to him — and how important it is to him that these stories are preserved and passed down to future generations. Not every Irish American shares this passion, of course: even in Paul's own family, the history gene seems to skip generations. Paul told me his own father did not care much for history, but I found it telling that his grandfather, Maurice (pronounced "Morris") McLoughlin, a lifelong resident of Brooklyn, was remembered at his death in 1936 in part as a drama critic and poet, but primarily as an "authority on old Brooklyn" who passed on that knowledge as a features writer for the *Brooklyn Daily Eagle*. "Deeply interested in Brooklyn lore," the *Eagle* reported when Maurice passed away, he "spent much of his time pouring [sic] over reference books in search of curious historical items. He was known to have a remarkable memory and numerous anecdotes and points of information were stored in his mind."

That last sentence could just as easily describe Maurice's grandson. While Paul McLoughlin's passion may not be Brooklyn history, but rather that of Irish and Catholic New York, his ancestor's infatuation with the past has clearly trickled down to him. That same fervor motivates countless amateur Irish American genealogists, whose painstaking work and generosity in making it public has so enriched these pages. As much as any academic, these history buffs are helping to ensure — one document and story at a time — that the saga of the Famine Irish in America, which recently appeared irretrievable, sees the light of day once more.

Conclusion

Although many Famine immigrants did well in America, earning and saving far more money than they had ever thought possible, only a handful of the 960,000 who passed through New York became fabulously wealthy. Yet those overachievers served as role models for the entire Famine generation. Their rags-to-riches stories were repeated ad nauseam in the Irish American press; wives held them up to their underachieving husbands as exemplars of ambition, hard work, and sobriety; and parents used tales of wealthy Irish immigrants to inspire their children to dream big. In time, the achievements that underpinned these stories would help to lay the foundation not just for Irish America, but also for the very concept of the American Dream.

One of these self-made tycoons was Hugh Collender, born in December 1828 on a farm just outside the small town of Cappoquin in County Waterford near the Cork border. Although a member of the Famine generation, Collender sought refuge in America for a different reason than most of his countrymen. In his teens, Collender had been apprenticed to a maker of window blinds, but he also became active in the small band of freedom fighters who joined with Thomas Francis Meagher in 1848 in an ill-fated attempt to spark the overthrow of British rule of Ireland. (This was the same Thomas Francis Meagher who would eventually employ the Lalor brothers at his New York newspaper and command James Cavanagh, Dr. William O'Meagher, Timothy Carr, and so many other

Famine immigrants in the Irish Brigade.) Their plan to attack a police barracks was discovered before it could be carried out, however, and Collender was arrested nonetheless for trespassing (apparently while surveilling an intended target) and served a month at hard labor for that crime. Upon his release, Collender became involved in further anti-British plots, but fearing arrest, he fled to New York, arriving there at the beginning of 1850.

The twenty-one-year-old Irish nationalist soon found work in his trade making window coverings and gained entrée into the social circle of New York's leading Irish nationalist exiles. And it was within that circle that he met the unlikely man who made his eventual prosperity possible: billiards champion Michael Phelan.

Ten years Collender's senior, Phelan was a native of County Kilkenny and had immigrated to New York as a seven-year-old in 1825. He and Collender probably became acquainted because Phelan also fancied himself a champion of revolution in Ireland, although

Billiards master Michael Phelan in about 1860.

it's not clear he ever did anything for the cause other than drink and shoot pool with the movement's most famous adherents. Phelan's father had made his living in New York as a billiard-hall operator but had been determined that Michael should have a more respectable calling and apprenticed him to a jeweler. Yet Michael had an abiding passion for billiards. He played every minute he could and by the time Collender landed in the United States, Phelan was the best player in North America, winning matches that drew hundreds of spectators.

Phelan soon stopped working as a jeweler and instead supported himself and his family by fronting New York billiard parlors. He was paid a salary (and perhaps a cut of the profits) to socialize at these establishments and shoot an occasional game with the awestruck customers.* Phelan eventually tried to operate pool halls of his own, yet these consistently failed. Hoping for better luck out west, he ventured to San Francisco, but lost nearly all his money there on what the press called "disastrous...speculations." Phelan returned to New York nearly broke but was able to open a Broadway billiard parlor by taking loans from what the Dun & Company credit rating agency deemed "parties...of questionable char[acter]." To make matters worse, whatever money came his way, the Dun investigators found, Phelan often squandered gambling.

To say that Collender became close with Michael Phelan and his family would be an understatement. In April 1853, the twenty-four-year-old Collender married Phelan's fifteen-year-old daughter, Julia (marrying that young was hardly more common in the 1850s than it is today), and at age seventeen she gave birth to Kate, the first of their seven children. The young couple and their baby lived

---

* American billiards in those days was played with four balls. Players scored points for striking their own ball so that it pocketed any of the other three or for caroming their ball off two or more of the others. But sensing that Americans wanted a game that was a bit easier and had more scoring, Phelan invented "pool," which eventually became the most popular billiard-table game.

with Michael, his wife, Ann, and the Phelans' two surviving younger children in a cheap frame house that the Phelans owned in the sparsely populated neighborhood of Yorkville, what is now Manhattan's Upper East Side. Living with Julia's parents may not have been ideal, but it enabled Collender's teenaged wife to get help with childcare from her mother, who was still very much in the thick of child rearing herself: Julia Collender's baby was only a few years younger than Julia's sister Maggie.

Living in such close quarters with his father-in-law had unexpected benefits for Hugh as well. He soon learned that the billiards master's pet peeve was the poor quality of the pool tables he was forced to play on and especially the inconsistent caroms off ineptly constructed bumpers. Phelan had ideas for how billiard-table "rails" could be constructed "to insure mathematical correctness of angles when played upon." But because the better bumpers would be costly to fabricate, table manufacturers were not interested in his ideas. Collender, however, was a more persuasive salesman. In 1856, he convinced Irish-born billiard-table maker Tobias O'Connor to take him on as a partner in return for the exclusive rights to his father-in-law's bumper designs, which Collender had patented. Phelan was paid a royalty on each table O'Connor made. In 1860, Phelan purchased O'Connor's share in the firm and became Collender's partner in the venture.

Phelan & Collender billiard tables quickly became all the rage. The novel bumpers made them a status symbol for serious and even semiserious players, who refused to patronize billiard parlors that did not feature the company's tables. The duo also made billiards more popular to play at home by designing models smaller than the then standard six-by-twelve feet. These tables were "sufficiently large to entertain the adult male," noted *Harper's Weekly*, yet "small enough to render billiard-playing easy to ladies and children, who can best appreciate the sanitary advantages of the gentle yet thorough exercise called forth at billiards."

Purchases by celebrities helped Phelan & Collender's sales as well. General Ulysses S. Grant ordered a simple table from the company's lower Manhattan showroom in 1867. But the duo, sensing a great chance for publicity, built the savior of the Union a spectacular showpiece, a five-and-a-half-by-eleven-foot table constructed "of solid blistered and highly polished black walnut" held together by gold plates. At the corners, Phelan & Collender placed "gilded… arms of the United States," while the sides were ornamented with the general's "USG" monogram. As expected, newspapers across the country carried stories about Grant's gorgeous billiard table and the company that had manufactured it. The general loved his table and two years later brought it with him when he moved into the White House, where he turned a space in the residence's sprawling glass conservatory—located where the West Wing would be built forty years later—into a billiard room.

Ordinary Americans loved Phelan & Collender billiard tables just as much as the president did. By the time Grant brought their handiwork to the White House, Phelan & Collender were selling more billiard tables than any other company in North America and had outgrown their manufacturing facility on Crosby Street in what is now the SoHo neighborhood of Manhattan. To keep up with demand, the duo built a massive five-story factory on Tenth Avenue that stretched from West Thirty-Sixth all the way to West Thirty-Seventh Street. *Harper's* called it "one of the sights of the metropolis." Yet within a decade, they had outgrown it too and opened an even larger facility in Stamford, Connecticut.

Phelan and Collender divided the responsibilities for running their huge operation in an unorthodox manner. Phelan was primarily the face of the operation and contributed advice on the design of the tables, cues, and balls. Collender made all the business decisions—a sensible strategy, given Phelan's track record. It was also a profitable one. In 1870, Dun & Company estimated that the business was worth $300,000 to $500,000, equal to about $8 to

public
is re-
y one
nufac-
within
have
e resi-
seem
twen-
was
yer in
there
is of
I, the
nufac-
hat of
(for-
LLEX-
source
ishing
twith-
e roy-
a oth-
r the
n and
wu as
'ollen-
y shut
e New
c, the
Gulf
Can-
nt an

also
knec
plea?
rails
duct
has
in
have
table
to s
chas
plish
macl
of M
it a
mini
est n
most
imm
story
Ave
and
is on
metr
three
cons
strac
wort
yenrl
nishi
partr
done
the f

ndred tables yearly. Fully iber go into dwelling-houses. nd of late years for billiard s mainly due to a reduction ard size used to be six feet llustrated on this page. Thanks to the invent- ive talent of Mr. H. W. COLLENDER, to whom, and also to his late partner, the lamented Mr. MICHAEL PHELAN, billiard players in this coun- try are indebted for all the more marked im- is an ornament. Mr. COLLENDER's improve- ment consists in dispensing with the centre legs, and so altering the shape of the frame that the table appears much smaller than the ordinary box-shaped affair. The absence of the centre up to the delicate process o both of which kinds of lab factories performed by ha chinery, the bulk of it d this factory, and patented,

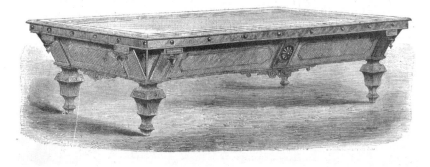

The Phelan & Collender billiard-table factory on Tenth Avenue and an image of the company's patented "Bevel" table, its bestseller and the standard against which all other tables came to be judged.

$13 million today. That made the two Irish immigrants wealthy even by New York standards. As was their wont, Collender judiciously saved and invested his share of the profits, while Phelan continued to spend and gamble ostentatiously.

When Phelan passed away in 1871 and Collender took over the business, his in-laws sued, complaining that Collender had cheated them out of their rightful share of the company's proceeds. That action, which could not have made Julia Phelan Collender very happy, dragged out over nearly a decade and ultimately failed, after which the Phelans began to sue one another instead. That's because Michael's widow, Ann, had, when she died in 1888, left almost all her $200,000 estate to Julia's sister Maggie. Ann's other surviving child, George, contested the will, claiming his mother was not of sound mind when she made it and that she and Maggie had conspired to disinherit him as punishment for marrying a Protestant. Maggie, through her attorney, replied that their mother had bankrolled several business ventures for George (including one manufacturing billiard tables) and that he had failed in all of them, accruing sizable debts that were still unpaid. George was so profligate, Maggie said, that *she* had been forced to support *his* three children and was still doing so. That was why Ann had decided to leave George a monthly annuity of $150 (about $5,000 in today's dollars) rather than a lump sum. After what the press accurately described as "a long and bitter contest," the judge ruled that Ann had been of sound mind when she made her will and that George was owed nothing more than the sum stipulated therein.

Meanwhile, the Collenders had moved out of New York to an eighty-acre estate on Long Neck Point in Darien, Connecticut — before it became an enclave of the wealthy — where Hugh commissioned a "massive manor house" built to his specifications overlooking Long Island Sound. It even boasted its own chapel, so that the Collenders could celebrate mass without having to rub elbows with Darien's Catholic riffraff (primarily the servants of the wealthy Protestants who lived there). In 1884, Hugh negotiated the merger of his company with the midwest's leading billiard-table manufacturer, the Brunswick-Balke Company, and served as the first president of the new billiard-table behemoth.

Hugh Collender toward the end of his life.

H. W. COLLENDER

One might imagine that Collender's stature in the insular world of billiards would have suffered after the death of his renowned partner, but that was not the case. Collender became a beloved billiards patriarch, with prizes and tournaments named in his honor. When he died in 1890, the onetime revolutionary left Julia an estate worth nearly $1 million, the equivalent of — at the very least — $33 million today. In fact, Hugh Collender may have made more money than any other Famine immigrant who arrived as an adult in the United States.

Americans scrutinizing the Famine Irish when Hugh Collender stepped ashore in 1850 would have had a hard time explaining his success. Most native-born Americans were convinced that the Famine refugees — predisposed to be "slothful and lazy" — lacked the capacity to thrive in their new homeland. Yet there were a few far-sighted observers who recognized that these newcomers *would* succeed. One of the most prominent was a Harvard professor and polymath named Francis Bowen. In the Civil War era, there were no academic departments at American universities, and the faculty had to teach a wide variety of subjects. Bowen took this requirement to extraordinary lengths. He published books and essays on history and philosophy, religion and poetry, and even made forays into the natural sciences as one of the first Americans to review Charles Darwin's *On the Origin of Species*. (Bowen deemed Darwin's theories "impossible" because they could be true only if the earth was millions of years old.)

Bowen was best known, however, for his writings on economics — in fact, he was the faculty member who added the subject to the Harvard curriculum. In the textbook Bowen wrote on the subject (then called "political economy"), he argued that unique features of the American economy made it one in which virtually anyone could succeed, no matter their education, religion, or previous experience. "There are innumerable openings" for advancement in America, Bowen argued, "which require only an adventurous spirit and a very moderate amount of capital or credit. The step between the situations of a journeyman and a master-mechanic, a clerk and a small tradesman, a farm-laborer and a small farmer, is a short one and very easily taken." If all else failed, Bowen noted, "there is always the resource of removing to the West, and becoming a pioneer in the settlement of government land" (as Peter Lynch and Michael Egan had done in Minnesota). These homesteads, Bowen pointed out, could be obtained for no money down, "and paid for out of the proceeds of subsequent harvests." Saying that these leaps up the socioeconomic ladder could be "very easily taken" was an exaggeration, yet Bowen's core insight, far ahead of its time, was exemplified by the Famine immigrants whose stories have been recounted in these pages.

But weren't Irish Catholics — conditioned by years of experience to believe that hard work brought no real reward and reared in a religion that supposedly taught acquiescence to one's lowly status — incapable of taking advantage of such opportunities? Bowen, despite living in New England, the epicenter of American nativism and anti-Catholicism, felt certain that this was not the case. Seeing opportunity all around him, wrote Bowen in his textbook, "even the Irish immigrant here soon loses his careless, lazy, and turbulent disposition, and becomes as sober, prudent, industrious, and frugal as his neighbors." That was because the Irish recognized that in America, in contrast to their native land under colonial rule, these qualities could bring them substantial financial rewards.

Bowen realized that every single person could not prosper in the United States. To fully reap the rewards that America had to offer required "health, strength, and...faculties of mind" that "Providence" had not distributed equally. But Bowen did believe that "every individual here has the power to make savings," and that such savings, combined with enough health, smarts, and good luck, made it possible for most people to succeed, and for many to truly thrive. There isn't "any obstacle to any individual's becoming rich, if he will, and almost to any amount that he will; — no obstacle, I say, but what arises from the dispensations of Providence." There were no impediments to wealth "but natural and inevitable ones; society interposes none, and none exist which society could remove. And ours is the only community on earth of which this can be said."

Ours is the only community on earth of which this can be said. With those words, Bowen was articulating the concept that would become known as the American Dream, the idea that in the United States alone, almost anyone could achieve financial prosperity and security. Although the phrase "American Dream" was not coined until the twentieth century, the concept behind it had been present in America since the arrival of the Puritans in the 1620s. Yet belief in the American Dream was put to the test in the mid-nineteenth century with the arrival of the Famine Irish. With so many Americans doubting that these newest immigrants were capable of self-improvement, was it possible that the land of opportunity had reached its limit?

Nativists, in fact, thought the Irish would destroy the American Dream by becoming the nation's first permanent underclass, something that would harm native-born Americans too by causing an increase in crime, taxes, and political corruption. Many found these predictions credible, as the meteoric rise of the Know Nothing Party at the end of the Famine migration made clear. But while the Famine immigration and the Know Nothing movement that resulted in part from it tested Americans' faith in the Dream concept, they could not destroy it. The Know Nothing movement quickly fizzled, as Northerners soon came to believe that slaveholders posed a graver threat to the nation than Catholic immigrants, and Southerners decided that the Republican Party represented the greatest danger to their prosperity.

The Republicans' first successful presidential candidate, Abraham Lincoln, was victorious in part because he refused to endorse any part of the Know Nothing agenda and he prominently espoused the tenets of the American Dream before and during his presidency. "There is not, of necessity, any such thing as the free hired laborer being fixed to that condition for life," wrote Lincoln in 1861, in his first State of the Union message. "The prudent, penniless beginner in the world, labors for wages awhile, saves a surplus with which to buy tools or land for himself; then labors on his own account another while, and at length hires another new beginner to help him." Lincoln knew this from his own experience, having grown up "poor" in various frontier farming settlements but then rising, as he told a regiment of soldiers in 1864, "to occupy this big White House. I am a living witness that any one of your children may look to come here as my father's child has."*

That such words applied to the Famine Irish might not have

---

* These words were never truer than they were in the 1850s and '60s. Of all the men ever to become president, the only three who truly grew up poor—Millard Fillmore, Abraham Lincoln, and Andrew Johnson—entered the White House in these two decades.

been obvious to all of Lincoln's listeners in the first half of the 1860s, but with the passage of time it became clear that even the Famine refugees had enjoyed the benefits of the American Dream. Seeking in 1878 to explain "the Irish success in America," a New Orleans newspaper observed that "by all obvious reasoning the advent of the Irish should have been a failure." First, "they were not welcomed. 'No Irish need apply'" was the sentiment everywhere. Second, "their religion [was] reviled," making it harder not only to find work, but also make business deals and gain social acceptance. Nonetheless, "step by step, they advanced." Even an Irishman who arrived in America in middle age without vocational skills, noted this newspaper, "set himself to work to acquire a trade at an age when the average Saxon dreams of retiring from business." Even more gratifying to the immigrants, observed the author, was seeing that their children "now occupy places at the bar, on the press, or in the avenues of trade, which would honor any people," and which place them "second in number and attainments to none in the land." Given the "poverty" in which they had begun their lives in America, the paper concluded, "this Celtic success...is truly miraculous."

That sentiment became widespread. Anti-Irish and anti-Catholic prejudice revived at times in the late nineteenth century, but such nativism never again included the idea that the Irish were lazy and incapable of advancing. Soon thereafter, when new immigrant groups such as Italians and eastern European Jews began arriving in the United States in large numbers, bringing with them even less experience with the Protestant work ethic than the Irish, native-born Americans (many now of Irish ancestry) did not question the newcomers' abilities to prosper. Americans might ignorantly disdain the new immigrants on the grounds that they were innately inferior to Anglo-Saxons, or would not make good citizens in a democracy, or would bring radicalism to America, or would never assimilate, or would take jobs and depress the wages of native-born workers. But they would never again argue that immigrants could not *prosper*. The Famine refugees had proven that there was no immigrant group too poor, too uneducated, or too unskilled to succeed in America.

———

How had the Famine immigrants achieved this improbable success? First, notwithstanding the assertions of native-born Americans then and historians ever since, the Famine Irish were not overwhelmingly forced into menial day labor upon arrival. Only about half of the male Famine immigrants began their lives in America in these low-paying, perilous positions. For every Famine immigrant who had to take day labor or similar work upon landing in New York, there was another who arrived with desirable vocational experience—training as a craftsman, or experience operating a small business, or a background working as a clerk behind a desk or counter—that allowed them to find comparable jobs in Manhattan. Then, as now, Americans assumed that the immigrants who arrived on America's shores must have been penniless paupers, the dregs of their homelands, when in fact such migrants have never made up a very large proportion of those who move to the United States. That is the case today, and that was the case for the Famine Irish, even though contemporaries failed to recognize that fact.

Second, those who did start out as day laborers were hardly trapped in those positions. Forty-one percent of men whose first American jobs are best described as unskilled and who were still alive ten years later ended their careers higher up the socioeconomic ladder than where they began, and three-quarters of these social climbers finished their working days in white-collar occupations. Some became clerks, salesmen, or civil servants, but the vast majority (three out of four) opened their own business, running a saloon, grocery, or other retail enterprise. Skilled craftsmen were not trapped in their occupations either—thousands of them opened retail establishments like saloons and groceries, and still more started businesses related to their artisanal trade. To say that unskilled and artisan Famine immigrants "seldom rose from the bottom of American urban society," as prominent scholars of the Irish experience in America have suggested for generations, is simply not true.

Further evidence that the Famine immigrants had more control over their fates than previously understood is found in their savings accounts. The Famine refugees saved a lot more in those accounts than their native-born neighbors imagined. Leaving aside those who emigrated as children (and therefore had the advantages of an American education) as well as those who died before living for a decade in the United States, we find that male Famine immigrants living in New York or Brooklyn saved, on average, $463 in their accounts, equal to about $17,000 today (the median high balance was $291).

Even if we take only the immigrants who started at the bottom of the socioeconomic ladder and *never climbed any higher*, the level of savings is still impressive. Men who remained in unskilled occupations for their whole lives saved on average $374, equal to more than a year's wages. Their median savings of $287 (about $11,000 today) was only barely lower than that of all male Famine immigrants. This amount of savings may not seem like much, but given how little they brought with them to America and the obstacles they faced, the Famine immigrants' level of savings is surprising. These figures are even more remarkable when we consider that today, 56 percent of Americans report not having even $1,000 in savings.

Another sign that the Famine immigrants were not "hapless beings" for very long, if ever, was their propensity to buy real estate. Among male Famine immigrants who began their American lives in New York, opened Emigrant Savings Bank accounts in the 1850s, and were still alive in 1870, 27 percent owned real estate, far more than historians have imagined. The surprising ability of the Famine immigrants to purchase their own homes has remained obscured primarily because scholars have focused their studies on America's biggest cities, where real estate was too expensive for all but the most successful newcomers. Only about 10 percent of the male Famine immigrants who were still living in New York owned land in 1870, whereas nearly half of those who had moved elsewhere had purchased homes. Among the movers, 42 percent of male Famine immigrants who relocated to New York City's suburbs (Long Island, Staten Island, Westchester County, and northeastern New Jersey) managed to buy a home by 1870, and 59 percent of the men who ventured beyond the New York City area owned real estate by that date. We know from their bank records that the surprising ability of those who left New York to buy property was not a result of having accumulated more money in New York than those who remained behind. Those who departed the New York metropolitan area had saved, before they left New York, less on average than those who remained.

There were limits, of course, to what the Famine immigrants could accomplish. Poor health was by far the biggest impediment to upward mobility. Hundreds of thousands of Famine immigrants died before they had an opportunity to climb the socioeconomic ladder. Many perished because they arrived weakened by years of malnutrition and hunger. Others succumbed because in New York they encountered illnesses like tuberculosis that were far more prevalent in crowded tenements than in sparsely populated rural Irish settlements. This was an era when even well-respected medical professionals like William O'Meagher ascribed illnesses to vapors and miasmas rather than bacteria and viruses, and the treatments they prescribed usually did more harm than good. Genetics and sheer luck often determined who lived and who died as the Famine immigrants began to find their way in America.

Women also faced systemic limitations to upward mobility. A lowly paid job as a domestic servant, laundress, or seamstress was the only realistic option for all but a tiny handful of Irish-born women in this era. There were many female business owners, but in almost every case these women either entered business in conjunction with a male kinsman or took over a business started by a spouse after he passed away. And as hatmaker Joanna Boyle and her daughter Annie discovered, men could, even after their deaths, use stipulations in their wills to keep female business proprietors dependent on the men who remained in their lives. As a result, upward mobility for Irish-born women in this period was almost always determined in conjunction with a father, brother, or husband. Irish immigrant families, however, would never have succeeded in improving their situations had it not been for the contributions that women made to household incomes as domestics or seamstresses, or by taking in boarders or laundry, and waiting on customers behind bars and shop counters.*

Despite feeling justifiable pride for having overcome so many obstacles, the Famine immigrants probably took even more pleasure in the achievements of their children. Knowing that their American-born offspring had more opportunities than they themselves had

---

* It should be noted that African Americans in the mid-nineteenth century faced far more systemic barriers to socioeconomic advancement than any Irish immigrant. There was virtually no occupation that an Irish immigrant could not and did not follow in antebellum New York, whereas well-entrenched social customs barred Black New Yorkers from all but a tiny handful of vocations. Lacking the right to vote and hold political office was also a crucial impediment to advancement that the Famine Irish did not face. Because Blacks could not vote, politicians felt no need to dole out patronage positions to them, and as we have seen, these jobs provided important footholds for climbing New York's occupational hierarchy. Lacking political rights, African Americans also did not receive the informal welfare that Irish Americans collected from Tammany Hall, and as a result when a crisis struck, Black New Yorkers had less of a safety net than Irish immigrants. A few writers have contended that the Irish were not truly considered "white" upon arrival in America and that therefore they faced the same disadvantages as African Americans. But if native-born Americans had viewed the Irish that way, then nativists would have demanded that the Irish be barred from voting on those grounds. Yet they never did so. Nativists might contend that the "Irish race" was inferior to the Anglo-Saxon "races," but even these bigots never contended that the Irish were not white.

enjoyed must have convinced most immigrants that coming to and settling in America had been worth the trials and tribulations they had suffered. Those included parting from parents and loved ones in Ireland and the guilt that might have come with it; the perilous ocean journey; the initial disorientation and homesickness after landing; the difficulties finding decent housing and appropriate employment; the deaths of family members from the diseases that ran rampant in New York tenements; and the insults they endured for being Irish or Catholic. Nonetheless, as the Famine Irish slowly assimilated over the years, transforming from Irishmen and -women in America into *Irish Americans*, the majority would have still occasionally longed for "home," the term they would have used for Ireland even decades after they had last set foot on Irish soil.

Most of the immigrants who felt this longing could not afford to leave work for a month or more to visit Ireland. "Ordinarily, therefore, only the rich or well-to-do can set foot on the 'ould sod,'" a newspaper noted. But in 1896, some enterprising Irish Americans came up with a way to bring the old sod to New York. That year was the fiftieth anniversary of the onset of the Great Famine and the huge immigration to America sparked by it. Looking back at how far the Irish American community had come in that half century, a group of prominent New Yorkers of Irish descent decided that the city needed a fitting monument to their achievements. But the dignitaries decided that the typical monuments of the day — statues and obelisks — would not suffice. Instead, they decided to build a palace.

The "Irish Palace," said its promoters, would be a living monument to Irish Americans. It would house a library with the great works of literature produced by Irish authors. It would also contain "a fine ballroom," a "large auditorium," a "gymnasium," a "labor bureau" for those needing assistance finding work, and meeting rooms "fitted up in good style" where "all the Irish organizations of the city" could hold their meetings and events. Finally, the palace would boast "a drill room" so that the city's Irish militia companies could train there, an armory to store their weapons, as well as a rifle range and riding academy so that these Irish American soldiers could hone their skills for the eventual liberation of Ireland. "Public spirited citizens of all nationalities," wrote the effort's organizers, "must applaud us for the conception of so grand an undertaking." The price tag that the group announced for the project was a whopping one million dollars, equal to about thirty-seven million today.

The first fund-raising event held to make the dream of the Irish Palace a reality was an Irish fair. Organizers announced that in exchange for a fifty-cent ticket, visitors to this fair could see a replica of Blarney Castle and "two pieces of the genuine 'Blarney Stone,'" artifacts from Clontarf, Swords Castle, the Hill of Tara, and "many other historic relics and curios." Each Irish county would also have its own booth featuring paintings of its famous sights and native sons as well as samples of its "antiquities" and distinctive handicrafts. "The aim," noted the *Times*, "will be to transport the visitor, as far as possible, into the very vicinity and local surroundings of Ireland's great historical events."

None of these features, however, turned out to be the most popular attraction at the fair. To fill the central space of the exhibition hall, the fair's organizers decided to place on the floor a giant map of Ireland's thirty-two counties, measuring twenty-five feet from top to bottom and nearly as far across. Newspaper magnate William Randolph Hearst sent an agent to traverse Ireland and collect soil from each part in sufficient quantities so that the space on the floor map depicting each county could be covered with actual soil from that locale. The giant map was surrounded by a fence, and one gained access (after paying an additional ten cents for the privilege) through "five-columned archways, surmounted by a huge green shamrock." The map was the hit of the fair, giving "great delight to thousands, who never thought to stand again on Irish soil."

In many cases, the immigrants were overwrought with emotion when they made it to the front of the line and finally set foot on their native sod. "One poor woman—Kate Murphy by name, and 80 years old—knelt down and kissed the soil of Fermanagh; then, crossing herself, proceeded to say her prayers, unmindful of the crowd around her," reported the *Irish World*. "While thus kneeling[,] a photographer took a flashlight picture of her. The flash was a revelation to the simple hearted creature, who seemed to think it a light from heaven, and was awed into reverential silence. When she finally stepped off the Irish soil she sighed sadly and clung to the fence, still gazing at 'Old Ireland.' She kept looking backward as she walked away, as if bidding a long farewell." Touching, smelling, even kissing that soil would have been a Proustian moment for this woman and for many of her fellow Famine immigrants, awakening a visceral sensation of being "home" and, with it, long-buried memories of Ireland and the loved ones (many no longer living, others not seen for decades) whom they had left behind. The ability to access those long-dormant emotions was surely worth every penny of the admission price.

—————

The experience of the Famine Irish in America, like that of Kate Murphy at the Irish fair, was bittersweet. There was sadness about the circumstances of their emigration and all that had been involuntarily left behind. And there were lofty dreams, like the building of an Irish Palace, that never came to fruition. Yet there was also the pride in all that *had* been accomplished—the obstacles overcome, the nest eggs put away, the businesses launched, the offspring set on the path to middle-class respectability or, in a few cases, great fortunes.

More than a century later, in the East Room of the White House on St. Patrick's Day with the Taoiseach (prime minister) of Ireland looking on, an American president whose great-great-great-grandfather had immigrated to the United States during the Famine invoked the story of Kate Murphy, noting that her heart and those of many Irish immigrants had clearly been torn between their love of America and their longing for the land they had left behind. Like so many other Americans with Irish roots, Barack Obama had learned that there was more to the story of the Famine immigrants than the familiar tale "of overcoming hardship through strength, and sacrifice, and faith, and family." As Obama noted, "the Irish did more than help build America,...they helped to sharpen the *idea* of America: the notion that no matter who you are, where you come from, what your last name is, in this country, you can make it." In that manner, the forty-fourth president recognized, the Famine immigrants had changed how Americans defined their nation and its ideals. One hundred seventy-five years after the Great Famine and the unprecedented influx of Irish refugees into the United States that it precipitated, Americans still "revel in that idea" — the grand promise of the American Dream and the notion that *anyone* can achieve it. In this sense, and in all Americans, the Famine generation lives on.

Acknowledgments

This book originated as a challenge issued by one of my colleagues at George Washington University. It was 2010, the history department was holding its faculty research seminar, and I was presenting my new research on the Irish-born customers of New York's Emigrant Savings Bank in the era of the Great Potato Famine. I had discovered the Emigrant Bank records while finishing work on my book *Five Points*, a history of the most famous (and infamous) Irish neighborhood in nineteenth-century America. The point of my paper was that the Famine immigrants had saved a lot more in their bank accounts than one would have imagined given their reputation for having remained locked in poverty, even after living for years in the United States, because they had come to America so poor, so lacking in educational and vocational skills, and had faced so much discrimination upon arrival.

That the immigrants had saved more than expected was pretty much inarguable—the data spoke for itself. But my colleagues wanted to know *why* the immigrants had done so well and in particular why, as I had described in my talk, some of the Irish had done better than others. I had found, for example, that immigrants from County Kerry had saved far more than those from neighboring Cork, even though their situations upon arrival were so similar. I had also discovered that those who started out in New York in unskilled occupations had actually saved *more* in their accounts than those who came to America with artisanal skills. What could explain these things? I replied that I did not have nearly enough data to answer such questions and that it would take an army of research assistants years to do enough research to answer them.

In response, Eric Arnesen, one of my colleagues, said I should apply for one of those big, prestigious grants that I had spent my years as department chair pestering my colleagues to pursue. One of those awards would pay for the army of research assistants I claimed to need. Yet applying for a grant was the last thing I wanted to do. I already had a book project lined up — a history of immigrant life in New York City called *City of Dreams* — that I was raring to get started on. But I had to admit that Eric was right; I *had* been nagging my colleagues to apply for such grants, even when, like me, they felt that doing so was a waste of time because the odds of winning were so slim. Consequently, I felt duty bound to try. I figured I could submit an application or two (my university would be pleased by my simply applying), get rejected, and then start work on *City of Dreams*. Because I lacked the statistical training to make use of the mountain of data I was proposing to collect, I lined up two economic historians (Cormac Ó Gráda and Simone A. Wegge) who possessed such skills to collaborate with me on the project should the grant application prove successful. No one was more surprised than me when, in the summer of 2011, I was informed that the National Endowment for the Humanities had awarded us $290,000 for our project.

In the decade that followed, three dozen students and a professional genealogist gathered more than a million pieces of information (much of it pdf's and jpeg's of historical documents found online) that traced the life stories of the thousands of Emigrant Savings Bank customers who opened accounts during the bank's first eight years of operation. There would have been even documents more had we not decided, fairly early in the process, to focus our efforts primarily on the bank's Irish-born customers who had come to America during the Famine.

Thus, the first people I need to acknowledge are the students who enlisted in my army of research assistants. They included Jenna Andrews, Sara Barrack, Theresa Baum, Ali Beachman, Caitlyn Borghi, Meagan Byrne, Julia Casanova-Moore, Madeline Crispell, Emily deRedon, James Feenstra, Holly Firlein, Bill Horne, Greg Hughes, Jon Keljik, Bob Lintott, Erika MacLeod, Madlyn Murtha, Michelle Ordway, Mika Ramachandran, Lauren Ricci, Megan Rohrer, Elizabeth Rosenwasser, Michael Salgarola, Rachel Scharf, Aly Seeberger, Emma Shindell, Melanie Strating, Whitney Tarella, Milica Taskovic, and Sam Wood. Meaghan Casey graduated too soon to join my ragtag band of warriors, but she contributed nonetheless through the research she had done under my supervision on her award-winning senior thesis on the Emigrant Bank's Irish-born depositors.

After *City of Dreams* was published in 2016, I resumed work on *Plentiful Country*, but decided at that point to transform my army of researchers into a smaller, more agile, more expert unit akin to Tom Cruise's Impossible Mission Force. (Cue the Lalo Schifrin theme music!) Katie Carper, Lindsay Chervinsky, and Hope McCaffrey did not know one another when, in the spring semester of 2010, they sat down in the same row of a GWU lecture hall on the first day of my class on the American Civil War. Nonetheless, these formidable scholars went on to manage my research project in its final years, each taking charge successively as, one by one, they enrolled in American history doctoral programs. Even after moving on to their own academic careers, however, they sometimes generously came out of retirement (much like the members of the Impossible Mission Force) to play key cameo roles when their particular expertise was needed or attrition had rendered the unit precariously small. Lindsay has gone on to become a well-known scholar of the American Presidency; Katie has established herself as one of the foremost authorities on the business of immigration in the nineteenth century; while Hope, the last of the three to enter a

Ph.D. program, will undoubtedly become equally well known in her area of expertise—women in nineteenth-century American politics. A fourth doctoral student, Lindsay D. Graham, did heroic work creating our project website, beyondragstoriches.org. That website was made possible in part by a grant from the Andrew W. Mellon Foundation (particularly appropriate given that Andrew's Mellon forebears were Irish immigrants from County Tyrone). And George Washington University generously funded these research assistants after my NEH funding ran out.

The most important contributor of research assistance to *Plentiful Country*, however, was genealogist extraordinaire Janet Wilkinson Schwartz. *Plentiful Country* is the third book of mine to which Janet has contributed, and as in those previous cases, this work is immeasurably better because of the incredible gems of research she uncovered—finds that time and again turned interesting or even fascinating stories into extraordinary ones. Janet found that Bartholomew O'Donnell supplemented his income by becoming a marathon race walker and that draper Hugh Collender became a billiard-table-manufacturing magnate. Janet also found the newspaper coverage of the court case that made it possible to trace the story of hat shop operators Terence and Joanna Condon Boyle. In other cases, Janet through her dogged detective work *disproved* unbelievable tales about the Famine immigrants that made it into the press in an era when accuracy was not a particularly high priority for journalists, thus saving me from embarrassing errors. I am truly grateful to Janet for devoting so many years to this project.

Once I began translating all that research onto the written page, another army—of friends and colleagues—came to my aid. My collaborations with Simone A. Wegge, Cormac Ó Gráda, and Dylan Connor on articles aimed at academic audiences helped me better understand and describe the significance of the information we had collected. Marion Casey shared the research of her students at New York University as well as her own encyclopedic knowledge of Irish

New York. Timothy Meagher and Deirdre Moloney offered advice on early drafts of the book's chapters. Karen Ward Mahar gave me editorial advice throughout the project, while Cormac Ó Gráda and Kevin Kenny were unbelievably generous with their time, offering thorough and thought-provoking critiques of every single chapter. My great friend, journalist Marianne Szegedy-Maszak, did not read any of the chapters, but edited many versions of my book proposal. Furthermore, during our many lunches, and later during our Covid walks, Marianne offered invaluable advice about the writing process. In particular, she many times suggested elegant solutions when I felt that my rendering of a scene had fallen flat. As I neared the finish line, Elizabeth Stack and John Ridge came through with research leads that helped me pull together the book's conclusion, while Patrick Williams and Jacob Anbinder read the very final version of the manuscript and saved me from many factual and stylistic embarrassments. At the last minute my uncle, Paul Anbinder, did a fabulous job scrutinizing the page proofs and saved me from many mistakes and infelicities.

Yet a book like *Plentiful Country* requires still more collaborators. Chris Robinson worked tirelessly with me on draft after draft of each map and infographic, until we got them just right. Margaret Sullivan was equally patient figuring out what I was looking for in the one original piece of artwork for the book, the image that sits between Part I and Part II, depicting the Irishman contemplating the climb up the socioeconomic ladder. The other illustrations were collected by the incomparable Gina Broze. And I was saved from many a transcription and citation error by fact checker Jane Ackerman.

Once the book was in production, I had had the assistance of an outstanding team at Little, Brown. I was trepidatious about working with a new editor this late in my career, but Alex Littlefield proved to be an insightful, imaginative collaborator who improved every aspect of *Plentiful Country*. Copy editor Trent Duffy saved me from countless mistakes, and editorial assistant Morgan Wu patiently kept track of my submissions and omissions. Betsy Uhrig managed the production process with wisdom and patience.

Twenty-five years ago, when I first had an inkling that my writing might appeal to a trade audience, I approached a literary agent named Philippa (who represented a friend of mine) in search of an agent of my own. After receiving my writing sample, she called me and minced no words in telling me why she would not represent me: "Tyler, you will NEVER write a trade book." That rejection was one of the best strokes of luck in my life, because it led me instead to Jill Grinberg, who for the past quarter century has been a great agent and an even greater friend. Jill's advice, wisdom, and encouragement has influenced every part of my writing career.

The most important support I have received, however, has come from my family. Writers are an obsessive/compulsive group if ever there was one, and family members bear the brunt of those behaviors. We obsess about our manuscripts and then feel compelled to write "for just a few more minutes," which quickly become hours more often than not. (They say that Graham Greene could get up in the morning, write exactly one hundred words — no more and no less — and then pour himself a drink and lounge on the Amalfi Coast for the rest of the day, but he was an exception.) I owe a huge debt to my family members — and in particular my wife, Lisa, and my children, Jacob, Dina, Maya, and Celia — for tolerating with such good grace all the times I said, "I can't, I have to write."

Finally, I must thank my parents, Madeline and Stephen Anbinder, for all they have done for me. They have been unrelenting cheerleaders, patient sounding boards, keen-eyed editors, and wonderful role models. This book is dedicated to them, with love and gratitude.

Illustration Credits

5: Captain Thomas D. Norris.
Courtesy New York State Military Museum

8: Captain Thomas D. Norris in 1894.
New York Irish-American, *courtesy New York State Library*

15: Depositors' names in the Emigrant Savings Bank test books.
New York Public Library

17: Thomas D. Norris's entry in the Emigrant Savings Bank test books.
New York Public Library

25: Replica of a Famine-era cabin.
Tyler Anbinder

33: Women planting potatoes in northeast Ireland.
Photograph reproduced courtesy Trustees of National Museums Northern Ireland, BELUM.Y.W.01.56.25

47: Woodcut of famished children.
© Illustrated London News Ltd / *Mary Evans*

47: Famine victims in British-ruled India, 1877.
Photo by Willoughby Wallace Hooper, courtesy Bridgeman Images

57: Five Points.
Collection of New-York Historical Society, PR-065-0440–0001

60: Ship leaving Liverpool.
Illustrated London News, *courtesy Tyler Anbinder*

66: New York City around 1850.
Courtesy Lionel Pincus and Princess Firyal Map Division, New York Public Library

69: A standard two-room tenement apartment in New York City, circa 1900.
Jessie Tarbox Beals / Museum of the City of New York

74: Help-wanted ads in the *New York Tribune*.
Courtesy Library of Congress Prints and Photographs Division

80: Bar in Crown's Grocery, Five Points.
New York Illustrated News, *courtesy Tyler Anbinder*

93: Print of the Old Brewery tenement.
John Gough, Platform Echoes, *courtesy Library of Congress*

95: Moving Day.
Harper's Weekly, *April 30, 1859, Lincoln Financial Foundation Collection*

100: 31 Baxter Street.
Frank Leslie's Illustrated Newspaper, *July 1, 1865, Lincoln Financial Foundation Collection*

104: An English gashouse, 1821.
Look and Learn / Peter Jackson Collection / Bridgeman Images

106: Advertisement for Edgar Farmer & Co.
Holbrook's Newark City Directory for 1877, Charles F. Cummings New Jersey Information Center

108: Depiction of a New York cartman.
Yale University Art Gallery

112: Depiction of an Irish servant.
Harper's Weekly, *December 7, 1867, Lincoln Financial Foundation Collection*

117: Female customers in the Emigrant Savings Bank.
Frank Leslie's Illustrated Newspaper, *March 13, 1880, Internet Archive*

131: Hat peddler as depicted in *Harper's Weekly*, September 19, 1868.
University of Michigan

131: Umbrella peddler as depicted in *Harper's Weekly*, September 19, 1868.
Tyler Anbinder

151: Depiction of a charcoal peddler.
Yale University Art Gallery

158: Deposit ledger for Bridget and Michael Quinn.
New York Public Library

161: Hudson Street, Ward Three, New York.
Collection of New-York Historical Society,
PR.020.FF.23

163: Depiction of iron molders.
State Library Victoria, Pictures Collection

165: Timothy Carr.
Courtesy Tim Carr

166: A dresser preparing a goat hide.
Alexander Watt, Leather Manufacture, 5th ed., courtesy University of California Libraries

166: Goat hides in sumac solution.
Alexander Watt, Leather Manufacture, 5th ed., courtesy University of California Libraries

169: A George P. Fox newspaper ad.
New York Freeman's Journal, *September 7, 1850, New York Public Library*

180: The "Improved Threshing Engine."
From the Collections of the Henry Ford

187: Jonathan Dillon.
Courtesy Michael and Sheila Sexton

187: Isabella Dillon.
Dillon/Stiles Family Archives

188: The inside of Abraham Lincoln's timepiece.
Division of Political and Military History, National Museum of America History, Smithsonian Institution

195: Commemorative portrait of James Cavanagh.
New York Irish-American, *January 12, 1901, courtesy New York State Library*

202: An advertisement for James Goodwin's paper business.
Reference Book and Directory of the Book and Job Printers *(1870), New York Public Library*

214: The Washington Hotel.
New York Public Library

225: John Mara.
Brooklyn Daily Eagle, *December 28, 1900, courtesy Brooklyn Public Library*

228: Castle Garden.
Tyler Anbinder

232: Advertisement in the *New York Herald.*
New York Herald, *November 21, 1890, Tyler Anbinder*

240: Advertisement for Callanan & Kemp.
New York Irish-American, *December 18, 1875, courtesy New York State Library*

240: Laurence Callanan.
George W. Engelhardt, New York the Metropolis, *New York Public Library*

243: Advertisement for William Doherty's carriage business.
New York Public Library

250: Michael Carroll's shop.
Harper's Weekly, *March 29, 1879, Tyler Anbinder*

252: Astor House.
Courtesy Library of Congress Prints and Photographs Division

256: "Mrs. Sandy Sullivan's Genteel Lodging-House."
New York Illustrated News, *February 18, 1860, Tyler Anbinder*

261: Nicolino Calyo, "The Mead, Ginger, and Root Beer Cart."
Yale University Art Gallery

270: A View in the Five Points.
New York Public Library

280: The Voting-Place, No. 488 Pearl Street.
Harper's Weekly, *November 13, 1858, Tyler Anbinder*

287: Walter Roche and his family.
Courtesy Robert Gibbons

291: A saloon on Water Street.
Frank Leslie's Illustrated Newspaper, *August 8, 1868, courtesy New York State Library*

297: Callaghan McSweeney.
Courtesy Ed and Connie McSweeny

297: Honoria McSweeney.
Courtesy Ed and Connie McSweeny

298: Painting of William Rudkin.
Courtesy Conor Welch

298: Painting of Catherine Connolly Rudkin.
Courtesy Conor Welch

302: Photo of Bernard "Barney" Woods.
Brooklyn Daily Eagle, *March 21, 1906, courtesy Brooklyn Public Library*

312: The New York Steam Sugar Refining Company's plant.
Collection of New-York Historical Society, PR.020.FF.27

315: Church of St. John.
John Gerald Berger, A History of St. Brendan's Parish

324: Depiction of the Battle of Wolf Mountain.
Frank Leslie's Illustrated Newspaper, *May 5, 1877, Denver Public Library / Wikipedia*

325: Edmond Butler.
The Illustrated American, *April 6, 1895, University of Iowa*

330: Threshing scene, Walsh County, North Dakota.
Courtesy Minnesota Historical Society

338: Patrick Drew.
Milwaukee Journal, *November 2, 1903, courtesy Milwaukee Public Library*

342: Advertisement in the San Francisco City Directory.
San Francisco Public Library

350: Garrett Bartnett's mug shot.

Courtesy San Quentin State Prison Records, California State Archives

356: Caroline Sinnamon and a student.

Courtesy Archives and Special Collections, Penfield Library, State University of New York at Oswego

366: Walter J. Bartnett.

Los Angeles Herald, *June 23, 1908, courtesy California Digital Newspaper Collection, Center for Bibliographic Studies and Research, University of California, Riverside*

367: Michael J. Kavanagh.

Courtesy Kathleen Kavanagh

368: Richard V. Oulahan.

Courtesy Herbert Hoover Presidential Library

370: Thomas J. Bradley.

Moses King, The Dewey Reception and Committee of New York City, *Columbia University Libraries*

374: Senator William R. Sharkey.

Courtesy Contra Costa County Historical Society

374: Charles Sharkey.

Courtesy Folsom State Prison Records, California State Archives

376: Captain Frank J. Killeen.

Buffalo Evening News, *March 10, 1917, Tyler Anbinder*

381: Letter detail.

Paul McLoughlin

384: Michael Phelan.

Michael Phelan, The Game of Billiards, *courtesy Library of Congress Prints and Photographs Division*

388: Phelan & Collender billiard-table manufactory and its patented Bevel table.

Harper's Weekly, *March 16, 1872, University of Michigan*

390: Hugh Collender.

Chicago Billiard Museum / Wikipedia

A Note on the Value of a Dollar

The Famine immigrants were obsessed with money—earning it, saving it, and sending it to loved ones in Ireland. As a result, this book contains many references to the amounts of money these newcomers saved in their bank accounts, spent on a home or farm, or bequeathed to their children. A curious reader naturally wants to know "How much is that worth in today's dollars?" Yet even economists who have devoted years to studying this question have a hard time determining the answer for dollar amounts from the 1840s and '50s, when the immigration resulting from the Great Irish Famine took place.

The most widely used method to determine the changing value of the dollar is to survey the price of a variety of consumer goods (like food, fuel, and clothing) and services (like rent and transportation) and calculate the rate at which those prices change over time. By that measure, $1 from the 1850s is worth about $38 today. (By "today," I mean the spring of 2023, the time of this writing; for simplicity's sake, I've used that term throughout the book.) But economic historians recognize that consumer prices are not always the best way to translate the value of dollar amounts from the past into contemporary terms. Wages in the United States, for example, have risen at a far faster rate than consumer goods. Thus, work as a New York day laborer—the prototypical job for a newly arrived Irishman in the 1850s—paid $1 per day in the 1850s but averaged $157 per day at the beginning of 2023, reflecting a much higher rate of inflation than that for consumer goods. And wage inflation for other occupations has been almost twice as high as for day labor.

Complicating matters further, these economists offer a third means of determining the value of dollar amounts from the past, one that is particularly relevant to *Plentiful Country* because it involves the value of "wealth held." Most of the dollar amounts referred to in this book are bank balances and real estate appraisals, which fall under this category. Economists tell us that $1 of wealth held in 1852 had the same "prestige value" (based on per capita gross domestic product) as $629 at the beginning of 2023.

So which multiplier should one use: 38 or 157 or 629?

In the end, I determined my answer by considering the moral of a story told in a guidebook for those immigrating to America in the early nineteenth century. According to the tale, an Irish immigrant was at work on a letter to his loved ones "back home" when his employer oversaw what he was writing. In the letter, the immigrant bragged that he was doing so well in America that he could now afford to eat meat twice a week, far more often than he had in Ireland. The employer asked the immigrant why he did not tell the truth, which was that he now ate meat "every day of the week,... three times a-day." The immigrant replied that "his friends would *disbelieve all* he had said" in the letter "if he had told them *that.*"

As we have seen, the average household savings at the Emigrant Savings Bank for the Famine immigrants who survived at least ten years in the United States was $463. If one uses the "wealth held" multiplier suggested by economic historians, that amount would equate to an average savings for Famine immigrants of $291,227 in today's dollars. Even using the more modest day-laborer-wage-inflation multiplier would result in the immigrants' average savings equaling, in modern terms, $72,691, an amount those familiar with the standard depiction of the Famine immigrants would also find difficult to believe. Consequently, so that readers will not "disbelieve all" I have written, *Plentiful Country* uses the most conservative multiplier available—38—to calculate the modern value of dollar figures from the 1850s, even though the best answer is probably higher. The modern values of dollar figures from other decades are calculated using the precise years involved and that same conservative method.

Those who wish to learn the details behind these calculations can do so at measuringworth.com.

A Note on Sources

One might wonder how I can write with such assurance about Irish Americans who were born two centuries ago. Doing so has been made possible by the digital revolution; in fact, almost all of the sources used in writing this book are available online. I relied most heavily on Ancestry.com, which requires a subscription but can be accessed for free in many libraries. Most Ancestry.com records are also accessible for free at Familysearch.org, but that site is not as user-friendly. Another important source for this book, city directories, can be found on those sites as well as Google Books, hathitrust .org, archive.org, and the website of the New York Public Library. Old newspapers were also crucial for the writing of *Plentiful Country*, and I accessed them via the subscription sites newspapers.com, genealogybank.org (which specializes in Irish American publications), and newspaperarchive.org. A free site that concentrates on New York State newspapers, including hard-to-find periodicals that are often not on the subscription sites, is known as Old Fulton Postcards. It is particularly difficult to use but contains some real gems available nowhere else. It can be accessed at fultonhistory.com, or in a slightly more user-friendly version at fultonsearch.org.

Anyone who examines the sources listed in the following notes will find that they often contradict one another, even on the most mundane facts, such as the spelling of immigrants' names, their years of birth, and what jobs they held at a given time. To sort through these contradictions and inaccuracies, I gave credence to contemporaneous documents over those written years later and I trusted family sources over those written by outsiders. But in many cases, I ultimately had to rely on my judgment, which has been honed by four decades of immersion in the historical records of the mid-nineteenth century. Still, that judgment is far from perfect, and I have lost count of the number of times that a story I felt sure I had gotten right had to be significantly revised when one of these websites uploaded a new set of documents, or a family member corrected a transcription error, revealing something that suddenly changed my understanding of an immigrant's life story. To let the reader know in every instance which facts I know with certainty and which are less clear, I would have to use "probably" and "apparently" in every paragraph, often many times. But I have chosen not to do so in order to not bore the reader.

I also need to briefly explain my method for citing New York City directories, those annual publications that listed the name, occupation, and address for most men (and a few women) in American cities. In most places, directories cover a calendar year and are easy to cite. But as we've seen, May 1 was the date on which virtually all residential leases ended in New York and huge numbers of residents changed addresses. The information for New York and Brooklyn directories was compiled in the weeks immediately after Moving Day, and then published midyear, with titles such as *Doggett's New York City Directory for 1850–1851*. I used city directories primarily to find an immigrant's occupation for the years between censuses. Because the directory for 1850–1851 contained that person's occupation as of May 1850, the year that directory was published, I have for clarity's sake cited all city directories by the date they were published. So, *Doggett's New York City Directory for 1850–1851* is cited, using my abbreviation method, as the 1850 *NYCDir*.

One might also wonder whether the Emigrant Savings Bank customers who are the subjects of this book are really representative of the Famine Irish overall. It is true that the Emigrant Bank's customers are not a perfect cross section of all Irish New Yorkers. If the initial American occupation for all male Famine immigrants could be determined, for example, the percentage of unskilled workers would likely be about 5 percentage points higher than that found among the Emigrant Bank's customers, and the total in the three white-collar categories combined would be about the same percentage lower. Nonetheless, recent studies by economic historians that use algorithms to trace the occupational trajectories of millions of Americans (and tens of thousands of Famine immigrants) report levels of upward occupational mobility that are just as high (in fact, a little higher) than that found with the Emigrant Savings Bank's customers. A detailed discussion of those studies and the question of representativeness can be found in Tyler Anbinder, Cormac Ó Gráda, and Simone A. Wegge, "'The Best Country in the World': The Surprising Social Mobility of New York's Irish-Famine Immigrants," *Journal of Interdisciplinary History* 53 (2023): 413–14.

Finally, some discussion is warranted about the source that underpins almost every biographical sketch in *Plentiful Country*, the test books of the Emigrant Savings Bank. To take full advantage of this unparalleled font of information on the life stories of New York's Famine immigrants, I led a team of students in a decade-long effort. First, we transcribed into a database the test book entries for the first 18,000 accounts opened at the bank. Then, we added to this database information we found in the bank's deposit ledgers, as well as data from ship manifests, censuses, city directories, and death records. (New York City's death certificates are in the process of being digitized as I write this, which explains why in some cases I can cite an immigrant's actual death certificate, but in others I can access only an incomplete transcription.) All this information is presented in two databases created in Microsoft Excel format. The larger of the two, which I call the Emigrant Savings Bank Depositor Database, contains every bit of information collected about the people who opened all 18,000 accounts, even those not opened by Famine immigrants. The other, the Emigrant Savings Bank Mobility Database, contains entries only on the 1,207 male Famine immigrants whose occupations in America I could trace for at least ten years. This was the database I used to calculate the rates of socioeconomic mobility cited throughout *Plentiful Country*. Both databases can be downloaded from Harvard University's Dataverse website, https://dataverse.harvard.edu/dataverse/anbinder, or at https://doi.org/10.7910/DVN/RYCAAU.

Endnotes

Abbreviations Used in These Notes

The sources most often cited in the notes that follow are entries in the manuscript population schedules of the federal and state census returns, because those census records are the best means of tracking the lives of ordinary Americans in the nineteenth century. These records are organized by state, then county, then township. Large towns were often divided into wards, and in big cities those wards were sometimes subdivided into districts. When a district was considered too large for a single census taker, districts were subdivided into divisions; these might be numerical ("first division") or directional ("western district"). Within each town, ward, district, and division, census marshals would give each building they visited a dwelling number and each residence within a dwelling was given a family number. All this information is needed to find a particular census entry from 1850 through 1870, so to streamline these notes, the abbreviations listed below have been utilized.

There are, however, a few exceptions. In 1870, Democrats complained (accurately, it turned out) that the Republicans in charge of the census had undercounted residents of heavily Democratic New York and Philadelphia. In those two cities, therefore, the census of 1870 was done a second time. This subsequent count was known as the "second enumeration." Because the second enumeration was done in haste, it contains less information about each resident and therefore when an immigrant appeared in both, I used the first 1870 enumeration. In most cases, census takers compiling the second enumeration of 1870 did not bother with dwelling and family numbers, but instead listed street addresses to prove they had visited every house. So when citing the second enumeration, a page number is provided. (Page numbers are not normally used to cite census entries because each census page usually has two — and sometimes even three — page numbers on it because government officials felt free to add them for their own purposes.) Beginning in 1880, the federal census stopped making reference to city wards and instead divided counties by enumeration districts, which is why those are specified for censuses from that year forward. Those later census pages sometimes contain assembly district numbers, which is why these must sometimes be included when citing censuses compiled after 1870.

Acct.	Account
AD	Assembly district
BklynDir	*Brooklyn City Directory*
BDE	*Brooklyn Daily Eagle*
Dir	Directory
DIST	District
DIV	Division
DW	Dwelling
ED	Enumeration district
Enum2	Second enumeration
ESB	Emigrant Savings Bank Records, New York Public Library
FAM	Family
KingsC	Kings County, New York
NYC	New York County (synonymous with "New York City" before 1892)
NYCen	New York State Census
NYCDeaths	New York City municipal deaths, 1795–1949, Familysearch.org

ENDNOTES

NYCDir	*New York City Directory*
NYCMA	New York City Municipal Archives
NYEP	*New York Evening Post*
NYH	*New York Herald*
NYIA	New York *Irish-American*
NYShips	Passenger lists of vessels arriving at New York, New York, 1820–1897, Record Group 36, National Archives, Ancestry.com
NYT	*New York Times*
NYTrib	*New York Tribune*
SF	San Francisco
USCen	Manuscript population schedules, United States Census, Record Group 29, National Archives
W	Ward

Introduction

3 *Thomas D. Norris:* Accts. 13011, 39712, and 109566, ESB; FAM420, DW159, DIST3, W9, NYC, 1855 NYCen; FAM475, DW114, DIST2, W1, NYC, 1860 USCen; FAM12, DW9, DIST5, W23, ED659, NYC, 1880 USCen; 1854 *NYCDir,* 532; 1860 *NYCDir,* 645; 1875 *NYCDir,* 998; 1876 *NYCDir,* 1028; 1884 *NYCDir,* 1308; 1885 *NYCDir,* 1431; 1886 *NYCDir,* 1463; 1887 *NYCDir,* 1476; 1891 *NYCDir,* 1021; "Letters from the Sixty-ninth," *NYIA,* July 6, 1861, 2; "Captain Thomas D. Norris," *NYIA,* Aug. 19, 1865, 3; "Divorces Granted Yesterday," *NYH,* Nov. 3, 1867, 10; "Tammany Primaries," *New York World,* Dec. 30, 1873, 5; "The Irish Classes in America," *NYIA,* Sept. 25, 1880, 8; "The Land League in America," *NYIA,* Feb. 12, 1881, 8; "Latest Election Returns," *New York Truth,* Nov. 11, 1882, 1 (Norris's salary); "Irish Classes in America," *NYIA,* Jan. 31, 1885, 5; "We Regret," *NYIA,* Jan. 10, 1886, 4; "Captain T. D. Norris," *NYIA,* May 14, 1894, 4; *Official Register of the United States Containing a List of the Officers and Employees in the Civil, Military, and Naval Service on the First of July, 1895* (Washington, DC, 1895), 1:189; "Obituary," *New York Irish World,* Jan. 27, 1900, 11; "Death of Capt. Thomas D. Norris," *An Claidheamh Solais,* Feb. 10, 1900, 7; will of Thomas D. Norris, Oct. 8, 1894, NY Wills and Probate Records, 1659–1999, Ancestry.com.

6 *"worse than death":* "A Soldier of the Union in Trouble," *NYTrib,* July 16, 1879, 2.

6 *"paper dealer":* FAM1914, DW1516, Morrisania, Westchester County, NY, 1870 USCen.

7 *"revenue officer":* "An Old Soldier's Troubles," *NYH,* July 16, 1879, 9.

8 *Anna O'Sullivan:* Marriage of Thomas D. Norris and Anna Sullivan [sic], Nov. 1, 1892, NY Extracted Marriage Index, 1866–1937, Ancestry.com; FAM489, DW175, ED519, KingsC, 1900 USCen.

8 *"ingratitude":* "Town Topics," *NYIA,* Feb. 24, 1883, 4.

8   "storekeeper": *Official Register of the United States, Containing a List of the Officers and Employés in the Civil, Military, and Naval Service on the First of July, 1889* (Washington, DC, 1889), 1:187.

9   "sanitarium": "Death of Thomas D. Norris," *BDE*, Jan. 14, 1900, 5.

9   "asphyxia": Death certificate for Mary Norris, July 18, 1900, KingsC, NYCMA.

9   "destitute": Mrs. M. O'Brien to Dear Sir, May 17, 1914, Thomas D. Norris Civil War pension file, Record Group 15, National Archives.

9   "endeared him to all": "Our Gaelic World," *New York Irish World*, Jan. 20, 1900, 10.

9   "in every respect": "Death of Capt. Thomas D. Norris," *NYIA*, Jan. 20, 1900, 1.

10 presented these immigrants: John Maguire, "Why Hollywood Gets the Irish So Wrong," BBC.com, Dec. 10, 2020.

10 "other opportunities": Oscar Handlin, *Boston's Immigrants: A Study in Acculturation* (1941; repr., Cambridge, MA, 1991), 55.

10 "exceptional Irishman": Ibid., 69.

10 "majority of Famine emigrants": Kerby A. Miller, *Emigrants and Exiles: Ireland and the Irish Exodus to North America* (New York, 1985), 314–15.

11 "poverty and hardship": Ibid., 315–16.

11 "before the Civil War": Kenneth A. Scherzer, "Immigrant Social Mobility and the Historian," in *A Companion to American Immigration*, ed. Reed Ueda (Malden, MA, 2006), 374.

11 "tables of the Irish gentry": Thomas Mooney, *Nine Years in America*, 2nd ed. (Dublin, 1850), 81.

11 "Any man or woman": Diarmaid Ó Muirithe, *A Seat Behind the Coachman: Travellers in Ireland, 1800–1900* (Dublin, 1972), 138–39.

11 "best country in the world": Eliza Quin to her "Dear Pearants," *Third Report from the Select Committee of the House of Lords on Colonization from Ireland* ([London], 1849), 128.

11 "deprivation": Miller, *Emigrants and Exiles*, 315.

11 "helplessness": Handlin, *Boston's Immigrants*, 125.

14 maiden names: Bonnie Ruberg, "What Is Your Mother's Maiden Name? A Feminist History of Online Security Questions," *Feminist Media Histories* 3, no. 3 (2017): 57.

16 Special Collections: "An Unexpected Treasure," *NYT*, Sept. 21, 1995, A22; Harry Keaney, "Immigrant Treasure Trove Found," *Irish Echo*, Sept. 20–26, 1995, 1, 18, 38.

19 "urban society": Miller, *Emigrants and Exiles*, 314.

20 "yearning to breathe free": Emma Lazarus, "The New Colossus," in *The Poems of Emma Lazarus*, 2 vols. (Boston, 1888), 1:203.

Chapter 1: "Enough to Sicken the Heart"

23 Cornelius Sullivan 'must have felt: Accts. 617, 2581, and 15839, ESB; manifest of the *West Point*, Mar. 29, 1851, NYShips; FAM354, DW81, DIST3, W6, NYC, 1855 NYCen.

23 English landlord: Gerard Lyne, *The Lansdowne Estate in Kerry Under W. S. Trench* (Dublin, 2001), xvii–xxxviii, lviii–lxvi, 3–20; Tyler Anbinder, "From Famine to Five Points: Lord Lansdowne's Irish Tenants Encounter North America's Most Notorious Slum," *American Historical Review* 107 (Apr. 2002): 356–60.

24 "half fed": Jonathan Binns, *The Miseries and Beauties of Ireland*, 2 vols. (London, 1837), 2:336.

24 "face of the globe": Thomas Campbell Foster, *Letters on the Condition of the People of Ireland* (London, 1846), 389.

24 *"in the street every morning"*: John O'Sullivan Diary, c. Mar. 1847, quoted in Gerard Lyne, "William Steuart Trench and the Post-Famine Emigration from Kenmare to America, 1850–1855," *Journal of the Kerry Archaeological and Historical Society* 25 (1992): 125n242.

24 *"starving hundreds that besiege me"*: John O'Sullivan to Charles Trevelyan, "February 1847," in House of Commons, *Correspondence from January to March, 1847, Relating to the Measures Adopted for the Relief of the Distress in Ireland: Commissariat Series [Second Part]* (London, 1847), 166.

24 *"living tomb"*: *Tralee Chronicle*, Jan. 16, 1847.

25 *taken to Cork*: W. Steuart Trench, *Realities of Irish Life* (London, 1869), 111–27; Lyne, "William Steuart Trench and the Post-Famine Emigration," 89–137; Anbinder, "From Famine to Five Points," 358–62.

25 *countless different shades of green*: A color version of the photo can be found at https://scholarspace.library.gwu.edu/downloads/3x816n34q?disposition=inline.

28 *"luxuriant fields"*: Peter Connell, *The Land and People of County Meath, 1750–1850* (Dublin, 2004), 127n1.

28 *half the Irish population*: Cormac Ó Gráda, *Ireland's Great Famine: Interdisciplinary Perspectives* (Dublin, 2006), 27.

29 *"endured by the Irish"*: Johann Kohl, *Travels in Ireland* (London, 1844), 87.

29 *"naked and famishing"*: Gustave de Beaumont, *Ireland: Social, Political, and Religious*, ed. W. C. Taylor, 2 vols. (London, 1839), 1:264–65.

29 *"slaves in the colonies"*: *Selection of Parochial Examinations Relative to the Destitute Classes in Ireland* (Dublin, 1835), 234.

30 *"lives"*: Joel Mokyr, *Why Ireland Starved: A Quantitative and Analytical History of the Irish Economy, 1800–1850* (London, 1983), 103.

31 *"small farmers"*: Cormac Ó Gráda, *Ireland Before and After the Famine: Explorations in Economic History, 1800–1925*, 2nd ed. (Manchester, Eng., 1993), 58–59.

31 *"smallholders"*: Mokyr, *Why Ireland Starved*, 18, 284.

31 *remaining 85 percent*: Estimates of this figure vary quite a bit. See *Atlas of the Great Irish Famine*, ed. John Crowley, William J. Smyth, and Mike Murphy (New York, 2012), 183 Thomas Larcom, "Observations on the Census of the Population of Ireland in 1841," *Journal of the Statistical Society of London* 6 (1843): 341; Cormac Ó Gráda, "Poverty, Population, and Agriculture, 1801–45," in *Ireland Under the Union, 1801–70*, ed. W. E. Vaughan, vol. 5 of *A New History of Ireland*, 9 vols. (Oxford, 1989), 5:114.

32 *"hampers on their backs"*: "The Condition of the People of Ireland," London *Times*, Nov. 18, 1845, 8.

33 *"wretched"*: *Poor Enquiry (Ireland): Appendix (E) Containing Baronial Examinations Relative to Food, Cottages and Cabins, Clothing and Furniture* (London, 1836), supplement, pp. 13, 81, 110, 123, 132, 151, 172, 185, 187, 192–93, 196, 213, 232, 236, 239, 284, 286, and 347. For the other quotations, see supplement, pp. 10, 27, 38, 88–89, 63, 75, 109, 159, 173, and 221.

34 *"in general very bad"*: Ibid., p. 49.

34 *"rolling in volumes"*: Ibid., p. 41.

34 *"fourth-class"*: *Report of the Commissioners Appointed to Take the Census of Ireland for the Year 1841* (Dublin, 1843), pl. 2.

34 *"almost ridiculous"*: *Poor Enquiry (Ireland): Appendix (E)*, supplement, p. 113. The remaining quotations in this paragraph are from pp. 65, 84, 181, 65, 22, 187, 90, and 113.

35 *"meat, eggs, or fish"*: Ibid., p. 20.

35 *"historically unique"*: Austin Bourke, *"The Visitation of God"? The Potato and the Great Irish Famine* (Dublin, 1993), 54.

35 *"the very worst"*: *Poor Enquiry (Ireland): Appendix (E)*, supplement, p. 13.

36 *"on all hands"*: Binns, *Miseries and Beauties of Ireland*, 1:50.

36 *"hungry months"*: Ciarán McCabe, *Begging, Charity, and Religion in Pre-Famine Ireland* (Liverpool, 2018), 27.

36 *"waiting months"*: Regina Sexton, "Diet in Pre-Famine Ireland," in *Atlas of the Great Irish Famine*, ed. Crowley, Smyth, and Murphy, 42.

36 *"oatmeal zones"*: Bourke, *"Visitation of God,"* 42–43.

36 *"strong potato profile"*: Sexton, "Diet in Pre-Famine Ireland," 43.

38 *"nation of paupers"*: De Beaumont, *Ireland: Social, Political, and Religious*, 1:270.

38 *"young men of Ireland"*: Kerby Miller, *Emigrants and Exiles: Ireland and the Irish Exodus to North America* (New York, 1985), 172.

38 *"peace and plenty"*: *Irish Immigrants in the Land of Canaan: Letters and Memoirs from Colonial and Revolutionary America, 1675–1815*, ed. Kerby Miller et al. (New York, 2003), 420–24.

40 *"state of destitution"*: James Grant, "The Great Famine in County Tyrone," in *Tyrone: History and Society*, ed. Charles Dillon and Henry A. Jeffries (Dublin, 2000), 595.

40 *"abundant harvest"*: N. Marshall Cummins, *Some Chapters of Cork Medical History* (Cork, 1957), 104.

40 *"stench"*: Trench, *Realities of Irish Life*, 100–102.

40 *"potato cholera"*: Dan Gallogly, "The Famine in County Cavan," in *The Famine in Ulster: The Regional Impact*, ed. Christine Kinealy and Trevor Parkhill (Belfast, 1997), 64.

40 *"putrefying vegetation"*: Cummins, *Some Chapters of Cork Medical History*, 104.

40 *"putrefied and rotten"*: Michelle O'Mahony, *Famine in Cork City: Famine Life at Cork Union Workhouse* (Cork, 2005), 74.

41 *"total failure of the potato crop"*: *Atlas of the Great Irish Famine*, ed. Crowley, Smyth, and Murphy, 451.

41 *"fearfully awful"*: Bryan McMahon, *The Great Famine in Tralee and North Kerry* (Cork, 2017), 75 (remaining Kerry quotations, 76–77).

41 *"wretched souls"*: *Atlas of the Great Irish Famine*, ed. Crowley, Smyth, and Murphy, 350.

42 *"into the graveyard"*: Gerard MacAtasney, *The Dead Buried by the Dying: The Great Famine in Leitrim* (Sallins, Ire., 2014), 165.

42 *"I gave Absolution"*: Cummins, *Some Chapters of Cork Medical History*, 106.

42 *"in the poor house"*: Anthony Begley and Soinbhe Lally, "The Famine in County Donegal," in *The Famine in Ulster*, ed. Kinealy and Parkhill, 82.

43 *"three each day"*: Mr. Gill to Mr. Russell, Feb. 25, 1847, in House of Commons, *Correspondence from January to March, 1847, Relating to the Measures*, 192.

43 *"almost to the bone"*: "The Scarcity," *British Magazine* 31 (Mar. 1847): 339.

43 *"snow falling thick"*: Grant, "Great Famine in County Tyrone," 595.

44 *"what are we to do?"*: *Atlas of the Great Irish Famine*, ed. Crowley, Smyth, and Murphy, 400.

44 *"half naked to their work"*: Ignatius Murphy, *A People Starved: Life and Death in West Clare, 1845–1851* (Dublin, 1996), 32–33.

44 *"death sentence to them"*: *Atlas of the Great Irish Famine*, ed. Crowley, Smyth, and Murphy, 422.

44 *"premature death"*: in *The Famine in Ulster*, ed. Kinealy and Parkhill, 40.

44 *"most appalling forms"*: Ibid.

44 *"stand or move a limb"*: Ibid., 54.

44 *"span him with my hand"*: Ibid., 53.

45 *"annals of human suffering"*: Ibid., 26.

45 *"agonies of famine"*: Pat Conaghan, *The Great Famine in South-West Donegal, 1845–1850* (Enniscrone, Ire., 1997), 12.

45 *"acme of misery has been reached"*: Ibid.

45 *"no provisions at all"*: Ibid., 66.

45 *"entirely gone"*: Ibid.

45 *"typhus fever, and death"*: Ibid., 95.

45 *"abyss of misery"*: Ibid., 92.

45 *"Bazaar of Beggars"*: *Atlas of the Great Irish Famine*, ed. Crowley, Smyth, and Murphy, 335.

45 *"save them from perishing"*: Ibid.

45 *"buried by the dying"*: MacAtasney, *Dead Buried by the Dying*, 128.

45 *"corpses in the morning"*: *Atlas of the Great Irish Famine*, ed. Crowley, Smyth, and Murphy, 310.

46 *"reduced to skeletons"*: Ibid., 349.

46 *"moaning piteously"*: William Bennett, *Narrative of a Recent Journey of Six Weeks in Ireland* (London, 1847), 27–28.

46 *"screaming with hunger"*: Ciarán Ó Murchadha, *Sable Wings over the Land: Ennis, County Clare, and Its Wider Community During the Great Famine* (Ennis, Ire., 1998), 93.

46 *"crawling skeletons"*: McMahon, *Great Famine in Tralee and North Kerry*, 93.

46 *"very climax of misery"*: Patrick Hickey, *Famine in West Cork: The Mizen Peninsula, Land and People, 1800–1852* (Cork, 2002), 186.

47 *"misery and horror"*: "Sketches in the West of Ireland," *Illustrated London News*, Feb. 13, 1847, 100.

47 *"the dying or the dead"*: Elihu Burritt, *A Journal of a Visit of Three Days to Skibbereen and Its Neighbourhood* (London, 1847), 8.

47 *"Black '47"*: Cormac Ó Gráda, *Black '47 and Beyond: The Great Irish Famine in History, Economy, and Memory* (Princeton, NJ, 1999), 3.

48 *"death and pestilence itself!"*: Robert Forbes, *The Voyage of the Jamestown on Her Errand of Mercy* (Boston, 1847), 22.

48 *"poor destitutes of this city"*: Geoffrey Elliott, *The Mystery of Overend and Gurney: A Financial Scandal in Victorian London* (London, 2006), 114; William Henry, *Famine: Galway's Darkest Years* (Cork, 2011), 69. Elliott and Henry transcribe the same quotation a bit differently.

49 *"system of relief"*: *Clare Journal* in Ó Murchadha, *Sable Wings over the Land*, 106.

49 *"an all-wise Providence"*: *Atlas of the Great Irish Famine*, ed. Crowley, Smyth, and Murphy, 86.

49 *"intended for a blessing"*: Ibid.

49 *"brutalizing the Irish"*: "The Scarcity," *British Magazine* 31 (Feb. 1847): 223.

49 *"well bred pigs"*: Forbes, *Voyage of the Jamestown*, 22.

50 *"ports for America"*: *Atlas of the Great Irish Famine*, ed. Crowley, Smyth, and Murphy, 339.

50 *"flying to America"*: MacAtasney, *Dead Buried by the Dying*, 136.

50 *"unprecedented extent"*: Murphy, *People Starved*, 38.

50 *"the spring ships"*: "The Scarcity," 227.

51 *"well-dressed, healthful"*: Henry, *Famine: Galway's Darkest Years*, 176–77.

51 *"comfortable farmers"*: MacAtasney, *Dead Buried by the Dying*, 258.

51 *"money and value"*: "Liberty and a Welcome for the Exil[e] of Ireland," *NYIA*, Aug. 26, 1849, 2.

51 *three times more likely*: Ó Gráda, *Ireland's Great Famine*, 165.

51 *"dread of fever"*: Hickey, *Famine in West Cork*, 222.

51 *"the Next World"*: *Atlas of the Great Irish Famine*, ed. Crowley, Smyth, and Murphy, 378.

52 *"state of our poor"*: McMahon, *Great Famine in Tralee and North Kerry*, 212.

52 *"horrors which abound"*: Ibid., 238.

52 *"studded with bodies of the dead"*: Henry, *Famine: Galway's Darkest Years*, 128.

52 *"Skibbereen, Dunmanway, Bantry"*: Lyne, "William Steuart Trench and the Post-Famine Emigration," 97.

53 *"little dickey"*: *Atlas of the Great Irish Famine*, ed. Crowley, Smyth, and Murphy, 217.

54 *Cain family*: Acct. 14436, ESB; FAM538, DW134, DIST6, W16, NYC, 1855 NYCen.

54 *"sibling emigration"*: MacAtasney, *Dead Buried by the Dying*, 260.

54 *"die of the hunger"*: Michael and Mary Rush to Mr. and Mrs. Thomas Barrett, Sept. 6, 1846, in *Further Papers Relative to Emigration to the British Provinces in North America* (London, 1847), 13.

Chapter 2: "The Best Country in the World"

55 *3 and 10 percent*: Gerard Moran, *Sending Out Ireland's Poor: Assisted Emigration to North America in the Nineteenth Century* (Dublin, 2004), 35–69.

55 *Cornelius Sullivan...from bucolic Tuosist*: Accts. 617, 2581, and 15839, ESB; manifest of the *West Point*, Mar. 29, 1851, NYShips; FAM354, DW81, DIST3, W6, NYC, 1855 NYCen; FAM1346, DW271, DIST2, W6, NYC, 1860 USCen; 1857 *NYCDir*, 804; 1858 *NYCDir*, 777; 1859 *NYCDir*, 825; 1860 *NYCDir*, 833; 1862 *NYCDir*, 846; 1863 *NYCDir*, 840; 1864 *NYCDir*, 857.

55 *"starving condition"*: "Destitute Emigrants," *NYEP*, Mar. 18, 1851, 2.

55 *"landed upon our shores"*: *New York Sun* quoted in "The Landlord Vagabonds of Ireland," *NYIA*, Mar. 29, 1851, 2.

56 *"tenants of the Marquis of Lansdowne"*: "Emigrant Lodgers," *New York Spectator*, June 9, 1851, 1.

56 *"farmer"*: Acct. 617, ESB.

58 *"hand to mouth"*: Thomas Mooney, *Nine Years in America*, 2nd ed. (Dublin, 1850), 85.

58 *"living tomb"*: *Tralee Chronicle*, Jan. 16, 1847.

61 *"Oh thou spot of earth"*: Cian T. McMahon, *The Coffin Ship: Life and Death at Sea During the Great Irish Famine* (New York, 2022), 98.

62 *"foulest stench"*: John Heagerty, *Four Centuries of Medical History in Canada*, 2 vols. (Toronto, 1928), 1:121.

62 *"alive with maggots"*: McMahon, *Coffin Ship*, 145.

64 *"No words can describe it"*: Ibid., 194.

65 *"people all crazy"*: Mooney, *Nine Years*, 80.

68 *"tenant house"*: "Chancery Sale," *NYEP*, Feb. 1, 1831, 3.

68 *"little low wooden houses"*: Mooney, *Nine Years*, 82.

70 *same neighborhoods*: Residential patterns based on ESB Depositor Database.

72 *Martin Dwyer*: Acct. 6951, ESB; manifest of the *Thomas P. Sage*, Feb. 16, 1853, NYShips.

72 *John Connolly*: Acct. 8135, ESB; manifest of the *Liverpool*, Nov. 9, 1849, NYShips.

72 *Michael J. Dunn*: Acct. 4446, ESB; manifest of the *Liverpool*, June 27, 1848, NYShips; FAM2048, DW634, W17, NYC, 1850 USCen.

ENDNOTES

72 *George Branagan:* Acct. 12598, ESB; manifest of the *John Bright,* Aug. 27, 1854, NYShips.

72 *Michael Brady:* Acct. 8686, ESB; manifest of the *Star of the West,* May 3, 1851, NYShips; FAM1410, DW303, DIV5, W11, NYC, 1860 USCen; FAM 376, DW45, DIST12, W11, NYC, 1870 USCen.

72 *Patrick Coffey:* Acct. 1793, ESB; manifest of the *Henry Clay,* Mar. 21, 1851, NYShips.

72 *Laurence Collins:* Acct. 2553, ESB; manifest of the *Samuel,* May 4, 1849, NYShips.

72 *bookkeeper Edward A. Kelly:* Acct. 12566, ESB; manifest of the *Yorkshire,* July 8, 1848, NYShips; FAM150, DW96, DIST1, W7, NYC, 1850 USCen.

72 *Martin O'Brien:* Acct. 8331, ESB; manifest of the *Fidelia,* Apr. 5, 1854, NYShips.

73 *"slothful and lazy":* "Troubles in Families," *Boston Transcript,* Feb. 4, 1852, 1.

73 *"No Irish need apply":* "Coachman Wanted," *NYTrib,* May 14, 1852, 1.

73 *"must be Protestant":* "Six Men Wanted," *NYTrib,* May 14, 1852, 1.

73 *"English, French, or German":* "New Intelligence Office," *NYTrib,* May 14, 1852, 1.

74 *"superstition and ignorance":* "Republicanism v. Monarchy," *NYIA,* Mar. 29, 1851, 2.

75 *"idle about our Atlantic cities":* "Hints on Irish Emigration," *New York Truth Teller,* Jan. 30, 1847, 27.

75 *"hapless beings":* "Irish Emigrants," *NYH,* Mar. 23, 1851, 2.

75 *"lazy and lounging": Daily News* quoted in "The Irishman as an Emigrant," *NYIA,* Dec. 28, 1850, 1.

75 *"steal, and starve":* "Immigrants Should Go West," *Middletown (CT) Constitution,* Feb. 14, 1855, 2.

76 *"Know-Nothing organization":* "The Know-Nothings," *NYTrib,* Nov. 16, 1853, 4. See also Tyler Anbinder, *Nativism and Slavery: The Northern Know Nothings and the Politics of the 1850s* (New York, 1992).

77 *"easy making money":* Eliza Quin to her "Dear Pearants," in *Third Report from the Select Committee of the House of Lords on Colonization from Ireland* ([London], 1849), 128.

77 *"working man at home":* Gerald MacAtasney, *The Dead Buried by the Dying: The Great Famine in Leitrim* (Sallins, Ire., 2014), 261–62.

77 *"can eat good beef":* Michael Coogan, letter to the editor, *NYIA,* July 30, 1853, 4.

77 *"on Christmas at home":* Bridget Rooney to Pat Rooney, Jan. 15, 1848, BR146/10/13, Broadlands Papers, University of Southampton.

77 *"the best Country in the world":* Quin to "Dear Pearants," 128.

78 *"in their coffins":* "Senior's Irish Voyages," *Dublin Review,* n.s., 12 (Jan. 1869): 7.

78 *James Deasy:* Accts. 17126, 24549, 37904, 50934, and 60729, ESB; p. 7, DW167, ED11, W7, NYC, Enum2, 1870 USCen; FAM32, DW30, ED294, Oyster Bay, Queens County, NY, 1880 USCen; FAM21, DW20, ED727, Oyster Bay, Nassau County, NY, 1900 USCen.

78 *Anna O'Shea:* Accts. 1025, 1450, 8620, and 10195, ESB; FAM3, DW251, DIST2, W10, NYC, 1855 NYCen; FAM65, DW52, DIST9, W12, NYC, 1870 USCen; FAM139, DW115, ED532, NYC, 1880 USCen; FAM59, DW58, ED127, Yonkers, Westchester County, NY, 1900 USCen; "Catholic Publisher Dies," *NYT,* Mar. 5, 1906, 9.

78 *Lawrence Grimes:* Acct. 3741, ESB; FAM350, DW64, ED149, NYC, 1880 USCen; FAM380, DW202, ED275, NYC, 1900 USCen.

78 *Maurice Spillane:* Accts. 3843 and 15579, ESB; FAM126, DW15, DIST5, W18, NYC, 1860 USCen; FAM323, DW64, ED327, NYC, 1880 USCen; FAM204, DW43, ED833, NYC, 1910 USCen.

79 *Anthony Abberton:* Acct. 11976, ESB; FAM1439, DW225, DIST5, W18, NYC, 1860 USCen; FAM42, DW8, ED503, NYC, 1880 USCen; FAM28, DW7, ED492, NYC, 1900 USCen.

79 *"chopped to death":* "Chopped to Death," *NYH,* July 7, 1871, 6.

79 *Rosanna and Michael J. J. Kavanagh:* Accts. 5148 and 5589, ESB; FAM188, DW98, W2, Albany, Albany County, NY, 1860 USCen; p. 45, DIST6, W21, NYC, Enum2, 1870 USCen; FAM283, DW23, ED421, NYC, 1880 USCen; FAM99, DW99, ED137, Clear Creek, Pottawatomie County, KS, 1900 USCen; *Portrait and Biographical Album of Jackson, Jefferson and Pottawatomie Counties, Kansas* (Chicago, 1890), 190, 193.

79 *"died within a short time":* "Dead in a Prison Pen," *NYH,* Apr. 8, 1881, 9.

83 *Edward A. Kelly, the Irish bookkeeper:* 1859 *NYCDir,* 455.

84 *Occupations Within One Year of Arrival:* These data were derived from (1) Irish-born adult males who opened an account at the Emigrant Savings Bank from 1850 to 1858 and within a year of their arrival in America; (2) Emigrant Bank customers who immigrated in 1849 or 1850 and who were found in the 1850 census; and (3) bank customers who immigrated in 1854 or 1855 and were found in the 1855 New York census. The 857 immigrants who constitute this dataset can be found at https://dataverse.harvard.edu/dataverse/anbinder.

86 *"miraculous":* "The Irish Success in America," *New Orleans City Item,* Aug. 21, 1878, 2.

Chapter 3: "All the Rude and Heavy Work"

89 *Bartholomew O'Donnell was walking in circles:* Accts. 1589 and 1669, ESB; entry for "Patt O'Donnell," manifest of the *Heather Bell,* Jan. 8, 1849, NYShips; FAM79, DW23, W6, NYC, 1850 USCen; FAM65, DW8, DIST2, W4, 1855 NYCen; FAM2414, DW1137, W10, KingsC, 1870 USCen; FAM151, DW58, DIST7, W12, KingsC, 1875 NYCen; FAM466, DW248, ED84, KingsC, 1880 USCen; 1864 *BklynDir,* 352; 1865 *BklynDir,* 315; 1876 *BklynDir,* 694; 1877 *BklynDir,* 698; 1878 *BklynDir,* 743; 1884 *BklynDir,* 990; 1885 *BklynDir,* 795; "The Walking Mania: An Octogenarian on the Track," *BDE,* Feb. 8, 1879, 4; "An Ancient Pedestrian," *Brooklyn Union-Argus,* Feb. 10, 1879, 3; "Unsuccessful: A Plucky Old Man on the Track," *BDE,* Feb. 23, 1879, 4; death certificate for "Bartholomew O. Donnell," KingsC, Oct. 5, 1889, NYCMA.

89 *Bartley:* Marriage certificate of Samuel Roberts and Margaret O'Donnell, Dec. 7, 1902, NYCMA.

91 *"No language can exaggerate":* The Old Brewery, and the New Mission House at the Five Points, By Ladies of the Mission (New York, 1854), 43.

91 *"wickedest house":* National Police Gazette in Edward Van Every, Sins of New York as "Exposed" by the Police Gazette (1930; repr., New York, 1972), 282.

95 *"Moving Day":* "New-York City; First of May — Moving Day," *NYT,* May 1, 1855, 1.

96 *"Unsuccessful: A Plucky Old Man on the Track":* "Unsuccessful," 4.

96 *"pedestrianism":* Matthew Algeo, Pedestrianism: When Watching People Walk Was America's Favorite Spectator Sport (Chicago, 2014).

96 *"industrious in his habits":* "Unsuccessful," 4.

97 *"In Summer time":* Ibid.

98 *"short of the outlay":* Ibid.

98 *"famed in song and story":* Old Brewery, 33.

98 *"rude and heavy work":* Thomas Mooney, Nine Years in America, 2nd ed. (Dublin, 1850), 84.

99 *Dominick Follis:* Acct. 9542, ESB.

99 *"suddenly gave way":* "Serious Accident," *NYT,* Aug. 9, 1852, 2.

99 *Richard Fitzgerald:* Acct. 6468, ESB; "Fatal Effects of the Heat," *Morning Courier and New-York Enquirer,* July 2, 1855, n.p.

ENDNOTES

100 *"was seriously hurt"*: "City Intelligence," *NYEP*, Apr. 30, 1850, 2.

100 *"blow on the head or from terror"*: "Terrible Calamities," *NYH*, Apr. 30, 1850, 1.

101 *"most frightful manner"*: Ibid.

101 *"tottering"*: Ibid.

101 *"tremendous crash"*: Ibid.

101 *"literally smashed together"*: "City Intelligence," 2.

102 *"mangled beneath casks of flour"*: "Terrible Calamities," 1

103 owed another $1,168: "Superior Court—General Term," *NYTrib*, Jan. 20, 1851, 6; "Home Department," *New York Spectator*, Mar. 27, 1851, 1.

103 *Mary Hourigan*: To hold a portion of their settlements, each widow was given an account at the Emigrant Savings Bank with $65.71. See accts. 610–615, ESB; FAM263, DW91, Eastern DIV, W1, NYC, 1850 USCen (Pratt); FAM148, DW42, W4, NYC, 1850 USCen (Barry).

103 *retorts*: Louis Bader, "Gas Illumination in New York City, 1823–1863" (Ph.D. diss., New York University, 1970), 29.

104 *Only one of the sixteen*: ESB Depositor Database.

105 *Maurice Spillane*: Accts. 3843 and 15579, ESB; FAM 126, DW15, W18, NYC, 1860 USCen; FAM420, DW108, DIST10, W16, NYC, 1870 USCen; FAM323, DW-64, ED327, NYC, 1880 USCen; FAM478, DW49, ED153, NYC, 1900 USCen; FAM204, DW43, ED833, NYC, 1910 USCen; entry for Maurice Spillane, Mar. 24, 1914, NYCDeaths.

105 *"public porters"*: "Public Porters and Handcartmen: Rates of Fare," *NYTrib*, Nov. 13, 1845, 4.

106 *25 percent more*: ESB Depositor Database; Tyler Anbinder, Cormac Ó Gráda, and Simone A. Wegge, "Networks and Opportunities: A Digital History of Ireland's Great Famine Refugees in New York," *American Historical Review* 124 (Dec. 2019): 1615.

106 *Timothy Cleary*: Accts. 4326, 10309, and 37915, ESB; FAM408, DW93, DIST2, W1, NYC, 1860 USCen; FAM313, DW43, ED378, NYC, 1880 USCen.

106 *William Cornwall from Clare*: Accts. 4208 and 8601, ESB; FAM177, DW69, DIST2, W5, KingsC, 1855 NYCen; FAM894, DW727, W8, KingsC, 1870 USCen; FAM267, DW187, ED62, KingsC, 1880 USCen.

106 *William Follis from Kilkenny*: Acct. 15979, ESB; FAM1572, DW501, W4, NYC, 1850 USCen; FAM178, DW20, ED5, NYC, 1880 USCen.

107 *Patrick Brennan*: Acct. 13254, ESB; FAM1136, DW1031, Jamaica, Queens County, NY, 1860 USCen; FAM1555, DW1342, Jamaica, Queens County, NY, 1870 USCen; FAM325, DW275, ED275, Jamaica, Queens County, NY, 1880 USCen; "Suicide of Louis King," *NYH*, Feb. 15, 1880, 13.

107 *Alex McConnerty*: Acct. 8022, ESB; FAM651, DW359, DIST2, W5, NYC, 1860 USCen; FAM139, DW28, DIST8, W6, NYC, 1870 USCen; FAM330, DW90, ED35, NYC, 1880 USCen; FAM126, DW54, ED261, KingsC, 1900 USCen; "Alexander McConnerty," *Brooklyn Times*, Apr. 19, 1917, 7; "Appraisals," *Brooklyn Times*, May 29, 1918, 9.

108 *"branch of the business"*: "The Public Cartmen of New-York," *NYTrib*, June 24, 1857, 7.

109 *cartmen saved 35 percent more than porters*: ESB Depositor Database.

109 *Robert Wilson*: Accts. 4797 and 13287, ESB; FAM2092, DW343, DIST1, W18, NYC, 1860 USCen; FAM3355, DW1949, W21, KingsC, 1870 USCen; 1874 *BklynDir*, 918; 1878 *BklynDir*, 1063.

109 *John McSweegan*: Acct. 13843, ESB; FAM354, DW120, DIST5, W13, NYC, 1855 NYCen; FAM114, DW89, DIV3, W14, NYC, 1860 USCen.

109 *John Hanlon*: Accts. 10362 and 43319, ESB; FAM74, DW34, DIST16, W9, NYC, 1870 USCen.

109 *paid the least:* Anbinder, Ó Gráda, and Wegge, "Networks and Opportunities," 1615.

109 *"plop down before you":* Mooney, *Nine Years in America,* 81, 86.

110 *John Brogan:* Acct. 6752, ESB; FAM482, DW270, DIST1, W8, NYC, 1855 NYCen; FAM2073, DW660, DIST9, W5, NYC, 1860 USCen.

110 *Terrence Connelly:* Acct. 13658, ESB; FAM2390, DW2209, Springfield, Hampden County, MA, 1860 USCen; FAM126, DW86, W3, Springfield, Hampden County, MA, 1870 USCen; FAM489, DW329, ED313, Springfield, Hampden County, MA, 1880 USCen.

110 *Thomas McCabe:* Accts. 12733 and 21295, ESB; FAM1100, DW422, DIST9, W17, NYC, 1860 USCen; p. 42, DIST5, W17, NYC, Enum2, 1870 USCen; FAM76, DW9, ED368, NYC, 1880 USCen; FAM295, DW57, ED529, NYC, 1900 USCen; "Deaths Reported Nov. 14," *NYT,* Nov. 15, 1902, 9.

110 *John Duffy:* Accts. 12352, 37037, 44015, and 62189, ESB; FAM1242, DW145, DIST1, W18, NYC, 1860 USCen; FAM170, DW17, ED219, NYC, 1880 USCen; entry for John Duffy, Dec. 16, 1909, NYCDeaths.

110 *Newell McMurray:* Accts. 13330 and 35384, ESB; FAM3041, DW688, DIST1, W5, NYC, 1860 USCen; 1864 *NYCDir,* 572; FAM459, DW212, DIST13, W9, NYC, 1870 USCen; FAM184, DW159, ED39, Jersey City, Hudson County, NJ, 1880 USCen; entry for Newell McMurray, Jan. 22, 1892, NYCDeaths.

111 *"servant girl":* Margaret Lynch-Brennan, *The Irish Bridget: Irish Immigrant Women in Domestic Service in America, 1840–1930* (Syracuse, 2009), 71.

113 *"master and slave": Glimpses of New-York City by a South Carolinian* (Charleston, 1852), 187.

113 *Mary Dougherty:* Accts. 3002 and 6109, ESB; FAM135, DW65, DIST1, W12, KingsC, 1855 NYCen; FAM516, DW591, Reid, Will County, IL, 1860 USCen; FAM175, DW169, Wesley, Will County, IL, 1870 USCen; FAM89, DW84, ED215, Wesley, Will County, IL, 1880 USCen.

113 *Margaret Barry:* Accts. 1316, 2947, 4184, 5825, 7853, and 8972, ESB; FAM1, DW154, DIST2, W2, KingsC, 1855 NYCen.

113 *"out to service":* Acct. 946, ESB. See also accts. 4184, 5826, and 9198, ESB.

113 *"washer":* Acct. 9199, ESB. See also FAM352, DW77, DIST1, W7, NYC, 1860 USCen.

113 *fourth Barry sister, Catherine:* Accts. 5825, 12514, and 38390, ESB; FAM352, DW77, DIST1, W7, NYC, 1860 USCen; FAM234, DW149, W16, KingsC, 1870 USCen; FAM406, DW220, ED184, KingsC, 1880 USCen; p. 19, DIST8, W19, KingsC, 1892 NYCen; "Died," *Brooklyn Times,* Nov. 23, 1897, 5.

114 *Mary Bradley:* Acct. 12090, ESB; manifest of the *Andrew Foster,* Apr. 19, 1852, NYShips; FAM968, DW347, DIST4, W7, NYC, 1855 NYCen; FAM559, DW276, DIST4, W7, NYC, 1860 USCen; p. 55, DW267, DIST10, W7, NYC, Enum2, 1870 USCen; FAM161, DW267, ED93, NYC, 1880 USCen.

114 *Margaret Heslin:* Accts. 10669 and 14754, ESB; FAM1013, DW530, W1, KingsC, 1850 USCen; FAM145, DW123, DIST1, W3, KingsC, 1855 NYCen; FAM581, DW401, W3, KingsC, 1870 USCen; FAM98, DW96, ED6, KingsC, 1880 USCen.

114 *Mary Ann Booth:* Acct. 9012, ESB; FAM316, DW241, W7, KingsC, 1850 USCen; FAM278, DW153, DIST1, W10, KingsC, 1860 USCen; FAM83, DW95, W6, KingsC, 1870 USCen; FAM17, DW17, DIST10, W6, KingsC, 1875 NYCen; FAM157, DW128, ED44, KingsC, 1880 USCen; will of Mary Ann Booth, Mar. 2, 1891, NY Wills and Probate Records, 1659–1999, Ancestry.com; "Married and Vanished," *Brooklyn Citizen,* June 21, 1893, 1.

115 *Ellen Cummiskey:* Accts. 1556, 16132, 24562, 50744, 90691, and 121305, ESB; FAM1965, DW1018, W5, NYC, 1850 USCen; FAM22, DW17, DIST4, W5, NYC,

1855 NYCen; FAM283, DW310, DIST2, W21, NYC, 1860 USCen; FAM245, DW147, DIST19, W21, NYC, 1870 USCen; FAM108, DW91, ED124, Morristown, Morris County, NJ, 1880 USCen; manifest of the *Neptune*, Dec. 21, 1855, NYShips ("Susan Commisky"); entries for James Gibney, 1876 *Meriden Dir*, 59, and 1880 *Meriden Dir*, 58; entry for Ellen Cummiskey, St. Patrick's Cemetery, Hale Collection of Cemetery Inscriptions, 1629–1934, Ancestry.com.

116 *Rose Bray from County Louth:* Acct. 16583, ESB; FAM431, DW108, DIST6, W8, NYC, 1855 NYCen; FAM953, DW692, DIST1, W21, NYC, 1860 USCen; FAM413, DW335, DIST18, W12, NYC, 1870 USCen; FAM123, DW107, ED535, NYC, 1880 USCen; "Charles O'Conor's Bequests," *NYT*, May 29, 1884, 5.

116 *"faithful attendant, Rose Bray":* "Charles O'Conor," *NYH*, Dec. 1, 1875, 10.

116 *Bridget White from Clare:* Accts. 15270 and 64705, ESB.

116 *Sarah Corrigan:* Acct. 17799, ESB; FAM2315, DW474, DIST1, W1, NYC, 1860 USCen; p. 30, DIST1, W1, NYC, Enum2, 1870 USCen.

117 *peak bank balance for servants:* ESB Depositor Database.

118 *Michael Connell:* Acct. 11799, ESB; FAM172, DW45, W4, NYC, 1850 USCen; FAM239, DW73, DIST4, W4, NYC, 1855 NYCen; FAM85, DW22, DIST2, W4, NYC, 1860 USCen; FAM15, DW2, ED32, NYC, 1880 USCen.

118 *41 percent:* ESB Mobility Database.

118 *Patrick Wallace:* Accts. 1680, 11800, and 29538, ESB; FAM353, DW53, ED347, NYC, 1880 USCen; "Died," *NYH*, Aug. 27, 1882, 13.

120 *John McMahon:* Accts. 3478, 9270, 21118, and 36351, ESB; manifest of the *Limerick Lass*, June 5, 1851, NYShips; FAM181, DW33, DIST3, W1, NYC, 1855 NYCen; FAM1025, DW211, DIST1, W1, NYC, 1860 USCen; FAM334, DW118, DIST7, W5, NYC, 1870 USCen; FAM274, DW90, ED92, NYC, 1880 USCen; FAM681, DW59, ED81, NYC, 1900 USCen; 1851 *NYCDir*, 350; 1852 *NYCDir*, 370; 1865 *NYCDir*, 628; 1866 *NYCDir*, 652; 1867 *NYCDir*, 667; 1868 *NYCDir*, 702; 1869 *NYCDir*, 715; 1880 *NYCDir*, 1001; 1881 *NYCDir*, 1047; 1890 *NYCDir*, 805; "N. Y. Real Estate Sales," *New York Evening Express*, Apr. 16, 1875, 4; "Died," *NYH*, Sept. 5, 1884, 9; "Died," *NYT*, May 31, 1907, 9.

120 *"intelligence":* 1864 *NYCDir*, 570.

120 *"50 Laborers Wanted":* "50 Laborers," *New York Sun*, July 16, 1866, 3. See also "50 Laborers," *New York Sun*, July 23, 1867, 3.

121 *Mary Dunahoe:* Accts. 2368 and 10606, ESB; FAM5, DW337, DIST2, W10, NYC, 1855 NYCen; FAM901, DW193, DIST5, W11, NYC, 1860 USCen; p. 9, DIST1, W11, NYC, Enum2, 1870 USCen; FAM173, DW25, ED373, NYC, 1880 USCen; FAM218, DW19, ED432, NYC, 1900 USCen; 1865 *NYCDir*, 1056; 1869 *NYCDir*, 1194; 1874 *NYCDir*, 1545; 1878 *NYCDir*, 1581; 1881 *NYCDir*, 1748; 1886 *NYCDir*, 2125; entry for Patrick Winters, Apr. 11, 1887, NYCDeaths.

122 *the O'Keefes:* Accts. 2534, 12767, 40838, and 57297, ESB; entries for Ellen Dwyre [sic], Michael Carroll, and James Keefe, manifest of the *City of Washington*, Mar. 31, 1851, NYShips; FAM208, DW49, DIST3, W1, NYC, 1855 NYCen; FAM1914, DW983, W12, KingsC, 1870 USCen; FAM228, DW169, DIST9, W10, KingsC, 1875 NYCen; FAM417, DW208, ED86, KingsC, 1880 USCen; 1874 *BklynDir*, 642; 1877 *BklynDir*, 701; 1878 *BklynDir*, 746 (as "O'Keeffe"); 1879 *BklynDir*, 772; 1882 *Bklyn-Dir*, 872; 1883 *BklynDir*, 937; 1884 *BklynDir*, 994; death certificate for Dennis O'Keefe, Sept. 11, 1884, NYCMA; "Died," *BDE*, Sept. 12, 1884, 3; "Died," *BDE*, Apr. 6, 1893, 5; "Ellen C. O'Keefe," *Brooklyn Standard Union*, May 21, 1919, 15.

122 *"tobacco factory":* "Colonel Roberts' Cadetship," *NYH*, June 28, 1872, 8.

123 *John O'Keefe, the one quoted:* FAM1660, DW342, DIST1, W1, NYC, 1860 USCen; FAM252, DW36, DIST3, W1, NYC, 1870 USCen; FAM339, DW62, ED6, NYC, 1880 USCen; "'Admiral' O'Keefe," *NYIA*, Oct. 5, 1872, 4; "A Poor Boy's Victory," *Cincinnati Enquirer*, June 30, 1872, 5; "'The Collarless O'Keefe,'" *San Francisco Bulletin*, July 11, 1872, 3; "'Admiral' O'Keefe," *NYH*, July 20, 1872, 8.

123 *"dirty clothes and unkempt hair":* "Colonel Roberts' Cadetship," 8.

124 *"freshies":* "The Naval Cadets," *NYH*, June 2, 1873, 8.

124 *James Conyers:* "Stoning a 'Nigger,'" *NYEP*, June 6, 1873, 2; "Row at Annapolis," *Portland Oregonian*, June 6, 1873, 1; "The War of Races at Annapolis," *Washington National Republican*, June 6, 1873, 1.

124 *"much was expected":* "Cadets Dismissed," *NYIA*, June 14, 1873, 1.

125 *"aged pedestrian heartily":* "O'Donnell's Task Finished," *NYT*, Mar. 20, 1879, 8.

125 *bequest to Margaret:* FAM488, DW330, ED426, KingsC, 1900 USCen; p. 4A, ED810, KingsC, 1900 USCen (Loretta, Willie, and Viola).

Chapter 4: *"Too Often Seen to Need Description"*

127 *John Griffin, who at age twenty-three:* Accts. 2032, 9176, 13732, 13912, and 18955, ESB; manifest of the *Heather Bell*, Jan. 8, 1849, NYShips; FAM425, DW52, DIST1, W4, NYC, 1855 NYCen; FAM702, DW301, DIST3, W4, NYC, 1860 USCen; 1856 *NYCDir*, 335; 1857 *NYCDir*, 336; 1859 *NYCDir*, 345; 1862 *NYCDir*, 348; entry for John Griffin, Nov. 11, 1863, NYCDeaths. For Michael Griffin, see FAM474, DW107, DIST1, W4, NYC, 1855 NYCen; FAM448, DW255, W4, Jersey City, Hudson County, NJ, 1860 USCen; FAM198, DW126, W5, Jersey City, Hudson County, NJ, 1870 USCen; death record for Michael Griffin, Aug. 6, 1876, NJ Deaths and Burials Index, 1798–1971, Ancestry.com.

130 *"chamois skins":* Accts. 17785, 27034, 37511, 43853, and 51220, ESB.

131 *"I want to sell to-day":* Alvin Harlow, *Old Bowery Days: The Chronicles of a Famous Street* (New York, 1931), 173.

131 *"Hannah":* Inscription for Hannah Griffin, Griffin family tombstone, Calvary Cemetery, Findagrave.com.

132 *Mary now took over:* 1866 *NYCDir*, 404; FAM76, DW15, DIST6, W4, NYC, 1870 USCen.

133 *John and Mary's son Jerry:* 1871 *NYCDir*, 450; 1874 *NYCDir*, 507; 1875 *NYCDir*, 517; 1876 *NYCDir*, 534; 1878 *NYCDir*, 572; 1879 *NYCDir*, 594; 1880 *NYCDir*, 606; 1883 *NYCDir*, 658; 1902 *NYCDir*, 545; acct. 115493, ESB; FAM404, DW53, ED29, NYC, 1880 USCen; FAM495, DW107, ED924, NYC, 1900 USCen; FAM312, DW42, ED1527, NYC, 1910 USCen; entry for Jeremiah Griffin, Mar. 15, 1911, NYCDeaths.

134 *quarter of the city's Irish peddlers:* ESB Depositor Database.

134 *James Cunningham:* Accts. 437, 719, 720, 781, 1853, 2119, 9704, 10040, 21066, 32881, 44487, and 115095, ESB; FAM1556, DW489, W14, NYC, 1850 USCen; FAM143, DW66, DIST1, W14, NYC, 1855 NYCen; 1846 *NYCDir*, 101; 1847 *NYCDir*, 109; 1849 *NYCDir*, 114; will of James Cunningham, Dec. 2, 1881, New York Probate Records, 1629–1971, Familysearch.org.

135 *James McGill:* Accts. 4736, 13904, and 15538, ESB; FAM1540, DW486, W14, NYC, 1850 USCen; FAM142, DW60, DIST1, W14, NYC, 1855 NYCen; FAM1526, DW362, DIST3, W14, NYC, 1860 USCen.

135 *James Bresland:* Accts. 621, 2064, 4483, and 9831, ESB; FAM1540, DW486, W14, NYC, 1850 USCen; FAM138 and FAM141, DW65, DIST1, W14, NYC, 1855 NYCen.

135 *"travelling merchant":* Acct. 779, ESB.

135 *Thomas Rolston arrived:* Acct. 2299, ESB; FAM46, DW45, Mill Creek Hundred, New
   Castle County, DE, 1850 USCen; FAM5082, DW4858, W18, Baltimore, Baltimore
   County, MD, 1860 USCen; marriage record of Thomas Rolston and Mary Young,
   Church of St. John the Evangelist, Philadelphia, Nov. 2, 1868, PA and NJ Church
   and Town Records, 1669–2013, Ancestry.com; FAM797, DW657, W18, Baltimore,
   Baltimore County, MD, 1870 USCen; FAM120, DW104, ED 179, W18, Baltimore,
   Baltimore County, MD, 1880 USCen; 1870 *Baltimore Dir,* 480; 1872 *Baltimore Dir,*
   488; 1878 *Baltimore Dir,* 551; 1885 *Baltimore Dir,* 1052; 1889 *Baltimore Dir,* 937;
   1893 *Baltimore Dir,* 1136; 1895 *Baltimore Dir,* 1144; 1904 *Baltimore Dir,* 1351;
   "Died," *Baltimore Sun,* Apr. 28, 1904, 4.

135 *James McShane:* Acct. 10141, ESB.

135 *James Dowd, Joseph Brogan, and James Burns:* Accts. 7304 (Dowd), 7686, 9741, and
   12522 (Brogan), and 3874, 9362, and 9379 (Burns), ESB.

136 *John Haffey, who emigrated in 1852:* Accts. 8691, 9691, 10040, 15009, and 32881, ESB.

136 *Ann and Mary Cunningham:* Accts. 9107 and 7810, ESB; FAM1550, DW364, DIST3,
   W14, NYC, 1860 USCen.

136 *"card factory":* FAM 1550, DW364, DIST3, W14, NYC, 1860 USCen.

136 *median savings of peddlers:* ESB Depositor Database.

136 *Margaret Cunningham Haffey:* FAM293, DW286, Canaan, Wayne County, OH, 1870
   USCen; FAM344, DW339, ED225, Pike Station, Wayne County, OH, 1880 USCen;
   FAM73, DW71, ED140, Creston, Wayne County, OH, 1900 USCen; "John Haffey,"
   Orrville (OH) Courier, Nov. 3, 1905, 6.

136 *Joseph Brogan:* Accts. 7686, 9741, and 12522, ESB; FAM904, DW934, Lees Creek,
   Crawford County, AR, 1860 USCen; FAM170, DW161, W2, Fort Smith, Sebastian
   County, AR, 1870 USCen; Brogan advertisement *Fort Smith Weekly Herald,* Nov.
   28, 1868, 2; "More Election News," *Tri-Weekly Fort Smith Herald,* Nov. 29, 1870, 3;
   "Joseph Brogan," *Fort Smith Herald,* Aug. 14, 1913, 1.

137 *older brother Walter:* Marriage of Walter Roulston [sic] and Mary J. Hamelton [sic],
   May 19, 1854, New York City Marriage Records, 1829–1940, Familysearch.org;
   FAM691, DW565, W18, Baltimore, Baltimore County, MD, 1870 USCen; FAM98,
   DW78, ED174, Baltimore, Baltimore County, MD, 1880 USCen; 1860 *Baltimore
   Dir,* 329; 1863 *Baltimore Dir,* 338; 1871 *Baltimore Dir,* 486; 1872 *Baltimore Dir,* 488;
   1878 *Baltimore Dir,* 551; 1885 *Baltimore Dir,* 1052; 1895 *Baltimore Dir,* 1144; "Walter
   H. Ralston," *Baltimore Sun,* Apr. 14, 1896, 7.

137 *Andrew Brice:* FAM451, DW49, DIST10, W11, NYC, 1855 NYCen; FAM1553,
   DW339, DIST5, W11, NYC, 1860 USCen; 1868 *NYCDir,* 129; 1871 *NYCDir,* 135;
   1877 *Cincinnati Dir,* 166; 1878 *Nashville Dir,* 137; 1878 *NYCDir,* 163; FAM385,
   DW120, ED596, NYC, 1880 USCen; "Obituary Notes," *NYH,* May 23, 1913, 7;
   "Appraisals of Estates," *NYTrib,* May 16, 1914, 15.

138 *"good retail profit":* Thomas Mooney, *Nine Years in America,* 2nd ed. (Dublin, 1850),
   84–85.

138 *Patrick Barrett:* Accts. 9054, 11632, 13604, and 36664, ESB; FAM59, DW46, DIST4,
   W22, KingsC, 1875 NYCen; FAM393, DW217, ED61, KingsC, 1880 USCen; 1878
   BklynDir, 39; 1879 *BklynDir,* 39; 1882 *BklynDir,* 45; 1884 *BklynDir,* 51; 1886 *Bklyn-
   Dir,* 46; 1888 *BklynDir,* 46; 1890 *BklynDir,* 49.

139 *"dropped dead":* "Dropped Dead on the L Platform," *BDE,* Dec. 24, 1893, 20.

139 *Andrew Brosnan:* Accts. 5292, 10445, and 27033, ESB; FAM791, DW170, DIST1,
   W1, NYC, 1860 USCen; 1866 *BklynDir,* 59; 1869 *BklynDir,* 69; FAM1647, DW837,
   W6, KingsC, 1870 USCen; FAM189, DW66, DIST8, W6, KingsC, 1875 NYCen;
   FAM291, DW101, ED42, KingsC, 1880 USCen; 1870 *BklynDir,* 78; 1877 *BklynDir,*

96; 1879 *BklynDir*, 104; 1882 *BklynDir*, 119; 1896 *BklynDir*, 161 (Patrick); entry for Andrew Brosnan, Oct. 25, 1881, NYCDeaths; "Real Estate Transfers," *BDE*, Nov. 4, 1892, 2.

139 *"long and tedious illness"*: "Died," *NYH*, May 28, 1868, 5.

140 *"free and clear"*: Will of Andrew Brosnan, Aug. 1, 1881, NY Wills and Probate Records, 1659–1999, Ancestry.com.

140 *Anastasia Mullen*: Acct. 6172, ESB.

140 *Bernard Hanratty*: Accts. 991, 7284, 10661, 14891, 17991, 25634, 31117, 62358, and 64732, ESB; "Died," *NYH*, July 1, 1865, 3; probate file for Bernard Hanratty, July 19, 1865, NY Wills and Probate Records, 1659–1999, Ancestry.com; FAM461, DW245, W3, Jersey City, Hudson County, NJ, 1870 USCen.

140 *Thomas Field*: Accts. 2942 and 33952, ESB; FAM121, DW47, W6, KingsC, 1850 USCen; FAM1365, DW1365, DIST1, W6, KingsC, 1855 NYCen; FAM105, DW74, DIST1, W1, KingsC, 1860 USCen; 1861 *BklynDir*, 136; 1862 *BklynDir*, 138; 1863 *BklynDir*, 150; entry for Ann Field, Feb. 4, 1859, NYCDeaths.

141 *younger brother Timothy*: Manifest of the *Continent*, July 15, 1851, NYShips; FAM1398, DW1398, DIST1, W6, KingsC, 1855 NYCen.

141 *"exhaustion of the brain"*: Entry for Thomas Fields [sic], July 29, 1863, NYC Index to Death Certificates, 1862–1948, Ancestry.com.

141 *cousin Timothy Jr.*: P. 147, DIST3, Randalls Island, W12, NYC, 1860 USCen.

141 *Edward Field*: FAM701, DW595, W7, KingsC, 1870 USCen; FAM544, DW539, DIST2, W7, KingsC, 1875 NYCen; FAM144, DW59, ED76, KingsC, 1880 USCen; FAM34, DW20, ED77, KingsC, 1900 USCen; FAM138, DW40, ED450, KingsC, 1930 USCen; entry for Edward Martin Fields, Dec. 30, 1935, NYC Index to Death Certificates, 1862–1948, Ancestry.com.

142 *Catherine Norris*: Acct. 1017, ESB; FAM147, DW31, DIST1, W6, NYC, 1855 NYCen.

142 *Honora Hickey*: Accts. 4912, 5586, 7708, 11901, 15855, 20131, 32415, and 42538, ESB; entry for Dennis Hickey, Mar. 9, 1859, NYCDeaths; FAM255, DW84, ED87, NYC, 1880 USCen; "A Man Kicked to Death," *NYH*, Sept. 9, 1869, 5; "Kicked to Death by a Woman," *NYH*, Sept. 10, 1869, 5.

142 *"notions stand"*: Acct. 4912, ESB.

142 *Ann supported them*: Accts. 4611, 7396, 17386, 23720, 30206, and 43045, ESB; FAM380, DW115, Eastern DIV, W1, NYC, 1850 USCen; FAM210, DW65, DIST1, W1, NYC, 1855 NYCen; FAM1150, DW235, DIST1, W1, NYC, 1860 USCen.

142 *Teresa peddled*: Acct. 2921, ESB; FAM2294, DW1000, W18, NYC, 1850 USCen.

143 *Jane McShane*: Accts. 14493, 15559, 22758, 33180, and 47385, ESB; FAM1196, DW128, DIST10, W11, NYC, 1855 NYCen; FAM1061, DW213, DIST8, W11, NYC, 1860 USCen.

143 *Catherine Murphy*: Accts. 554, 6620, 11982, and 54577, ESB; FAM812, DW645, W12, NYC, 1850 USCen; FAM202, DW131, W2, NYC, 1860 USCen.

143 *"toy store"*: FAM77, DW705, DIST20, W11, NYC, 1870 USCen.

143 *Catherine O'Connell*: Accts. 7202, 15729, and 65741, ESB.

143 *Catherine Dowd*: Accts. 14127, 19471, and 24056, ESB; FAM1759, DW357, DIST1, W1, NYC, 1860 USCen; FAM250, DW234, ED90, Belleville, Essex County, NJ, 1880 USCen.

143 *"long and painful illness"*: "Died," *New York World*, Apr. 8, 1867, 5.

143 *"home saloon"*: FAM385, DW337, Belleville, Essex County, NJ, 1870 USCen.

143 *Honora Shea*: Accts. 4737 and 9438, ESB; manifest of the *American Eagle*, Mar. 28, 1851, NYShips; FAM87, DW16, DIST5, W6, NYC, 1855 NYCen; FAM1334, DW268, DIST2, W6, NYC, 1860 USCen.

ENDNOTES

144 *41 percent ended their careers:* ESB Mobility Database.

145 *Peter Bryson:* Accts. 5186, 49696, and 66251, ESB; FAM166, DW166, La Junta, Mora County, NM, 1870 USCen; FAM134, DIST6, W7, KingsC, 1875 NYCen; 1879 *Bklyn-Dir*, 116.

145 *Hugh Conaghan:* Accts. 5055 and 16028, ESB; FAM11, DW4, DIST31, W19, NYC, 1870 USCen.

145 *Thomas McClafferty:* Acct. 4002, ESB; manifest of the *City of Washington*, Mar. 31, 1852, NYShips; manifest of the *United Kingdom*, May 9, 1865, NYShips; 1874–5 *Seneca Falls and Waterloo Village (NY) Dir*, 174; FAM326, ED101, Seneca County, NY, 1900 USCen; entry for Thomas McClafferty, May 9, 1902, Seneca County, NY Census of Inmates in Almshouses and Poorhouses, 1830–1920, Ancestry.com; entry for Thomas McClafferty, Aug. 19, 1902, NY State Death Index, 1852–1956, Ancestry.com.

145 *"pack peddler":* FAM541, DW533, Waterloo, Seneca County, NY, 1870 USCen.

146 *peddlers accumulated no less in savings:* ESB Depositor Database.

147 *"trouts in abundance":* William Roulston, "The Parish of Upper Badoney, County Tyrone in 1814," *Familia: Ulster Genealogical Review* 26 (2010): 145.

148 *"cold dreary region":* Ibid.

149 *Daniel Kane from the hamlet:* Accts. 487, 1648, 1660, 10976, and 29893, ESB; 1842 *NYCDir*, 179; 1844 *NYCDir*, 190; 1847 *NYCDir*, 225; FAM1273, DW537, DIST6, W7, NYC, 1850 USCen; FAM122, DW23, DIST8, W7, NYC, 1855 NYCen.

149 *Patrick Moss:* Acct. 3665, ESB; FAM1274 (mislabeled as "Norris"), DW537, DIST6, W7, NYC, 1850 USCen; FAM318, DW92, DIST6, W13, NYC, 1855 NYCen; 1842 *NYCDir*, 236; 1850 *NYCDir*, 363.

149 *"fire brick manufactory":* William Perris, *Maps of the City of New-York* (New York, 1852), pl. 19.

152 *"to need description":* "City Street Characters," *Ballou's Dollar Monthly Magazine*, Feb. 1859, 108.

152 *Patrick Devlin from the hamlet:* Accts. 13842 and 58212, ESB; 1856 *NYCDir*, 217; FAM1705, DW410, DIST5, W13, NYC, 1860 USCen; p. 37, DW649, DIST14, W7, NYC, Enum2, 1870 USCen.

152 *James, James, John, Michael, and Patrick:* For James Devlin, son of Owen, see accts. 8753, 32314, 46168, 56834, 70033, and 156563, ESB; FAM12, DW7, DIST8, W7, NYC, 1855 NYCen; FAM1432, DW343, DIST5, W7, NYC, 1860 USCen. For James, son of James, see accts. 14349, 14350, 22353, 24319, 32352, 36322, and 53734, ESB. For John, see accts. 13841 and 25781, ESB. For Michael, see accts. 14349, 22353, 24319, and 36322, ESB; FAM775, DW148; DIST8, W7, NYC, 1855 NYCen. For Patrick, see accts. 13481, 14832, and 25781, ESB.

152 *Charles and Francis McConnell:* Accts. 2849, 4725, 15255, 15256, and 56679, ESB.

152 *Alexander Fisher:* Accts. 8348, 11945, 14009, 22863, 29288, 42296, and 51603, ESB; FAM2081, DW569, W13, NYC, 1850 USCen; FAM499, DIST4, W13, NYC, 1855 NYCen; FAM1709, DW454, DIST2, W13, NYC, 1860 USCen.

153 *Peter Devlin:* Accts 8341 and 17377, ESB; FAM2374, DW2286, Northfield, Richmond County, NY, 1860 USCen; FAM430, DW447, Northfield, Richmond County, NY, 1870 USCen; FAM215, DW186, ED306, Richmond County, NY, 1880 USCen; "Died," *NYH*, Feb. 28, 1890, 1.

153 *James Devlins from Fallagh:* Acct. 8753, ESB; FAM657, DW149, DIST10, W7, NYC, 1870 USCen; FAM13, DW4, ED133, NYC, 1880 USCen; FAM56, DW55, ED297, NYC, 1900 USCen; 1880 *NYCDir*, 373; 1882 *NYCDir*, 396; 1887 *NYCDir*, 469; 1895 *NYCDir*, 343; "Building Plans Filed," *NYTrib*, Apr. 29, 1897, 8.

153 *other James Devlin and his brother Michael:* Acct. 14349, ESB; 1849 *NYCDir,* 126; 1860 *NYCDir,* 223; 1862 *NYCDir,* 224; 1864 *NYCDir,* 228; 1868 *NYCDir,* 276; 1870 *NYCDir,* 298; 1876 *NYCDir,* 331; 1879 *NYCDir,* 367; 1880 *Jersey City Dir,* 111; 1882 *Jersey City Dir,* 128; 1889 *Jersey City Dir,* 153; entries for Michael Devlin, July 7, 1890, and James Devlin, Feb. 19, 1899, NJ Deaths and Burials Index, 1798–1971, Ancestry.com; affidavit of John H. Devlin, Mar. 15, 1901, estate record of James Devlin, Hudson County, NJ Wills and Probate Records, 1739–1991, Ancestry.com.

153 *"charcoal factory":* "To Contest the Election," *NYTrib,* Apr. 12, 1890, 1.

153 *"suddenly insane":* "Victim of Religious Mania," *Jersey City News,* Feb. 4, 1895, 3.

154 *Charles McConnell:* Accts. 2849, 15255, 15256, and 56679, ESB; FAM2081, DW569, W13, NYC, 1850 USCen; FAM499, DIST4, W13, NYC, 1855 NYCen; FAM1300, DW402, DIST1, W5, KingsC, 1860 USCen; 1861 *BklynDir,* 280; 1862 *BklynDir,* 279; 1863 *BklynDir,* 299; 1866 *BklynDir,* 363; entry for Charles McConnell, Apr. 11, 1871, NYCDeaths; "Died," *NYH,* Apr. 13, 1871, 5; will of Charles McConnell, Apr. 4, 1871, KingsC, NY Wills and Probate Records, 1659–1999, Ancestry.com.

154 *John Conway:* Accts. 2382 and 9483, ESB; FAM1710, DW411, DIST5, W7, NYC, 1860 USCen; FAM645, DW147, DIST10, W7, NYC, 1870 USCen; FAM160, DW43, ED98, NYC, 1880 USCen.

154 *two Patrick Devlins:* Accts. 13841, 13842, 14833, 25781, and 58212, ESB; FAM1705, DW410, DIST5, W7, NYC, 1860 USCen; FAM653, DW468, DIST10, W7, NYC, 1870 USCen; 1856 *NYCDir,* 217; 1862 *NYCDir,* 224; 1864 *NYCDir,* 228; 1868 *NYCDir,* 276; 1879 *NYCDir,* 367; "Died," *New York Sun,* Nov. 8, 1879, 3.

154 *Charles Clarke:* Accts. 8332, 14883, 16421, 21643, 25391, 29906, and 57551, ESB; FAM966, DW232, DIST5, W7, NYC, 1860 USCen.

154 *Edward Fox:* Accts. 8345, 8737, 11941, and 11942, ESB; FAM58, DW17, DIST8, W7, NYC, 1855 NYCen; FAM968, DW232, DIST5, W7, NYC, 1860 USCen.

154 *"severe illness":* "Died," *NYH,* Nov. 20, 1869, 9.

154 *Michael Clark:* Accts. 7869, 22335, and 23052, ESB; FAM721, DW238, DIST2, W10, NYC, 1860 USCen; FAM539, DW111, DIST1, W7, NYC, 1870 USCen.

155 *"one of the best":* "Canada's Dalradian Plans to Dig Deep for Northern Irish Gold," *Reuters,* Nov. 27, 2017. See also "'How Much Is a Life Worth': Northern Irish Community Split over Gold-Mining Plans," *The Guardian,* July 28, 2020.

Chapter 5: "I Was Never Out of Work for Twenty-Four Hours"

156 *Michael Quinn was born in 1817:* Accts. 15313 and 15754, ESB; "Tons of Type," *Cleveland Herald,* reprinted in *Altoona Times,* Aug. 5, 1884, 1; manifest of the *Jacob A. Westervelt,* June 3, 1851, NYShips; manifest of the *Yorkshire,* Sept. 18, 1855, NYShips; 1856 *NYCDir,* 673; 1857 *NYCDir,* 677; 1858 *NYCDir,* 653; 1860 *NYCDir,* 700; 1861 *NYCDir,* 694; FAM930, DW357, DIST3, W4, NYC, 1860 USCen; FAM279, DW253, W1, Erie, Erie County, PA, 1870 USCen; FAM184, DW169, ED146, Erie, Erie County, PA, 1880 USCen.

157 *"consumption":* "Died," *NYIA,* Feb. 19, 1859, 3.

159 *"Father Quinn":* "Personal Intelligence," *NYH,* Aug. 15, 1884, 4.

159 *"at the case":* "More than 50 Years at the Case," *Atlanta Constitution,* Aug. 7, 1884, 5.

159 *"all the fast days":* Ibid.

159 *"emigration agent":* 1888 *Erie Dir,* 168; 1890 *Erie Dir,* 203.

160 *"Old People's Home":* "Evening Echoes," *Meadville (PA) Republican,* Dec. 20, 1899, 4.

161 *James W. Pratt:* Accts. 12268, 12339, and 17247, ESB; manifest of the *Harvest Queen,* Oct. 18, 1855, NYShips; FAM321, DW297, W7, KingsC, 1870 USCen; FAM362, DW246, ED213, KingsC, 1880 USCen.

161 *Edward Butler:* Acct. 8735, ESB; manifest of the *Caleb Grimshaw*, Sept. 11, 1848, NYShips; FAM897, DW304, W4, NYC, 1850 USCen; FAM420, DW90, DIST1, W4, NYC, 1855 NYCen; FAM2711, DW2589, Greenburgh, Westchester County, NY, 1860 USCen; FAM382, DW268, Dobbs Ferry, Westchester County, NY, 1870 USCen; "Colonel Edward Butler," *New York Irish World*, Feb. 10, 1877, 8.

162 *Henry Martin:* Accts. 13292 and 38026, ESB; FAM721, DW238, W6, NYC, 1850 USCen; FAM505, DW126, DIST6, W16, NYC, 1855 NYCen; FAM1719, DW624, DIST2, W16, NYC, 1860 USCen; FAM43, DW10, DIST4, W22, NYC, 1870 USCen.

162 *James Dowling:* Acct. 6516, ESB; manifest of the *Cambridge*, Sept. 11, 1848, NYShips; FAM563, DW59, DIST8, W17, NYC, 1860 USCen; 1867 *NYCDir*, 285; "Died," *NYH*, July 26, 1868, 6.

162 *Timothy Carr, a native of County Kerry:* Accts. 9511 and 45921, ESB; FAM219, DW41, DIST3, W1, NYC, 1855 NYCen; FAM457, DW100, DIST1, W1, NYC, 1860 USCen; p. 50, DIST11, W10, NYC, Enum2, 1870 USCen; FAM335, DW53, ED203, NYC, 1880 USCen; 1864 *NYCDir*, 147; 1867 *NYCDir*, 169; 1879 *NYCDir*, 231; 1890 *NYCDir*, 201; 1895 *NYCDir*, 220; 1899 *NYCDir*, 198; 1901 *NYCDir*, 209; "The First Battle of Bull Run," *NYIA*, June 7, 1884, 4; "The Old Armorer Hurt," *New York World*, Sept. 27, 1890, 9; "The Fighting 69th," *New York World*, Apr. 24, 1889, 28; "Death of a 69th Regiment Veteran," *NYIA*, Nov. 23, 1901, 4; will of Timothy Carr, June 7, 1901, NY Wills and Probate Records, 1659–1999, Ancestry.com.

164 *"foot it with the best":* "The Sixty-Ninth Dances," *New York Sun*, July 14, 1886, 1.

165 *Felix Toole:* Accts. 8535 and 15170, ESB; FAM186, DW50, DIST6, W7, NYC, 1855 NYCen; FAM70, DW22, DIST3, W11, NYC, 1860 USCen; 1867 *NYCDir*, 1032; FAM86, DW25, DIST11, W13, NYC, 1870 USCen; FAM222, DW43, ED134, NYC, 1880 USCen.

165 *John Riordan:* Accts. 386, 2814, 12645, and 42437, ESB; manifest of the *Columbia*, Apr. 5, 1850, NYShips.

165 *Daniel Cunningham:* Accts. 3873, 5772, and 37204, ESB; FAM656, DW128, DIST5, W4, NYC, 1855 NYCen; FAM53, DW12, DIST2, W4, NYC, 1870 USCen.

166 *"the Swamp":* Frank Norcross, *A History of the New York Swamp* (New York, 1901), 200–208.

167 *Daniel Devlin:* Manifest of the *Hawksbury*, Aug. 9, 1833, NYShips; FAM351, DW286, DIST4, W12, NYC, 1855 NYCen; FAM796, DW516, DIST3, W12, NYC, 1860 USCen; William E. Devlin, "Shrewd Irishmen: Irish Entrepreneurs and Artisans in New York's Clothing Industry, 1830–1880," in *The New York Irish*, ed. Ronald H. Bayor and Timothy J. Meagher (Baltimore, 1996), 183–86.

167 *best-known was George P. Fox:* Accts. 5978, 6094, and 10334, ESB; marriage of George Fox and Mary Rowley, Nov. 16, 1834, England Marriages, 1538–1973, Familysearch.org; FAM118, DW53, W5, NYC, 1850 USCen; FAM403, DW207, DIST1, W8, NYC, 1855 NYCen; FAM540, DW293, DIST3, W15, NYC, 1860 USCen; FAM625, DW197, DIST2, W15, NYC, 1870 USCen; FAM302, DW98, ED162, NYC, 1880 USCen; 1846 *NYCDir*, 146; 1847 *NYCDir*, 155; 1848 *NYCDir*, 156; 1849 *NYCDir*, 161; Fox advertisement, *New York Citizen*, Dec. 2, 1854, 765; "Died," *NYH*, May 27, 1885, 9; entry for George Patrick Fox, May 24, 1885, NYCDeaths.

168 *"exceedingly moderate charges":* Advertisement, *New York Atlas*, Dec. 17, 1848, 3.

168 *"Fashionable Tailoring Establishment":* Advertisement, *New-York Freeman's Journal and Catholic Register*, Sept. 7, 1850, 8.

168 *"garments gratis":* George P. Fox, *Fashion: The Power That Influences the World*, rev. ed. (New York, 1871), 242.

169 *"blue dress coat":* Ibid., 203.

170 *"perfect fitting pantaloons"*: Advertisement, *New-York Freeman's Journal and Catholic Register*, 8.

170 *"progressively rise[n]"*: Advertisement, *New York Evening Mirror*, Feb. 13, 1855, 2.

170 *"a great brag"*: Entry for George P. Fox, NY, vol. 209, p. 96, R. G. Dun & Co. credit report volumes, Baker Library, Harvard Business School.

170 *"tricky"*: Ibid.

170 *"Beau Brummel"*: "Influence of Dress on Morals," *Cincinnati Times*, May 6, 1872, 1.

170 *"material universe"*: Fox, *Fashion*, xx.

171 *Thomas Bannon*: Accts. 11349, 14392, 16651, and 36422, ESB; FAM570, DW216, DIST4, W8, NYC, 1855 NYCen; FAM602, DW101, DIST3, W4, NYC, 1860 USCen; FAM374, DW72, DIST10, W14, NYC, 1870 USCen; FAM371, DW52, ED50, NYC, 1880 USCen; service record of Thomas Bannon, Companies D and K, 95th NY Infantry Regiment, National Archives; entry for Bridget Bannon, Mar. 8, 1886, NYCDeaths; entries for Thomas Bannon, Register of Members of National Homes for Disabled Volunteer Soldiers, Togus Branch (p. 7958) and Roseburg Branch (p. 10847), Ancestry.com. For John Bannon, see FAM570, DW216, DIST4, W8, NYC, 1855 NYCen; FAM1299, DW478, W1, Boston, Suffolk County, MA, 1865 MA Census; FAM102, DW44, ED1172, Boston, Suffolk County, MA, 1900 USCen.

172 *Michael Flanagan*: Accts. 16230 and 46218, ESB; FAM761, DW145, DIST4, W6, NYC, 1860 USCen; FAM346, DW70, DIST2, W14, NYC, 1870 USCen; FAM290, ED216, NYC, 1880 USCen; 1855 *NYCDir*, 290; 1884 *NYCDir*, 554; entry for Mary Flanigan [sic], Mar. 18, 1886, NYCDeaths; "Died," *NYH*, Mar. 19, 1886, 9; entry for Michael Flanagan, July 22, 1887, NYCDeaths; "Died," *NYH*, July 24, 1887, 13.

172 *"get no money"*: Acct. 16230, ESB.

173 *Tailors saved*: Tyler Anbinder, Cormac Ó Gráda, and Simone A. Wegge, "Networks and Opportunities: A Digital History of Ireland's Great Famine Refugees in New York," *American Historical Review* 124 (Dec. 2019): 1615.

173 *60 percent more*: Ibid.

173 *Patrick Costello*: Accts. 1070, 3125, 3877, and 16611, ESB; FAM316, DW204, Eastern DIST, W15, NYC, 1850 USCen; FAM1299, DW318, DIV3, W14, NYC, 1860 USCen; FAM388, DW180, DIST9, W18, NYC, 1870 USCen; FAM413, DW96, ED189, NYC, 1880 USCen; 1882 *NYCDir*, 330.

173 *Andrew Delany*: Acct. 4092, ESB; manifest of the *Fingal*, Nov. 7, 1848, NYShips; p. 1, DW528, DIST17, W21, NYC, Enum2, 1870 USCen; FAM214, DW111, ED474, NYC, 1880 USCen; 1882 *NYCDir*, 385.

174 *Jeremiah Crowley*: Accts. 12421 and 38696, ESB; FAM1822, DW416, DIST6, W18, NYC, 1860 USCen; FAM1675, DW1366, W4, Cambridge, Middlesex County, MA, 1870 USCen; FAM45, DW30, ED721, Cambridge, Middlesex County, MA, 1900 USCen.

174 *John Burke from rural County Limerick*: Acct. 6515, ESB; FAM1031, DW445, DIST1, W7, NYC, 1850 USCen; FAM325, DW98, DIST10, W17, NYC, 1860 USCen.

174 *John Cleary*: Acct. 4288, ESB; FAM926, DW345, DIST1, W7, NYC, 1855 NYCen; FAM464, DW119, DIV2, W4, NYC, 1860 USCen; p. 35, FAM29, DW313, DIST10, W21, NYC, Enum2, 1870 USCen; 1875 *NYCDir*, 230; 1876 *NYCDir*, 236; 1877 *NYCDir*, 241.

174 *John Burke, this one from County Westmeath*: Accts. 4267 and 17697, ESB; FAM2099, DW534, DIST3, W14, NYC, 1860 USCen; FAM300, DW144, DIST13, W19, NYC, 1870 USCen; FAM264, DW123, ED631, NYC, 1880 USCen; 1853 *NYCDir*, 103; 1859 *NYCDir*, 124; 1871 *NYCDir*, 159; 1876 *NYCDir*, 180; 1885 *NYCDir*, 249; 1892 *NYCDir*, 190; entry for John Burke, July 15, 1892, NYCDeaths.

175 *James Cassidy*: Accts. 4074, 8010, 15935, 20220, and 30282, ESB; FAM797, DW288, DIST6, W8, NYC, 1855 NYCen; FAM68, DW34, DIV3, W8, NYC, 1860 USCen;

FAM22, DW9, DIST11, W8, NYC, 1870 USCen; 1864 *NYCDir*, 152; 1865 *NYCDir*, 164; 1866 *NYCDir*, 172; 1867 *NYCDir*, 175; 1868 *NYCDir*, 182; 1870 *NYCDir*, 196; "Died," *NYH*, May 21, 1870, 6.

175 *John Kernan:* Accts 4481, 5030, and 40386, ESB; FAM1314, DW349, W11, NYC, 1850 USCen; FAM1040, DW730, W8, KingsC, 1855 NYCen; FAM771, DW627, DIST3, W11, KingsC, 1860 USCen; FAM5, DW3, ED 230, KingsC, 1880 USCen; 1875 *BklynDir*, 483; 1889 *BklynDir*, 654; "Obituary," *BDE*, Feb. 13, 1896, 4; "Wills Filed for Probate," *BDE*, Feb. 21, 1896, 1.

175 *Arthur Thompson:* Accts. 7968 and 10330, ESB; FAM276, DW118, DIST2, W10, NYC, 1855 NYCen; FAM886, DW187, DIST8, W11, NYC, 1860 USCen; p. 69, DW116, DIST10, W17, NYC, Enum2, 1870 USCen.

176 *Richard Daly:* Accts. 7037 and 48188, ESB; FAM166, DW139, DIST4, Deerpark, Orange County, NY, 1865 NYCensus; FAM1748, DW1321, Deerpark, Orange County, NY, 1870 USCen; FAM134, DW121, Deerpark, Orange County, NY, 1875 NYCen.

176 *John Wharton from County Carlow:* Accts. 8215, 25990, and 41176, ESB; FAM944, DW590, DIST1, W12, NYC, 1860 USCen; FAM260, DW212, DIST13, W12, NYC, 1870 USCen; p. 20B, ED9, W1, KingsC, 1900 USCen; p. 2B, ED30, AD18, KingsC, 1905 NYCen; 1867 *NYCDir*, 1097; 1871 *NYCDir*, 1221; 1873 *NYCDir*, 1381; 1877 *NYC-Dir*, 1495; 1879 *NYCDir*, 1599; 1882 *NYCDir*, 1737; 1889 *NYCDir*, 2112; entry for Ann Maria Wharton, Apr. 8, 1890, NYCDeaths; entry for John Wharton, Jan. 10, 1901, NY Census of Inmates in Almshouses and Poorhouses, 1830–1920, Ancestry .com; entry for John Wharton, May 31, 1908, NYCDeaths.

176 *Some journeymen moved just one rung:* The work lives of all immigrants described in this paragraph are documented in the ESB Mobility Database.

178 *variety of possibilities was almost endless:* Ibid.

178 *"undertakers' trimmings":* FAM52, DW37, ED222, KingsC, 1880 USCen.

178 *Paul J. Hurley:* Acct. 12965, ESB; p. 33, DIST14, W10, NYC, Enum2, 1870 USCen; FAM221, DW42, ED209, NYC, 1880 USCen; 1861 *NYCDir*, 419; 1864 *NYCDir*, 434; 1867 *NYCDir*, 508; 1875 *NYCDir*, 688; death certificate for Paul J. Hurley, Feb. 14, 1893, NYCMA.

178 *William Barry:* Acct. 11610, ESB; FAM1169, DW281, DIST3, W11, NYC, 1860 USCen; FAM229, DW133, DIST7, W10, KingsC, 1875 NYCen; FAM452, DW177, ED85, W10, KingsC, 1880 USCen.

178 *Thomas Kelly:* Acct. 17729, ESB; FAM1027, DW142, DIST5, W18, NYC, 1860 USCen; FAM848, DW401, W1, Jersey City, Hudson County, NJ, 1870 USCen; FAM184, DW69, ED35, Jersey City, Hudson County, NJ, 1880 USCen.

178 *John Carey from Fermanagh:* Accts. 2412 and 24446, ESB; FAM542, DW271, DIST1, W17, KingsC, 1860 USCen; FAM767, DW376, W17, KingsC, 1870 USCen; FAM482, DW207, DIST2, W17, KingsC, 1875 NYCen; 1870 *BklynDir*, 105.

179 *Francis C. Graves:* Accts. 1348, 7072, and 10769, ESB; FAM507, DW235, DIST1, W11, KingsC, 1860 USCen; FAM1555, DW1578, DIST1, Hartford, Hartford County, CT, 1870 USCen; FAM465, DW176, ED12, Hartford, Hartford County, CT, 1880 USCen; FAM185, DW100, ED153, Hartford, Hartford County, CT, 1900 USCen; FAM118, DW94, ED164, Hartford, Hartford County, CT, 1910 USCen; 1863 *BklynDir*, 181; 1864 *BklynDir*, 164; 1887 *Hartford Dir*, 107; 1888 *Hartford Dir*, 113; 1895 *Hartford Dir*, 145; *Official Gazette of the United States Patent Office* (Washington, DC, 1883), 289; "No. 48,313, Paper Feeding Device," *Canadian Patent Office Record* 23 (Mar. 1895): 177.

179 *John Sinnamon:* Acct. 10942, ESB; FAM716, DW186, DIST1, W6, NYC, 1855 NYCen; FAM62, DW51, W8, Oswego, Oswego County, NY, 1870 USCen; FAM25, DW24,

ED258, Oswego, Oswego County, NY, 1880 USCen; "Oregon Items," *San Francisco Bulletin*, Jan. 10, 1876, 1; 1856 *Oswego Dir*, 50; 1861 *Oswego Dir*, 131; 1869 *Oswego Dir*, 222; 1870 *Oswego Dir*, 189; 1873 *Oswego Dir*, 255; 1880 *Oswego Dir*, 252; 1882 *Oswego Dir*, 315; *Annual Report of the Commissioner of Patents for the Year 1880* (Washington, DC, 1881), 186, "Dead in Glasgow," *Oswego Palladium*, July 21, 1894, 5; "The Suspicious Affair in Glasgow," *Glasgow Herald*, July 23, 1894, 4.

180 *"in a disreputable house"*: "An American Murdered," *NYH*, July 22, 1894, 10.

180 *"slums of Glasgow"*: "Cable Personal and Political," *NYH*, July 24, 1894, 9.

181 *Francis Brady*: Acct. 10371, ESB; FAM1514, DW1482, Elyria, Lorain County, OH, 1860 USCen; FAM63, DW64, W2, Fremont, Sandusky County, OH, 1870 USCen; FAM61, DW51, ED83, W4, Fremont, Sandusky County, OH, 1880 USCen; FAM437, DW416, ED74, Fremont, Sandusky County, OH, 1900 USCen.

181 *"a pioneer merchant tailor"*: "Death at Fremont," *Cleveland Leader*, May 19, 1905, 2.

181 *Richard Sharkey*: Accts. 10753 and 16845, ESB; FAM1828, DW599, DIST4, W21, NYC, 1860 USCen; FAM70, DW107, Little York, Nevada County, CA, 1870 USCen; FAM73, DW72, ED98, Sierra, Sierra County, CA, 1880 USCen; "Richard Sharkey Dead," *Marysville (CA) Appeal*, Dec. 3, 1898, 3.

181 *William Stapleton*: Accts. 3624 and 4353, ESB; FAM399, DW270, W5, NYC, 1850 USCen; FAM3307, DW3431, Joliet, Will County, IL, 1860 USCen; FAM361, DW339, W1, Joliet, Will County, IL, 1870 USCen; FAM218, DW206, ED197, W1, Joliet, Will County, IL, 1880 USCen; 1872 *Joliet Dir*, 94; 1877 *Joliet Dir*, 182; 1881 *Joliet Dir*, 195; 1885 *Joliet Dir*, 288; 1888 *Joliet Dir*, 353; 1889 *Joliet Dir*, 375; 1892 *Joliet Dir*, 482.

181 *"doing a good bus[iness]"*: Entry for William Stapleton, IL, vol. 229, p. 213, R. G. Dun & Co. credit report volumes, Baker Library, Harvard Business School.

182 *"city collector"*: "Tax Sale Notice," *Joliet Signal*, Apr. 24, 1866, 2–3.

182 *"best men in the city"*: "A. Cagwin Having Declined," *Joliet Signal*, Mar. 29, 1881, 1.

182 *Patrick Keady*: Accts. 10869 and 29146, ESB; FAM1224, DW689, DIST2, W10, KingsC, 1855 NYCen; FAM604, DW474, DIST1, W6, KingsC, 1860 USCen; FAM244, DW258, W6, KingsC, 1870 USCen; FAM301, DW262, ED44, KingsC, 1880 USCen; FAM299, DW111, ED61, KingsC, 1900 USCen; "General News," *NYTrib*, Apr. 8, 1864, 4; "Several Gentlemen," *Brooklyn Times*, Oct. 11, 1866, 2; "From New York," *Buffalo Commercial Advertiser*, Apr. 29, 1867, 2 (tenement reform); "Won by an Epigram," *Brooklyn Times*, Dec. 31, 1898, 2; "Justice Keady Dead," *BDE*, Oct. 7, 1908, 20.

182 *Michael Smee continued*: Accts. 4633, 8637, 11938, and 19831, ESB; FAM230, DW75, W12, KingsC, 1870 USCen; FAM404, DW309, ED7, Claverack, Columbia County, NY, 1880 USCen.

182 *Richard Casey*: Accts. 1028 and 4894, ESB; FAM1115, DW1086, DIST10, SF, SF County, CA, 1860 USCen; FAM651, DW386, DIST3, W10, SF, SF County, CA, 1870 USCen; FAM11, DW7, ED101, SF, SF County, CA, 1880 USCen; 1887 *SF Dir*, 309; "Casey," *San Francisco Examiner*, Sept. 12, 1888, 5.

183 *Robert Edgeworth*: Acct. 5885, ESB; FAM1104, DW393, W6, Jersey City, Hudson County, NJ, 1870 USCen; FAM39, DW14, ED16, Jersey City, Hudson County, NJ, 1880 USCen; 1896 *Jersey City Dir*, 220.

183 *William M. Dowling*: Accts. 12936, 17666, and 32100, ESB; FAM1305, DW205, DIST5, W18, NYC, 1860 USCen; FAM268, DW253, W4, Lansing, Ingham County, MI, 1870 USCen; FAM290, DW268, ED130, Lansing, Ingham County, MI, 1880 USCen; "It Happened Back in 1882," *Lansing State Journal*, May 27, 1932, 6; 1883 *NYCDir*, 440; 1886 *NYCDir*, 505.

ENDNOTES

183 *"hard to find"*: "Death of Wm. M. Dowling," *Passaic (NJ) News*, Nov. 30, 1895, 1.

183 *Jonathan Dillon*: Manifest of the *Liverpool*, Mar. 24, 1845, NYShips; FAM2018, DW500, W6, NYC, 1850 USCen; FAM216, DW138, DIST2, W12, NYC, 1855 NYCen; FAM614, DW573, W7, Washington, DC, 1860 USCen; FAM269, DW199, DIST4, W15, NYC, 1870 USCen; FAM414, DW379, DIST5, W19, KingsC, 1875 NYCen; FAM130, DW128, ED85, Mt. Vernon, Westchester County, NY, 1900 USCen; 1864 *BklynDir*, 109; 1867 *NYCDir*, 270; 1871 *NYCDir*, 291; 1874 *BklynDir*, 205; 1877 *NYCDir*, 347; 1882 *NYCDir*, 405; 1884 *NYCDir*, 426; 1892 *Mt. Vernon and New Rochelle Dir*, 61; 1899 *Mt. Vernon Dir*, 83; 1905 *NYCDir*, 349; "Insolvent Debtors," *Dublin Freeman's Journal*, Jan. 11, 1833, 1 (debts of Dillon's father); "When Sumter Was Fired On," *Washington Evening Star*, Oct. 9, 1902, 19; entry for Jonathan Dillon, June 23, 1907, NYCDeaths; "Timeless Lincoln Memento Is Revealed," *NYT*, Mar. 11, 2009, C1.

184 *Joseph Dillon*: Manifest of the *Carroll from Carrollton*, Dec. 20, 1836, NYShips; FAM1077, DW650, W4, KingsC, 1850 USCen; 1845 *NYCDir*, 106; "Death of Colonel Joseph J. Dillon," *NYII*, Dec. 24, 1865, 8.

184 *Isabella Martin Dillon*: "The Alhamra," *NYH*, Oct. 19, 1846, 2; "Musical," *NYH*, Oct. 20, 1846, 2; marriage of Jonathan Dillon and Isabella Martin, Feb. 27, 1848, New York City Compiled Marriage Index, Ancestry.com; "Italian Opera—Astor Place," *NYEP*, Nov. 1, 1848, 3; "Obituary," *Mt. Vernon (NY) Chronicle*, Aug. 28, 1896, 2.

184 *"never out of work"*: "Who Has Lincoln's Watch," *NYT*, Apr. 30, 1906, 7.

185 *"only Union sympathizer"*: Ibid.

185 *"English lever watch"*: Ibid.

185 *"we have a government"*: T. J. Stiles, "The Secret Message," *The Atlantic*, Mar. 2009.

Chapter 6: "Never Was There a Brighter Brain"

191 *James Cavanagh from Carrick-on-Suir*: Accts. 2533, 3534, 4623, 11766, 17531, 18008, and 42041, ESB; manifest of the *Envoy*, NYShips, Jan. 22, 1851; FAM227, DW42, DIST3, W1, NYC, 1855 NYCen; FAM559, DW119, DIST1, W1, NYC, 1860 USCen; FAM347, DW120, W6, KingsC, 1865 NYCen; FAM497, DW454, W6, KingsC, 1870 USCen; FAM309, DW115, ED45, KingsC, 1880 USCen; p. 19, ED22, W6, KingsC, 1892 NYCen; FAM368, DW121, ED64, KingsC, 1900 USCen; 1854 *NYCDir*, 131; 1855 *NYCDir*, 149; 1858 *NYCDir*, 142; 1860 *NYCDir*, 149; 1866 *BklynDir*, 87; 1879 *BklynDir*, 155; 1881 *BklynDir*, 167; 1886 *BklynDir*, 176; 1888 *BklynDir*, 182; 1889 *BklynDir*, 192; 1890 *BklynDir*, 184; 1896 *BklynDir*, 228; 1898 *BklynDir*, 230; "Wanted—Four Good Journeyman Carpenters," *NYH*, May 8, 1862, 8; "Wanted—By a Respectable Married Woman," *NYH*, June 21, 1864, 5; "The May Elections: Official Canvass," *NYH*, June 1, 1870, 12; "The Vote in Brooklyn," *New York World*, Nov. 4, 1875, 1; "Jacobs and Cavanagh," *NYH*, Feb. 12, 1876, 3; *Official Register of the United States Containing a List of the Officers and Employees in the Civil, Military, and Naval Service on the First of July, 1895* (Washington, DC, 1895), 1:58; "Obituary," *BDE*, Jan. 7, 1901, 3.

192 *"That depends"*: "General Cavanagh Dead," *New York Irish World*, Jan. 12, 1901, 3.

192 *"ever witnessed"*: Susannah Ural Bruce, *The Harp and the Eagle: Irish-American Volunteers and the Union Army, 1861–1865* (New York, 2006), 120.

193 *"Fighting Little Major"*: "General James Cavanagh Dead," *NYIA*, Jan. 12, 1901, 4.

193 *"perfect slaughter-pen"*: D. P. Conyngham, *The Irish Brigade and Its Campaigns* (Boston, 1869), 342–44.

193 *"severely wounded"*: Report of Brig. Gen. Thomas F. Meagher, Dec. 20, 1862, in *The War of the Rebellion: A Compilation of the Official Records of the Union and Confederate Armies* (Washington, DC, 1888), ser. 1, 21:244.

193 *"a truer heart"*: Ibid.

195 *"honorable service"*: "General Cavanagh Dead," 3.

196 *"they are suited"*: Thomas Mooney, *Nine Years in America*, 2nd ed. (Dublin, 1850), 91.

196 *upon arrival in America:* See the database of jobs held by male Famine immigrants within one year of arrival in the United States at https://dataverse.harvard.edu /dataverse/anbinder, as well as the ESB Mobility Database.

197 *Robert Lewis from Dublin:* Acct. 4039, ESB; FAM413, DW284, DIST8, W12, NYC, 1870 USCen; p. 42, DIST17, W12, NYC, Enum2, 1870 USCen; FAM232, DW138, ED635, NYC, 1880 USCen; 1871 *NYCDir,* 676; 1873 *NYCDir,* 765; 1885 *NYCDir,* 1125; "Obituary Notes," *NYT,* May 21, 1899, 7.

197 *dry goods clerk:* FAM1599, DW639, DIST9, W19, NYC, 1860 USCen.

198 *John Devins:* Accts. 4346, 12926, 16440, 32170, and 39610, ESB; manifest of the *Marmion,* Dec. 4, 1849, NYShips; FAM15, DW21, W1, Racine, Racine County, WI, 1860 USCen; FAM475, DW284, W15, KingsC, 1870 USCen; FAM423, DW351, ED225, KingsC, 1880 USCen.

198 *William Durack:* Acct. 2728, ESB; FAM1095, DW543, W21, KingsC, 1870 USCen; FAM342, DW115, ED215, KingsC, 1880 USCen; FAM205, DW120, ED304, Chicago, Cook County, IL, 1900 USCen; 1860 *NYCDir,* 251; 1882 *BklynDir,* 312; 1889 *Chicago Dir,* 536.

198 *Alexander Furlong:* Acct. 5879, ESB; FAM176, DW44, DIST1, W3, NYC, 1855 NYCen; entry for Alexander Furlong, June 16, 1857, NY Church and Civil Deaths, 1824–1962, Familysearch.org.

199 *John Brown:* Accts. 10613, 21045, and 23260, ESB; manifest of the *Forfarshire,* NYShips, May 12, 1848; FAM1847, DW844, DIST3, W16, NYC, 1860 USCen; FAM1587, DW1021, W20, KingsC, 1870 USCen; FAM22, DW19, ED199, KingsC, 1880 USCen; "Died," *BDE,* Dec. 8, 1882, 3; "Deaths," *Brooklyn Citizen,* Mar. 6, 1893, 5.

199 *$3,000 per year: The City Record,* Jan. 29–30, 1874, 103–4, 109–11; *The United States Treasury Register…July 1, 1873* (Washington, DC, 1873), 116.

199 *Richard Oulahan:* Accts. 3867, 21678, and 35802, ESB; FAM1133, DW133, DIST1, W18, NYC, 1860 USCen; FAM1494, DW1408, W5, Washington, DC, 1870 USCen; FAM144, DW126, ED74, Washington, DC, 1880 USCen; 1863 *NYCDir,* 668; 1865 *Washington Dir,* 292; *United States Treasury Register…July 1, 1873,* 29; *Official Register of the United States…First of July, 1891* (Washington, DC, 1892), 1:56; "Death of a Famous Irishman," *Washington Evening Star,* June 12, 1895, 9; "Maj. Richard Oulahan Dead," *Washington Post,* June 13, 1895, 2.

200 *Thomas E. Foran:* Accts. 17043 and 31434, ESB; FAM1436, DW232, DIST8, W17, NYC, 1860 USCen; p. 23, DW1217, DIST8, W19, NYC, Enum2, 1870 USCen; FAM158, DW27, ED448, NYC, 1880 USCen; 1856 *NYCDir,* 286; 1858 *NYCDir,* 278; 1868 *NYCDir,* 367; 1869 *NYCDir,* 372; 1872 *NYCDir,* 399; 1873 *NYCDir,* 431; 1887 *NYCDir,* 635; 1888 *NYCDir,* 644; "Died," *NYH,* June 13, 1891, 1.

201 *James Goodwin:* Accts. 7729, 9872, 13077, and 22559, ESB; manifest of the *Edward Stanley,* Aug. 19, 1854, NYShips; FAM738, DW366, W17, NYC, 1850 USCen; FAM1, DW59, DIST1, W2, KingsC, 1855 NYCen; FAM105, ED49, Toxteth Park, Lancashire, 1871 UK Census; FAM236, DW216, ED34, New Marlborough, Berkshire County, MA, 1880 USCen; FAM482, ED609, W12, NYC, 1910 USCen; 1861 *NYCDir,* 330; 1864 *NYCDir,* 341; 1867 *NYCDir,* 399; 1870 *NYCDir,* 457; 1875 *NYCDir,* 499; 1879 *NYCDir,* 572; 1880 *NYCDir,* 584; 1887 *NYCDir,* 734; 1889 *BklynDir,* 465;

1891 *NYCDir*, 511; 1894 *NYCDir*, 523; 1910 *NYCDir*, 552; entries for James Goodwin, James Goodwin & Co., and Goodwin, Cobb & Co., NY, vol. 194, p. 795 and p. 800 subpages A21, A29, A42, A75, and A101, R. G. Dun & co. credit report volumes, Baker Library, Harvard Business School; "Business Failures in Massachusetts," *NYT*, Feb. 24, 1876, 2; "Business Interests," *Boston Post*, Apr. 11, 1876, 3; "Manufacturing News," *Lowell Courier*, July 19, 1876, 2; "New England News," *Boston Evening Transcript*, Feb. 3, 1877, 3; "Business Troubles," *Boston Evening Transcript*, Oct. 23, 1882, 1; Byron Weston, "History of Paper Making in Berkshire County," *Collections of the Berkshire Historical and Scientific Society* 2 (1895): 13; "Obituary," *Paper Trade Journal* 52 (Jan. 26, 1911): 38.

201 *"tricky" and "cunning"*: Entry for Goodwin, Cobb & Co., NY, vol. 194, p. 795, R. G. Dun & Co. credit report volumes.

202 *Peter McCullough*: Accts. 5119, 9970, 14548, 15984, 16983, and 46490, ESB; FAM1048, DW375, W16, NYC, 1850 USCen; FAM318, DW97, DIST8, W16, NYC, 1855 NYCen; FAM1458, DW561, DIST1, W22, NYC, 1860 USCen; FAM223, DW129, ED471, NYC, 1880 USCen; FAM96, DW14, ED479, NYC, 1900 USCen; 1857 *NYCDir*, 520; 1861 *NYCDir*, 534; 1864 *NYCDir*, 554; 1867 *NYCDir*, 648; 1869 *NYCDir*, 694; 1871 *NYCDir*, 716; entry for Delia McCullough, Aug. 5, 1896, NYC-Deaths; entry for Peter McCullough and Catherine Hoar, June 19, 1898, New York City Marriage Records,1829–1938, Familysearch.org; entry for Peter McCullough, Feb. 15, 1904, NYCDeaths; will of Peter McCullough, Aug. 14, 1902, NY Wills and Probate Records, 1659–1999, Ancestry.com; "Must Pay for the Wake," *New York Sun*, Feb. 12, 1907, 1; *Report of Cases Heard and Determined in the Appellate Division of the Supreme Court of the State of New York* (Albany, 1908), 122:888, 920.

203 *"retired"*: FAM257, DW181, DIST13, W22, NYC, 1870 USCen.

203 *"steaks and other meats"*: "Sues for $71 He Spent at a Relative's Wake," *NYT*, Dec. 7, 1906, 7.

204 *"immoral"*: "Wakes Denounced in Court," *NYT*, Oct. 17, 1907, 18.

204 *"delicatessen in their nature"*: Supreme Court, Appellate Division — First Department: Joseph J. McCullough, Plaintiff-Respondent, Against Charles McCready and Richard S. Treacy...Papers on Appeal from Order (New York, 1907), 30.

204 *George Hargan*: Accts. 5977, 6954, 12723, 13760, 13761, 14556, and 33001, ESB; manifest of the *Marion*, Apr. 12, 1847, NYShips; FAM1898, DW564, W4, NYC, 1850 USCen; FAM1115, DW247, DIST2, W4, NYC, 1855 NYCen; 1849 *NYCDir*, 192; 1853 *NYCDir*, 301; 1855 *NYCDir*, 361; 1858 *NYCDir*, 344; "New York Common Council," *NYH*, Mar. 16, 1853, 8; George Hargan, letter to the editor, *NYT*, Aug. 1, 1856, 8; George Hargan, letter to the editor, *NYT*, Aug. 7, 1856, 3; "Academy of Music," *NYH*, July 12, 1858, 4; "George Hargan," *NYH*, Aug. 30, 1858, 3; "Died," *NYH*, Mar. 2, 1863, 5.

205 *William O'Meagher*: Accts. 5981, 9579, and 27950, ESB; FAM277, DW163, DIST2, W6, NYC, 1855 NYCen; FAM1086, DW234, DIST4, W6, NYC, 1860 USCen; FAM13, DW8, DIST10, W18, NYC, 1870 USCen; 1857 *NYCDir*, 636; 1858 *NYCDir*, 614; 1860 *NYCDir*, 657; 1879 *NYCDir*, 1162; 1891 *NYCDir*, 1041; *Physicians and Surgeons of America: A Collection of Biographical Sketches* (Concord, NH, 1896), 224; "Death of Coroner O'Meagher," *NYT*, Feb. 25, 1896, 6.

206 *Henry Madden*: Acct. 4181, ESB; manifest of the *Mary Florence*, Apr. 5, 1849, NYShips; FAM1378, DW1007, W10, Albany, Albany County, NY, 1860 USCen; FAM286, DW207, Eastern DIST, W10, Albany, Albany County, NY, 1865 NYCen; FAM103, DW45, W1, Albany, Albany County, NY, 1870 USCen; "Died," *Albany Argus*, November 4, 1870, 1.

206 *"well known schoolmaster"*: "Fatal Result," *Albany Argus*, November 3, 1870, 4.

206 *John and Stephen McMahon*: Accts. 4760 and 10697, ESB; manifest of the *Sarah Milledge*, May 13, 1848, NYShips; FAM496, DW233, W10, NYC, 1850 USCen; FAM1003, DW267, DIST3, W10, NYC, 1855 NYCen; FAM369, DW42, ED241, NYC, 1900 USCen; FAM368, DW42, ED714, NYC, 1910 USCen; p. 17, ED5, AD3, Pocantico Hills, Mt. Pleasant, Westchester County, NY, 1915 NYCen; FAM163, DW131, Pocantico Hills, Westchester Country, NY, 1920 USCen; death certificate of Brother Stephen McMahon, Feb. 28, 1912, Pennsylvania Death Certificates, 1906–1968, Ancestry.com.

207 *"magnetic personality"*: M. D. Azarie, "Brother Justin," *Catholic Educational Review* 3 (1912): 411.

208 *"giants"*: Brother Angelus Gabriel, *The Christian Brothers in the United States, 1848–1948* (New York, 1948), 581.

208 *Josephine Cowen from Dublin*: Acct. 7103, ESB.

208 *Josephine Gibbons from Clare*: Acct. 10242, ESB.

208 *Emma Kingsbury*: Acct. 8662, ESB.

208 *Margaret Antisell, who emigrated from Dublin*: Accts. 5500 and 5501, ESB; FAM1218, DW809, DIST2, W4, KingsC, 1860 USCen; FAM1941, DW1086, W9, KingsC, 1870 USCen; FAM267, DW167, ED73, KingsC, 1880 USCen.

208 *Margaret Smithson from Dublin*: Acct. 5356, ESB.

208 *Michael J. Sause from Tipperary*: Accts. 1167 and 17650, ESB; FAM2395, DW514, DIST4, W18, NYC, 1855 NYCen; FAM750, DW267, DIST6, W18, NYC, 1860 USCen; p. 32, DW237, DIST5, W17, NYC, Enum2, 1870 USCen; FAM82, DW49, ED733, NYC, 1900 USCen; 1863 *NYCDir*, 756; 1864 *NYCDir*, 772; 1866 *NYCDir*, 884; 1867 *NYCDir*, 902; 1870 *NYCDir*, 1060; 1877 *NYCDir*, 1235; 1886 *NYCDir*, 1711; 1892 *NYCDir*, 1244; "Walks About Town," *New York Dispatch*, Apr. 25, 1880, 5; "Professor Sause's Masquerade," *New York Truth*, Jan. 12, 1883, 4; "Lyceum Opera House," *New York Age*, Apr. 5, 1890, 3; Judson Sause, *The Art of Dancing*, 5th ed. (Chicago, 1889).

209 *"enjoyable in the city"*: "To Retire from His Profession," *New York Dispatch*, Jan. 25, 1885, 5.

209 *"any other living man"*: "Some Flashlight Glimpses of the World at Large," *Atlanta Journal*, July 31, 1897, 4.

209 *"He died happy"*: "Old Dancing Teacher Dead," *NYT*, Apr. 14, 1906, 11.

209 *Anthony Geraghty*: Accts. 2418 (Thomas's), 5021, 10850, and 13569, ESB; FAM479, DW121, DIST9, W11, NYC, 1860 USCen; p. 5, DW209, DIST13, W12, NYC, Enum2, 1870 USCen; FAM62, DW41, ED591, NYC, 1880 USCen; 1858 *NYCDir*, 301; 1859 *NYCDir*, 320; 1864 *NYCDir*, 327; "Irish-American Obituary," *NYIA*, July 9, 1887, 5.

210 *"popular with his pupils"*: "Obituary Notes," *NYT*, June 19, 1887, 5.

210 *Edward Delaney*: Accts. 9813 and 9814, ESB; FAM313, DW259, DIST4, W12, NYC, 1855 NYCen; FAM407, DW299, DIST3, W12, NYC, 1860 USCen; FAM463, DW236, DIST16, W12, NYC, 1870 USCen; 1883 *NYCDir*, 414; "Deaths," *NYH*, May 21, 1883, 9.

210 *Daniel Quinn*: Acct. 7328, ESB; FAM506, DW178, DIST4, W16, NYC, 1855 NYCen; FAM1201, DW512, DIST2, W20, NYC, 1860 USCen; FAM105, DW23, DIST4, W20, NYC, 1870 USCen; FAM218, DW48, ED384, NYC, 1880 USCen.

211 *Daniel D. McCarthy*: Accts. 10616 and 13727, ESB; manifest of the *Osceola*, May 31, 1849, NYShips; FAM760, DW235, DIST5, W14, NYC, 1855 NYCen; FAM391, DW75, DIST10, W14, NYC, 1870 USCen; FAM246, DW209, ED306, Northfield,

Richmond County, NY, 1880 USCen; p. 8, DIST20, W14, KingsC, 1892 NYCen; 1858 *NYCDir*, 498; 1859 *NYCDir*, 530; *Metropolitan Catholic Almanac for 1861* (Baltimore, 1861), 233; 1861 *NYCDir*, 528; 1862 *NYCDir*, 540; 1863 *NYCDir*, 536; 1865 *NYCDir*, 603; 1867 *NYCDir*, 641; 1878 *NYCDir*, 895; *History of Richmond County*, ed. Richard M. Bayles (New York, 1887), 435; "Death List of a Day," *NYT*, June 1, 1898, 7.

211 *Gerald, the younger of the two:* Accts. 16338, 30428, and 38608, ESB; FAM121, DW102, DIST1, W10, KingsC, 1855 NYCen; FAM1237, DW751, DIST2, W12, KingsC, 1860 USCen; FAM6, DW6, W12, KingsC, 1865 NYCen; FAM806, DW584, W6, KingsC, 1870 USCen; W. F. Lyons, *Brigadier-General Thomas Francis Meagher: His Political and Military Career* (New York, 1886), 26; "Death of Gerald R. Lalor, Esq.," *NYIA*, Oct. 21, 1871, 4.

212 *Richard Lalor also ended:* Accts. 6785 and 14932, ESB; FAM121, DW102, DIST1, W10, KingsC, 1855 NYCen; FAM1237, DW751, DIST2, W12, KingsC, 1860 USCen; FAM6, DW6, W12, KingsC, 1865 NYCen; FAM806, DW584, W6, KingsC, 1870 USCen; FAM277, DW82, DIST10, W6, KingsC, 1875 NYCen; FAM296, DW128, ED43, KingsC, 1880 USCen; 1852 *BklynDir*, 268; 1853 *BklynDir*, 304; 1862 *BklynDir*, 242; 1863 *NYCDir*, 490; 1867 *NYCDir*, 587; 1869 *BklynDir*, 372; 1870 *BklynDir*, 404; 1872 *BklynDir*, 425; 1877 *BklynDir*, 516; Michael Cavanagh, *Memoirs of Gen. Thomas Francis Meagher* (Worcester, MA, 1892), 346; William D. Murphy, *Biographical Sketches of the State Officers and Members of the Legislature of the State of New York in 1862 and '63* (Albany, 1863), 186; death certificate for Richard J. Lalor, June 28, 1884, NYCMA; "Richard J. Lalor," *NYIA*, July 12, 1884, 5.

212 *Dick:* "Death of Richard J. Lalor," *BDE*, June 29, 1884, 1.

212 *John Irvine, born in County Fermanagh:* Accts. 6070, 9429, 20659, 35720, 38123, 49450, 51241, 53230, 55024, and 62268, ESB; FAM811, DW261, W6, NYC, 1850 USCen; FAM2044, DW417, DIST1, W1, NYC, 1860 USCen; FAM931, DW328, DIST6, W7, NYC, 1870 USCen; FAM59, DW14, ED85, NYC, 1880 USCen; FAM132, DW19, ED70, NYC, 1900 USCen; 1867 *NYCDir*, 514; 1869 *NYCDir*, 548; 1872 *NYCDir*, 592; 1876 *NYCDir*, 402; 1878 *NYCDir*, 709; 1885 *NYCDir*, 926; 1890 *NYCDir*, 623; 1891 *NYCDir*, 664; 1897 *NYCDir*, 632; death certificate for Margaret Irvine, Nov. 16, 1872, NYCMA; "Deaths," *NYH*, Apr. 8, 1889, 1; John J. Irvine, Nov. 28, 1900, New York City Death Index, 1892–1898, 1900–1902, Ancestry.com.

212 *"Arwin":* FAM5, DW108, DIST6, W6, NYC, 1855 NYCen.

213 *"pickle maker":* Acct. 9429, ESB.

214 *Peter J. Faye:* Acct. 17539, ESB; FAM1, DW1, Eastern DIV, W1, NYC, 1850 USCen; FAM10, DW5, DIST1, W2, NYC, 1855 NYCen; "A Member (20 Years) of the Stock Exchange," *NYH*, Dec. 15, 1880, 11; "Obituary Notes," *NYTrib*, May 30, 1884, 5; "Brokers at Peter Faye's Funeral," *NYT*, June 2, 1884, 2.

214 *"custodian of money":* "Old Peter Faye," *NYH*, May 30, 1884, 8.

215 *"natural-born statesman":* "Financial and Commercial," *New York World*, Nov. 19, 1870, 3.

215 *"stock-exchange deals":* "Old Peter Faye," 8.

215 *James Verdon:* Acct. 13352, ESB; FAM195, DW195, Warren, Somerset County, NJ, 1850 USCen; FAM347, DW347, Warren, Somerset County, NJ, 1860 USCen; FAM18, DW17, Warren, Somerset County, NJ, 1870 USCen.

216 *Michael Quigley:* Acct. 4611, ESB; FAM380, DW115, Eastern DIST, W1, NYC, 1850 USCen; FAM210, DW65, DIST1, W1, NYC, 1855 NYCen; FAM1287, DW267, DIST1, W1, NYC, 1860 USCen; FAM14, DW9, DIST1, W1, NYC, 1870 USCen; FAM146, DW57, ED40, W6, KingsC, 1880 USCen; 1856 *NYCDir*, 673; 1857 *NYCDir*, 675; 1860 *NYCDir*, 698; 1861 *NYCDir*, 694; 1865 *NYCDir*, 791; 1866 *NYCDir*,

821; 1870 *NYCDir*, 984; 1871 *NYCDir*, 932; 1872 *NYCDir*, 981; 1875 *NYCDir*, 1081; 1878 *NYCDir*, 1183; 1880 *NYCDir*, 1263; 1883 *NYCDir*, 1362; 1883 *BklynDir*, 1003; "Police Intelligence," *NYH*, Aug. 2, 1856, 1; "$10 Reward," *NYH*, Sept. 25, 1857, 2; "Police Intelligence," *NYH*, Jan. 29, 1858, 5; "Metropolitan Politics," *NYH*, Oct. 31, 1861, 12; "Vote for Members of Assembly," *NYH*, Nov. 6, 1861, 10; "Political Matters," *New York Sunday Dispatch*, Jan. 18, 1863, 5; "Died," *NYH*, Aug. 20, 1874, 9; "City Items," *New York World*, Nov. 3, 1875, 8.

216 *"of immense strength"*: "His Place at the Oar Vacant," *NYH*, Nov. 3, 1883, 5.

216 *"ever came to this port"*: "A Famous Battery Boatman Dead," *New York World*, Nov. 3, 1883, 4.

216 *"arm and fist"*: "His Place at the Oar Vacant," 5.

217 *"proper punishment"*: "A First Ward Rowdy," *NYT*, Apr. 15, 1877, 5.

218 *"cirrhosis of liver & kidneys"*: Death certificate for Michael Quigley, Oct. 31, 1883, NYCMA.

218 *Patrick Drury*: Accts. 14692, 20159, and 29515, ESB; FAM628, DW 595, New Utrecht, KingsC, 1860 USCen; FAM423, DW367, New Utrecht, KingsC, 1870 USCen; FAM534, DW473, ED262, New Utrecht, KingsC, 1880 USCen; p. 11, DIST2, New Utrecht, KingsC, 1892 NYCen; "A Very Foolish Constable," *BDE*, Feb. 5, 1889, 4; "Constable Drury's Mistake," *Brooklyn Times*, June 12, 1890, 1.

218 *James M. Brann*: Accts. 1329, 9957, 10398, and 36386, ESB; marriage of J. M. Brann and Sarah McEvoy, NJ Marriages, 1678–1985, Familysearch.org; FAM1021, DW695, W4, Jersey City, Hudson County, NJ, 1860 USCen; FAM194, DW133, ED18, Jersey City, Hudson County, NJ, 1880 USCen; FAM186, DW96, ED96, Jersey City, Hudson County, NJ, 1900 USCen; 1854 *Jersey City Dir*, 16; 1868 *Jersey City Dir*, 46; 1875 *Jersey City Dir*, 66; 1876 *Jersey City Dir*, 64; 1881 *Jersey City Dir*, 60; 1883 *Jersey City Dir*, 69; 1885 *Jersey City Dir*, 80; 1888 *Jersey City Dir*, 79; 1893 *Jersey City Dir*, 121; 1896 *Jersey City Dir*, 118; entries for James M. Brann, NY, vol. 351, p. 1237 and p. 1300 subpage A68, R. G. Dun & Co. credit report volumes, Baker Library, Harvard Business School; "Wholesale Libel Suits," *NYH*, Sept. 12, 1876, 5; "County Courts," *Jersey City Evening Journal*, Dec. 12, 1876, 4; "A Clergyman in an Awkward Position," *NYT*, Feb. 13, 1877, 2; "A Remarkable Trial," *NYH*, Feb. 13, 1877, 5; "Hudson County's Clerk," *NYH*, Jan. 26, 1878, 10; "A Defaulting County Clerk," *NYT*, Jan. 27, 1878, 2; "County Clerk Brann Returns," *NYH*, Mar. 27, 1878, 8; "Jim Brann's Record," *Sunday Tattler and Jersey City Express*, Sept. 5, 1886, 2; "Injured on the Trolley," *Jersey City News*, Sept. 14, 1895, 2; "Obituary Notes," *New York Sun*, Sept. 10, 1907, 2.

218 *"Western States...and Canada"*: "James M. Brann and His Slanderers," *Freehold (NJ) Monmouth Herald and Inquirer*, Feb. 13, 1862, 3.

219 *"than any other man"*: "A Final Effort in Jersey City," *NYH*, Aug. 5, 1875, 3.

219 *"most remarkable case"*: "Brann Justified," *NYH*, Feb. 15, 1877, 5.

219 *"a lunatic asylum"*: "A Defaulting County Clerk," *Paterson (NJ) Guardian*, Jan. 26, 1878, 2.

220 *James Buckley*: Acct. 14068, ESB; manifest of the *Devonshire*, Apr. 7, 1851, NYShips; FAM1, DW47, DIST1, W2, KingsC, 1855 NYCen; FAM229, DW76, W2, KingsC, 1865 NYCen; FAM2439, DW1258, W21, KingsC, 1870 USCen; 1857 *BklynDir*, 44 (Julia Buckley); "The City and County Government," *BDE*, May 8, 1860, 2; "Official County Canvass," *BDE*, Nov. 28, 1864, 1; "The Election Fraud Inquiry: Sixty Politicians Indicted," *BDE*, Dec. 18, 1869, 2; "The Election Indictments," *BDE*, Mar. 24, 1870, 14; "The Election Indictments," *BDE*, Mar. 31, 1870, 13; "Justice Buckley Indicted," *NYH*, Oct. 7, 1872, 5.

ENDNOTES

220 *"in the Democratic ranks"*: "The Lower Courts," *BDE*, Apr. 28, 1865, 2.

220 *"presence of the citizens"*: "The Election Indictments," *BDE*, Mar. 12, 1870, 3.

221 *"while upon the bench"*: "Brooklyn," *NYTrib*, Oct. 7, 1872, 8.

221 *"congestion of [the] brain"*: Death certificate for James Buckley, Oct. 9, 1872, NYCMA.

221 *Mary McCauley Buckley*: FAM105, DW46, DIST3, W21, KingsC, 1875 NYCen; FAM608, DW229, ED91, KingsC, 1880 USCen; p. 23, DIST7, W11, KingsC, 1892 NYCen; "Lively Cooks," *BDE*, June 6, 1885, 6; "Sheriff-Elect Walton Makes Appointments," *BDE*, Dec. 20, 1899, 20; death certificates for Julia Buckley Meade, June 22, 1902, and Mary E. Buckley, Feb. 4, 1907, NYCMA.

221 *cleaner*: Block H, ED2, AD10, KingsC, 1905 NYCen.

222 *average policeman saved more*: Tyler Anbinder, Cormac Ó Gráda, and Simone A. Wegge, "Networks and Opportunities: A Digital History of Ireland's Great Famine Refugees in New York," *American Historical Review* 124 (Dec. 2019): 1615.

223 *Felix Hayes from Kerry*: Accts. 10208, 18859, and 24206, ESB; FAM585, DW121, DIST2, W1, NYC, 1855 NYCen; FAM178, DW61, ED12, NYC, 1880 USCen; 1861 NYCDir, 375; *Report of the Police Department of the City of New York for the Year Ending December 31, 1886* (New York, 1887), 11; entry for Felix Hayes, Sept. 8, 1893, NYCDeaths.

223 *"stupidity,"*: "What Came of an Officer's Stupidity," *NYT*, July 19, 1879, 8.

223 *Patrick Crinnion*: Acct. 55842, ESB; p. 54, DW261, DIST16, W20, NYC, Enum2, 1870 USCen; FAM62, DW16, ED409, NYC, 1880 USCen; 1867 *NYCDir*, 230; 1871 *NYCDir*, 246; 1898 *NYCDir*, 274; "Twenty-Ninth Precinct," *City Record* (Jan. 31, 1879): 156; *Report of the Police Department of the City of New York for the Year Ending December 31, 1899* (New York, 1900), 113; death certificate for Patrick Crinnion, Dec. 30, 1907, NYCMA.

223 *"good machinist"*: "They All Know Crinnion," *NYH*, May 12, 1895, 14.

223 *"Paddy the Horse"*: "Obituary," *New York Sun*, Dec. 31, 1907, 3.

224 *John Mara*: Acct. 8718, ESB; FAM1498, DW798, W6, KingsC, 1870 USCen; FAM152, DW89, ED17, KingsC, 1880 USCen; FAM246, DW200, ED436, KingsC, 1900 USCen; entries for John Mara, U.S. Army Register of Enlistments, Ancestry.com; "Real Estate Transfers," *BDE*, Apr. 5, 1890, 2; "Seven New Captains for This Borough," *Brooklyn Citizen*, Dec. 28, 1900, 2; "Two Brooklyn Police Captains Ask to Retire," *Brooklyn Times*, Jan. 17, 1903, 4; death certificate for John Mara, Sept. 10, 1908, NYCMA; "Obituary," *Brooklyn Citizen*, Sept. 12, 1908, 4.

224 *"close-mouthed fellow"*: "The Observer's Grab Bag," *Brooklyn Times*, Dec. 13, 1900, 8.

226 *name was Hubert D. Glynn*: Accts. 1936, 5232, and 7754, ESB; FAM1995, DW789, DIST2, W22, NYC, 1860 USCen; FAM242, DW73, DIST6, W22, NYC, 1870 USCen; FAM404, DW334, DIST2, New Lots, KingsC, 1875 NYCen; FAM215, DW174, ED260, New Lots, KingsC, 1880 USCen; "Marriages and Deaths," *NYH*, May 21, 1867, 9; "His First Vacation," *New York World*, Oct. 20, 1885, 8; "City and Suburban News," *NYT*, Oct. 26, 1885, 8; will of Hubert D. Glynn, NY Wills and Probate Records, 1659–1999, Ancestry.com.

226 *"for the Catholic priesthood"*: "Hubert D. Glynn," *NYIA*, Dec. 10, 1894, 4.

226 *"special Irish supervisor"*: Ibid.

227 *"Emigrant Landing Depot"*: "Special Notices," *NYT*, Aug. 3, 1855, 5.

228 *"opened its gates"*: "Hubert D. Glynn," 4.

228 *"genial"*: Ibid.

228 *"his kind deeds"*: "Heir to a Fortune," *New York Daily Graphic*, Sept. 14, 1887, 598.

Chapter 7: "Getting On Very Well"

230 *accomplishments of Andrew Kerwin:* Accts. 691, 2851, 8910, 8959, 9369, 15048, 15134, 15858, 16130, 16131, 16137, 19580, and 26813, ESB; FAM6, DW83, DIST2, W21, NYC, 1855 NYCen; FAM466, DW261, DIST10, W19, NYC, 1870 USCen; FAM532, DW124, ED565, NYC, 1880 USCen; FAM331, DW270, ED483, NYC, 1900 USCen; 1848 *NYCDir*, 230 (John Kerwin); "City and Suburban News," *NYT*, July 20, 1878, 8.

231 *"master mason":* FAM635, DW168, DIST4, W21, NYC, 1860 USCen.

231 *"made considerable money":* Entry for Andrew Kerwin, NY, vol. 381, subpage A276, p. 200, R. G. Dun & Co. credit report volumes, Baker Library, Harvard Business School.

232 *"small house in the city":* Christopher Gray, "East of Sutton Place, a Little Known Enclave," *NYT*, Feb. 18, 1996, sect. 9, 7.

236 *Bernard Mulgrew:* Acct. 16053, ESB; 1854 *NYCDir*, 538; 1856 *NYCDir*, 598; 1860 *NYCDir*, 621; 1862 *NYCDir*, 630; 1864 *NYCDir*, 637; "Died," *NYH*, Mar. 22, 1876, 9.

236 *Robert Yates:* Accts. 7904, 13338, 14527, and 27763, ESB; FAM689, DW465, DIST2, W4, KingsC, 1860 USCen; FAM12, DW8, ED25, KingsC, 1880 USCen; FAM47, DW41, ED313, KingsC, 1900 USCen.

236 *Edmund Butler from tiny Rathnagard:* Accts. 11842, 16104, 65666, and 65667, ESB; FAM322, DW85, DIST1, W1, NYC, 1855 NYCen; FAM47, DW15, DIST2, W1, NYC, 1860 USCen; FAM492, DW138, W1, KingsC, 1870 USCen; "Death of Edmund Butler," *BDE*, Feb. 23, 1894, 4.

236 *"stevedoring firms":* "Candidates," *BDE*, Oct. 30, 1882, 4.

236 *"over a hundred men":* "Michael E. Butler," *BDE*, Oct. 30, 1882, 4.

237 *Thomas Meagher:* Accts. 15959 and 121119, ESB; manifest of the *Aberdeen*, Nov. 25, 1850, NYShips; FAM1190, DW245, DIV1, W1, NYC, 1860 USCen; p. 17, DIST7, W1, NYC, Enum2, 1870 USCen; FAM279, DW32, ED3, NYC, 1880 USCen; 1856 *NYCDir*, 564; 1860 *NYCDir*, 585; 1861 *NYCDir*, 582; 1863 *NYCDir*, 589; 1865 *NYC-Dir*, 601; 1866 *NYCDir*, 688; 1870 *NYCDir*, 822; 1876 *NYCDir*, 929; "Died," *NYH*, Nov. 4, 1869, 8.

237 *"agent":* 1864 *NYCDir*, 601.

238 *"softening of the brain":* Death certificate for Thomas Magee [sic], Mar. 31, 1882, NYCMA.

238 *Lawrence J. Callanan:* Acct. 16506, ESB; FAM218, DW53, DIST1, W1, NY, 1860 USCen; FAM20, DW8, DIST1, W3, NY, 1870 USCen; FAM146, DW117, ED174, NYC, 1880 USCen; FAM201, DW119, ED825, NYC, 1910 USCen; 1857 *BklynDir*, 51; 1859 *NYCDir*, 135; "Transfer of Real Estate—New York," *New York World*, June 26, 1875, 3; "Died," *NYH*, May 11, 1873, 7 (John Callanan); "Died," May 28, 1873, 4 (Elizabeth Callanan); "Died," June 3, 1873, 8 (Peter Callanan); "To Let—New House," *NYH*, Dec. 11, 1887, 2; "Blocking the Sidewalks," *NYIA*, Feb. 15, 1890, 2; "Save Battery Park," *NYIA*, May 2, 1891, 4; "Looking for a Candidate," *NYH*, Sept. 26, 1894, 6; "Appraisals of Estates," *NYTrib*, Oct. 22, 1914, 9.

238 *"under strict discipline and no favors":* New York State's Prominent and Progressive Men, ed. Mitchell C. Harrison, 3 vols. (New York, 1902), 3:54.

239 *"a fortune":* "Obituary," *Simmons' Spice Mill*, Nov. 1913, 1072.

240 *"most prominent":* "Catholic Liquor Dealers," *NYTrib*, July 20, 1894, 4.

241 *"park was saved":* "L. J. Callanan Dead," *NYT*, Oct. 18, 1913, 13.

241 *William Cruise and his wife, Julia:* DW131, ED1ii, St. Martin, Liverpool, Lancashire, England, 1851 UK Census, Ancestry.com; FAM55, DW12, DIST2, W5, NYC, 1855

NYCen; FAM201, DW55, W1, KingsC, 1870 USCen; FAM155, DW118, DIST1, W5, KingsC, 1875 NYCen; 1858 *NYCDir*, 188; 1860 *NYCDir*, 197; 1867 *BklynDir*, 134; 1868 *BklynDir*, 135; 1874 *BklynDir*, 174; 1879 *BklynDir*, 214; death certificates for Julia Cruise, Oct. 16, 1878, and William Cruise, May 22, 1880, NYCMA.

242 *"We'll hang him"*: Adrian Cook, *The Armies of the Streets: The New York City Draft Riots of 1863* (Lexington, KY, 1974), 135.

242 *"save my boy"*: Ibid., 136.

243 *Patrick Fitzpatrick:* Accts. 6010 and 45971, ESB; FAM114, DW22, ED487, NYC, 1880 USCen.

243 *Blacksmith Patrick McCusker:* Accts. 6189, 14377, and 69812, ESB; FAM659, DW252, DIST14, W19, NYC, 1870 USCen.

243 *Andrew Maloney:* Accts. 16987, 21520, 21975, and 28347, ESB; FAM700, DW364, DIST4, W7, NYC, 1860 USCen.

243 *William Doherty became the owner:* Acct. 2561, ESB; manifest of the *Probus*, Nov. 7, 1848, NYShips; FAM303, DW113, DIST6, W20, NYC, 1855 NYCen; FAM1134, DW677, DIST3, W21, NYC, 1860 USCen; FAM185, DW166, Westchester, Westchester County, NY, 1870 USCen; FAM241, DW223, ED127, Westchester County, NY, 1880 USCen; advertisement for William Doherty's business, *Curtin's Westchester County Directory for 1871–1872* (New York, 1871), 15; entry for William H. Doherty, Feb. 18, 1900, New York City Extracted Death Index, 1862–1948, Ancestry.com; William S. Pelletreau, *Historic Homes and Institutions and Genealogical and Family History of New York*, 4 vols. (New York, 1907), 4:165–66.

244 *James Slattery:* For the careers of the immigrants in this paragraph (other than McGreevy), see ESB Depositor Database.

244 *James McGreevy:* FAM46, DW18, DIST2, W6, KingsC, 1855 NYCen; FAM161, DW84, DIST3, W6, KingsC, 1860 USCen; FAM1373, DW814, W6, KingsC, 1870 USCen.

244 *Michael Murray:* For the careers of the immigrants in this paragraph, see ESB Depositor Database.

244 *Michael Doyne:* Accts. 4707, 7891, 27728, and 35636, ESB; FAM6, DW2, W17, KingsC, 1850 USCen; FAM1316, DW1206, Morrisania, Westchester County, NY, 1860 USCen; FAM614, DW533, Morrisania, Westchester County, NY, 1870 USCen; will of Michael Doyne, Jan. 6, 1872, NY Wills and Probate Records, 1659–1999, Ancestry.com; "Died," *NYH*, July 19, 1873, 2.

245 *John Sidley:* For the careers of the immigrants in this paragraph (other than Farrell), see ESB Mobility Database.

245 *Farrell is the rare:* Acct. 3819, ESB; manifest of the *Isaac Wright*, July 1, 1850, NYShips; FAM439, DW233, W5, KingsC, 1850 USCen; FAM1607, DW937, DIST2, W10, KingsC, 1860 USCen; FAM151, DW82, W10, KingsC, 1870 USCen; FAM67, DW20, ED78, KingsC, 1880 USCen; 1863 *BklynDir*, 146; 1864 *BklynDir*, 133; "Lucy Farrell," *Brooklyn Standard Union*, Dec. 1, 1906, 12.

246 *"highly respected"*: "Peter Farrell Laid at Rest," *Brooklyn Citizen*, Feb. 17, 1894, 2.

246 *Thomas, Peter, and Patrick Muldoon:* Accts. 6893, 9918, 11756, 11775, 15385, 22839, 39106, and 40978, ESB; manifest of the *City of Washington*, Nov. 22, 1852, NYShips; FAM489, DW245, DIST4, W9, and FAM233, DW67, DIST1, W9, and FAM126, DW46, DIST89, W9, all NYC, 1855 NYCen; FAM126, DW46, DIST89, W9, NYC, 1855 NYCen; 1856 *NYCDir*, 598; 1857 *NYCDir*, 600; 1859 *NYCDir*, 617; entries for Peter Muldoon, May 21, 1868, Thomas Muldoon, Feb. 26, 1873, and Alice Muldoon, Apr. 15, 1880, NYCDeaths; entry for Patrick Muldoon, May 10, 1903, New York State Death Index, 1880–1956, Familysearch.org.

ENDNOTES

246 *brother Peter McLoughlin:* 1834 *NYCDir,* 461; 1837 *NYCDir,* 410; 1841 *NYCDir,* 468; 1845 *NYCDir,* 236; "Death of Peter McLoughlin," *New-York Freeman's Journal,* Feb. 11, 1854, 5; "Sale of the Estate of Peter McLoughlin," *NYT,* Feb. 28, 1864, 8.

246 *"best country in the World":* Peter McLoughlin to his "Dear Brother Patt," Sept. 1, 1829, copy held by Paul McLoughlin, Boulder, CO. Extracts from the letter, with some variations from the original, can be found in Peter P. McLoughlin, *Father Tom: Life and Lectures of Rev. Thomas P. McLoughlin* (New York, 1919), 10.

247 *"good bank A/C":* Entry for Thomas Muldoon, NY, vol. 264A, p. 103, R. G. Dun & Co. credit report volumes, Baker Library, Harvard Business School.

247 *"habits are not the best":* Ibid., p. 102.

247 *"failed":* Ibid., vol. 293, p. 3046.

247 *cousin John McLoughlin:* Accts. 9918 and 13670, ESB; manifest of the *Margaret,* Apr. 25, 1849, NYShips; FAM655, DW538, W22, KingsC, 1870 USCen; FAM14, DW9, ED230, KingsC, 1880 USCen; 1861 *NYCDir,* 551; "John McLoughlin," *NYH,* Nov. 30, 1890, 15.

248 *Constantine Duffy:* Accts. 420 and 5695, ESB; manifest of the *Waterloo,* Apr. 6, 1848, NYShips; FAM51, DW14, DIST9, W11, NYC, 1855 NYCen; FAM332, DW271, DIST15, W12, NYC, 1870 USCen; 1850 *NYCDir,* 154; 1862 *NYCDir,* 247–48; 1864 *NYCDir,* 251–52; 1869 *NYCDir,* 308; "Died," *NYH,* Sept. 28, 1873, 7; "Obituary Notes," *NYH,* Feb. 16, 1882, 3; "The Duffy Will Case," *New York Sun,* Jan. 15, 1890, 8.

248 *Eugene McSwyny:* Accts. 1823, 1824, 4023, 15548, 15549, 15555, and 17355, ESB; FAM78, DW29, DIST4, W7, NYC, 1860 USCen; FAM230, DW155, DIST5, W19, NYC, 1870 USCen; 1852 *NYCDir,* 403; 1860 *NYCDir,* 559; 1862 *NYCDir,* 567; 1870 *NYCDir,* 785; 1871 *NYCDir,* 744; "A Fatal Fall," *New York Evening Express,* Jan. 10, 1872, 4; entry for Eugene McSwyny, NY, vol. 212, p. 349, R. G. Dun & Co. credit report volumes, Baker Library, Harvard Business School.

248 *"master draper":* Manifest of the *James Wright,* Aug. 16, 1850, NYShips.

249 *"McSwyny & Co., Drygoods":* 1851 *NYCDir,* 353.

249 *"not much acquainted":* Entry for Eugene McSwyny, vol. 146, p. 81, R. G. Dun & Co. credit report volumes.

249 *"responsible nor reliable":* Ibid., vol. 217, p. 828.

249 *"severest snow-storm":* "Winter in Earnest," *NYTrib,* Dec. 27, 1872, 1.

250 *"undamaged condition":* Common Council advertisement, *NYIA,* Apr. 14, 1855, 3.

251 *Bernard Sheridan:* Accts. 9822, 11489, 11778, 30501, and 35415, ESB; DW8, DIST6, W6, NYC, 1855 NYCen; FAM422, DW66, DIST4, W6, NYC, 1860 USCen; FAM292, DW39, DIST11, W6, NYC, 1870 USCen; 1854 *NYCDir,* 754; 1875 *NYCDir,* 1221.

251 *"Lanty" Ryan:* Accts. 13788, 15891, 52625, 53733, and 81506, ESB; FAM728, DW141, DIST4, W6, NYC, 1860 USCen; FAM71, DW25, DIST8, W7, NYC, 1870 USCen; FAM108, DW74, ED1614, Bronx County, NY, 1910 USCen; FAM503, DW57, ED3-628, Bronx County, NY, 1930 USCen; 1858 *NYCDir,* 695; "Deaths," *NYT,* Mar. 24, 1933, 17.

251 *"dealer in paper":* FAM153, DW40, ED91, NYC, 1880 USCen.

251 *Daniel and Susan Bradley:* Accts. 5409, 7526, and 18187, ESB; FAM537, DW166, DIST3, W14, NYC, 1855 NYCen; FAM940, DW258, DIST3, W14, NYC, 1860 USCen; FAM96, DW25, ED80, NYC, 1880 USCen; 1868 *NYCDir,* 120; "Obituary Notes," *NYT,* May 22, 1912, 13.

253 *"famous Seventh ward":* "Daniel Bradley Is Dead," *New York Sun,* May 21, 1912, 9.

253 *Francis McMahon:* Acct. 789, ESB; FAM137, DW15, DIST1, W18, NYC, 1860 USCen; 1851 *NYCDir,* 350; 1852 *NYCDir,* 400; 1854 *NYCDir,* 462; 1860 *NYCDir,* 555; 1864 *NYCDir,* 570.

253 *Tim Slattery:* Acct. 15430, ESB; FAM822, DW553, DIST2, W9, KingsC, 1860 USCen; FAM569, DW507, Flatbush, KingsC, 1870 USCen.

253 *John Dennison:* Acct. 17601, ESB; FAM1098, DW461, DIST2, W11, KingsC, 1855 NYCen; FAM659, DW347, DIST2, W11, KingsC, 1860 USCen; FAM36, DW12, W11, KingsC, 1865 NYCen; FAM878, DW581, W9, KingsC, 1870 USCen.

254 *James Boyce:* Accts. 15140, 15141, and 32430, ESB; FAM428, DW69, DIST4, W6, NYC, 1860 USCen; FAM234, DW20, ED45, NYC, 1880 USCen; "A Juvenile Thief," *New York Sun,* Aug. 22, 1865, 4; entry for James Boyce, Feb. 23, 1881, NYCDeaths.

254 *Jeremiah and Honora Perry:* Accts. 2038, 7715, and 7961, ESB; FAM480, New Hudson, Allegany County, NY, and FAM1314, DW277, DIV1, W1, NYC, 1860 USCen; 1853 *NYCDir,* 546; 1854 *NYCDir,* 558; 1855 *NYCDir,* 655.

255 *Philip McQuade:* Acct. 2986, ESB; manifest of the *Jane H. Glidden,* Jan. 18, 1848, NYShips; FAM317, DW74, W4, 1850 USCen; FAM780, DW125, DIST5, W6, NYC, 1855 NYCen; FAM106, DW16, DIST3, W6, NYC, 1860 USCen; 1854 *NYCDir,* 465; 1864 *NYCDir,* 575; 1867 *NYCDir,* 672; 1868 *NYCDir,* 707; "Died," *NYH,* July 27, 1868, 7.

255 *Ann Giltenan Delany:* Accts. 5048 and 8315, ESB; FAM1201, DW372, DIST1, W20, NYC, 1855 NYCen; FAM1631, DW487, DIST3, W20, NYC, 1860 USCen; p. 48, DW245, DIST16, W20, NYC, Enum2, 1870 USCen.

255 *Kate Sullivan:* Accts. 6524 and 10876 (Mary), ESB; FAM859, DW135, DIST5, W6, NYC, 1855 NYCen; FAM1136, DW227, DIST2, W6, NYC, 1860 USCen; FAM522, DW77, ED41, NYC, 1880 USCen; "Information Wanted—Of Mary Shay," *NYH,* Mar. 19, 1855, 7; "Backgrounds of Civilization," *New York Illustrated News,* Feb. 18, 1860, 216; 1862 *NYCDir,* 846 (Alex); 1863 *NYCDir,* 840; entry for Alex Sullivan, July 23, 1862, NYCDeaths.

257 *"two or three deep":* "Abodes of the Poor," *NYT,* July 1, 1859, 2.

257 *"place was quite sweet":* Samuel B. Halliday, *The Lost and Found: Or, Life Among the Poor* (New York, 1860), 207.

257 *Jeremiah Tannian:* Accts. 1951 and 3604, ESB; FAM530, DW63, ED29, NYC, 1880 USCen; 1878 *NYCDir,* 1392; entry for Jeremiah Tannahan, Dec. 9, 1883, NYCDeaths.

258 *"health failing":* Jeremiah Tannahan, Apr. 18, 1883, New York Census of Inmates in Almshouses and Poorhouses, 1830–1920, Ancestry.com.

258 *Henry McAleenan:* Accts. 7446 and 19359, ESB; FAM919, DW217, DIST2, W6, NYC, 1860 USCen; p. 54, DIST14, W16, NYC, Enum2, 1870 USCen; FAM233, DW211, ED578, NYC, 1880 USCen; FAM18, DW13, ED776, NYC, 1900 USCen; 1858 *NYCDir,* 510, 1862 *NYCDir,* 524; 1872 *NYCDir,* 703; 1881 *NYCDir,* 953; 1891 *NYCDir,* 775.

258 *"keen at a bargain":* Entry for Henry McAleenan, NY, vol. 323, subpage A210, p. 900, R. G. Dun & Co. credit report volumes, Baker Library, Harvard Business School.

258 *"practically a wilderness":* "Pawnbroker Gave $2,000,000 to his Family of Six," *NYH,* Dec. 2, 1913, 8.

259 *Francis, Patrick, and John Morgan:* Accts. 17465, 17635, 24835, and 25718 (Francis), ESB; FAM1706, DW395, W11, NYC, 1850 USCen; FAM210, DW37, DIST2, W4, NYC, 1855 NYCen; FAM56, DW21, DIST4, W20, and FAM138, DW79, DIST4, W20, and FAM2, DW1, DIST6, W20, all NYC, 1860 USCen; FAM168, DW130, DIST10, AD15, W20, and FAM349, DW177, DIST21, W20, and FAM476, DW208, DIST1, W22, all NYC, 1870 USCen; FAM286, DW48, ED469, NYC, 1880 USCen; 1853 *NYCDir,* 496 (Francis); 1856 *NYCDir,* 590–91; 1864 *NYCDir,* 629; 1876

NYCDir, 975–76; 1889 NYCDir, 1413; "Obituary Notes," NYT, Mar. 6, 1901, 9; "Alfred Morgan, 81: Businessman Bought White Rock in 50's," NYT, Feb. 27, 1988, 12.

259 "rootbrewer": 1854 NYCDir, 508.

259 "gingerpop": Ibid., 507.

259 "sarsaparilla": 1860 NYCDir, 612.

259 "waters": 1873 NYCDir, 926.

260 "cash business, both ways": Entry for Morgan & Brother, NY, vol. 276, p. 1338, R. G. Dun & Co. credit report volumes, Baker Library, Harvard Business School.

260 "wealthy": Ibid.

260 "liked and respected": "Obituary," American Bottler 35, no. 5 (May 15, 1915): 42.

261 John and Maria Regan: Accts. 7093, 9653, 15052, 24120, 42271, 49271, and 52288, ESB; FAM565, DW278, W1, Hoboken, Hudson County, NJ, 1860 USCen; FAM43, DW11, DIST3, W1, NYC, 1870 USCen; FAM554, DW224, ED45, Hoboken, Hudson County, NJ, 1880 USCen; 1861 Jersey City and Hoboken Dir, 252; 1867 NYCDir, 850; 1874 Jersey City and Hoboken Dir, 563; 1880 Jersey City and Hoboken Dir, 296; "Died," NYH, Nov. 25, 1880, 9.

262 "boy to open oysters": "WANTED — A boy," NYH, July 19, 1867, 3.

262 "smart boy": "WANTED — A smart boy," NYH, Aug. 18, 1879, 7.

262 discriminatory laws: Norma Basch, In the Eyes of the Law: Women, Marriage, and Property in Nineteenth-Century New York (Ithaca, NY, 1982), 42–223.

263 Joanna Condon Boyle: Accts. 13294, 14916, 17276, 20066, 22350, 27051, and 29193, ESB; FAM951, DW339, DIST6, W16, NYC, 1855 NYCen; FAM1767, DW650, DIST2, W16, NYC, 1860 USCen; FAM625, DW276, DIST1, W16, NYC, 1870 USCen; 1872 NYCDir, 126; will of Terence Boyle, Feb. 18, 1862, and "Inventory and Appraisement of the Personal Estate of Terence Boyle," filed Sept. 5, 1863, both in NY Wills and Probate Records, 1659–1999, Ancestry.com.

263 "Mrs. Boyle's Millinery": "Surrogate's Court," New York Transcript, Dec. 22, 1864, 2.

264 "Boyle's Millinery": Ibid.

265 Orphan Annie: FAM111, DW97, ED340, NYC, 1880 USCen; FAM181, DW133, ED689, Queens County, NY, 1900 USCen; sheet 12B, ED1144, NYC, 1910 USCen; "Augustine Healy," Brooklyn Standard Union, Apr. 17, 1903, 2; death certificate for Anna Loretta Healy, Oct. 20, 1919, NYCMA.

267 Occupational Mobility of Male Famine Immigrant Business Owners: ESB Mobility Database.

268 "best country in the World": Peter McLoughlin to his "Dear Brother Patt," Sept. 1, 1829.

Chapter 8: "Few Men Better Known"

269 John Lane survived: Accts. 11910, 28565, 32716, 43678, and 61817, ESB; FAM81, DW23, DIST10, W16, NYC, 1870 USCen; FAM408, DW73, ED328 (Lanes), and FAM40, DW14, ED247 (Feeneys), NYC, 1880 USCen; 1855 NYCDir, 479; 1857 NYCDir, 473; 1858 NYCDir, 458; 1860 NYCDir, 489; 1864 NYCDir, 503; 1869 NYCDir, 630; 1876 NYCDir, 775; 1890 NYCDir, 717; entry for Daniel Lane, Dec. 4, 1895, NYCDeaths; "Knife, Pistol and Slungshot," NYH, Dec. 4, 1880, 9; "Bravos in Court," New York Sun, Dec. 23, 1880, 3; "Fell upon Him with a Club," NYH, Mar. 30, 1891, 10; "Wants His Son Sent to Prison," New York World, June 17, 1893, 5; "Fought by the Deathbed," New York Sun, June 4, 1894, 3; "Both the Lane Boys at the Funeral," New York World, June 6, 1894, 1; entries for Michael Lane, Dec. 23,

1880, Oct. 29, 1884, and Apr. 4, 1891, Sing Sing Prison Admission Registers, 1865–1939, Ancestry.com.

271 *"scapegrace of the family":* "Fought by Death Beds," *New York Press,* June 4, 1894, 5.

271 *"score of neighbors":* Ibid.

272 *"struggled out into the hall":* Ibid.

273 *Francis Lawler:* For the careers of the immigrants in this paragraph, see ESB Depositor Database.

273 *John Green:* Ibid.

273 *Michael Murphy:* Acct. 15807, ESB; manifest of the *Albert Gallatin,* Sept. 19, 1855, NYShips; 1856 *NYCDir,* 604; 1858 *NYCDir,* 587; 1865 *NYCDir,* 710; "Funeral of a Prominent Politician," *New York World,* Dec. 25, 1883, 8.

274 *Patrick Reynolds:* Acct. 1760, ESB; manifest of the *Waterloo,* Aug. 10, 1849, NYShips; FAM90, DW29, W6, NYC, 1850 USCen; FAM474, DW122, DIST4, W6, NYC, 1855 NYCen; FAM729, DW174, DIST3, W6, NYC, 1860 USCen; FAM49, DW18, DIST7, W6, NYC, 1870 USCen; "Trial for Murder," *NYTrib,* Nov. 16, 1852, 3; "Deaths," *New York Sun,* June 6, 1866, 2.

274 *Michael J. Higgins:* Accts. 2177, 3686, 6150, 7855, 8830, 10167, 22520, and 22521, ESB; FAM1892, DW562, W4, NYC, 1850 USCen; FAM1, DW1, DIST2, W4, NYC, 1855 NYCen; "Died," *NYTrib,* Jan. 4, 1861, 3.

275 *"one first-rate oysterman":* "Wanted—At Higgins' Saloon," *New York Sun,* Mar. 21, 1857, 3.

275 *James and Margaret Meehan:* Accts. 5166, 7714, 11309, 13776, 14243, 14770, and 17474, ESB; FAM303, DW72, W6, NYC, 1850 USCen; FAM143, DW29, DIV2, DIST3, W6, NYC, 1855 NYCen; 1850 *NYCDir,* 344; 1856 *NYCDir,* 565; entry for James Meehan, May 6, 1857, NYCDeaths.

275 *Thomas Fenton:* Accts. 8502, 12661, 44393, and 69023, ESB; FAM1485, DW1002, DIST3, W12, NYC, 1860 USCen; FAM100, DW71, DIST18, W12, NYC, 1870 USCen; FAM216, DW147, ED533, NYC, 1880 USCen; "Died," *New York Sun,* Apr. 27, 1897, 7; marriage certificate for Thomas Fenton and Ellen E. Murphy, Oct. 13, 1898, NYCMA; entry for Thomas Fenton, Sept. 26, 1899, NYCDeaths; will of Thomas Fenton, Aug. 26, 1897, NY Wills and Probate Records, 1659–1999, Ancestry.com; "Safe's Contents Not for Widow," *NYTrib,* July 14, 1901, 7.

276 *Thomas Murphy:* Accts. 3092, 3706, 8402, and 12256, ESB; FAM375, DW65, DIST5, W6, NYC, 1855 NYCen; FAM1584, DW316, DIST2, W6, NYC, 1860 USCen; 1860 *NYCDir,* 629.

277 *James and Patrick Simmons:* Acct. 6644, ESB; FAM482, DW127, DIST4, W16, NYC, 1860 USCen; FAM355, DIST2, W2, KingsC, 1875 NYCen; FAM258, DW124, ED11, KingsC, 1880 USCen; 1860 *NYCDir,* 788; 1866 *BklynDir,* 517; 1867 *BklynDir,* 564; 1868 *BklynDir,* 573; "Loss of Time," *Brooklyn Union-Argus,* Dec. 15, 1881, 4; "Died," *BDE,* Mar. 19, 1885, 3.

278 *saloonkeeper's political clout:* J. Frank Kernan, *Reminiscences of the Old Fire Laddies* (New York, 1885), 47–54; William M. Ivins, *Machine Politics and Money in Elections in New York City* (New York, 1887), 7–27; Charles Stelzle, *A Son of the Bowery: The Life Story of an East Side American* (New York, 1926), 47–48; Matthew Breen, *Thirty Years of New York Politics Up-To-Date* (New York, 1899), 249–52, 255–57.

279 *private welfare system:* John W. Pratt, "Boss Tweed's Public Welfare Program," *New-York Historical Society Quarterly* 45 (1961): 396–411.

279 *James McGillin:* Accts. 21540 and 56679, ESB; FAM499, DW15, DIST4, W13, NYC, 1855 NYCen; FAM1709, DW454, DIST2, W13, NYC, 1860 USCen; FAM127, DW65, ED11, KingsC, 1880 USCen; 1864 *BklynDir,* 275.

279 *"Knights of the Round Table"*: "Death of James McGillin," *BDE*, Oct. 2, 1889, 6.

279 *"Murty" O'Sullivan*: Accts. 16840 and 30116, ESB; FAM685, DW140, DIST2, W6, NYC, 1860 USCen; 1860 *NYCDir*, 662; 1862 *NYCDir*, 847; 1864 *NYCDir*, 858; 1865 *NYCDir*, 947; "Daniel O'Sullivan," *NYIA*, Dec. 31, 1859, 2; "Deaths," *New York Sun*, Aug. 1, 1864, 2; "Death of Captain Mortimer O'Sullivan," *New York World*, Aug. 2, 1864, 8.

280 *"large four horse"*: "The Kenmare Hurlers," *NYIA*, Mar. 26, 1859, 2.

282 *the O'Connor brothers*: Accts. 1703, 4348, 4491, 4553, 6560, 7561, 33991, and 54179, ESB; manifest of the *Abby Pratt*, Apr. 2, 1849, Passenger Lists of Vessels Arriving at New Orleans, 1820–1902, Ancestry.com; FAM750, DW241, Western DIST, W1, NYC, 1850 USCen; FAM777, DW146, DIST2, W1, NYC, 1855 NYCen; FAM300 ("Connor"), DW80, DIST1, W1, NYC, 1855 NYCen; FAM2139, DW433, DIST1, W1, NYC, 1860 USCen; FAM441, DW86, DIST1, W1, and FAM563, DW93, DIST1, W1, NYC, 1870 USCen; FAM155, DW25, ED4, and FAM216, DW42, ED4, NYC, 1880 USCen; 1859 *NYCDir*, 647 (David); Entry for Daniel O'Connor, NY, vol. 276, p. 1337, R. G. Dun & Co. credit report volumes, Baker Library, Harvard Business School; "Died" (Julia), *NYH*, Feb. 22, 1861, 8; entry for Margaret O'Connor, 10 Washington Street, "Metropolitan Board of Health," *BDE*, Aug. 15, 1867, 3; "Died" (Elizabeth), *NYH*, Jan. 7, 1873, 9; "First Ward Desperadoes," *NYH*, June 23, 1876, 5; "They Lead No Gang," *NYH*, June 25, 1876, 4; death certificate for Elizabeth O'Connor, Jan. 5, 1873, NYCMA; entry for Daniel David O'Connor, May 7, 1891, NYCDeaths.

282 *"Kerry Block"*: "Factious First Warders," *NYH*, June 24, 1876, 3.

283 *"held full sway"*: Ibid.

283 *"fight soon began"*: Ibid.

284 *But Walter Roche*: Acct. 8355, ESB; manifest of the *New World*, May 25, 1848, NYShips; FAM1468, DW362, W6, 1850 USCen; FAM538, DW234, DIST2, W6, NYC, 1855 NYCen; FAM1037, DW202, DIST4, W6, NYC, 1860 USCen; FAM72, DW56, ED672, NYC, 1880 USCen; 1853 *NYCDir*, 589; 1854 *NYCDir*, 601; 1856 *NYCDir*, 701; 1890 *NYCDir*, 1050; "The Walter Roche Guard," *NYIA*, Dec. 2, 1854, 3; "Died," *NYH*, Dec. 14, 1904, 1.

284 *"concert-saloon"*: "Yesterday," *NYTrib*, Dec. 18, 1869, 6.

285 *full-scale riot ensued*: Tyler Anbinder, *Five Points: The 19th-Century New York Neighborhood That Invented Tap Dance, Stole Elections, and Became the World's Most Notorious Slum* (New York, 2001), 278–92.

286 *founded savings banks*: "The Guardian Savings Bank" and "Tweed's Banks," *NYT*, Nov. 18, 1871, 4–5; "The Ring Savings Banks," *NYT*, Nov. 19, 1871, 4; "Recalling the Ring Frauds," *NYTrib*, Nov. 22, 1877, 8; Jeffrey D. Broxmeyer, "Political Capitalism in the Gilded Age: The Tammany Bank Run of 1871," *Journal of the Gilded Age and Progressive Era* 16 (2017): 44–64.

287 *"nod and wink"*: "A Review of the Tammany Candidates," *NYTrib*, Oct. 30, 1869, 5.

288 *wisely held*: "To Sell Doherty Land," *NYTrib*, Mar. 6, 1907, 1.

288 *"Lakes of Killarney"*: "Supervisor Roche," *NYH*, June 23, 1870, 3.

289 *none to be seized*: "The Secret Accounts: Proofs of Undoubted Frauds Brought to Light," *NYT*, July 22, 1871, 1; "The Secret Accounts: Second Series," *NYT*, July 24, 1871, 1; "The Secret Accounts: Third Series," *NYT*, July 26, 1871, 1; "Arrest of Walter Roche," *NYTrib*, Feb. 14, 1872, 8; "Walter Roche to Be Arrested Again," *NYTrib*, Feb. 24, 1872, 8; "Walter Roche Bailed," *NYTrib*, Feb. 27, 1872, 1; "Walter Roche: History of His Swindles," *NYT*, Mar. 11, 1872, 8; "The Courts…Walter Roche Arraigned," *NYH*, Feb. 19, 1874, 9; "The Bowling Green Savings Bank," *NYT*, Feb.

26, 1874, 2; "A Heavy Verdict Against Walter Roche," *NYTrib,* June 18, 1874, 2; "Depositors' Grief," *New York World,* Sept. 28, 1883, 4.

290 *"their naked persons":* Timothy J. Gilfoyle, *City of Eros: New York City, Prostitution, and the Commercialization of Sex, 1790–1920* (New York, 1992), 49–50.

290 *Mark and Mary Ann Driscoll:* Accts. 5546, 6621, 6965, 9023, 11428, 17591, 18432, and 19592, ESB; FAM244, DW55, DIST6, W14, NYC, 1855 NYCen; FAM530, DW140, DIST2, W4, NYC, 1860 USCen; 1860 *NYCDir,* 244; 1863 *NYCDir,* 245; 1868 *NYCDir,* 290; "Brutality and Violence in the City," *NYT,* Nov. 20, 1857, 1; "The Late Murders," *NYT,* Nov. 21, 1857, 1, 8; Mark Driscoll, letter to the editor, *NYT,* Nov. 26, 1857, 5; "The Water-Street Murder," *NYT,* Nov. 28, 1857, 5; "United States Marshal's Office," *NYTrib,* Sept. 9, 1863, 8; "Police Intelligence," *NYH,* Feb. 9, 1866, 2; entry for Mark Driscoll, Mar. 2, 1866, Sing Sing Prison Admission Registers, 1865–1930, Ancestry .com; Adrian Cook, *The Armies of the Streets: The New York City Draft Riots of 1863* (Lexington, KY, 1974), 238; entry for Mark Driscoll, Feb. 6, 1868, NYCDeaths.

292 *"Mary Driscoll":* "Mixing Her Whiskey with Water," *NYTrib,* June 19, 1880, 1.

292 *Christopher "Kit" Burns:* FAM462, DW124, DIST4, W4, NYC, 1855 NYCen; FAM535, DW145, DIST2, W4, NYC, 1860 USCen; FAM161, DW35, DIST1, W4, NYC, 1870 USCen; 1856 *NYCDir,* 121; 1860 *NYCDir,* 126; "Dedication of Kit Burns' Dog-Pit," *NYTrib,* Feb. 8, 1870, 5.

293 *"fallen women":* Directory to the Charities of New York, 1874 (New York, 1874), 42.

293 *Pete Dawson:* Accts. 1322, 7404, 11529, 13609, and 15192, ESB; FAM535, DW146, DIST3, W4, NYC, 1855 NYCen; p. 79, Village of Sing Sing, Town of Ossining, Westchester County, NY, 1860 USCen; 1853 *NYCDir,* 178; 1855 *NYCDir,* 469; 1858 *NYCDir,* 202; "The Case of Peter Dawson," *NYT,* July 22, 1858, 4, 8; "Mayor's Police," *NYT,* July 24, 1858, 1; "A King in the Penitentiary," *NYT,* July 26, 1858, 4; "Let No More Dawsons Be Punished," *NYT,* July 27, 1858, 4; "Brooklyn Intelligence," *NYT,* Dec. 16, 1858, 5; "A Curious Case," *New York Evening Express,* Oct. 9, 1862, 4; entry for Peter Dawson, "Report...Transmitting the Pardons, Commutations and Restorations to Citizenship, by the Governor, During the Year 1864," Assembly Document 134, *Documents of the Assembly of the State of New York, Eighty-Eighth Session* (Albany, 1865), n.p.

293 *"winning address":* "Peter Dawson and His Troubles," *NYT,* July 16, 1858, 4.

294 *"get the money":* "A Notorious House of Prostitution Broken Up," *NYT,* July 15, 1858, 3.

295 *"wept like a child":* "The Exit of Pete Dawson," *NYT,* Dec. 24, 1858, 8.

295 *"$5,000 of Pete's money":* "The Case of 'Pete' Dawson," *NYT,* Dec. 23, 1858, 1.

295 *"big Irishman":* "Peter Dawson," *New York Evening Express,* Dec. 27, 1858, 3.

295 *Callaghan McSwiney:* Accts. 9895, 9896, 9905, 14037, 14079, and 15104, ESB; manifest of the *Garland,* Oct. 22, 1850, NYShips; FAM893, DW190, DIST5, W11, NYC, 1860 USCen; 1851 *NYCDir,* 353; 1854 *NYCDir,* 466; 1860 *NYCDir,* 559; 1862 *NYCDir,* 567; 1865 *NYCDir,* 633; entry for Callaghan McSweeny, 1864, IRS Tax Assessment Lists, 1862–1918, Ancestry.com; "Died," *NYH,* Dec. 22, 1861, 5 (Honoria); "Obituary," *NYH,* Aug. 31, 1865, 8.

296 *"strength of mind":* "O'Callahan J. M'Swiney, Esq.," undated clipping from an unidentified newspaper, courtesy of McSweeny descendant Angela O'Sullivan.

297 *William Rudkin:* Acct. 875, ESB; 1849 *Dublin Almanac,* 582; manifests of the *Hemisphere,* Apr. 15, 1851, and *Lafayette,* July 9, 1851, NYShips; FAM427, DW310, DIST3, W11, KingsC, 1855 NYCen; FAM175, DW137, DIST3, W10, KingsC, 1860 USCen; FAM281, DW293, W6, KingsC, 1870 USCen; 1861 *BklynDir,* 378; 1870 *BklynDir,* 622; "Obituary," *NYIA,* Nov. 8, 1873, 5.

298 *"flavoring extracts"*: "William Rudkin, Chemist," 1864 broadside in the possession of Rudkin descendant Conor Welch.

299 *"old Rudkin"*: Entry for William Rudkin, NY, vol. 235, p. 1128, R. G. Dun & Co. credit report volumes, Baker Library, Harvard Business School.

299 *Peter McGoldrick*: Accts. 836, 7105, 28838, 33016, and 48757, ESB; FAM2078, DW1490, W20, KingsC, 1870 USCen; FAM2, DW92, DIST4, W20, KingsC, 1875 NYCen; 1866 *BklynDir*, 214; 1869 *BklynDir*, 436; 1875 *BklynDir*, 589; 1879 *BklynDir*, 666; 1887 *BklynDir*, 753; entry for Peter McGoldrick, Sept. 1866, IRS Tax Assessment Lists, 1862–1918,,Ancestry.com; "The Day in Brooklyn," *NYH*, Jan. 14, 1867, 8; "Dissolution of Partnership," *BDE*, July 15, 1870, 3; "Washington and Park Avs., s.w. cor.," *Real Estate Record and Builder's Guide*, Apr. 1, 1871, 159; "Obituary," *New York Irish World*, June 18, 1892, 5; "Ann Gallagher McGoldrick," *BDE*, Nov. 9, 1907, 14.

299 *Irish poteen*: Rebecca Dalzell, "The Whiskey Wars That Left Brooklyn in Ruins," *Smithsonian Magazine*, Nov. 18, 2014.

300 *"four elegant mansions"*: Untitled, *BDE*, Aug. 1, 1871, 3.

300 *Bernard Woods was another*: Acct. 11454, ESB; manifest of the *Western World*, June 21, 1851, NYShips; FAM544, DW268, DIST1, W14, KingsC, 1855 NYCen; FAM1453, DW591, DIST2, W14, KingsC, 1860 USCen; FAM1482, DW487, W14, KingsC, 1870 USCen; FAM357, DW130, ED115, KingsC, 1880 USCen; 1861 *BklynDir*, 480; 1868 *BklynDir*, 686; 1878 *BklynDir*, 1072; 1882 *BklynDir*, 1260; 1896 *BklynDir*, 1614; "Bernard Woods," *BDE*, Mar. 20, 1906, 3; "Bernard Woods Dead," *BDE*, Mar. 21, 1906, 4; "Obituary," *New York Sun*, Mar. 21, 1906, 5.

301 *"coal bins"*: *Higginson's Insurance Maps of the City of Brooklyn* (Brooklyn, 1868), 4:67.

301 *"power in politics"*: "Obituary," *NYIA*, Mar. 24, 1906, 5.

301 *"athletic hall"*: *Higginson's Insurance Maps*, 4:77.

301 *"Madison Square Garden"*: "Only Four Going to the End of the Race," *NYTrib*, Dec. 1, 1882, 3.

303 *Michael Halpin*: Acct. 4809, ESB; manifest of the *Senator*, Apr. 3, 1848, NYShips; FAM1579, DW547, DIST1, W16, NYC, 1850 USCen; FAM116, DW37, DIST1, W16, NYC, 1855 NYCen; FAM1913, DW863, DIST3, W16, NYC, 1860 USCen; 1850 *NYCDir*, 217; 1854 *NYCDir*, 306; 1856 *NYCDir*, 348; 1858 *NYCDir*, 337; 1860 *NYCDir*, 359; 1861 *NYCDir*, 356; 1862 *NYCDir*, 363; 1864 *NYCDir*, 367; 1865 *NYCDir*, 403; 1866 *NYCDir*, 420; "Democratic General Committee," *NYH*, June 4, 1858, 8; "City Politics," *NYH*, Nov. 18, 1859, 1; "16th Ward," *NYH*, Dec. 20, 1860, 6; "Tammany General Committee for 1864," *New York World*, Jan. 4, 1864, 8; entry for Michael Halpin, July 25, 1866, NYCDeaths; "Died," *NYH*, Jan. 1, 1869, 7; Michael Halpin probate records (esp. images 277–80, 454–71, and 546–51), New York Wills and Probate Records, 1659–1999, Ancestry.com.

304 *"this line of business"*: Entry for Michael Halpin, NY, vol. 266, p. 388, R. G. Dun & Co. credit report volumes, Baker Library, Harvard Business School.

305 *"heavy Curtains"*: "Wm. Witters, Auctioneer," *NYH*, Oct. 31, 1866, 3.

305 *"Wines and Liquors"*: "Executors' Sale," *NYH*, Oct. 30, 1866, 9.

305 *Thomas "Hugh" Keane*: Acct. 11180, ESB; manifest of the *Guy Mannering*, July 22, 1850, NYShips; FAM732, DW233, DIST5, W14, NYC, 1855 NYCen; FAM284, DW64, DIST2, W4, NYC, 1860 USCen; FAM686, DW114, DIST3, W4, NYC, 1870 USCen; FAM144, DW35, ED32, NYC, 1880 USCen; 1855 *NYCDir*, 441; 1860 *NYCDir*, 451; 1864 *NYCDir*, 463; 1871 *NYCDir*, 595; 1873 *NYCDir*, 672; 1882 *NYCDir*, 851; 1892 *NYCDir*, 733; entry for Hugh Keane, NY, vol. 314, subpage A9, p. 5200, as well as p. 5131, R. G. Dun & Co. credit report volumes, Baker Library, Harvard

Business School; marriage certificate for Hugh Keane and Mary Connell, Feb. 8, 1885, NYCMA; "Hugh Keane Democratic Association of the Fourth Ward," *NYH*, May 16, 1870, 10; "Died," *NYH*, Apr. 14, 1884, 9; "Died," *NYH*, Oct. 25, 1887, 1; "For Sale or Exchange," *NYH*, June 9, 1889, 2; Stamford house described in advertisement in *NYTrib*, Aug. 8, 1891, 9; "Mrs. H. L. Keane Sues Her Husband," *NYTrib*, Aug. 30, 1894, 4; "Mrs. Keane Sues," *New York Sun*, Aug. 30, 1894, 8; "Says Keane Cheated Her," *NYH*, Aug. 30, 1894, 7; "Gives His Wife the Slip," *NYH*, Sept. 2, 1894, 5; *Keane v. Keane, Reports of Cases Heard and Determined in the Supreme Court of the State of New York*, vol. 93 (New York, 1895), 159–61. For Keane's real estate business, see "Adjourned Sale," *NYH*, Aug. 28, 1866, 11; "For Sale—A Country Seat," *NYH*, Apr. 22, 1867, 11; "For Sale—On Madison," *NYH*, Apr. 20, 1871, 8; "For Sale Cheap for Cash," *NYH*, Dec. 29, 1871, 2; "O. K.," *New York Sun*, Feb. 24, 1872, 1.

306 *"imposing looking blonde"*: "Keane's Wife Sues," *New York Evening World*, Aug. 29, 1894, 2.

306 *"handsome house"*: "Accused Her of Flirting," *NYH*, Aug. 10, 1892, 11.

306 *"scrupulously neat and polite"*: Ibid.

306 *"not a cent"*: "Keane Must Help His Wife," *NYH*, Aug. 12, 1892, 5.

307 *"$7 and up"*: "Dressmaker," *NYH*, Apr. 14, 1909, 19. For Helen's life after her divorce, see marriage certificate of Charles Gremillot and Helen A. Keane, Sept. 25, 1904, NYCMA; FAM173, ED604, NYC, 1910 USCen; entry for Helen Gremillot, Mar. 14, 1911, New York Extracted Death Index, 1862–1948, Ancestry.com.

Chapter 9: "Well-Cultivated Fields and a Good Bank Account"

312 *family of Peter Lynch*: Accts. 1067, 2797, 2798, 3576, 8852, 11674, 14200, and 79101, ESB; FAM1349, DW519, W8, NYC, 1850 USCen; FAM1897, DW1897, St. Paul, Ramsey County, MN, 1857 MN census; FAM877, DW877, Faxon, Sibley County, MN, 1860 USCen; FAM4, DW4, Faxon, Sibley County, MN, 1870 USCen; line 4, p. 2, Faxon, Agriculture Schedules, 1870 USCen; FAM83, DW83, ED100, Faxon, Sibley County, MN, 1880 USCen; FAM66, Faxon, Sibley County, MN, 1885 MN census; FAM173, Belle Plaine, Scott County, MN, 1895 MN census; FAM67, DW66, Belle Plaine, Scott County, MN, 1900 USCen; p. 9, ED12, Belle Plaine, Scott County, MN, 1905 MN census; entries for James and Peter Lynch, Apr. 2 and 5, 1891, Faxon, Sibley County, MN County Deaths, 1850–2001, Familysearch.org; entries for Mary and Jane Lynch, Jan. 30, 1907, MN Death Records and Certificates, 1900–1955, Familysearch.org; will and probate records for Peter Lynch, MN Wills and Probate Records, 1801–1925, Ancestry.com; "Died at Belle Plaine," *Minneapolis Irish Standard*, Feb. 2, 1907, 5; "Deaths," *Minneapolis Star*, Jan. 5, 1926, 11.

312 *"Illinois"*: Manifest of the *Sea*, Dec. 8, 1846, NYShips.

315 *"frame dwelling"*: Rev. Edward D. Neill, *History of the Minnesota Valley* (Minneapolis, 1882), 435.

319 *John and Honora Killeen*: FAM309, DW313, Porter, Niagara County, NY, 1860 USCen; FAM437, DW455, Porter, Niagara County, NY, 1865 NYCen; FAM85, DW77, Niagara Falls, Niagara County, NY, 1870 USCen; FAM329, DW292, Niagara Falls, Niagara County, NY, 1875 NYCen; FAM258, DW216, ED172, Buffalo, Erie County, 1880 USCen; FAM277, DW234, ED217, Buffalo, Erie County, NY, 1900 US Cen; 1883 *Buffalo Dir*, 475; 1901 *Buffalo Dir*, 746; 1907 *Buffalo Dir*, 746; "Mrs. Honora Killeen," *Buffalo Morning Express*, Dec. 26, 1907, 6; *Memorial and Family History of Erie County, New York*, 2 vols. (Buffalo, 1906–1908), 2:91–92.

320 *"best-known residents"*: "John Killeen's Funeral to Be Held Thursday," *Buffalo Enquirer*, Jan. 4, 1911, 3.

321 *Christopher Burke*: Acct. 17533, ESB; manifest of the *Princess Alice*, Jan. 17, 1848, NYShips; FAM416, DW191, DIST2, W18, NYC, 1855 NYCen; FAM762, DW738, Macon, Bibb County, GA, 1860 USCen; 1851 *NYCDir*, 86; "Painting," *Macon (GA) Weekly Telegraph*, Nov. 22, 1859, 3; "The First Bale," *Macon Telegraph and Messenger*, July 15, 1876, 7; "The Funeral of Mr. C. Burke," *Atlanta Constitution*, Aug. 22, 1884, 4.

321 *Henry Lovi*: FAM1312, DW1347, W13, Chicago, Cook County, IL, 1870 USCen.

321 *"moderate prices"*: "Painting," *Macon Daily Telegraph*, Nov. 11, 1865, 4.

321 *"popular Irishmen"*: "The News of Macon," *Savannah Morning News*, Aug. 22, 1884, 1.

322 *"realms of teeming fertility"*: "Important to Emigrants," *NYIA*, Apr. 23, 1859, 2.

323 *Edmond Butler*: Accts. 6717 and 16735, ESB; FAM718, DW356, W14, NYC, 1850 USCen; FAM266, DW216, DIST2, W7, KingsC, 1860 USCen; p. 5, FAM7, DW4, Fort Wallace, Wallace County, KS, 1870 USCen; FAM42, DW42, W19, ED201, Baltimore, Baltimore County, MD, 1880 USCen; "Lieutenant-Colonel Edmond Butler," in William H. Powell and Edward Shippen, *Officers of the Army and Navy Who Served in the Civil War* (Philadelphia, 1892), 65; *Progressive Men of the State of Montana*, 2 vols. (Chicago, 1903), 1:76–77.

324 *"from decimation"*: "General Miles' Expedition Against Crazy Horse," *Leavenworth (KS) Times*, Mar. 24, 1877, 2.

326 *"some 3,000 Irish"*: "Important to Emigrants," *NYIA*, Apr. 23, 1859, 2.

326 *Michael and Ellen Egan*: Accts. 2263 and 14005, ESB; FAM871, DW871, Faxon, Sibley County, MN, 1860 USCen; FAM10, DW11, Faxon, Sibley County, MN, 1870 USCen; line 10, pp. 1–2, Faxon, Agriculture Schedules, 1870 USCen; FAM54, DW54, ED100, Faxon, Sibley County, MN, 1880 USCen; FAM20, Faxon, Sibley County, MN, 1885 MN census; p. 2, schedule 3, W3, Minneapolis, Hennepin County, MN, 1895 MN Census; FAM177, DW143, ED28, Minneapolis, Hennepin County, MN, 1900 USCen; Neill, *History of the Minnesota Valley*, 434; entries for Ellen Egan, Aug. 19, 1898, and Michael Egan, Aug. 2, 1902, MN Birth and Death Records, 1866–1916, Familysearch.org; gravestone for Ellen and Michael Egan, St. Thomas Cemetery, Jessenland, MN, Findagrave.com; estate records of Michael Egan, probated Sept. 6, 1902, Sibley County, MN Wills and Probate Records, 1801–1925, Ancestry.com.

326 *"worked on a railroad"*: Neill, *History of the Minnesota Valley*, 434.

327 *"oaks for a roof"*: Ibid.

328 *Patrick Dolan*: Acct. 4417, ESB; FAM449, DW166, DIST7, W7, NYC, 1855 NYCen; FAM228, DW243, Hudson, Walworth County, WI, 1860 USCen; FAM49, DW50, Linn, Walworth County, WI, 1870 USCen; FAM128, DW126, ED129, Alden, McHenry County, IL, 1880 USCen; FAM162, DW162, ED145, Alden, McHenry County, IL, 1900 USCen.

329 *Adam Strain*: Accts. 11131 and 13156, ESB; FAM1, DW1, DIST4, W14, NYC, 1855 NYCen; FAM1276, DW1497, Westfield, Marquette County, WI, 1860 USCen; FAM33, DW33, Oxford, Marquette County, WI, 1870 USCen; FAM40, DW40, ED226, Oxford, Marquette County, WI, 1880 USCen; "Death of Adam Strain," *Montello-Marquette (WI) Sun*, Mar. 4, 1882, 5.

329 *"a good neighbor"*: "Death of Adam Strain," 5.

330 *Felix Quinn*: Accts. 16406, 38676, and 39222, ESB; FAM2, DW2, Colchester, Delaware County, NY, 1860 USCen; FAM78, DW68, W9, KingsC, 1865 NYCen; FAM507, DW540, W21, KingsC, 1870 USCen; FAM270, DW228, DIST2, W22,

KingsC, 1875 NYCen; FAM597, DW267, ED440, KingsC, 1900 USCen; 1857 *Bklyn-Dir*, 300; 1861 *BklynDir*, 357; 1864 *BklynDir*, 339; 1868 *BklynDir*, 509; 1870 *BklynDir*, 587; 1876 *BklynDir*, 746; probate records for Felix Quinn, Kings County Estate Files, 1866–1923, Familysearch.org; "Mrs. Frances L. Harding," *Brooklyn Tablet*, Feb. 21, 1963, 9.

331 *James Moriarty:* Accts. 14149 and 30497, ESB; FAM490, DW453, W3, Greencastle, Putnam County, IN, 1870 USCen; FAM197, DW177, W3, ED159, Greencastle, Putnam County, IN, 1880 USCen; "James Moriarty," *Greencastle Banner*, July 5, 1877, 3.

331 *John Forhan:* Accts. 9512 and 15884, ESB; FAM1083, DW318, DIST6, W18, NYC, 1860 USCen; FAM649, DW604, Greencastle, Putnam County, IN, 1870 USCen; FAM75, DW72, ED156, Greencastle, Putnam County, IN, 1880 USCen; "Deaths," *Indiana State Sentinel*, Jan. 27, 1892, 8.

331 *Bartholomew "Batt" Finn:* Accts. 8162, 9797, and 17009, ESB; FAM1085, DW318, DIST6, W18, NYC, 1860 USCen; FAM624, DW582, Greencastle, Putnam County, IN, 1870 USCen; FAM78, DW78, ED155, Greencastle, Putnam County, IN, 1880 USCen; FAM651, DW600, ED40, Center Township, Delaware County, IN, 1900 USCen; FAM146, DW142, ED34, Muncie, Delaware County, IN, 1910 USCen; "Real Estate Transfers," *Greencastle Banner*, Nov. 6, 1873, 3; "Centenarian Passes Away at East Chicago," *Muncie Evening Press*, July 9, 1915, 5; "Former Muncie Man Dies, Nearing Century Mark," *Muncie Morning Star*, July 10, 1915, 5.

331 *"passing freight":* "Death on the Rail," *Indianapolis News*, July 3, 1877, 2.

332 *"specimen of manhood":* "A Former Greencastle Man Dies at Age of 106 Years," *Greencastle Herald*, July 12, 1915, 1.

332 *"senility":* Death certificate of Bartholomew Finn, July 8, 1915, IN Death Certificates, 1899–2017, Ancestry.com.

332 *Daniel Curtin:* Acct. 6329, ESB; FAM180, DW183, Hudson, Summit County, OH, 1860 USCen; FAM150, DW147, Hudson, Summit County, OH, 1870 USCen; FAM181, DW166, ED173, Hudson, Summit County, OH, 1880 USCen.

332 *Robert Baxter:* Acct. 2385, ESB; FAM956, DW887, W6, Detroit, Wayne County, MI, 1860 USCen; FAM360, DW349, DIST2, W6, Detroit, Wayne County, MI, 1870 USCen; FAM913, DW880, W12, ED310, Detroit, Wayne County, MI, 1880 USCen.

332 *Robert Armstrong:* Acct. 7671, ESB; FAM478, DW474, W3, Milwaukee, Milwaukee County, WI, 1860 USCen; FAM1193, DW1038, W1, Milwaukee, Milwaukee County, WI, 1870 USCen; FAM267, DW260, ED95, Milwaukee, Milwaukee County, WI, 1880 USCen; death certificate of Robert Armstrong, Nov. 27, 1890, Milwaukee Deaths, 1854–1911, Ancestry.com; "Death Was Accidental," *Milwaukee Journal*, Nov. 28, 1890, 2.

332 *"vault":* "Found Dead in a Vault," *Milwaukee Journal*, Nov. 27, 1890, 3.

332 *William White and Bridget Flanagan White:* Accts. 1, 3989, and 10798, ESB; FAM1656, DW752, DIST1, W7, NYC, 1850 USCen; FAM631, DW270, DIST1, W7, NYC, 1855 NYCen; FAM1059, DW1060, W1, Bloomington, McLean County, IL, 1860 USCen; FAM345, DW336, Bloomington, McLean County, IL, 1870 USCen; FAM219, DW212, ED165, Bloomington, McLean County, IL, 1880 USCen; entry for William White, W6, ED165, Bloomington, Mortality Schedules, 1880 USCen; FAM162, DW153, ED91, Bloomington, McLean County, IL, 1900 USCen; 1868 *Bloomington Dir*, 165; 1872 *Bloomington Dir*, 311; "Real Estate Transfers," *Bloomington Daily Pantagraph*, May 4, 1870, 4; "The Death Messenger," *Bloomington Leader*, Jan. 8, 1880, 4; "Happy Family Reunion," *Bloomington Weekly Pantagraph*, Aug. 28, 1903, 18.

333 *"very active"*: "Mrs. William White," *Bloomington Weekly Pantagraph*, July 30, 1909, 8.

333 *"cheap, for cash"*: "For Sale," *Bloomington Daily Pantagraph*, Mar. 5, 1864, 4.

333 *brother Patrick Flanagan*: FAM243, DW240, Normal, McLean County, IL, 1870 USCen; line 25, p. 1, Normal, Agriculture Schedules, 1870 USCen; line 6, p. 12, ED166, Normal, Agriculture Schedules, 1880 USCen; "City and County," *Bloomington Weekly Pantagraph*, Apr. 16, 1880, 3.

333 *"quite successful"*: *The History of McLean County, Illinois* (Chicago, 1879), 833.

333 *"Irish citizens of the county"*: "City and County," 3.

334 *"oldest of Bloomington's residents"*: "Mrs. William White," 8.

334 *John L. Vaughan*: Acct. 8919, ESB; FAM462, DW439, Dubuque, Dubuque County, IA, 1860 USCen; FAM124, DW128, W4, Dubuque, Dubuque County, IA, 1870 USCen; FAM150, DW157, ED176, Dubuque, Dubuque County, IA, 1880 USCen; 1865 *Dubuque Dir*, 107; 1869 *Dubuque Dir*, 228; 1875 *Dubuque Dir*, 220; 1878 *Dubuque Dir*, 156; 1881 *Dubuque Dir*, 193; 1883 *Dubuque Dir*, 192; 1884 *Dubuque Dir*, 390; 1889 *Dubuque Dir*, 219; 1890 *Dubuque Dir*, 402; entries for Hoare and Vaughan, IA, vol. 18, p. 142, subpages D6, F32, and F34, and for John L. Vaughan, IA, vol. 19, p. 256, R. G. Dun & Co. credit report volumes, Baker Library, Harvard Business School; "Dissolution Notice," *Dubuque Times*, Sept. 30, 1866, 4; "Assignees Notice in Bankruptcy," *Dubuque Times*, Sept. 23, 1873, 4; "The City," *Dubuque Times*, May 2, 1884, 6.

335 *"served an apprenticeship"*: "Over the Dark River," *Dubuque Herald*, Feb. 26, 1893, 8.

335 *James Hoare*: Acct. 14205, ESB; FAM462, DW439, Dubuque, Dubuque County, IA, 1860 USCen; entry for James Hoare, IA, vol. 18, p. 142, subpage F34, R. G. Dun & Co. credit report volumes, Baker Library, Harvard Business School; "Death of James Hoare," *Dubuque Herald*, Dec. 25, 1868, 4.

335 *"habitual drunkards"*: Entry for Hoare and Vaughan, vol. 18, p. 142 subpage D6, R. G. Dun & Co. credit report volumes.

336 *Michael R. Curran*: Acct. 11966, ESB; FAM1487, DW550, DIST5, W20, NYC, 1855 NYCen; FAM905, DW344, DIST4, W20, NYC, 1860 USCen; FAM672, DW672, W4, Kansas City, Jackson County, MO, 1870 USCen; FAM 438, DW356, ED2, Kansas City, Jackson County, MO, 1880 USCen; FAM171, DW136, ED86, Denver, Arapahoe County, CO, 1900 USCen; 1858 *NYCDir*, 191; 1860 *NYCDir*, 201; 1867 *NYCDir*, 238; 1869 *NYCDir*, 250; 1870 *NYCDir*, 268; 1870 *Kansas City (MO) Dir*, 153; 1872 *Kansas City Dir*, 113; 1874 *Kansas City Dir*, 114; 1875 *Kansas City Dir*, 108; 1876 *Kansas City Dir*, 112; 1880 *Kansas City Dir*, 190; 1881 *Kansas City Dir*, 155; 1882 *Kansas City Dir*, 129; 1885 *Kansas City Dir*, 162; 1886 *Kansas City Dir*, 222; entry for Michael R. Curran, NY, vol. 216, p. 712, R. G. Dun & Co. credit report volumes, Baker Library, Harvard Business School; "Candidates," *Kansas City (MO) Times*, Aug. 4, 1872, 2; *History of Colorado*, ed. Wilbur Fiske Stone, 4 vols. (Chicago, 1918–1919), 3:652–54; "J. A. Curran Leaves $125,000 to Widow," *Denver Post*, Nov. 21, 1932, 4.

337 *Patrick Drew*: Acct. 5114, ESB; manifest of the *William D. Sewall*, Apr. 11, 1850, NYShips; FAM446, DW148, W3, NYC, 1850 USCen; FAM1133, DW1148, W1, Milwaukee, Milwaukee County, WI, 1860 USCen; FAM875, DW713, W1, Milwaukee, Milwaukee County, WI, 1870 USCen; FAM106, DW103, ED95, Milwaukee, Milwaukee County, WI, 1880 USCen; FAM240, DW216, ED14, Milwaukee, Milwaukee County, WI, 1900 USCen; "Hon. Patrick Drew," *Milwaukee News*, Oct. 31, 1875, 2; entries for Patrick Drew, Wisconsin Wills and Probate Records, 1800–1987, Ancestry.com.

337 *"largest buildings were erected"*: "Old Contractor Dies," *Milwaukee Journal*, Nov. 2, 1903, 4.

338 *John D. Durkin:* Accts. 11225, 14961, 15417, 15901, 16422, 16929, 17056, 17549, 18570, 19140, and 19741, ESB; FAM30, DW19, DIST1, W10, NYC, 1855 NYCen; FAM111, DW92, W7, Syracuse, Onondaga County, NY, 1860 USCen; roster of prisoners, line 26, p. 91, W4, Auburn, NY, 1865 NYCen; "Circuit Court of Oyer and Terminer," *Syracuse Standard,* June 7, 1862, 3; "Murder of Dr. Durkin," *Syracuse Standard,* June 3, 1867, 3; "The Durkin Murder Trial," *Carbondale (PA) Advance,* May 9, 1868, 3.

338 *"consumption doctor":* Acct. 14961, ESB.

339 *"most costly character":* "Circuit Court of Oyer and Terminer," 3.

339 *"big pile of money":* "Durkin Murder Trial," *Scranton Republican,* Jan. 25, 1868, 4.

340 *Members of the Canty family:* Accts. 536, 556, 557, 802, 803, 879, 3214, 4701, and 7269, ESB; manifest of the *Speed,* May 28, 1847, NYShips; FAM1323, DW421, and FAM1952, DW613, W6, NYC, 1850 USCen; lines 1–5, p. 103, SF, SF County, CA, 1852 CA Census; FAM384, DW131, DIST1, W6, NYC, 1855 NYCen; FAM767, DW762, DIST5, and FAM1516, DW1238, DIST7, and FAM1188, DW1129, DIST10, all SF, SF County, CA, 1860 USCen; 1854 *SF Dir,* 113; 1856 *SF Dir,* 32, 182; 1859 *SF Dir,* 81; 1860 *SF Dir,* 86; 1861 *SF Dir,* 90; 1865 *SF Dir,* 109.

341 *Ruddock family:* Accts. 1918, 3206, and 13389, ESB; FAM1071, DW115, DIST10, W11, NYC, 1855 NYCen; FAM3986, DW4184, and FAM4119, DW4317, Township 3, Tuolumne County, CA, 1860 USCen; FAM562, DW532, W1, and FAM1360, DW901, DIST3, W10, SF, SF County, CA, 1870 USCen; FAM143, DW98, ED3, and FAM48, DW37, ED182, and FAM161, DW119, ED213, all SF, SF County, CA, 1880 USCen; FAM49, DW38, ED182, and FAM36, DW26, ED305, SF, SF County, CA, 1900 USCen; FAM380, DW312, ED306, AD45, SF, SF County, CA, 1910 USCen; 1864 *SF Dir,* 345; 1867 *SF Dir,* 420; 1871 *SF Dir,* 563; 1874 *SF Dir,* 573; 1879 *SF Dir,* 757; 1880 *SF Dir,* 785; 1881 *SF Dir,* 907; 1891 *SF Dir,* 1193; 1910 *SF Dir,* 1468; "Real Estate Matters," *San Francisco Examiner,* Feb. 2, 1875, 3; "Mortgages Recorded," *San Francisco Examiner,* Mar. 24, 1877, 3; "Real Estate Matters," *San Francisco Examiner,* Apr. 28, 1879, 3; "Died," *San Francisco Examiner,* Feb. 6, 1879, 3; "Died," *San Francisco Call,* June 2, 1903, 13; "Died," *San Francisco Call,* Dec. 20, 1905, 14; "Died," *San Francisco Examiner,* Oct. 7, 1910, 4.

341 *"placer claims":* Oscar T. Shuck, *History of the Bench and Bar of California* (Los Angeles, 1901), 921.

342 *"liquor saloon":* 1860 *SF Dir,* 86.

343 *"stock-raising and lumbering":* *History of Mendocino County, California* (San Francisco, 1880), 667.

344 *William Fivey:* Acct. 16775, ESB; FAM1343, DW539, DIST9, W17, NYC, 1860 USCen; FAM1329, DW881, DIST3, W10, SF, SF County, CA, 1870 USCen; FAM47, DW37, ED144, SF, SF County, CA, 1880 USCen; 1868 *SF Dir,* 216; 1871 *SF Dir,* 250; 1874 *SF Dir,* 249; 1877 *SF Dir,* 328; 1880 *SF Dir,* 333; 1883 *SF Dir,* 442.

344 *Michael Arthur:* Acct. 7650, ESB; FAM2233, DW2345, Eureka, Sierra County, CA, 1860 USCen; FAM102, DW102, Eureka, Sierra County, CA, 1870 USCen.

344 *Laurence Burd:* Acct. 2605, ESB; FAM377, DW121, DIST1, W6, NYC, 1855 NYCen; FAM887, DW720, DIST4, W10, SF, SF County, CA, 1870 USCen; "Deaths," *San Francisco Chronicle,* Feb. 20, 1877, 4.

345 *Michael F. Cummings:* FAM793, DW104, W18, NYC, 1860 USCen; 1867 *SF Dir,* 152; 1871 *SF Dir,* 188; 1874 *SF Dir,* 62a; 1875 *SF Dir,* 221; 1879 *SF Dir,* 241; 1880 *SF Dir,* 247; 1887 *SF Dir,* 372; 1891 *SF Dir,* 421; 1893 *Sacramento Dir,* 179.

345 *John M. Foy:* Accts. 6525, 12396, and 62603, ESB; FAM248, DW154, Yonkers, Westchester County, NY, 1870 USCen; FAM26, DW24, ED129, SF, SF County, CA, 1880 USCen; 1857 *NYCDir,* 293; 1867 *NYCDir,* 357; 1870 *NYCDir,* 407; 1878 *SF Dir,*

332; 1883 *SF Dir*, 453; 1890 *SF Dir*, 506; 1891 *SF Dir*, 558; "Foy," *San Francisco Call*, Dec. 6, 1904, 14.

345 *"pure chemicals"*: 1881 *SF Dir*, 13.

345 *David G. Bartnett*: Accts. 12281 and 17934, ESB; FAM267, DW51, DIST4, W20, NYC, 1855 NYCen; FAM1063, DW1094, Township 3, Contra Costa County, CA, 1870 USCen; FAM544, DW399, ED47, Pacheco, Contra Costa County, CA, 1880 USCen; FAM19, DW19, ED411a, Contra Costa County, CA, 1900 USCen; FAM262, DW261, ED166, Township 5, Contra Costa County, CA, 1910 USCen; "Pioneer of Pacheco Passes from Long and Useful Life," *Concord (CA) Transcript*, Feb. 28, 1918, 1; "All Bartnett Estate Given to Children," *Martinez (CA) Gazette*, May 9, 1918, 1.

345 *"India Rubber Factory"*: FAM15, DW8, W12, NYC, 1850 USCen.

346 *"hub of Pacheco"*: "Barnett [sic] Estate Set at $520,721," *Oakland Tribune*, Feb. 27, 1956, 18.

346 *John, a book peddler back east*: Accts. 6388 and 8939, ESB; FAM1268, DW299, DIST4, W18, NYC, 1855 NYCen; FAM793, DW104, W18, NYC, 1860 USCen; FAM5, DW5, Douglas, San Joaquin County, CA, 1870 USCen; FAM130, ED115, Douglas, San Joaquin County, CA, 1880 USCen; line 7, p. 11, ED115, Douglas, Agriculture Schedules, 1880 USCen; "Dashes Here and There," *Stockton Evening Mail*, Feb. 2, 1883, 3.

346 *Ellen and her husband, John Griffin*: Accts. 6480 and 8787, ESB; FAM1272, DW299, DIST4, W18, NYC, 1855 NYCen; FAM289, DW278, Castoria, San Joaquin County, CA, 1860 USCen; FAM1, DW1, Douglas, San Joaquin County, CA, 1870 USCen; FAM130, ED115, Douglas, San Joaquin County, CA, 1880 USCen; line 6, p. 11, ED115, Douglas, Agriculture Schedules, 1880 USCen; FAM53, DW52, ED101, Douglas, San Joaquin County, CA, 1900 USCen; "A Fatal Cancer," *Stockton Evening Mail*, May 14, 1881, 3.

346 *"ability and sagacity"*: George M. Tinkham, *History of San Joaquin County, California* (Los Angeles, 1923), 1600.

346 *Patrick Cummings*: Acct. 8939, ESB; FAM1268, DW299, DIST4, W18, NYC, 1855 NYCen; FAM101, DW74, ED92, SF, SF County, CA, 1880 USCen; "A Row in the Station-House," *San Francisco Chronicle*, Jan. 12, 1871, 3; "The Gage of Battle," *San Francisco Evening Bulletin*, Mar. 6, 1871, 3; "An Attorney Drowned," *San Francisco Examiner*, Dec. 5, 1884, 2.

347 *Ellen Canty Regan's brothers*: FAM180, DW162, ED155, SF, SF County, CA, 1880 USCen; FAM983, DW670, precinct 2, W10, SF, SF County, CA, 1870 USCen; FAM36, DW15, ED124, SF, SF County, CA, 1880 USCen; FAM154, DW131, ED105, SF, SF County, CA, 1910 USCen; 1865 *SF Dir*, 109; 1871 *SF Dir*, 143; 1877 *SF Dir*, 191; 1880 *SF Dir*, 187; 1890 *SF Dir*, 281; "Died," *San Francisco Examiner*, Oct. 30, 1882, 4; "Deaths," *San Francisco Chronicle*, Dec. 25, 1889, 7.

347 *final Canty sibling, Ellen*: FAM1396, DW1237, DIST2, W8, SF, SF County, CA, 1870 USCen; FAM11, DW98, ED92, SF, SF County, CA, 1880 USCen; "Jeremiah Regan's Estate," *San Francisco Evening Bulletin*, Dec. 9, 1881, 3.

348 *"clear to the bone"*: "Terrible and Fatal Accident," *San Francisco Alta California*, quoted in *Napa County Weekly Reporter*, June 26, 1858, 2.

350 *Garrett Bartnett*: FAM945, DW853, Jamaica, Queens County, NY, 1860 USCen; FAM1138, DW1172, Township 3, Contra Costa County, CA, 1870 USCen; "A Vile and Cowardly Outrage," *Pacheco Contra Costa (CA) Gazette*, July 9, 1870, 2; entries for Garrett Bartnett, CA Prison and Correctional Records, 1851–1950, Ancestry .com; entry for Garrett Bartnett, May 6, 1907, CA Death Index, 1905–1939, Ancestry.com.

351 *Daniel who, with his wife, Mary Brickley Donovan:* Acct. 1827, ESB; manifest of the *St. George,* Nov. 1, 1850, NYShips; FAM152, DW152, Iowa City, Johnson County, IA, 1856 IA census; FAM2673, DW2814, Iowa City, Johnson County, IA, 1860 USCen; FAM81, DW81, W4, Iowa City, Johnson County, IA, 1870 USCen; FAM321, DW302, ED227, Iowa City, Johnson County, IA, 1880 USCen; 1868 *Iowa City Dir,* 45; Daniel and Mary Donovan's death dates are from Findagrave.com.

352 *Patrick Donovan:* Acct. 6719, ESB; manifest of the *Marmion,* Oct. 15, 1853, NYShips; FAM152, DW152, Iowa City, Johnson County, IA, 1856 IA census; FAM408, DW458, Graham, Johnson County, IA, 1860 USCen; FAM23, DW23, Cedar, Johnson County, IA, 1870 USCen; FAM64, DW64, ED235, Graham, Johnson County, IA, 1880 USCen; FAM124, DW123, ED77, Graham, Johnson County, IA, 1900 USCen; line 18, pp. 1–2, Cedar, Agriculture Schedules, 1870 USCen; line 2, p. 6, Graham, Agriculture Schedules, 1880 USCen; *History of Johnson County, Iowa... from 1836 to 1882* (Iowa City, 1883), 811; will and probate records of Patrick Donovan, Iowa Wills and Probate Records, 1758–1997, Ancestry.com.

353 *"best known men in Johnson County":* "Death Record of a Day," *Iowa State Press* (Iowa City), Jan. 14, 1901, 3.

Chapter 10: "A Respectable Life"

354 *"economic bottom":* Hasia R. Diner, "'The Most Irish City in the Union': The Era of the Great Migration, 1844–1877," in *The New York Irish,* ed. Ronald H. Bayor and Timothy J. Meagher (Baltimore, 1996), 94–95.

354 *"parents' status":* Kerby Miller, *Emigrants and Exiles: Ireland and the Irish Exodus to North America* (New York, 1985), 315.

355 *"occupational rank":* William J. Collins and Ariell Zimran, "The Economic Assimilation of Irish Famine Immigrants to the United States," *Explorations in Economic History* 74 (2019): 9.

355 *Gertrude Ryan:* FAM23, DW19, ED594, NYC, 1900 USCen; FAM108, DW74, ED1614, Bronx County, NY, 1910 USCen; FAM218, DW48, ED160, Bronx County, NY, 1920 USCen; FAM502, DW57, ED628, Bronx County, NY, 1930 USCen.

355 *"quick consumption":* "Obituary," *St. Paul Globe,* Jan. 29, 1889, 4. See also FAM2, DW2, W1, Hastings, Dakota County, MN, 1870 USCen; FAM69, DW65, 195, Hastings, Dakota County, MN, 1880 USCen.

356 *Caroline "Carrie" Sinnamon:* p. 3, ED1, W8, Oswego, 1892 NYCen; "Funerals," *Oswego Palladium-Times,* Aug. 3, 1947, 4; Dorothy Rogers, *Oswego: Fountainhead of Teacher Education* (New York, 1961), 142.

356 *"model teacher":* History of the First Half Century of the Oswego Normal and Training School (Oswego, NY, 1913), 94.

357 *Minnie Ledwith:* "Mrs. Ledwith, 80; Teacher 50 Years," *BDE,* Feb. 20, 1938, 11.

357 *Felix Quinn's remaining daughters:* FAM597, DW267, ED440, KingsC, 1900 USCen; FAM555, DW316, ED775, KingsC, 1910 USCen; FAM376, DW249, ED551, Queens County, NY, 1930 USCen; "Mrs. Frances L. Harding," *Brooklyn Tablet,* Feb. 21, 1963, 9.

357 *Michael Smee moved:* Accts. 4633, 8637, 9831, 11938, and 19831, ESB; FAM230, DW75, W12, KingsC, 1870 USCen; FAM10, DW9, DIST4, W12, KingsC, 1875 NYCen; FAM404, DW309, ED7, Claverack, Columbia County, NY, 1880 USCen.

357 *"finishers":* FAM130, DW127, ED9, Claverack, Columbia County, NY, 1900 USCen. See also FAM100, DW73, ED6, Claverack, Columbia County, NY, 1910 USCen; FAM183–84, DW115, ED13, Claverack, Columbia County, NY, 1920 USCen;

FAM45, DW37, ED9, Claverack, Columbia County, NY, 1930 USCen; FAM392, ED11-9, Philmont, Columbia County, NY, 1940 USCen; "Miss Maria Smee," *Hudson Columbia Republican*, Feb. 9, 1909, 1; "Philmont Woman Dead," *Hudson Evening Register*, Apr. 24, 1917, 5; "Miss Amelia Smee," *Hudson Columbia Republican*, Dec. 18, 1917, 16.

357 *Michael Boyne:* FAM395, DW305, ED7, Claverack, Columbia County, NY, 1880 USCen; p. 6, ED4, Claverack, Columbia County, NY, 1905 NYCen; p. 8, ED4, Claverack, Columbia County, NY, 1915 NYCen; p. 6, ED5, Claverack, Columbia County, NY, 1925 NYCen; "Items of Interest from a Neighboring Village," *Hudson Columbia Republican*, May 29, 1902, 5; "Executor's Sale," *Hudson Columbia Republican*, Oct. 22, 1903, 8; "Edward M. Boyne," *Concord (NH) Monitor*, July 30, 1964, 8.

358 *"shoddy":* "Purchased a Factory," *Hudson Columbia Republican*, Dec. 9, 1910, 5.

358 *cement plant manager:* FAM106, DW83, ED95, Catskill, Greene County, NY, 1910 USCen; p. 4, ED1, Catskill, Greene County, NY, 1915 NYCen; FAM297, DW234, ED54, and FAM92, DW72, ED56, Catskill, Greene County, NY, 1920 USCen; FAM210, ED1006, NYC, Greene County, NY, 1930 USCen; FAM205, ED34-20, Dewitt, Onondaga County, NY, 1940 USCen.

358 *one child, Margaret:* "Cowan Pleads Guilty," *BDE*, June 25, 1901, 3; "Statement by Mrs. Cowan," *BDE*, July 2, 1901, 9; FAM70, DW42, ED979, KingsC, 1910 USCen; FAM28, DW11, ED226, KingsC, 1920 USCen; marriage certificate of Samuel Roberts and Margaret O'Donnell, Dec. 2, 1902, and death certificate of Margaret Roberts, May 31, 1921, NYCMA.

359 *boarders:* FAM488, DW330, ED426, KingsC, 1900 USCen.

359 *"wife":* "Charge of Bigamy Made Against Cowan," *BDE*, May 16, 1901, 7.

359 *"fool":* "Cowan's Excuse for Bigamy," *Brooklyn Times*, June 26, 1901, 6.

359 *Italian noblemen:* "New York's New Countess," *Philadelphia Inquirer*, Jan. 29, 1891, 3; "Mrs. Julia Agnes Collender," *NYH*, Apr. 21, 1922, 9.

360 *well-known lawyer:* "Ex-City Court Justice Dies," *Brooklyn Tablet*, Mar. 1, 1952, 5.

360 *textile manufacturer:* "Mrs. John W. Kehoe," *NYT*, Feb. 27, 1948, 21.

360 *Brooklyn surgeon:* "Dr. William V. Pascual, 65, Prominent Surgeon, Dies," *BDE*, Sept. 27, 1944, 15.

360 *dental supplies:* "Alfred G. Rowan Dies," *Long Beach (NJ) Record*, Nov. 24, 1934, 1.

360 *"welfare worker":* "Corinne Roche," *New York Daily News*, Mar. 22, 1955, 34.

360 *Bill Quigley:* FAM65, DW46, ED210, KingsC, 1910 USCen; "Harbor Lights," *BDE*, Mar. 19, 1952, 29.

360 *"famous Battery boatman":* "Old Timers," *BDE*, May 26, 1946, 22.

360 *sons of tailor George P. Fox:* FAM625, DW197, DIST2, W15, NYC, 1870 USCen.

360 *"real estate operator":* "Andrew J. Kerwin, Former Builder, 76," *NYT*, Nov. 15, 1944, 27.

360 *Daniel J. Sullivan:* P. 21, DW106, DIST1, W14, NYC, Enum2, 1870 USCen; FAM428, DW206, ED100, KingsC, 1880 USCen; death certificate of Daniel Sullivan, June 13, 1884, NYCMA; "Two Suicides in Brooklyn," *NYT*, June 13, 1884, 5.

361 *"religious insanity":* "Fatal Religious Insanity," *Brooklyn Union*, June 13, 1884, 1.

361 *John D. Norris:* FAM153, DW78, ED178, SF, SF County, CA, 1910 USCen; 1897 *Denver Dir*, 817; 1907 *NYCDir*, 1234; 1908 *SF Dir*, 1340; "Fast Artillery Work in and About Manila," *BDE*, Mar. 27, 1899, 3.

361 *sons of Hubert D. Glynn:* Death certificates for James F. Glynn, Apr. 14, 1902, and William Glynn, Mar. 11, 1943, NYCMA; entry for Henry H. Glynn, Oct. 16, 1882, NYCDeaths; FAM171, DW95, ED464, KingsC, 1900 USCen; entries for James F. Glynn, 1887 *BklynDir*, 419, 1889 *BklynDir*, 460, 1897 *BklynDir*, 553, and 1900 *BklynDir*, 556.

362 *station agent:* FAM39, DW38, ED41, Cox Station, Charles County, MD, 1880 USCen; FAM115, DW106, ED243, Baltimore, Baltimore County, MD, 1900 USCen.

362 *Jeremiah Griffin:* Acct. 115493, ESB; FAM404, DW53, ED29, NYC, 1880 USCen; FAM495, DW107, ED924, NYC, 1900 USCen; FAM312, DW42, ED1527, NYC, 1910 USCen; 1876 *NYCDir*, 534; 1878 *NYCDir*, 572; 1883 *NYCDir*, 658; 1902 *NYCDir*, 545; 1905 *NYCDir*, 557.

362 *lace buyer Robert Lewis:* "Dr. Robert Lewis," New York *Daily News*, Dec. 21, 1939, 53; "Thomas W. Lewis," *New York Sun*, June 13, 1933, 25.

362 *The youngest, Eugene Devlin:* FAM215, DW186, ED306, Northfield, Richmond County, NY, 1880 USCen; FAM34, DW27, ED602, Richmond County, NY, 1900 USCen; FAM189, DW158, ED1303, West New Brighton, Richmond County, NY, 1910 USCen; FAM269, DW29, ED158, Bronx County, NY, 1920 USCen; FAM318, DW44, AD2, ED163, Bronx County, NY, 1930 USCen; "Revolution in Methods of Cooking Provokes Ardent Praise of McCann," *Brooklyn Times*, Feb. 27, 1926, 16; death certificate for Eugene Devlin, Apr. 2, 1948, NYCMA.

362 *Eugene's brother William Devlin:* FAM169, DW50, ED8, NYC, 1900 USCen; FAM15, DW15, ED1303, Richmond County, NY, 1910 USCen; FAM223, DW179, ED1564, Richmond County, NY, 1920 USCen; "Fire Chief Devlin May Die," *New York Sun*, Sept. 21, 1911, 1.

362 *"ice carnival at Montreal":* "Gave Themselves Up," *New York Sun*, Apr. 18, 1895, 8.

363 *"a respectable life":* Ibid.

363 *"shot over the side":* "Chief Devlin Dies of Fire Injuries," *NYT*, Sept. 25, 1911, 9.

363 *So, too, was Michael Murphy:* P. 19, DIST3, W7, NYC, Enum2, 1870 USCen; FAM188, DW56, ED87, NYC, 1880 USCen; "French Lashes Murphy," *New York World*, June 24, 1894, 5; "Police Captain Murphy Dead," *NYT*, Aug. 1, 1895, 7.

363 *"floral cradle":* "Police Corruption," *NYEP*, Feb. 3, 1886, 1.

364 *"acute disease of the liver":* "Police Captain Murphy Dead," *New York World*, Aug. 1, 1895, 7.

364 *Alfred Y. Morgan:* FAM208, DW103, ED556, NYC, 1920 USCen; "Fall from Office Window Is Fatal," *BDE*, Jan. 11, 1926, 3.

364 *went by John Commins:* FAM200, DW191, ED124, Oakland, Alameda County, CA, 1910 USCen; FAM89, DW86, ED74, Oakland, Alameda County, CA, 1920 USCen; FAM149, DW137, ED114, Oakland, Alameda County, CA, 1930 USCen; FAM281, DW875, ED61-26, Oakland, Alameda County, CA, 1940 USCen; 1895 *Oakland Dir*, 143; 1902 *Oakland Dir*, 127; 1911 *Oakland Dir*, 270; 1918 *Oakland Dir*, 323; 1923 *Oakland Dir*, 464; 1937 *Oakland Dir*, 202; 1940 *Oakland Dir*, 204; "Wife Ejected from Her Home," *San Francisco Call*, Aug. 16, 1902, 8; "Obtains Divorce from Young Wife," *San Francisco Chronicle*, Oct. 23, 1902, 7.

364 *"wealthy real estate man":* "Undisturbed by Many Accusers," *San Francisco Examiner*, Aug. 26, 1902, 9.

365 *Anna ended up:* DW483, ED27-46, Pacific Grove, Monterey County, CA, 1940 USCen; "Request of Mother Granted by Judge," *San Francisco Examiner*, Nov. 15, 1902, 7; entry for Anna Viers Griffin, May 21, 1958, CA Death Index, 1940–1997, Ancestry.com.

365 *Walter J. Bartnett:* FAM140, DW134, ED207, SF, SF County, CA, 1900 USCen; p. 16A, DW91, DIST506, AD11, NYC, 1930 USCen; "Two New Men Who Are Coming to Great Prominence in California," *Santa Cruz Surf*, Jan. 25, 1906, 1; "Bartnett Is Guilty," *Washington Post*, June 23, 1908, 1; "Banker Sentenced," *NYT*, July 2, 1908, 6; "Brown, Angered by Le Breton, Tells Bartnett's Part in Looting," *San Francisco Chronicle*, Aug. 30, 1908, 1; "Walter J. Bartnett Free Man in East," *San Francisco*

Examiner, Apr. 9, 1909, 2; "Bartnett Wins in Court of Appeal," *San Francisco Chronicle*, Dec. 21, 1910, 4; "W. J. Bartnett Freed of Bank Indictment," *San Francisco Examiner*, Mar. 16, 1911, 1; "Depositors See Plans Collapse," *San Francisco Call*, July 30, 1911, 1; "Depositors Sue Bank Wrecker for $15,000,000," *San Francisco Call*, July 19, 1913, 14; "When Western Pacific Iron Horses Drank the Waters of the Pacific," *Oakland Tribune*, July 9, 1916, 3; "Walter Bartnett, Attorney, Is Dead," *NYT*, July 14, 1935, 22; Walter J. Bartnett, *The Federation of the World*, 2nd ed. (San Francisco, 1906).

365 *"going mad"*: "Banker Going Mad in Jail," *NYT*, Jan. 24, 1908, 1.

366 *surviving child, Michael J. Kavanagh*: FAM8, DW8, and FAM99, DW99, ED137, Pottawatomie County, KS, 1900 USCen; *Portrait and Biographical Album of Jackson, Jefferson and Pottawatomie Counties, Kansas* (Chicago, 1890), 190–93; "Paint Now," *Westmoreland (KS) Recorder*, Aug. 27, 1903, 4; "Blaine Postmaster," *Westmoreland Recorder*, Jan. 17, 1907, 4; "M. J. Kavana[g]h Dead," *Westmoreland Recorder*, May 28, 1908, 4.

366 *Edward Graves*: *Commemorative Biographical Record of Hartford County, Connecticut* (Chicago, 1901), 1395–96; "Col. E. M. Graves Dead," *Hartford Courant*, June 1, 1905, 6.

366 *Richard V. Oulahan*: "Oulahan Appointed Press Bureau Head," *Washington Times*, Aug. 3, 1908, 4; "Passing of Oulahan Mourned by World," *Washington Post*, Dec. 31, 1931, 1; "Death of Oulahan Is Mourned Here," *NYT*, Jan. 1, 1932, 22; "Editorial Comment on Richard V. Oulahan's Death," *NYT*, Jan. 1, 1932, 22; Donald A. Ritchie, *Press Gallery: Congress and the Washington Correspondents* (Cambridge, MA, 1991), 195–218.

367 *"A man of distinguished appearance"*: "Oulahan Intimate of Many Presidents," *NYT*, Dec. 31, 1931, 7.

367 *"unfailing charm"*: "Richard V. Oulahan," *Washington Post*, Dec. 31, 1931, 6.

367 *"intimate friend"*: "Oulahan Intimate of Many Presidents," 7.

367 *"most intelligent adviser"*: Ritchie, *Press Gallery*, 217.

367 *"could bestow"*: "Oulahan Intimate of Many Presidents," 7.

368 *Richard Francis Xavier Smith*: *A Biographical Dictionary of Leading Living Men of the City of St. Louis and Vicinity*, ed. Albert Nelson Marquis (Chicago, 1912), 561.

368 *John A. Donovan*: FAM12, DW12, ED88, W2, Iowa City, Johnson County, IA, 1910 USCen; FAM92, DW74, ED93, W1, Iowa City, Johnson County, IA, 1920 USCen.

368 *"coffee second to none"*: Advertisement, *Iowa City Press*, May 1, 1920, 6.

368 *Daniel C. Stapleton*: FAM128, DW76, ED66, District of Columbia, 1920 USCen; 1895 *Omaha Dir*, 521; "City and County News," *North Platte Semi-Weekly Tribune*, June 2, 1914, 1; "Last Rites Are Held for D. C. Stapleton," *Washington Times*, May 4, 1920, 17; "$100,000 Left to Widow," *Washington Post*, May 23, 1920, 11; passport application of Ellen Stapleton, Aug. 13, 1919, U.S. Passport Applications, 1795–1925, Ancestry.com.

368 *John and James McCabe*: *Prominent Men of Staten Island, 1893* (New York, 1893), 210.

369 *John C. Burke*: FAM871, DW429, W17, KingsC, 1870 USCen; "Obituary," *Brooklyn Standard Union*, Dec. 6, 1919, 19.

369 *Michael E. Butler*: "Michael E. Butler," *BDE*, Oct. 30, 1882, 4; "Michael E. Butler Found Dead in Bed," *Brooklyn Times*, Aug. 3, 1926, 3–4; "Michael E. Butler Fortune to Children," *Brooklyn Times*, Aug. 13, 1926, 1.

369 *"political chieftain"*: "Michael E. Butler, Retired Political Leader, Expires," *Brooklyn Standard Union*, Aug. 3, 1926, 1.

ENDNOTES

369 *John J. Fitzgerald:* "Democrats Name Five Gold Men for Congress," *BDE*, Oct. 9, 1900, 15; "John J. Fitzgerald, Ex-County Judge and Leader in Congress, Dead at 80," *BDE*, May 14, 1952, 15.

369 *Thomas J. Bradley:* FAM121, DW41, DIST23, W11, NYC, 1870 USCen; FAM612, DW69, ED292, NYC, 1900 USCen; "Names Men for Congress," *NYT*, Oct. 6, 1896, 1; "Oh, Where Was Bradley Then?" *New York Sun*, Oct. 31, 1898, 3; "Records of New York Members of Congress," *NYT*, June 17, 1900, 5.

369 *"Bright and popular":* "Ex-Congressman Bradley Dead," *NYT*, Apr. 3, 1901, 9.

370 *"Life's glories":* Ibid.

370 *"alcoholic ward":* "T. J. Bradley at Bellevue," *NYT*, Jan. 2, 1901, 1.

370 *Arthur Kerwin:* FAM405, DW398, ED88, Los Angeles, Los Angeles County, CA, 1930 USCen; 1903 *SF Dir*, 1026; 1905 *SF Dir*, 1045; 1914 *SF Dir*, 1054; "West Pointer Succumbs at Soldiers' Home," *Los Angeles Times*, June 27, 1935, sect. II, 1.

371 *Paul B. Malone:* "Gen. Paul Malone, Army Teacher, Author," *Washington Post*, Oct. 18, 1960, B4.

371 *"O'Ryan's Roughnecks":* "Gen. O'Ryan Dead; Headed the 27th," *NYT*, Jan. 31, 1961, 29.

371 *Thomas P. McLoughlin:* FAM655, DW538, W22, KingsC, 1870 USCen; "Father McLoughlin Dead," *BDE*, Feb. 17, 1913, 2; Peter P. McLoughlin, *Father Tom: Life and Lectures of Rev. Thomas P. McLoughlin* (New York, 1919), 82; Tyler Anbinder, *Five Points: The 19th-Century New York Neighborhood That Invented Tap Dance, Stole Elections, and Became the World's Most Notorious Slum* (New York, 2001), 418–19.

372 *John T. Woods:* "All Flatbush to Honor Father John T. Woods," *BDE*, Dec. 13, 1908, 6; "Specially Honored by Residents of Flatbush," *Brooklyn Chat*, Jan. 5, 1924, 1, 4; "Mons. John T. Woods Dies in Hospital After Operation," *BDE*, May 8, 1924, 1.

372 *"beloved":* "Mons. John T. Woods Laid to Rest in Holy Cross," *Brooklyn Chat*, May 17, 1924, 6.

372 *"fast horses":* "William V. Collender," *NYH*, Feb. 13, 1890, 10.

373 *eldest son, Frank:* Entry for Frank P. Drew, Feb. 3, 1890, Milwaukee Deaths, 1854–1911, Ancestry.com.

373 *"sojourn in the South":* "Milwaukee Matters," *Milwaukee Weekly Wisconsin*, July 28, 1888, 5.

373 *Thomas David Drew:* FAM71, DW77, ED18, Milwaukee, Milwaukee County, WI, 1910 USCen; p. 10, "The Territories," 1901 census of Canada, Ancestry.com.

373 *"acute alcoholism":* Death certificate of Thomas D. Drew, Nov. 18, 1915, Washington State Board of Health, Familysearch.org.

373 *John I. Drew:* FAM71, DW77, ED18, Milwaukee, Milwaukee County, WI, 1910 USCen; FAM31, DW27, ED213, Milwaukee, Milwaukee County, WI, 1920 USCen; FAM19, DW16, ED224, Milwaukee, Milwaukee County, WI, 1930 USCen; "Drew Indicted by Grand Jury at Milwaukee," *Eau Claire Leader-Telegram*, Feb. 19, 1933, 10; "Sudden Death Removes Drew of Milwaukee," *Kenosha News*, July 18, 1934, 2.

374 *fourth son, Joe:* "Joseph Sharkey Succumbs Here," *Contra Costa (CA) Gazette*, Dec. 21, 1938, 1.

374 *"floor leader":* "The Senator Had Colorful Life, Rich Experiences," *Contra Costa (CA) Gazette*, July 26, 1948, 1, 8.

375 *sixth brother, Charles:* "Sharkey Convicted," *Los Angeles Times*, Nov. 14, 1902, 3; line 19, p. 17A, ED49, Marin County, CA, 1910 USCen; line 78, p. 3B, ED81, Sacramento County, CA, 1920 USCen; entry for Charles Sharkey, May 3, 1920, Applications for Seaman's Protection Certificates, 1916–1940, Ancestry.com.

375 *"considerable"*: "Attacked After Winning at Cards," *San Francisco Chronicle*, Sept. 3, 1902, 4.

375 *Michael and Thomas*: "Michael Killeen Dead," *Buffalo Evening News*, Aug. 15, 1904, 7; "Veteran Dispatcher Succumbs to Kidney Disease After Long Struggle," *Salida (CO) Mail*, Mar. 1, 1904, 1.

375 *third brother, James*: "James W. Killeen Dies at His Home," *Salt Lake City Tribune*, Jan. 20, 1913, 6.

376 *But Frank Killeen*: "Capt. Killeen of the Notorious 3d Goes to the 13th," *Buffalo Enquirer*, Sept. 6, 1901, 1; "F. J. Killeen, Retired Police Captain, Dies," *Buffalo Evening News*, Mar. 10, 1917, 1; "Frank J. Killeen," *Buffalo Times*, Mar. 10, 1917, 3; "Frank J. Killeen Died Yesterday," *Buffalo Enquirer*, Mar. 10, 1917, 4.

376 *"notorious third precinct"*: "Evidence of Protected Vice Is Ready for the Grand Jury," *Buffalo Courier*, Feb. 17, 1902, 7.

376 *"gambling resort"*: "Protected Vice Is Now to Be Assailed by the Anti-Saloon League," *Buffalo Enquirer*, Nov. 20, 1901, 10.

377 *Henry W. Killeen*: *Memorial and Family History of Erie County, New York*, 2 vols. (Buffalo, 1906–1908), 2:91–92; "Henry W. Killeen," *NYT*, Apr. 27, 1943, 24.

377 *"big brain"*: "Henry W. Killeen, Brilliant Buffalo Lawyer, Is Dead," *Buffalo Evening News*, Apr. 27, 1943, 10.

379 *"worst thing"*: Kathleen Kavanagh, email to the author, Feb. 4, 2023.

380 *"MacSwiney Chalice"*: "The MacSwiney Chalice," *Catholic New York*, Mar. 10, 2021.

381 *at age sixty*: "Death of Peter McLoughlin, Esq." *New-York Freeman's Journal*, Feb. 11, 1854, 5.

382 *"old Brooklyn"*: "M. E. McLoughlin, Ex-Eagle Writer, Dies in Bay State," *BDE*, July 24, 1936, 11.

Conclusion

383 *One of these self-made tycoons was Hugh Collender*: FAM271, DW178, DIST2, W12, NYC, 1855 NYCen; FAM 1439, DW553, DIST9, W17, NYC, 1860 USCen; FAM184, DW112, DIST14, W16, NYC, 1870 USCen; FAM52, DW47, ED151, Darien, Fairfield County, CT, 1880 USCen; entry for "Hugonium Collender," Dec. 24, 1828, Cappoquin, County Waterford, Ireland Roman Catholic Parish Baptisms, Findmypast.com; entry for Hugh Collender, Dec. 29, 1848, Ireland Prison Registers, 1790–1924, Ancestry.com; entries for Phelan & Collender and Hugh Collender, NY, vol. 267, p. 500, subpages A4, A17, A21, A25, and F, R. G. Dun & Co. credit report volumes, Baker Library, Harvard Business School; "Married," *NYIA*, May 7, 1853, 4; "Hugh W. Collender," *NYH*, Apr. 2, 1890, 6; "Collender," *New York Irish World*, Apr. 12, 1890, 5; "H. W. Collender's Will," *Stamford Advocate*, July 11, 1890, 4; *The Great Industries of the United States: Being an Historical Summary of the Origin, Growth, and Perfection of the Chief Industrial Arts of This Country* (Hartford, 1872), 396–404; Michael Cavanagh, *Memoirs of Gen. Thomas Francis Meagher: Comprising the Leading Events of His Career* (Worcester, 1892), 263. For the lawsuit between the two families, see *Court of Appeals: Hugh W. Collender, Respondent, Against George E. Phelan, Ann A. Phelan..., Appellants* (New York, 1879), 1–333; H. E. Sickles, *Report of Cases Decided in the Court of Appeals of the State of New York* (Albany, 1880), 366–73.

384 *champion Michael Phelan*: Accts. 14634, 15282, 15334, 16014, and 17350, ESB; FAM2840, DW1674, Williamsburg, KingsC, 1850 USCen; FAM271, DW178, DIST2, W12, NYC, 1855 NYCen; FAM1440, DW554, DIST9, W17, NYC, 1860

USCen; FAM75, DW64, ED340, NYC, 1880 USCen; 1848 *NYCDir*, 323; 1850 *NYC-Dir*, 398; 1853 *NYCDir*, 549; "Phelan: The Great Billiard Professor," *NYIA*, Aug. 17, 1850, 2; "Challenge at Billiards," *NYH*, Dec. 8, 1852, 6; "The Copartnership," *NYH*, Mar. 2, 1860, 7; "Evolution in Billiards," *NYTrib*, Feb. 24, 1879, 6; "Mother and Son," *NYH*, July 25, 1888, 5; "Mrs. Phelan's Will Sound," *BDE*, Aug. 25, 1889, 15; Patrick R. Redmond, *The Irish and the Making of American Sport, 1832–1920* (Jefferson, NC, 2014), 88 (invents "pool").

385 *"disastrous…speculations"*: "Death of Capt. M. Phelan," *NYIA*, Oct. 14, 1871, 4.

385 *"parties…of questionable char[acter]"*: Entry for Michael Phelan, NY, vol. 267, p. 438, R. G. Dun & Co. credit report volumes, Baker Library, Harvard Business School.

386 *"insure mathematical correctness"*: "Improved Billiard Tables and Cushions," *New York Irish News*, Apr. 12, 1856, 2.

386 *"the adult male"*: "Billiards and Its Appliances," *Harper's Weekly*, Mar. 16, 1872, 224.

387 *"polished black walnut"*: "Billiard-table for Gen. Grant," *NYT*, May 15, 1867, 5.

387 *"sights of the metropolis"*: "Billiards and Its Appliances," 224.

389 *"long and bitter contest"*: "Old Mrs. Phelan's Money," *NYH*, July 12, 1888, 2.

389 *"massive manor house"*: Maggie Gordon, "Long Neck Point," *Darien (CT) News*, Apr. 29, 2014.

391 *"impossible"*: "On the Origins of Species," *North American Review* 90 (Apr. 1860): 493.

391 *"innumerable openings"*: Francis Bowen, *The Principles of Political Economy Applied to the Condition, the Resources, and the Institutions of the American People* (Boston, 1856), 200.

392 *"frugal as his neighbors"*: Ibid, 123.

392 *"faculties of mind"*: Ibid, 122–23.

392 the American Dream: Jim Cullen, *The American Dream: A Short History of an Idea That Shaped a Nation* (New York, 2003), 4.

393 *"condition for life"*: The Collected Works of Abraham Lincoln, ed. Roy P. Basler, 9 vols. (New Brunswick, NJ, 1953), 5:52.

393 *"poor"*: Cullen, *American Dream*, 76.

393 *"occupy this big White House"*: *Collected Works*, 7:512.

394 *"Irish success in America"*: "The Irish Success in America," *New Orleans City Item*, Aug. 21, 1878, 2.

396 *"seldom rose"*: Kerby Miller, *Emigrants and Exiles: Ireland and the Irish Exodus to North America* (New York, 1985), 314.

396 *$463 in their accounts*: ESB Mobility Database.

396 *$1,000 in savings*: "56% of Americans Can't Cover a $1,000 Emergency Expense with Savings," CNBC.com, Jan. 19, 2022. One might reasonably argue that we ought to count *every* Famine immigrant in such calculations, even those who died soon after arriving in America or who for some other reason could not be tracked for ten years. If we include all Famine immigrants, regardless of how long their accounts were open, how long they lived in New York, and how long they survived in America, the average savings of those who were day laborers when they opened their accounts was $280 (about $11,000 today) and their median savings was $164 (about $6,000 today).

396 *27 percent owned real estate*: ESB Mobility Database.

399 *"'ould sod'"*: "May Tread the Old Sod," *Chicago Chronicle*, Nov. 21, 1897, 29.

399 *"Irish Palace"*: "For an Irish Palace," *NYIA*, Jan. 4, 1897, 4.

399 *"fine ballroom"*: Ibid.

399 *"large auditorium"*: "The Great Irish Fair," *NYIA*, Mar. 1, 1897, 5.

400 *"'Blarney Stone'"*: "At the Irish Fair," *New York Irish World*, May 22, 1897, 6.

400 *"relics and curios"*: "Irish Fair Opens To-Night," *NYT*, May 10, 1897, 2.
400 *"huge green shamrock"*: "At the Irish Fair," 6.
401 *"Kate Murphy by name"*: Ibid.
402 *"faith, and family"*: "Remarks by President Obama and Prime Minister Kenny of Ireland at St. Patrick's Day Reception," Mar. 17, 2015, https://obamawhitehouse.archives.gov/the-press-office/2015/03/17/remarks-president-obama-and-prime-minister-kenny-ireland-st-patricks-day. For Obama's Irish ancestry, see Chris Colin, "Rediscovering Obama's Irish Roots," *New Yorker*, Dec. 10, 2016.

A Note on the Value of a Dollar

415 *$1 from the 1850s is worth about $38 today:* This multiplier for calculating the value of a dollar from the 1850s varies for each year due to the swings in the economy and the resulting inflation and deflation. Using the consumer price calculator created by economic historians at measuringworth.com to determine what a dollar from each year of the 1850s was worth in the spring of 2023 results in an average answer of $38.
416 *"wealth held"*: https://www.measuringworth.com/calculators/ppowerus/.
416 *"back home"*: *Counsel for Emigrants, and Interesting Information from Numerous Sources Concerning British America, the United States, and New South Wales* (Aberdeen, 1838), ix.

Index

Note: Italic page numbers refer to illustrations.

About the Author

Tyler Anbinder is an emeritus professor of history at George Washington University, where he taught courses on the history of American immigration and the American Civil War era. He is the author of three award-winning books and of numerous articles, including one on immigrants and the Civil War draft that was awarded the Hubbell Prize for the best article in *Civil War History* for 2006. Additionally, Anbinder has held the Fulbright Commission's Thomas Jefferson Distinguished Chair in American History at the University of Utrecht in the Netherlands and has won three prestigious research grants from the National Endowment for the Humanities. He loves playing tennis with his friends and hiking with his children. Raised in New York, he has lived for the past thirty years in Arlington, Virginia.